Also in the Variorum Collected Studies Series:

ELIYAHU ASHTOR
Studies on the Levantine Trade in the Middle Ages

ELIYAHU ASHTOR
East-West Trade in the Medieval Mediterranean

ETAN KOHLBERG
Belief and Law in Imāmī Shī'ism

R.B. SERJEANT
Customary and Shari'ah Law in Arabian Society

R.B. SERJEANT
Studies in Arabian History and Civilisation

GEORGE MAKDISI
History and Politics in Eleventh-Century Baghdad

GEORGE MAKDISI
Religion, Law and Learning in Classical Islam

FRANZ ROSENTHAL
Science and Medicine in Islam

FRANZ ROSENTHAL
Muslim Intellectual and Social History

WILFERD MADELUNG
Religious Schools and Sects in Medieval Islam

HALIL INALCIK
Studies in Ottoman Social and Economic History

HARRY A. MISKIMIN
Cash, Credit and Crisis in Europe, 1300–1600

ANDRÉ-E. SAYOUS
Commerce et finance en Méditerranée au Moyen Age

JOHN H. PRYOR
Commerce, Shipping and Naval Warfare in the Medieval Mediterranean

Technology, Industry and Trade

Professor Eliyahu Ashtor

Eliyahu Ashtor

Technology, Industry and Trade

The Levant versus Europe, 1250–1500

Edited by B. Z. Kedar

Routledge
Taylor & Francis Group
LONDON AND NEW YORK

First published 1992 by Variorum, Ashgate Publishing

Published 2017 by Routledge
2 Park Square, Milton Park, Abingdon, Oxon, OX14 4RN
711 Third Avenue, New York, NY 10017, USA

Routledge is an imprint of the Taylor & Francis Group, an informa business

A CIP catalogue record for this book is available
from the British Library and the
US Library of Congress.

ISBN 13: 978-0-86078-323-7 (hbk)

COLLECTED STUDIES SERIES CS372

CONTENTS

This volume contains x + 331 pages

PUBLISHER'S NOTE

The articles in this volume, as in all others in the Collected Studies Series, have not been given a new, continuous pagination. In order to avoid confusion, and to facilitate their use where these same studies have been referred to elsewhere, the original pagination has been maintained wherever possible.

Each article has been given a Roman number in order of appearance, as listed in the Contents. This number is repeated on each page and quoted in the index entries.

It has not been possible to reproduce all the illustrations originally included in these articles; in some cases new illustrations have been substituted.

PREFACE

Eliyahu Ashtor, who died on November 2, 1984, concentrated in his last years on three broad, interrelated issues. The central of these was the trade between the Catholic West and the Muslim East. His work in this sphere culminated in his *Levant Trade in the Later Middle Ages* (Princeton, 1983), which reached him just a few months before his death. Variorum Reprints published two collections of related articles: the first, *Studies on the Levantine Trade in the Middle Ages*, appeared in 1978; the second, *East-West Trade in the Medieval Mediterranean*, was brought out posthumously in 1986.

The second broad issue was the role of the Jews in the economy of the medieval Mediterranean. Ashtor had touched upon this already at the age of 19, in a Zionist pamphlet he had written in Vienna in 1933, and in later years he repeatedly returned to it. A selection of his articles on this subject was brought out in 1983 by Variorum Reprints under the title *The Jews and the Mediterranean Economy, 10th–15th Centuries*. A posthumously published article, "The Jews in the Mediterranean Trade in the Later Middle Ages",[1] comes close to being a summation of Ashtor's views on this issue, and is reprinted at the end of the present volume.

The third broad issue – the relationships between the decline of technology and industry in the Muslim Levant and their progress in Western Europe in the later Middle Ages – came into focus in Ashtor's work only in the last decade of his life. The present collection includes eight studies on this subject which were published between 1977 and 1989. It should be underlined that Ashtor's work in this field was cut short by his death. He did succeed in amassing an impressive amount of variegated information, and in proposing divers causal links between demographic trends, types of regime, economic policies, and attitudes toward innovation on the one hand, and technology and industry on the other, but he was not given the opportunity to write any comprehensive monograph. Nevertheless, the information he gathered and the relationships he suggested may prove to be of considerable importance for future research.

I would like to thank the editors and publishers of the journals and books in which the articles originally appeared for permission to reprint those works in the present volume. The opportunity has been taken to correct a number of misprints in the texts themselves, in particular in Study VIII. My thanks also to Mr Ariel Viterbo for compiling the index.

B.Z. KEDAR

Mount Scopus,
September, 1991

[1] For a full list of Ashtor's publications see *Asian and African Studies* 22 (1988), 11–33.

I

Le Proche-Orient au Bas Moyen Age. Une région sous-développée

Une économie en déclin

Un coup d'œil très rapide sur les structures économiques du Proche-Orient musulman au Bas Moyen Age suggérera l'idée qu'il s'agit d'une région sous-développée. Ce sont des pays dans lesquels la part de la population vivant de l'agriculture est très élevée, voilà un trait caractéristique des pays sous-développés. Ils exportent des matières premières et importent des produits industriels. Le revenu per capita est très bas. Les ressources du sol (forces hydrauliques) ne sont pas mises au profit de la production de façon adéquate, les capitaux ne sont pas investis dans son développement.

Pourtant, en comparant les structures économiques du Proche Orient au Bas Moyen Age avec les aperçus que donnent les économistes du sous-développement on constate que ceux-ci ne concordent pas avec les données qu'on repère dans les sources historiques du Proche-Orient médiéval.

Selon les conceptions des économistes, les régions sous-développées sont des pays ayant une économie de subsistance jusqu'à l'établissement d'échanges avec des pays industrialisés. La productivité ayant été très faible, il n'y a pas eu de progrès économique [1]. Après l'« ouverture » qui a lieu pour la plupart après une longue période de domination coloniale, des entrepreneurs étrangers développent certains secteurs de l'économie, mais néanmoins la différence entre le revenu per capita

[1] H. Myint, *The Economics of the developing countries,* Londres 1964, p. 115.

dans les pays sous-développés et dans les pays industrialisés augmente. Les activités des entrepreneurs étrangers ont pour conséquence que les divers secteurs de l'économie nationale deviennent des économies parallèles. Le secteur organisé par les entrepreneurs étrangers et dirigé vers l'exportation, se distingue par son niveau technologique plus élevé et par son organisation économique plus moderne [2]. La vie des couches de la population qui travaillent pour l'exportation change considérablement. Des paysans produisant seulement pour l'exportation achètent les denrées dont ils ont besoin. On passe à une économie-argent [3]. Pourtant les entrepreneurs étrangers établissent de véritables monopoles dans les secteurs qu'ils dominent [4]. Le développement d'un secteur à économie-argent est accompagné d'autres changements: des nouvelles structures administratives, introduites par le régime colonial et les entreprises étrangères, l'organisation de services sanitaires, amenant la diminution de la mortalité et la croissance de la population. Ce dernier phénomène est un trait caractéristique des pays «en cours de développement» [5]. La façon de vivre, les goûts changent. On acquiert des produits industriels qui sont importés par les entrepreneurs et dont on n'avait pas besoin autrefois.

W. W. Rostow a élaboré un modèle de développement économique qui comprend diverses époques bien définies [6]. La première époque c'est la société primitive, hiérarchique, à bas niveau technologique. Puis une élite emploie des capitaux économisés pour faire des innovations technologiques et pour préparer des cadres d'ouvriers spécialisés. Il s'ensuit le grand «départ». On développe une ou deux industries importantes et toujours croissantes. A la même époque on établit un régime politique et social qui est très favorable au développement économique. Puis il y a l'adoption des nouvelles méthodes de production par tous les autres secteurs de l'économie et enfin, dernière époque,

[2] *Ibidem,* p. 40.

[3] *Ibidem,* p. 76.

[4] *Ibidem,* p. 121.

[5] *Ibidem,* p. 23 et s.; IDEM, *An interpretation of economic backwardness,* Oxford Economic Papers 1954, réimprimé dans A. W. AGARWALA - J. P. S. SINGH, *The Economics of underdevelopment,* Oxford University Press 1958, p. 107 et s.

[6] *The Stages of economic growth, a non-communist manifesto,* Cambridge University Press 1960.

«l'âge de la consommation des produits de premier ordre par les masses». On emploie généralement les voitures et les téléviseurs.

Hélas, ces conceptions des économistes modernes qui envisagent seulement les économies et l'intensification de la production à notre époque ne sont pas appropriées pour comprendre la vie économique en d'autres époques. Il faut élaborer d'autres modèles de sous-développement.

a) *Un modèle de sous-développement au Moyen Age*

Pour le Moyen Age, comme pour l'époque moderne, le sous-développement économique est une conception relative aux rapports entre diverses régions. Car jusqu'à ce qu'un certain pays fut mis en contact avec d'autres pays plus développés, personne ne se rendait compte de la différence entre leurs niveaux et ceux-ci n'avaient aucune influence sur la vie économique de la région moins développée. Pourtant à des époques plus reculées, la région subissant l'influence ou même la domination économique des étrangers pouvait être un pays à économie agraire, primitive, de subsistance, mais aussi un pays dont l'économie se trouvait au même niveau que celui d'où venaient les étrangers, ou, enfin, un pays autrefois développé et puis décadent. A notre époque, les pays dits sous-développés sont pour la plupart très faibles au point de vue militaire, c'est un aspect de leur infériorité technologique. Mais autrefois les pays avec lesquels les étrangers nouaient les relations pouvaient aussi être des puissances fortes. Une deuxième différence entre l'«ouverture» des pays sous-développés à notre époque et au Moyen Age se rapporte aux étrangers qui intervenaient dans leur vie économique. Tandis qu'à notre époque les étrangers qui s'emparent d'un certain secteur de l'économie des pays moins développés sont des financiers-marchands-industriels, au Moyen Age (qui ne se terminait pas partout, on le sait, en même temps), ils appartenaient à des couches différentes: ils étaient des chevaliers-militaires-nomades ou des marchands (qui n'étaient pas des industriels). Les étrangers appartenant à ces deux couches pouvaient devenir des entrepreneurs dans les régions où ils s'emparaient de l'économie. L'intervention d'étrangers appartenant à ces classes si diverses dans des économies si différentes produisait donc un éventail de méthodes d'exploitation.

Il se passait très souvent que les militaires (chevaliers-nomades) s'emparaient d'une région dont l'économie était primitive. L'établissement de leur domination aboutissait le plus souvent à l'exploitation accomplie d'un secteur ou d'un nombre très réduit de secteurs de l'économie nationale. La conquête de l'Amérique centrale et méridionale par les Espagnols était un tel cas. Le continent américain était alors, sans doute, une région dont l'économie était très primitive [7]. Les agriculteurs ne connaissaient pas le blé et n'employaient pas la charrue, ni les animaux de trait ni les bêtes de somme [8], La roue y était inconnue [9]. Les industries étaient peu développées [10]. On employait pour le tissage des métiers très simples [11]. La métallurgie était elle aussi très primitive [12]. Les Inca ne savaient pas écrire [13]. Qn n'employait pas d'argent dans les échanges [14]. Bref, malgré l'enthousiasme que les grands travaux de construction ont inspiré à des écrivains modernes, c'était une civilisation au niveau de l'époque de la pierre [15]. Un auteur moderne compare la culture des Incas avec la civilisation sumérienne [16]. Les nouveaux maîtres de l'Amérique, des militaires typiques, s'emparent de grands lots de terre et, en employant tous les moyens, fondent de véritables latifundia [17]. Ils ont recours à la corvée et au simple esclavage [18]. Les Espagnols se lancent aussi dans l'exploitation des richesses minières, sans se soucier de la vie des ouvriers. Par contre, ils ne développent pas des industries textiles ou d'autres, ils préfèrent l'importation des textiles

[7] V. R. ROMANO, *Les mécanismes de la conquête coloniale: les conquistadores,* Paris 1936, p. 57.

[8] S. G. MORLEY, *The Ancient Maya,* Stanford University Press 1946, p. 74, 82.

[9] *Ibidem,* p. 90.

[10] *Ibidem,* p. 432, 434.

[11] *Ibidem,* p. 406; A. H. VERRILL - R. VERRILL, *America's ancient civilizations,* New York 1963, p. 78, 84; V. W. v. HAGEN, *Das Reich der Inkas,* Vienne 1958, p. 101.

[12] S. G. MORLEY, *The Ancient Maya,* cit., p. 453.

[13] V. W. v. HAGEN, *Das Reich der Inkas,* cit. p. 85.

[14] *Ibidem,* p. 88.

[15] S. G. MORLEY, *The Ancient Maya,* cit., p. 448.

[16] V. W. v. HAGEN, *Das Reich der Inkas,* cit., p. 113.

[17] A. JARA, *Tierras nuevas, expansión territorial y ocupación del suelo en America (siglos XVI-XIX),* Mexico 1969, p. 28, 62.

[18] CH. E. CHAPMAN, *Colonial Hispanic America,* New York 1933, p. 151.

anglais [19]. C'est le comportement typique des militaires qui se sont emparés d'un grand empire à économie primitive.

Les marchands qui nouaient, au Moyen Age, des relations avec d'autres pays dont l'économie était peu développée, représentaient très souvent des régions relativement industrialisées. Les pays outre-mer où ils allaient faire le commerce étaient la plupart des cas dominés par une couche de militaires aguerris. Dans ce cas les marchands, italiens et autres, se contentaient de poursuivre des activités purement commerciales. Mais le besoin d'une protection efficace des factoreries les amenait souvent à envisager la fondation de colonies indépendantes, jouissant d'autonomie complète et soutenues par les forces de la mère-patrie [20]. Voilà les cas de la Crète et de Chypre, des colonies vénitiennes, et de Chios et de Phocée, devenues colonies génoises. Pourtant il y avait aussi des contacts avec des pays dont l'économie n'était pas du tout inférieure. Ces relations étaient de véritables échanges: on acquérait chez les étrangers les produits qu'on n'avait pas. Les Chinois et les Japonais achetaient aux Européens, au XVIe siècle, des canons et des horloges mécaniques [21]. Enfin, troisième possibilité, les marchands étrangers prenaient contact avec des pays dont l'économie était en déclin. Ces contacts aboutissaient à l'accélération de leur décadence. Car les marchands importaient les produits des pays plus développés et donnaient le coup de grâce aux industries indigènes.

Cet éventail n'est pas encore complet. Car il y avait des régions qui subissaient des interventions successives de puissances économiques étrangères, par exemple d'abord celles des militaires qui aspiraient à l'exploitation des ressources naturelles ou d'un secteur de l'économie nationale et puis celles des marchands qui offraient les produits des pays plus développés et amenaient la ruine des manufactures locales, ou vice-versa.

L'histoire économique du Proche-Orient au Moyen Age et à l'époque ottomane est un exemple typique de telles interventions successives.

[19] *Ibidem*, p. 146 et s.

[20] J. Hicks, *A theory of economic history*, Oxford University Press 1969, p. 51.

[21] C. M. Cipolla, *Guns and sails*, Londres 1965, p. 109; Idem, *Clocks and culture 1300-1700*, Londres 1967, p. 80 et ss.

On peut y distinguer, grosso modo, trois époques, chacune étant de la même durée, à peu près, voire de 350-400 ans.

Au milieu du VIIe siècle, des marchands arabes, les Ḳuraish de La Mecque, conquéraient la plupart du Proche-Orient, des pays ayant de vieilles industries et une économie monétaire. Les nouveaux maîtres fondaient de nouvelles industries, comme celle du papier, et développaient les anciennes, comme celle des textiles et du sucre. Ils avaient le plus grand intérêt au progrès technologique. La circulation de bonnes monnaies augmentait. Par suite de la conquête arabe, la monnaie d'or se répand en Irak et dans la Perse. Les échanges commerciaux entre les pays appartenant autrefois à des empires divers sont alors plus intenses. Le développement démographique se caractérise par une croissance remarquable pendant trois siècles et demi en Irak et quatre cent ans en Egypte.

L'essor économique du Proche-Orient musulman parvint à sa fin au bout de 350 ans, vers l'an 1000 en Irak et dans les pays voisins et cinquante ans plus tard aussi en Egypte. La domination politique d'une société militaire, s'établissant au-dessus de la couche bourgeoise, amena la stagnation économique. Les militaires turcs qui étaient devenus les seigneurs incontestés de tous les pays orientaux, tendaient à l'exploitation économique de ces pays de vieilles civilisations. La paysannerie est opprimée plus qu'autrefois [22], l'abandon des terres et la diminution de la population commencent. Comme dans les pays sous-développés à l'époque moderne la plupart de la population doit dépenser plus de la moitié du revenu pour l'alimentation [23]. Pourtant celle-ci est si pauvre qu'on peut croire aux jérémiades des chroniqueurs arabes qui parlent du grand nombre des victimes des épidémies. Car la sous-alimentation de vastes couches de la population avait pour conséquence qu'elles succombaient facilement aux maladies endémiques et épidémiques [24]. Le nouveau régime plus hiérarchique que la société arabe des Omayyades

[22] V. ma *Social and economic history of the Near East in the Middle Ages,* Londres 1976, p. 171 et s., 182 et s.

[23] V. mon article *Essai sur l'alimentation des diverses classes sociales dans l'Orient médiéval,* dans «Annales E. S. C.», XXIII (1968), p. 1031 et s. et cf. R. E. Baldwin, *Economic development and growth,* New York 1966, p. 4 et ss.

[24] V. mon article cité ci-dessus p. 1050 et ss.

n'était pas favorable au développement industriel. La rapacité des militaires qui voulaient aussi exploiter les industries amenait leur déclin. L'établissement de monopoles et le prélèvement de nombreux impôts engendraient la stagnation technologique et la décadence des industries [25]. Par suite de la diminution de la population le prix du travail augmentait, les industries n'étaient plus profitables, on fermait les manufactures. A la fin du XIIe siècle et au début du XIIIe siècle, après la terrible famine et épidémie en 1201-1202, les industries textiles de l'Egypte s'écroulèrent presque. Les fameuses manufactures de Tinnīs et de Dabīḳ devaient être fermées. L'importation de textiles européens commença. Un autre symptôme de sous-développement qui se dégage avec netteté des sources arabes est le déclin de la spécialisation du travail, considérée par Adam Smith comme premier facteur de la productivité avancée. Tandis qu'à l'époque des Croisades la spécialisation du travail était en Egypte plus grande que jadis à Rome [26], on ferma au XIVe siècle les manufactures royales (ṭirāz) au Caire, à en croire al-Maḳrīzī [27]. Celles-ci disparues, la production industrielle se poursuivait seulement au niveau artisanal.

Depuis la fin du XIVe siècle, les économies du Proche-Orient sont en pleine décadence. Un orientaliste a soutenu que l'économie du Proche-Orient est devenue à cette époque une économie-nature après avoir été une économie-argent à l'époque des califes [28]. Cette assertion est probablement exagérée, mais l'affirmation de B. Lewis qui parle du grand essor du Proche-Orient à ladite époque grâce aux revenus du commerce des épices l'est encore plus [29]. En effet, l'intensification des échanges commerciaux entre le Proche-Orient et l'Europe méridionale qui eut lieu dans le dernier tiers du XIVe siècle signifiait, pour employer le langage des économistes, l'« ouverture » d'une région sous-dé-

[25] V. *Social and economic history,* p. 178, 215 et s., 247.

[26] S. D. Goitein, *The main industries of the Mediterranean area as reflected in the records in the Cairo Geniza,* dans JESHO, IV (1961), p. 168.

[27] Al-Khiṭaṭ II, p. 98 l. 31; v. aussi Ibn Khaldūn, *The Muqaddimah*, tr. F. Rosenthal, II, Pricenton University Press 1967, p. 67.

[28] A. Poliak, *Les révoltes populaires en Egypte à l'époque des Mamelouks*, dans REI, VIII (1934), p. 252.

[29] V. son article *The Arabs in eclipse,* (dans le recueil de) C. M. Cipolla, *The Economic decline of empires,* Londres 1970, p. 113.

veloppée. Le régime féodal, type turc-proche-oriental, qui avait remplacé une économie marchande, industrielle et monétaire, et non pas une économie basée sur l'esclavage (d'après le modèle de Marx) avait accéléré le déclin démographique. L'«ouverture» n'était pas la suite d'une domination coloniale qui avait amélioré les services médicaux et organisé les services de transport. Puisque la population diminuait, il n'y avait pas de chômage, comme dans les pays sous-développés à notre époque. L'importation de produits industriels n'amenait pas le licenciement d'ouvriers, comme suite de la modernisation de la production. Mais la demande plus réduite, par suite de la dépopulation, avait pour conséquence un changement dans la production agricole: on agrandissait les secteurs qui produisaient pour l'exportation, on diminuait la production des denrées. Comme c'est le cas dans les pays sous-développés à notre époque, l'exportation n'était pas diversifiée, mais consistait en deux, trois articles [30]. Le secteur de l'agriculture qui produisait pour l'exportation n'était pas organisé par les étrangers, restant des marchands-acheteurs, et il n'y avait pas de changements technologiques dans la production. C'est ce qui se passe aussi à notre époque dans certaines régions sous-développées [31]. Etant donné que le volume de l'exportation de certaines matières premières produites dans le Proche-Orient, au contraire des régions sous-développées à notre époque, ne rapportait qu'une part réduite du revenu national, les conséquences qu'avaient pour la vie monétaire les ventes des produits indigènes, payés en argent comptant, étaient elles aussi plus modiques que dans les régions sous-développées à notre époque. Toutefois l'«ouverture» amenait un changement considérable de la vie économique. Elle était un facteur «deségalisant», bien que moins qu'à l'époque moderne [32]. Les couches en contact avec les étrangers et touchant des payements en argent comptant pour les produits vendus concevaient de nouvelles idées et changeaient leurs goûts. L'importation de produits étrangers devient un véritable dumping. On importe des produits agricoles, qui sont meilleurs que les indigènes, et surtout des produits industriels, des

[30] R. E. Baldwin, *Economiè development*, cit., p. 12.
[31] *Ibidem*, p. 53.
[32] Cf. H. Myint, *An interpretation of economic backwardness*, p. 110.

textiles et d'autres. C'est le coup de grâce pour les industries locales, décadentes depuis longtemps. Voilà un phénomène caractéristique de l'«ouverture» de quelques régions sous-développées à notre époque, où les métiers indigènes déclinent [33]. Pourtant dans le Proche-Orient médiéval c'était la ruine à peu près totale des grandes industries, produisant autrefois pour l'exportation et à l'échelle pré-capitaliste.

La ruine des industries est accompagnée d'autres phénomènes caractéristiques de l'«ouverture» des régions sous-développées. Les Orientaux ont recours aux services de transport organisés par les armateurs italiens. C'est ce qui se passait dans l'empire byzantin, lors de son déclin [34]. La balance commerciale des échanges entre le Proche-Orient et l'Europe méridionale et avec l'Inde d'autre part devient déficitaire, le revenu per capita diminue. Voici un autre trait caractéristique de l'économie des pays sous-développés [35]. En plus, le budget de l'Etat est surchargé de dépenses militaires, la déflation, suite de l'approvisionnement diminué de métaux précieux, augmente [36]. L'appauvrissement général s'accentue. La débâcle monétaire et industrielle est totale. Des pays d'une vieille civilisation languissante par suite de la dépopulation chronique, comme jadis l'empire romain [37], sont mûrs pour la domination étrangère.

b) *Déclin démographique*

Le phénomène le plus important de l'histoire sociale et économique du Proche-Orient à la basse-époque était, on l'a déjà relevé, la dépopulation. Elle s'accélère à la fin du XIVe siècle.

[33] *Ibidem*, p. 120.

[34] CH. DIEHL, *The economic decline of Byzantium*, dans C. M. CIPOLLA, *The economic decline of empires*, cit., p. 94 et s.

[35] H. MYINT, *The economics of the developing countries*, cit., p. 11.

[36] V. ma monographie *Les métaux précieux et la balance des payements du Proche-Orient à la basse époque*, Paris 1971, p. 97 et ss.

[37] La vieille thèse de Seeck et des autres savants qui expliquaient le déclin de l'empire romain par la dépopulation a été reprise dans l'excellente monographie de A. E. R. BOAK, *Manpower shortage and the fall of the Roman empire in the West*, Ann Arbor 1955.

Les source arabes nous fournissent plusieurs dates sur le nombre des villages de l'Egypte au Bas Moyen Age [38]. Les voici:

1375	2.163
1434	2.170
1460	2.365
1477	2.121

Ces données, desquelles on écartera le renseignement se rapportant à l'année 1460 qui est certainement erroné, indiquent une lente progression de la dépopulation. Mais les renseignements qu'on trouve dans le livre d'Ihn al-Djī'ān sur le rapport de l'impôt foncier sont plus instructifs. Cet auteur, qui écrivit en 1477 en s'appuyant sur les données dans la comptabilité du Trésor, nous fournit des totaux pour toutes les provinces. Il indique aussi, à plusieurs reprises, le rapport plus élevé à une époque antérieure. Le prince Omar Toussoun a conclu que ces indications se réfèrent au cadastre fait par le sultan al-Malik an-Nāṣir Muḥammad en 1315, tandis que les autres données datent de l'an 1375, comme le dit l'auteur [39]. Bien que ce savant se soit trompé en croyant que les revenus sont indiqués en dinars réels (et non en «dinārs djaishī», une monnaie de compte ou plutôt unité fiscale tout-à-fait imaginaire) [40], il est en effet très probable que les passages dans lesquels l'auteur parle des revenus «d'autrefois» se rapportent à l'époque d'al-Malik an-Nāṣir Muḥammad. Pourtant Ibn al-Djī'ān nous fournit des renseignements sur les revenus du Trésor à trois dates. Car en faisant l'addition des revenus des divers villages (fiefs etc.) dans chaque province on obtient toujours un total plus petit que celui indiqué par l'auteur. Or il paraît que ces données se rapportent à l'époque de l'auteur.

[38] Les données se référant aux années 1375 et 1477 sont les totaux des indications fournies par Ibn al-Djī'ān, v. ci-dessous. Pour les années 1434 (à être corrigé dans ma Social and economic history p. 303 où on lit 2122, ainsi que 2322 doit être corrigé en 2163) et 1460 v. Ibn Taghrībirdī, *an-Nudjūm az-zāhira* (éd. Popper), VI, p. 717 et Idem, *Ḥawādith* (éd. Popper), p. 333.

[39] *Mémoire sur les finances de l'Egypte depuis les pharaons jusqu'à nos jours,* Le Caire 1924, p. 138.

[40] Ce qu'a justement reproché A. N. Poliak, *Histoire des relations agraires en Egypte, en Syrie et en Palestine à la fin du Moyen Age et à l'époque moderne* (en hébreu), Jérusalem 1940, p. 23.

Ce qui semble confirmer cette hypothèse est le fait que les indications relatives au rapport de l'impôt foncier que nous fournit un autre auteur arabe, écrivant vers l'an 1400, sont pour la plupart des cas semblants aux totaux notés par Ibn al-Djī'ān pour chaque province. Or cet autre auteur, Ibn Duḳmāḳ, n'avait pas accès au cadastre, mais s'appuyait sur diverses autres sources d'information, comme le démontrent les nombreuses lacunes qu'il laissait dans son manuscrit, espérant obtenir plus tard des informations manquantes [41]. La comparaison des totaux qu'on obtient par l'addition des données qu'on trouve dans les livres de ces deux auteurs pour quelques provinces de l'Egypte septentrionale et méridionale, ne laisse aucun doute quant au déclin considérable de la production agricole, par suite de la dépopulation et de l'abandon des terres. Les voici:

	Nombre de villages	Total	Autrefois en plus	Addition des rapports des villages
al-Ḳalyūbīya				
Ibn al-Djī'ān p. 8 et ss.	59	419.850	26.650	345.100
Ibn Duḳmāḳ V, p. 47 et ss.	54	381.440 [42]		
an-Nastarāwa				
Ibn al-Djī'ān p. 137 et s.	6	43.500	4.000	29.900
Ibn Duḳmāḳ V, p. 113 et s.	12	51.000 [43]		
al-Buḥaira				
Ibn al-Djī'ān p. 116 et ss.	222 [44]	741.294 $^2/_3$	153.223	612.054
Ibn Duḳmāḳ V, p. 101 et ss.	293	859.904 [45]		

[41] Le livre d'Ibn al Djī'ān, *at-Tuḥfa as-sanīya bi-asmā al-bilād al-miṣrīya* a été publié par B. Moritz, Būlāḳ 1898 et v. les sommaires en tableaux (d'après un autre manuscrit) chez S. de Sacy, *Relation de l'Egypte par Abd-Allatif,* Paris 1810, p. 593 et ss. et chez A. N. Poliak, *Histoire des relations agraires,* cit., p. 90 et s.; le livre d'Ibn Duḳmāḳ, *al-Intiṣār li-wāsiṭat 'iḳd al-amṣār* fut aussi publié par Moritz, Būlāḳ 1893.

[42] C'est le revenu de 52 villages connu de l'auteur.

[43] C'est le revenu de 9 villages connu de l'auteur.

[44] En comptant les villages enregistrés nous trouvons 229.

[45] C'est le revenu de 272 villages connu de l'auteur.

al-Ikhmīmīya

Ibn al-Djī'ān p. 188 et ss.	24 [46]	243.925¹/₈	3.450	184.249
Ibn Duķmāķ V, p. 25 et ss.	35	187.980 [47]		

al-Ķūsīya

Ibn al-Djī'ān p. 190 et ss.	40	414.663,5	26.500	363.150
Ibn Duķmāķ V, p. 28 et ss.	44	405.241¹/₆ [48]		

Passons au rapport total. En calculant les 9.428.292 dinars djaishī que rapportaient toutes les provinces de l'Egypte à l'époque d'al-Malik an-Nāṣir Muḥammad selon une moyenne de 7-10 dirhams [49] on obtient 3.964.624 dinars. D'autre part, on lit dans la grande chronique d'Ibn Iyās que le revenu du gouvernement égyptien (sc. de l'impôt foncier) se montait à la fin de l'époque mamlouke à 1.300.000 dinars, 300.000 irdabbs de froment et 300.000 irdabbs d'orge [50]. L'addition de l'impôt payé en argent comptant et en nature donne 1.550.000 dinars (ashrafīs!) [51]. La diminution du revenu, étroitement liée à la dépopulation, ressort avec netteté de la comparaison de ces données avec une relation d'Ibn Iyās sur le rapport de l'impôt foncier au début de l'époque mamlouke, sous le règne du sultan Baibars. Il aurait été, à en croire cet auteur, de 12 millions de dinars [52]. Certainement il s'agit de dinars djaishī et la somme indiquée par l'auteur était l'équivalent de 9,1 mill. de dinars réels. On ne croira pas que la diminution formidable du rapport de l'impôt foncier était seulement la conséquence de la corruption, de l'inefficacité de l'administration et de l'amoindrissement des biens ruraux donnés aux militaires en fiefs.

On ne peut pas citer, pour démontrer la dimension de la dépopula-

[46] L'auteur dit toutefois p. 5: 26 villages.

[47] C'est le revenu de 27 villages connu de l'auteur.

[48] C'est le revenu de 42 villages connu de l'auteur.

[49] V. AL-MAĶRĪZĪ, *al-Khiṭaṭ*, II, p. 218 1. 11 - p. 219 1. 6 (à être corrigé chez A. N. POLIAK, *Some notes on the feudal system of the Mamlūks*, dans JRAS, 1937, p. 100 note 1).

[50] Ed. Būlāķ III, p. 266 (texte fautif dans l'édition Kahle-Mustafa V, p. 402).

[51] Pour le prix du blé v. *Social and economic history of the Near East in the Middle Ages*, p. 313 et pour la proportion des prix du blé et de l'orge v. mon *Histoire des prix et des salaires dans l'Orient médiéval*, Paris 1969, p. 301.

[52] V, p. 404.

tion en Syrie, des sources pareilles aux livres d'Ibn al-Djī'ān et d'Ibn Duḳmāḳ. Mais des renseignements trouvés dans des sources littéraires et documentaires ne laissent aucun doute: elle était aussi grande qu'en Egypte. L'écrivain arabe Khalīl aẓ-Ẓāhirī (m. 1468) raconte qu'à son époque il y avait dans la province de Safed (la Galilée) environ 1200 villages [53]. Selon les recensements que firent les Turcs en 1525/26 leur nombre n'était que 231! [54] Or Khalīl aẓ-Ẓāhirī connaissait la province de Safed probablement très bien, car durant quelque temps (en 1438 du moins) il y était un haut fonctionnaire [55]. Même en supposant que cette relation se rapporte à une époque plus reculée, c'est un témoignage éloquent. Dans une autre province syrienne, la province de Tripoli, les Ottomans s'apercevaient, en 1519/20, peu de temps après la conquête du pays, de ce que plusieurs villages qui comptaient autrefois 3000 habitants n'en avaient plus que 800 [56]. Il est probable que des habitants s'étaient enfuis lors de ce premier recensement ottoman, mais on ne croirait pas que ce phénomène explique la diminution tout à fait énorme de la population agraire dans la province de Tripoli.

Quant au nombre des habitants de la Syrie à l'époque mamlouke nous sommes toutefois réduits à des évaluations qui s'appuient sur diverses hypothèses. A. N. Poliak en faisant de telles hypothèses a conclu que la population de la Syrie entière (le Liban et la Palestine y comprises) s'élevait avant la Peste Noire à 900.000 âmes [57]. D'autre part, on peut citer des sources plus sûres pour le début de l'époque ottomane. L'historien turc O. L. Barkan qui a entrepris une recherche systématique des recensements faits par les Ottomans en Syrie après la conquête du pays, a calculé, en multipliant le nombre des feux par 5, que le total se montait en 1520-1535 à 571.360 [58]. Pourtant ce total comprend la population de plusieurs provinces de l'Asie Mineure (Adana, Uzeyr,

[53] *Zubdat kashf al-mamālik,* éd. Ravaisse, p. 44.

[54] B. Lewis, *Studies in the Ottoman archives,* dans BSOAS, XVI (1954), p. 475.

[55] V. Brockelmann, GAL², II, p. 167.

[56] R. Mantran - J. Sauvaget, *Règlements fiscaux ottomans, La Syrie,* Beyrouth 1951, p. 80.

[57] *The demographic evolution of the Middle East, dans Palestine and the Middle East,* X (1938), p. 201.

[58] *Essai sur les données statistiques des registres de recensement dans l'empire ottoman aux XVe et XVIe siècles,* dans JESHO, I (1957/58), p. 20.

Tarsus et Sis). La population de la Syrie, vers l'an 720, avait probablement été à peu près de 4 millions [59].

Si l'on suppose que la Palestine comptait, au XIVe siècle, un quart de la population totale de la Syrie, elle se serait montée avant la Peste Noire à 225.000 (si l'hypothèse de Poliak s'avérait juste) et après cette catastrophe démographique – 150.000. En multipliant par 5 le nombre des feux dans les quatre sandjaks palestiniens (Safed, Nabulus, Jérusalem et Ghaza) (et en excluant les «naḥiyas» galiléennes qui appartiennent aujourd'hui au Liban, c'est-à-dire Tibnīn, Tyr et Shaḳīf) on déduira du recensement de 1553/54 – 205.000 [60]. La population de la Palestine avant la conquête turque et la reprise démographique qui y faisait suite n'a pas pu être beacoup plus grande que 120-130.000 [61]. C'était le nadir démographique de la Palestine à l'époque historique.

c) *Déclin de l'agriculture*

Le recul démographique était accompagné par la diminution de la production agricole, les données recueillies par Ibn al-Djī'ān et par Ibn Duḳmāḳ le démontrent clairement. La demande de céréales dans les pays du Proche-Orient eux-mêmes diminuait et, d'autre part, on n'exportait plus de grandes quantités de blé à Rome et à Byzance comme autrefois. La production de blé en Egypte, bien que diminuée, était encore suffisante pour qu'on pût souvent en exporter en d'autres pays, en Syrie, au Hidjaz, à Chypre, à Rhodes, à Venise, Gênes et Raguse. La Syrie exportait elle aussi du blé à Chypre et ailleurs [62]. La courbe des-

[59] H. Lammens, *La Syrie*, I, Beyrouth 1921, p. 120.

[60] V. B. Lewis, *Studies in the Ottoman archives* 1. c. Ce savant a employé le coefficient 7-8 ce qui ne correspond même pas au nombre d'âmes dans les familles arabes de la Palestine à l'époque du régime mandataire anglais.

[61] Le professeur R. Bachi, *The population of Israel*, Jérusalem 1978, p. 23, 362 est enclin à supposer qu'elle se montait à 140-150.000. Mais il se peut que le nombre des âmes par famille ait été inférieur à 5 (et en effet le prof. Bachi dit lui-même que son total est peut-être un peu trop élevé).

[62] V. *Ḥawādith*, p. 251 et s. (des centaines de milliers d'irdabbs sont exportés en 1456 en Syrie et «aux îles des Francs») et v. les renseignements cités dans mon article *Quelques problèmes que soulève l'histoire des prix dans l'Orient médiéval, Studies in memory of Gaston Wiet,* Jérusalem 1977, p. 216 ss.

cendante du prix du blé est certainement une preuve de la surabondance [63]. Mais puisque la production avait diminué il arrivait, lors des sécheresses, qu'on devait en importer. Plusieurs renseignements de source arabe et dans des documents vénitiens et ancônitains portent témoignage de l'importation de blé en Egypte et en Syrie [64].

Le déclin de l'agriculture proche-orientale n'était pas seulement quantitatif, il était aussi qualitatif. C'est ce qu'on conclura de l'importation de grandes quantités d'huile d'olive. La différence entre le prix de l'huile indigène (syrien) et de l'huile importée en Egypte de l'Europe démontre que l'huile européenne était beaucoup plus estimée.

On importait en Egypte de l'huile des Pouilles [65], de la province de Naples [66], de la Provence [67], de la Catalogne [68], de Majorque [69], de Séville [70], de la Tunisie [71] et de la Tripolitaine [72]. De même on importait de l'huile européenne en Syrie, qui jadis l'exportait en Europe occidentale. Au début du XIVe siècle le gouvernement mamlouk s'efforçait encore d'empêcher l'importation d'huile européenne par des droits protecteurs [73], mais cent ans plus tard on devait apparemment y renoncer. Au XVe siècle, les Vénitiens y vendaient de l'huile des Pouilles [74].

[63] *Ibidem*, p. 212.

[64] V. les sources citées dans ledit article p. 215 s. et v. aussi ARCHIVIO DI STATO ANCONA, *Notai*, Angelo di Domenico VIII, f. 102a f., 232a/233b, 238b (a. 1469); ARCHIVIO DI STATO VENEZIA, *Senato*, Mar IX, f. 78a (a. 1471, mais se rapportant à 1470).

[65] ASV, *Giudici di petiziòn, Sentenze a giustizia* (cité dorénavant G. P., Sent.) 150, f. 71 b et ss. (a. 1466) (pour 4160 ducats!) 176, f. la et ss. (a. 1478) et v. mon article *New data for the history of Levantine Jewries in the fifteenth century*, dans «Bulletin of the Institute of Jewish Studies», III (1975), p. 97 et ss.

[66] Importation par Amalfitains: ASV, *Cancelleria Inferiore, Notai*, Ba 222, Antoniello de Vataciis (cité Vat.) sub 2 juillet 1404; par Gaëtans: *Ibidem* sub 18 juillet 1406; par Génois: *Ibidem* sub 28 déc. 1405; par Vénitiens: *Cronaca Morosini*, ms. Vienne 8331/32, c. 340 (a. 1417).

[67] Vat. sub 1 sept. 1401 (par Génois), 9 déc. 1405; ASV, *Cancelleria Inferiore, Notai*, Ba 211, Nicolo Turiano V, f. 2a et s. (vendu au «marchand du sultan»).

[68] Vat. sub 1 déc. 1400.

[69] ASV, *Cancelleria Inferiore, Notai*, Ba 83, Cristoforo del Fiore I, f. 16a et ss. (a. 1434, acheté à Rhodes et importé par des Vénitiens).

[70] ARCHIVIO DI STATO GENOVA, *Notai*, 312, Andreolo Caito IV, c. 87a et s., 211a et s., 216b (a. 1393); *Notai*, 405, Bartolomeo Gatti X, part 1, c. 63b et ss. (a. 1407).

[71] G. P., *Sent.*, 34, f. 11a et ss. 48, f. 85a et ss. (de Sfax).

[72] G. P., *Sent.*, 48, f. 102a et ss. 74, f. 9b et ss.; v. aussi 52, f. 9b et ss. (de la Berbérie).

[73] 10,5% contre 3,3% pour d'autres produits importés à Damas, PEGOLOTTI, *Pratica della mercatura*, éd. Evans, p. 90.

[74] G. P., *Sent.*, 52, f. 85b.

L'importation d'huile en Egypte et en Syrie était au Bas Moyen Age un grand négoce. Marchands de toutes les nations de l'Europe méridionale s'y adonnaient, des Vénitiens [75], des Génois [76], des Catalans [77] et d'autres encore [78].

L'huile qu'on importait de l'Europe méridionale se vendait toujours beaucoup plus cher que l'huile indigène. Tandis qu'un ḳinṭār djarwī (de 90 kg) d'huile indigène coûtait en Egypte, au XVe siècle, la plupart du temps 3-4 dinars (puis ashrafīs), l'huile espagnole se vendait 7-8 [79].

Le volume de l'importation de l'huile européenne dans le Proche-Orient devait être considérable. Citons quelques documents: deux marchands génois importèrent, en 1405, à Alexandrie de l'huile d'Andalousie (de Séville) qui fut vendue pour 6.382 dinars [80]. Deux Vénitiens échangèrent, en 1488, à Alexandrie 959 «botti» d'huile contre du poivre. La valeur de l'huile était probablement de 23.000 ducats [81]. Le témoignage le plus important, quant au volume de l'importation d'huile européenne en Egypte, est certainement l'affirmation faite par le sultan Ḳānṣūh al-Ghaurī lors des pourparlers avec un ambassadeur vénitien en 1512. Le sultan soutient que les Vénitiens apportaient «autrefois», c'est-à-dire à la fin du XVe siècle, à Alexandrie chaque année 3-4000 boutes d'huile d'olive [82]. Or cette quantité aurait représenté la valeur de 72-96.000 ducats. D'autre part, on n'oubliera pas que les Vénitiens

[75] ASV, *Senato,* Misti 34, f. 47b (a. 1373); Vat. I, f. 5a (a. 1399); G. P., *Sent.* 34, f. 37a et ss. (a. 1419), 39a et s. (a. 1404) 46, f. 25b et ss. (a. 1427 environ) 56, f. 78b et ss. (a. 1426) 74, f. 51b et ss. (a. 1435 environ) 188, f. 180b et ss. (a. 1488).

[76] ASV, *Cancelleria Inferiore, Notai,* Ba 230, Nicolo Venier B, 2, f. 32b et s. (a. 1421) et v. ci-dessous.

[77] Vat. sub 10 jan. 1406.

[78] V. outre les sources citées ci-avant les indications dans *Histoire des prix et des salaires,* pp. 268 et s., 318 et s.

[79] V. mon article *Quelques problèmes que soulève l'histoire des prix dans l'Orient médiéval,* tableau IV; des prix à être ajoutés:

nov. 1347	dinars	Lettere a Pignol Zucchello (Venise 1957), no. 56
1434	8 duc. de Rhodes	Nic. Turiano V, f. 2a et s.
1472	6 duc.	ASG, 2774c, f. 20a

Sur l'équivalence du ḳinṭār djarwī v. art. cit. note 85.

[80] Vat. sub 29 déc. 1405.

[81] G. P., *Sent.,* 188, f. 180b et ss.

[82] Reinaud, *Traités de commerce entre la république de Venise et les derniers sultans mamelouks d'Egypte,* dans JA 1829, II, p. 32 cf. 28.

n'étaient pas les marchands européens qui apportaient aux échelles de l'Orient les plus grandes cargaisons d'huile. C'étaient probablement les Génois. Quoiqu'il en soit, pour un pays, comme l'Egypte, dont le revenu du Trésor se montait alors à 1 million et demi de ducats, c'étaient des importations de valeur formidable. On ne peut pas sous-estimer leur poids pour la balance commerciale.

Pourtant la décadence de l'agriculture proche-orientale était si avancée qu'on dût aussi importer d'autres produits agricoles de l'Europe. Un tel produit était le miel. L'importation de miel en Egypte commençait déjà à la fin du XIIIe siècle. Car Marino Sanuto «le Vieux», écrivant dans la première décennie du XIVe siècle, parle de l'importation de miel en Egypte [83]. Puis, au XVe siècle, on l'importait surtout de la Grèce et des îles de l'archipel. On peut évoquer de nombreux textes littéraires et documents qui se réfèrent à l'importation de miel de Crète [84], de Rhodes [85], de Salonique [86], de Coron [87] et de Corfou [88]. Dans les listes de prix à Alexandrie datant de la neuvième décennie du XIVe siècle et de la première moitié du XVe siècle on repère le miel «del Golfo» (apparemment de la Dalmatie) et «delle isole» (probablement des îles grecques) et dans une autre liste qui date, selon ce qui semble, de 1420-25, - le miel «blanc», «del Golfo» et «de Coron» [89]. De même on vendait en Egypte du miel de plusieurs provinces de l'Italie, de la Sicile [90], des Pouilles [91], de Gaëte [92] et de la Lombardie [93]. Les

[83] *Secreta fidelium crucis,* Jérusalem 1972, p. 24.

[84] *Traité d'Emmanuel Piloti sur la Passage en Terre Sainte* (1420), éd. P. H. Dopp, Louvain 1958, p. 154, 158.

[85] Nic. Turiano IV, f. 58b. et s. (a. 1428).

[86] Piloti, p. 143.

[87] G. P., *Sent.,* 82, f. 9a et ss. (a. 1437); liste des prix dans les Archives Datini datée d'Alexandrie du 24 juillet 1386, Archivio di Stato di Prato, Quaderni di carichi di navi e di valute di mercanzie, 1171.

[88] Piloti, p. 151; G. P., *Sent.* 116, f. 68b et ss. (a. 1451); v. aussi Piloti, p. 157: importation de l'archipel et p. 138, 140 sur l'importation de miel de la Turquie.

[89] Liste de prix Datini du 24 juillet 1386 d'Alexandrie; N. da Uzzano, *Pratica della mercatura,* (dans) Pagnini, *Della decima,* IV, p. 111.

[90] Vat. sub mars 1405 (l'acte ne porte pas une date précise).

[91] ASV, *Senato,* Misti 34, f. 47b.

[92] Vat. sub 18 juillet 1406.

[93] ASV, *Proc. S. Marco,* Commissarie miste, Comm. Biegio Dolfin, Ba 181, fasc. 23 (a. 1418); Piloti, p. 150.

marchands français et d'autres importaient en Egypte du miel de la Provence [94]. On offrait à Alexandrie aussi du miel de la Catalogne [95] et de la Tunisie [96]. Plusieurs documents ont trait à l'importation de miel européen en Syrie. Dans des listes de prix à Alexandre qui datent du début du XVe siècle on trouve des indications touchant le miel de Turtose, de Cenades et de Mequinanza (en Catalogne) [97]. Les actes d'un procès à Venise se rapportent à l'importation de miel à Tripoli, en 1444 environ [98]. Les Vénitiens étaient toujours très actifs dans cette branche du commerce levantin [99].

Comme l'huile d'olive européenne, le miel était considérablement plus cher que l'indigène. Tandis que le ḳinṭār (djarwī) de miel indigène coûtait en Egypte, au XVe siècle, en moyenne 3-4 dinars, le prix du miel européen se montait, à la fin du XIVe siècle, à 4-6 dinars et après l'an 1425 à 6-8 ashrafīs (ou ducats). Les renseignements qu'on trouve dans diverses sources démontrent aussi que le prix du miel importé était en hausse au XVe siècle [100].

d) *Le Proche-Orient - exportateur de matières premières, la production du coton*

Le déclin, quantitatif et qualitatif, de la production agricole dans les pays du Proche-Orient non seulement donnait lieu à l'importation de produits agricoles de l'Europe, mais amenait aussi un changement de cultures. Quand la demande de céréales diminuait, on passait, dans divers districts de l'Egypte et de la Syrie, de la culture du blé à la plantation du coton.

[94] Vat. sub 4 oct. 1404 et 9 déc. 1405 (de Montpellier), 2 déc. 1399 (de Narbonne) et v. aussi sub 9 déc. 1399, 20 mai 1401; Nic. Venier B, 2, f. 42b et s. (a. 1421, par Génois).

[95] Crist. del Fiore I, f. 16a et s. (a. 1424, «catalan» et «de Mequinanza» importé par des Vénitiens de Rhodes).

[96] G. P., *Sent.* 34, f. 11a et ss. (a. 1422, importé par des Vénitiens). V. aussi les sources citées dans *Histoire des prix et des salaires*, p. 269.

[97] *Quelques problèmes que soulève l'histoire des prix dans l'Orient médiéval*, p. 224 s.

[98] G. P., *Sent.* 102, f. 63a et ss.

[99] Vat. I, f. 5a (a. 1399); G. P., *Sent.* VII, f. 80b et s. (a. 1403) (importation de miel valant 2400 ducats) 11, f. 18a et ss. (a. 1403) 56, f. 78b et ss. (a. 1426).

[100] *Quelques problèmes que soulève l'histoire des prix*, p. 224 s.

Il paraît que les plantations de coton aient été en Egypte, à l'époque des califes abbasides et des premièrs Fatimides, insignifiantes. Les tissus de coton qui datent de cette époque et portent des inscriptions démontrant qu'ils étaient destinés à des dignitaires égyptiens, étaient pour la plupart importés d'autres pays [101]. Les documents qui témoignent sans doute qu'on plantait, à cette époque, du coton en Egypte sont très rares [102]. Mais les sources de l'époque mamlouke ne laissent aucun doute qu'on agrandissait les plantations déjà dans la deuxième moitié du XIIIe siècle et au début du XIVe siècle. Marino Sanuto «le Vieux» mentionne le coton parmi les produits qu'on exportait de l'Egypte [103] et le pèlerin irlandais Simeon Semeonis, qui vint en 1323 en Egypte, décrit les plantations de coton, qu'il voyait près de la ville de Fūwa, dans la Basse-Egypte [104]. Ḥamdallāh Mustaufī, un auteur persan qui écrivit vers l'an 1340, parle lui aussi de la plantation de coton en Egypte [105]. Puis, à la fin du XIVe siècle et au début du XVe siècle, les plantations de coton et son exportation augmentaient considérablement, à en juger d'après de nombreux renseignements dans diverses sources. L'auteur crétois Emanuel Piloti parle des vastes plantations de coton dans la province de Gharbīya [106] et un Allemand, qui parcourut l'Egypte à la fin du XVe siècle, raconte qu'il voyait les plantations en faisant le voyage de Ḳaṭyā à Ghaza [107]. Ce voyageur dit aussi qu'on exportait le coton égyptien à Venise. Toutefois, on fera mieux de ne pas exagérer en traitant de l'agrandissement des plantations de coton en

[101] V. R. Pfister, *L'introduction du coton en Egypte musulmane,* dans «Revue des arts asiatiques», XI, (1937), p. 170, 172; C. J. Lamm, *Cotton in medieval textiles of the Near East,* Paris 1937, p. 172 et ss., 241; et cf. D. Müller-Wodarg, *Die Landwirtschaft Ägyptens in der frühen Abbāsidenzeit, Der Islam,* 1957, p. 39.

[102] V. un tel document: D. S. Margoliouth - E. J. Holmyard, *Arabic documents from the Monneret collection,* dans Islamica, IV (1931), no. 4, p. 268 et ss. Pour la fin de l'époque fatimide v. aussi un passage dans la géographie d'al-Idrīsī où il parle de l'exportation de tissus de coton d'Alexandrie en Cyrénaïque: *Description de l'Afrique et de l'Espagne,* éd. Dozy-de Gǫeje, Leyde 1866, p. 136, trad. p. 163.

[103] *Secreta fidelium crucis,* p. 24.

[104] *Itinerarium Symonis Semeonis ab Hybernia ad Terram Sanctam,* éd. M. Esposito, Dublin 1960, p. 64.

[105] *The geographical parts of the Nuzhat-al-qulūb,* éd. Guy Le Strange, Leyde 1915, p. 244.

[106] *Ibidem,* p. 69.

[107] *Die Pilgerfahrt des Ritters Arnold v. Harff,* Cologne 1860, p. 159.

Egypte au Bas Moyen Age. Car dans des nombreuses relations des chroniqueurs arabes sur les hausses des prix on cherche en vain le prix du coton, tandis qu'on repère plusieurs indications du prix du lin [108]. Par contre, l'auteur d'un Guide des marchands qui recueillait ses matériaux vers 1420 mentionne le coton parmi les produits égyptiens importés à Gênes [109]. En effet, dans la deuxième moitié du XIVe siècle et au XVe siècle, le commerce du coton était animé en Egypte, selon ce qu'on lit dans la Topographie d'al-Maḳrīzī [110]. Ce sont surtout les registres de la Douane de Gênes et les bulletins des facteurs de la firme Francesco Datini qui témoignent du grand volume de l'exportation du coton égyptien à la fin du XIVe siècle et au début du XVe siècle. Il paraît en effet que les Génois étaient les grands exportateurs du coton égyptien. De nombreux documents démontrent que déjà en 1366-1369 il n'y avait presque pas de bateau génois qui arrivait d'Alexandrie sans apporter une cargaison de coton valant quelques milliers de ducats [111]. On repère de lourdes cargaisons de coton égyptien aussi dans les inventaires qu'ont dressés les facteurs de Fr. Datini des bateaux faisant voile d'Alexandrie à Gênes dans les deux dernières décennies du XIVe siècle. Les Vénitiens, d'autre part, à peu près monopolisaient l'exportation du coton de la Syrie.

Le coton exporté en Italie était destiné à la production des fûtaines. Une part fut réexpédiée en Allemagne méridionale où la production des fûtaines avait pris un grand essor à cette époque. L'Egypte était donc devenue un pays qui exportait la matière première pour l'industrie textile en Europe. Il est vrai qu'elle avait exporté aussi à l'époque des Croisades du lin en Tunisie et ailleurs. Mais à cette époque c'était un article parmi beaucoup d'autres (industriels y compris) qu'on exportait. Au tournant du XIVe siècle l'exportation des produits industriels de l'Egypte était devenue insignifiante.

[108] V. mon article *L'évolution des prix dans le Proche Orient à la basse époque*, dans JESHO, IV (1961), p. 36.

[109] N. DA UZZANO, *Pratica della mercatura*, cit., p. 191.

[110] AL-KHIṬAṬ II, p. 101 l. 28.

[111] V. mon article dans le *volume II* del *commercio levantino di Genova nel secondo Trecento, Studi e testi di storia (Civico Istituto Colombiano, Saggi e documenti I)*, Génes 1978, p. 397, 398, 399, 400, 401, 403, 413.

Pourtant l'exportation du coton syrien l'emportait de beaucoup sur celle du coton égyptien.

Le coton s'était répandu en Syrie au Xe siècle. Un géographe arabe écrivant à la fin de ce siècle témoigne de la plantation de coton dans la province d'Alep [113] et en Palestine [114]. Mais à cette époque on y importait aussi des cotonnades de la Haute-Mésopotamie, où la production de coton avait pris un grand essor sous le règne des Ḥamdanides [115]. Dans diverses sources de l'époque des Croisades mention est faite des plantations de coton et du commerce de coton en Palestine et dans la Syrie du Nord. Une lettre judéo-arabe trouvée dans la gueniza du Caire a trait au commerce du coton à Ascalon, à l'époque fatimide [116]. Un auteur latin, qui écrivit dans la première moitié du XIIIe siècle, parle de l'industrie des cotonnades en Syrie [117]. Il paraît toutefois que seulement dans la Syrie septentrionale les plantations de coton constituaient alors un secteur important de l'agriculture. Car un écrivain arabe voulant mettre en relief la croissance de la demande des produits de l'agriculture, faisant suite elle-même à la croissance démographique dans cette région sous le règne de Nūr ad-dīn (1146-73), mentionne le prix du coton comme un article très important [118]. Les contrats que faisaient les Vénitiens dans la première moitié du XIIIe siècle avec les princes musulmans de la Syrie du Nord démontrent eux aussi que cette part du pays était alors le foyer du coton [119]. Dans d'autres régions le coton jouait apparemment un rôle plutôt réduit. La géographe al-Idrīsī, écrivant au milieu du XIIe siècle, ne le mentionne pas parmi les produits agricoles de la Syrie [120]. Des auteurs latins qui décrivaient la Pa-

[113] AL-MUḲADDASĪ, p. 181.

[114] P. 180. Probablement les tissus exportés d'Alep dont parle l'auteur étaient des cotonnades.

[115] IBN ḤAUḲAL, *Ṣūrat al-arḍ*, éd. Kramers, p. 222. Sur les plantations de coton dans ce pays à ladite époque v. op. cit., p. 213; AL-IṢṬAKHRĪ, p. 74 (où on lit que le coton était le produit principal d'un district); AL-MUḲADDASĪ, p. 141, 145.

[116] V. m. *Histoire des prix et des salaires dans l'Orient médiéval*, p. 251.

[117] J. DE VIRTRY, *Hist. Hierosolomitana*, ap. *Bongars, Gesta Dei per Francos,* I, Hannover 1611, p. 1099.

[118] IBN AL-'ADĪM, *Zubdat al-ḥalab bi-ta' rīkh Ḥalab,* II, Damas 1951-54, p. 285, 341; cf. *Recueil des historiens des Croisades, Hist. Orientaux, Hist. arabes*, III, p. 690.

[119] V. HEYD, *Histoire du commerce du Levant,* I, p. 376 et s.

[120] J. GILDEMEISTER, *Idrīsī's Palästina u. Syrien,* dans Beilage zu ZDPV, VIII (1885), p. 11.

lestine dans la deuxième moitié du XIIIe siècle et dans la première moitié du XIVe siècle, n'en parlent pas non plus, en traitant des régions où il fut plus tard le produit principal [121]. Al-Ḳalḳashandī, sans doute en citant Ibn Faḍlallāh al-'Umarī, un auteur de la première moitié du XIVe siècle, ne souffle pas un mot sur le coton de Syrie [122]. Mais quand les agriculteurs de la Galilée et des districts voisins perdaient les marchés qui étaient jadis les villes sur la côte, détruites par les Mamlouks à la fin du XIIIe siècle, beaucoup passaient de la culture des céréales à la plantation du coton, partiellement ou complètement. C'est ainsi que s'explique probablement l'envoi d'une ambassade vénitienne au gouverneur de la Galilée en 1304 [123]. Le voyageur maghrebin Ibn Baṭṭūṭa mentionne l'exportation de «vêtements de Jérusalem» en des pays lointains, en Afrique orientale [124], en Turquie [125] et au Turkestan [126]. Il s'agissait sans doute de cotonnades. Au cours du XIVe siècle la production de coton augmentait dans tous les pays du Proche-Orient. La plus petite demande de céréales, par suite des dévastations par les Mongols et les ravages des épidémies, contraignant les paysans à ce changement. Comme en Haute-Mésopotamie, où on agrandissait considérablement, à la fin du XIIIe siècle et au début du XIVe siècle, les plantations de coton [127], on les augmentait en Syrie du Nord. Lattakie était devenue à la fin du XIVe siècle, une ville marchande d'où on exportait de grandes quantités de coton [128]. En Palestine la production du

[121] V. Burchardus de Monte Sion, *Descriptio Terrae Sanctas,* éd. Laurent, Peregrinatores medii aevi quatuor, Leipzig 1864, p. 50 sur la vallé d'Esdraelon; L. de Suchem, *De itinere Terrae Sanctae,* Stuttgart 1851, p. 48 sur les environs d'Acre, p. 94 sur le Mont Gilboa et aussi p. 102 sur la Plaine de la Biḳā' en Syrie méridionale.

[122] *Ṣubḥ al-a'shā,* IV, p. 86 et s. (traduction erronée chez Gaudefroy-Demombynes, *La Syrie,* Paris 1923, p. 24).

[123] Thomas-Predelli, *Diplomatarium Veneto-Latinum,* I, p. 30 et s.

[124] II, p. 186.

[125] II, p. 311.

[126] III, p. 33 et s. Les doutes de Serjeant, v. BSOAS, XXVI, p. 656 (proposant de lire «de Maqdishu» en lieu de «Ḳudsi» ne sont pas justifiés, étant donné que l'auteur arabe parle aussi de l'exportation de cet article dans d'autres chapitres traitant de régions lointaines de l'Afrique orientale).

[127] Plusieurs auteurs de cette époque mentionnent les plantations de coton dans des lieux où il n'y en avait pas autrefois, v. Marco Polo, éd. H. Yule, 3e éd. (Londres 1921), I, p. 60 et s., 62 note 5; Ḥamdallāh Mustaufī, cit., p. 102 et s., 103, 106.

[128] ASV, *Senato,* Misti 38, f. 32a (a. 1383).

coton augmentait progressivement. De nombreux documents vénitiens en témoignent et on peut aussi évoquer des textes arabes [129]. A Jérusalem il y avait au XVe siècle un grand marché de coton [130]. Mais ce sont surtout les cadastres faits par les Ottomans, au début de leur domination, qui portent témoignage de ce changement. Le cadastre de la province de Safed, fait en 1525/26, comprend les indications suivantes touchant l'impôt d'un quart (de la récolte) [131]:

	Blé	Orge	Coton
District d'Acre	23 ghirāras	10 ghirāras	25 ķinṭārs
District de Nazareth	15 ghirāras	6 ghirāras	4 ķinṭārs

Le cadastre de la province (sandjaķ) de Safed (Galilée) fait en 1555/56 contient les données suivantes touchant les impôts en argent comptant (en aspres) [132]:

	Blé	Orge	Coton
Kafr Yāsīf	6.500	2.100	6.000
Kābūl	3.900	700	1.800

[129] Qu'on veuille considérer les citations suivantes comme supplément à celles qu'on trouve dans mon article *The Venetian cotton trade in Syria in the later Middle Ages*, «Studi Medievali», 1976, p. 680 et s.

[130] Mudjīr ad-dīn al-'Ulaimī, *al-Uns al-djalīl bi-ta'rīkh al-Ķuds wa'l-Khalīl*, Le Caire 1283, p. 383.

[131] B. Lewis, *Studies in the Ottoman archives*, dans BSOAS, XVI, p. 489; cf. Idem, *Nazareth in the sixteenth century according to the Ottoman tapu registers*, (dans) *Arabic and Islamic Studies in honor of Hamilton A. R. Gibb*, Londres 1965, p. 417. La ghirāra employée dans la Galilée était de 208,8 kg blé et le ķinṭār de 180 kg, cf. sur la ghirāra damascène W. Hinz, *Islamische Masse u. Gewichte*, Leiden 1955, p. 37 et Strauss dans REI, 1949, p. 55 note 1 et sur le ķinṭār de Damas *Tarifa*, Venise 1925, p. 26; B. de Paxi, *Tariffa di pexi e mesure*, Venise 1503, c. 5b: 600 livres vén. (sottili); et v. encore N. da Uzzano, *Pratica della mercatura*, cit. p. 113: 600 livres et cf. aussi W. Hinz, p. 26, 30.

[132] B. Lewis, *Notes and documents from the Turkish archives*, Jérusalem 1952, p. 18.

Ces données ne laissent aucun doute quand au grand rôle du coton dans la production agricole de la Galilée à la fin de l'époque mamlouke et au début de l'époque ottomane. Mais on trouve dans les documents publiés par B. Lewis de semblables données aussi dans le cadastre d'autres districts. Le cadastre du district de Jaffa, fait en 1525/26, comprend les indications suivantes touchant l'impôt «du tiers» [133]:

Blé	Orge	Coton
6 ghirāras	7 ghirāras	5 ķinṭārs

Tous ces renseignements, recueillis de sources différentes, indiquent le grand essor de la plantation de coton en Syrie et en Palestine à la fin du Moyen Age.

Il n'y a pas de doute que ce phénomène était accompagné du développement de l'industrie des cotonnades. Elle fleurissait en plusieurs villes et bourgades. A la même époque qu'Ibn Baṭṭūṭa mentionne les cotonnades de Jérusalem, l'auteur persan Ḥamdallāh Mustaufī parle de l'industrie cotonnière de Damas [134].

Pourtant les autorités mamloukes entravaient les activités des industriels par l'imposition de taxes sur la vente de la matière première et des tissus. Bon nombre d'inscriptions ciselées sur les portes de Grandes Mosquées et ailleurs portent témoignage de l'abolition de ces impôts, stigmatisés par les pieux musulmans comme «mukūs», taxes illégales (parce que non mentionnées dans le Coran). Mais, hélas, la répétition de ces solennelles abolitions démontre qu'on les renouvelait toujours.

En 1465 on abolissait l'impôt prélevé au marché du coton dans la bourgade transjordanienne de 'Adjlūn [135], – on en apprend qu'on plantait du coton aussi dans cette région. Une inscription de l'année

[133] B. Lewis, *Jaffa in the 16th century, according to the Ottoman taḥrīr registers,* Necati Lugol Armagan, Ankara 1969, p. 437. La ghirāra employée dans ce district était la ghirāra de Jérusalem équivalant à 625,4 kg de blé, le ķinṭār était de 250 kg, il W. Hinz, *Islamische Masse,* p. 29, 38 et Strauss dans REI, 1949, p. 55 note 1.

[134] *Ibidem,* p. 242 cf. p. 250.

[135] M. Van Berchem, *Arabische Inschriften aus Syrien,* Mittheilungen u. Nachrichten des Deutschen Palästina-Vereins 1903, p. 68.

1489 a trait à l'abolition d'une telle taxe à Hamah [136]. On peut aussi évoquer une inscription à Alep, datant de 1497 [137]. D'autres inscriptions se rapportent à l'abolition de taxes imposées sur le tissage des cotonnades ou leur vente. Deux inscriptions alépines se réfèrent à la taxe prélevée sur les tissus importés du village chrétien d'al-Ḳārā. L'une porte la date de 1412 [138], l'autre celle de 1442 [139]. Or il n'y a pas de doute que ces tissus étaient des cotonnades [140]. On ne se trompera pas non plus en soutenant que deux inscriptions de Hims, l'une de 1491 et l'autre de 1513, se rapportent aux cotonnades, bien qu'il y soit parlé de tissus simplement [141].

Le prix du travail relativement élevé, par suite de la dépopulation, et l'oppression fiscale par le gouvernement rendaient impossible que l'industrie cotonnière de Syrie devînt un grand secteur produisant pour l'exportation. Il est vrai que les marchands italiens acquiéraient à la fin du XIVe siècle des quantités considérables de cotonnades («bocassins») en Syrie, mais par rapport à la production de coton dans ce pays c'était une industrie avortée. C'est pourquoi une grande part du coton fut vendue aux marchands étrangers, pour la plupart aux Vénitiens, pour servir de matière première à l'industrie textile de la Lombardie et de l'Allemagne.

Qu'était le volume de l'exportation du coton syrien à laquelle se rapportent de si nombreux documents vénitiens?

Un auteur arabe qui écrivit dans la huitième décennie du XIVe siè-

[136] J. Sauvaget, *Décrets mamlouks de Syrie,* dans BEO, III (1933), no. 19 (p. 4 et s.) cf. L. A. Mayer, *Saracenic Heraldry*, Oxford 1933, p. 89 et s.

[137] Bischof, *Kitāb Tuḥaf al-anbā fī ta'rīkh Ḥalab ash-shahbā*, Beyrouth 1880, p. 133; cf. Kāmil al-Ghazzī, *Nahr adh-dhahab,* III, Alep 1923-26, p. 238. Une autre inscription alépine, de l'an 1442, a trait à l'abolition d'un droit prélevé sur le lin, v. Bischof, *Kitāb Tuḥuf al-anbā*, cit., p. 130 et Kāmil al-Ghazzī, *Nahr adh-dhahab*, III, p. 228. Voilà un témoignage de l'introduction du lin en Syrie (où on ne le cultivait pas à l'époque des califes, v. *Ṣubḥ al-a'shā* 1. c.) après le déclin de la culture du blé.

[138] Rāghib aṭ-Ṭabbākh, *I'lām an-nubalā*, II, Alep 1923-26, p. 454; G. Wiet, *Répertoire des décrets mamlouks de Syrie, Mélanges offerts à R. Dussaud,* II, Paris 1939, p. 523 (mo. 18).

[139] J. Sauvaget, *Décrets mamlouks de Syrie,* BEO III, no. 30 (p. 16 et ss.).

[140] V. C. J. Lamm, *Cotton in medieval textiles*, cit., p. 228 qui ne connaît que cette dernière inscription.

[141] M. Sobernheim, *Die Inschriften der Moschee von Ḥimṣ, Festschrift zu C. F. Lehmann-Haupts sechzigstem Geburtstag,* Vienne-Leipzig 1921, p. 228 et s. (no. 1), 232 et s. (no. 5).

cle, raconte que l'impôt sur l'exportation du coton d'Acre, port de la Galilée, était alors affermé pour 50,000 dirhams l'an. Supposant que l'impôt se montait à 5-7%, cette relation indiquerait que la valeur des cargaisons exportées de la Galilée s'élevait à un total de 35,000 dinars par an [142]. En faisant de ce renseignement des conclusions quant au total de l'exportation du coton de Syrie, on doit toutefois prendre en considération que son exportation de la Galilée était alors apparemment à son apogée. Car il paraît qu'on en exportait relativement moins au milieu et dans la deuxième moitié du XVe siècle. Deuxièmement, on doit relever que le prix du coton était à cette époque plus élevé que cent ans plus tard [143].

On trouve de précieux renseignements sur l'exportation du coton de Syrie dans les chroniques vénitiennes du XVe siècle. Les chroniqueurs nous fournissent des indications quant à l'argent et la valeur des cargaisons envoyées chaque année par les coques en Syrie. Or le service des coques étant principalement destiné à l'exportation du coton, on aura de bonnes raisons de supposer que la plupart servait de moyen de payement pour l'achat du coton. Voici quelques données:

Convois de coques vénitiennes allant en Syrie

		Nombre des coques	Cargaisons (argent comptant, marchandises, en ducats)		Source
1417	foire de mars	7	150.000	100-150.000	Morosini c. 326
		5			Dolfin c. 302a [144]
	septembre	5	ensemble	180.000	Morosini c. 331
		6	ensemble	260.000	Dolfin c. 310b, 302b
1418	foire de mars	7	ensemble	60.000	Morosini c. 345
	septembre	?	ensemble	35-40.000	Morosini c. 351
1419	foire de mars	5	ensemble	80.000 [145]	Morosini c. 355
	septembre	10	ensemble	150.000	Morosini c. 359

[142] B. Lewis, *An Arabic account of the province of Safed,* dans BSOAS, XV (1963), p. 483 et cf. mon article *Profits from trade with the Levant in the fifteenth century,* dans BSOAS, XXXVIII (1975), p. 266, 271.

[143] V. mon article *The Venetian cotton trade in Syria in the later Middle Ages*, p. 701 et ss.

[144] Ms. Marciana, Ital. VII DCCXCIV.

[145] Le chroniqueur relève la modicité de cet investissemnt.

1420	foire de mars	10-11	ensemble	80-100.000	Morosini c. 367
	septembre	4	ensemble	65-70.000	Morosini c. 373
1421	foire de mars	5 [146]	ensemble	?	Morosini c. 377
	septembre	3	ensemble	185.000	Morosini c. 380
1422	foire de septembre	2	ensemble	20-25.000	Morosini c. 388
1423	foire de mars	8	ensemble	?	Morosini c. 393
	septembre	2	70-75.000	20-25.000	Morosini c. 400
1424	foire de mars	7-8	ensemble	?	Morosini c. 406
1442	foire de septembre	6 + 2 en Egypte	ensemble	400.000	Dolfin c. 391b [147]

Ces données, pas très nombreuses, il est vrai, indiqueraient que les 12 coques qui partaient de Venise chaque année, en moyenne, pour la Syrie, transportaient de l'argent et des marchandises valant la plupart du temps 200-250.000 ducats. Certainement il y avait, dans la première moitié du XVe siècle, des années dans lesquelles l'investissement dans cette branche du commerce levantin de Venise s'élevait à 400-500.000 ducats, comme en 1442, une année après la suspension temporaire du service des galées levantines par le Sénat vénitien. On doit donc modifier l'évaluation du volume du commerce levantin de Venise à cette époque: on constate que l'exportation du coton syrien jouait déjà à cette époque un rôle beaucoup plus grand qu'on n'a cru. D'autre part il y avait des années dans lesquelles l'investissement était beaucoup plus petit. Deuxièmement, on n'oubliera pas qu'une part de l'investissement était destinée à l'achat d'autres produits (v. ci-dessous). D'autre part, quelques cargaisons de coton arrivaient à Venise aussi en dehors des convois qui fréquentaient les ports de Syrie lors des foires en mars et en septembre. Mais il n'y a pas de doute qu'elles étaient relativement insignifiantes.

Quoiqu'il en soit, la production de coton, servant de matière première pour les industries de fûtaine en Europe, était devenue un secteur très important de l'économie syrienne. Si le rapport de l'impôt foncier en Egypte avait diminué, à la fin de l'époque mamlouke, à 1 million et demi d'ashrafīs (égaux à ducats), le revenu national de la Sy-

[146] Puis l'auteur parle de 4 coques seulement.

[147] Le chroniqueur relève la valeur exceptionnelle des cargaisons.

rie était sans doute réduit de beaucoup. Une branche d'exportation rapportant 150-200.000 ducats par an avait donc une grande importance pour l'économie du pays. Voilà un trait caractéristique de sous-développement [148].

Quelques documents démontrent que les marchands vénitiens nouaient des relations commerciales avec les producteurs eux-mêmes et, d'autre part, on sait, qu'à l'intérieur du secteur agraire des pays proche-orientaux un changement s'était produit à cette époque: les biens ruraux qui étaient de propriété privée (mulk, et non pas des fiefs) avaient augmenté considérablement. Dans un acte judiciaire se rapportant aux activités de marchands vénitiens au début du XVe siècle il est parlé de l'achat de coton chez les «villani» près d'Alep [149]. Le contrat conclu entre Venise et le sultan du Caire en 1442 comprend la permission de s'habiller comme les musulmans au cas où on parcourait les villages (sc. en Syrie) pour l'achat du coton [150]. Sans doute ces contacts avaient pour conséquence le développement d'un secteur à économie-argent, une enclave dans une économie dans laquelle une grande part des payements se faisait en nature. C'est un phénomène caractéristique de l'«ouverture» de régions sous-développées [151]. Les agriculteurs qui vendaient le coton, changeant leurs coutumes, achetaient aux marchands étrangers des produits importés de l'Europe. Dans la comptabilité de la firme vénitienne Alvise Baseggio-Polo Caroldo, qui exportait du coton de la Galilée, on repère sous la date avril 1480 une note touchant la vente de «panni bressani» (draps de la ville de Brescia), échangés contre du coton avec Omar Masari de Kafr Kana (un village près de Nazareth) [152]. Voilà un phénomène de l'«ouverture».

e) *Le déclin des industries - les savonneries*

La déclin démographique et la hausse du prix du travail dans toutes les régions du Proche-Orient avaient amené, à la fin du XIVe siècle et

[148] H. Myint, *The Economics of the developing countries,* cit., p. 26.
[149] G. P., *Sent,* 15, f. 48a et ss. (procès en 1408).
[150] J. Wansbrough, *Venice and Florence in the Mamluk commercial privileges,* dans BSOAS, XXVIII (1965), p. 504, trad. p. 518.
[151] R. E. Baldwin, *Economic development and growth,* cit., p. 50.
[152] ASV, *Proc. di S. Marco,* Commissarie miste, Ba 117, fasc. 16, Comm. Baseggio.

au début du XVe siècle, la décadence de la plupart des vieilles industries. Ce phénomène était aussi la conséquence de la grande difficulté d'obtenir de bonnes matières premières à bon marché et surtout de la stagnation technologique, elle-même suite fâcheuse des monopoles.

Sans doute le déclin des industries textiles était le plus grave. Il avait pour conséquence un véritable dumping de tissus produits en divers pays de l'Europe méridionale et occidentale [153]. La décadence de l'industrie du sucre diminuait elle aussi considérablement le rapport en bonne monnaie étrangère dont jouissait le Proche-Orient autrefois. Car jusqu'à la fin du XIVe siècle l'Egypte et la Syrie en exportaient de grandes quantités en Europe méridionale. Le déclin de cette industrie était sans doute la suite de la stagnation technologique [154]. L'industrie du papier, introduite dans le Proche-Orient à la fin du VIIIe siècle, avait le même sort. Par conséquent on importait en Egypte et en Syrie, au XVe siècle, de la mélasse et du papier de l'Europe méridionale [155].

Qu'il nous soit permis de renvoyer aux articles dans lesquels nous avons traité en long du déclin de ces industries et d'esquisser ici le développement de deux autres manufactures.

L'industrie du savon fleurissait en Syrie depuis l'époque précédant les Croisades. La géographe al-Muḳaddasī mentionne le savon parmi les articles qu'on exportait, au Xe siècle, de la Palestine [156]. Les savonneries de la ville de Raḳḳa, à la frontière de la Haute-Mésopotamie et de la Syrie, étaient aussi connues pour l'excellente qualité de leurs produits. On les imitait selon ce que raconte un auteur juif du XIe siècle en Syrie [157]. Alep était, à l'époque des Croisades, un foyer de cette industrie.

[153] J'ai traité de ce sujet dans ma communication *Les lainages dans l'Orient médiéval, Atti della II Settimana di studi dell'Istituto F. Datini*, Florence 1976, p. 657 et ss.; v. aussi mon article *L'importation de textiles occidentaux dans le Proche Orient musulman au Bas Moyen Age (1370-1517), Studi in memoria di F. Melis*, II, Naples 1978, p. 303 ss.

[154] V. mon article *Levantine sugar industry - an example of technological decline*, dans «Israel Oriental Studies», VII (1977), p. 245 ss., 270 s.

[155] V. dans l'article cité dans la note précédente p. 260 ss.

[156] *Aḥsan at-taḳāsīm*, p. 180; trad. A. Miquel, Damas 1963, p. 218.

[157] Dozy, *Supplément* I, p. 817. L'auteur est *Yūsuf b. Isḥāk Ibn Baklaresh*, v. Brockelmann GAL² I, p. 641 Suppl. I, p. 889. Quant à l'explication du nom «raḳḳī» il n'y a pas lieu aux doutes, v. E. Wiedemann, *Aufsätze zur arabischen Wissenschaftsgeschichte*, II, Hildesheim 1970, p. 402 et v. Mehren (v. ci-dessous) qui propose l'émendation 'araḳī!

Un auteur arabe relate qu'on exportait le savon alépin en Byzance et en Irak. Il relève aussi le grand volume de la production [158]. Sans doute les savonniers avaient leurs secrets professionnels. C'est ainsi que s'explique que dans un manuscrit arabe de la Bodléienne les instructions pour la fabrication du savon sont écrites en syriaque [159]. On écoulait, aux XIe et XIIe siècles, du savon syrien et palestinien en Egypte [160], car le savon qu'on fabriquait en Egypte était de moindre qualité. C'était du savon fait de l'huile extraite des semences de rave, de colza et de laitue [161]. Mais on importait en Egypte aussi du savon de la Tunisie (et peut-être des autres pays du Maghreb). Plusieurs documents judéo-arabes trouvés dans la gueniza du Caire en portent témoignage [162]. Les savonneries syriennes fleurissaient aussi dans la première moitié du XIVe siècle. Le géographe ad-Dimishḳī parle de la fabrication du savon à Nābulus où on imitait les produits des savonneries de Raḳḳa [163]. Le voyageur maghrébien Ibn Baṭṭūṭa raconte qu'on produisait à Sarmīn, dans la Syrie septentrionale, du savon briqueté, qu'on exportait à Damas et au Caire, et aussi du savon parfumé pour laver les mains. Ce savon était coloré en rouge et en jaune [164].

Comme les autres industries, les savonneries souffraient de l'oppression fiscale. Les impôts prélevés par les Mamlouks renchérissaient la matière première, l'huile d'olive, et les frais de la production. En plus

[158] IBN ASH-SHIḤNA, *ad-Durr al-muntakhab*, Beyrouth 1909, p. 25 et v. p. 165 sur la taxe prélevée sur les savonneries en 1212/13; p. 249 le khan du savon; cf. la traduction française de J. SAUVAGET, *Les perles choisies*, Beyrouth 1933, p. 147, 194, 198. et v. aussi IBN SHADDĀD, *La description d'Alep*, éd. D. Sourde, Damas 1953, p. 152.

[159] Ms. Bodléienne Or. 68 (je suis reconnaissant au docteur J. Sadan pour avoir attiré mon attention sur ce manuscrit).

[160] V. le feuillet de la comptabilité d'un épicier (du XIe siècle) que j'ai cité in extenso dans mon article *Matériaux pour l'histoire des prix dans l'Egypte médiévale*, dans JESHO, VI (1963), p. 161.

[161] 'ADBALLAṬĪF, *Relation de l'Egypte*, p. 311.

[162] V. mon article *Documents pour l'histoire économique et sociale des juifs dans le Proche-Orient* (en hébreu), Zion VII (1941/42), p. 153; S. D. GOITEIN, *A Mediterranean society*, I, University of California Press 1967, p. 154, 184; IDEM, *Letters of medieval Jewish traders*, Princeton University Press 1973, p. 26, 45, 136 et ss., 140.

[163] *Nukhbat ad-dahr*, éd. Mehren Saint-Pétersbourg 1866, p. 200; trad. Mehren, Copenhague 1874, p. 270 et s. (où on trouve la traduction: savon fin!)

[164] I, p. 145 et s.

les autorités mamloukes avaient souvent recours à l'achat forcé de grandes quantités d'huile (le système du «ṭarḥ»). Il va sans dire que cette méthode de remplir les caisses du Trésor ruinaient les industries. Le témoignage des inscriptions et des chroniques arabes est éloquent. Citons-en quelques-unes: en 1440 on abolit à Ḥimṣ la ferme du courtage de l'huile, c'est-à-dire on proclama que le commerce de cet article serait libre, et non pas soumis aux exactions d'un fermier [165]. Deux inscriptions datant de 1453 et de 1461 ont trait à l'abolition de l'impôt prélevé à Alep sur la vente de l'huile du district de 'Azāz [166]. De longues relations de l'historien arabe Mudjīr ad-dīn al-'Ulaimī traitent de l'achat de grandes quantités d'huile d'olive, imposé en 1491, 1493 et 1495 aux habitants de Jérusalem et de Hébron. En effet l'auteur raconte que depuis 1485 le commerce de l'huile n'était pas libre. Pourtant on contraignait seulement les savonniers de Jérusalem et de Ramla à l'achat d'une certaine quantité (au gouvernement, qui l'avait érigé en monopole). Puis en 1491 tous les habitants de Jérusalem et de Hébron devaient acheter de l'huile à un prix élevé de trois fois sa valeur. En 1493 les autorités imposaient l'achat forcé, aux savonniers seulement, à Jérusalem, Hébron, Ghaza et Ramla. Puis en 1495 on contraignait encore une fois tous les habitants de ces villes, paraît-il, à l'achat de grandes quantités d'huile à un prix très élevé [167].

Quelques inscriptions annoncent l'abolition des impôts sur la vente d'huile et de savon et de leur achat forcé. En 1433 on abolit ces exactions à Hamah [168]. Evoquons aussi deux inscriptions de Tripoli qui se rapportent à l'achat forcé d'huile et de savon. Elles datent de 1453 et de 1502 [169].

Le savon qu'on produisait en Syrie était pour la plupart le savon

[165] M. v. OPPENHEIM, *Inschriften aus Syrien, Mesopotamien und Kleinasien I: Arabische Inschriften,* bearbeitet v. Maz van Berchem, Leipzig 1909, no. 5, p. 9 et ss.

[166] BISCHOF, *Tuḥaf al-anbā,* p. 131, 133 et s.; KĀMIL AL-GHAZZĪ, *Nahr adh-dhahab,* III, p. 229 et s., 231.

[167] *al-Uns al-djalīl,* p. 686 et s., 694 et s., 702.

[168] J. SAUVAGET, *Décrets mamlouks de Syrie,* dans BEO, III, no. 17, p. 1 et s.

[169] *Matériaux pour un Corpus inscriptionum Arabicarum II,* part 1, par M. SOBENNEIM, Le Caire 1909, no. 25, p. 59 et s., 32 p. 76 et ss.

«dur», à base de soude [170]. C'était le même savon qui était plus tard produit dans la Provence et à Venise et connu comme «savon de Marseille» ou «de Venise» (aussi en allemand «Kernseife») [171]. On obtenait la soude de la cendre de deux plantes du genre des Chénopodiacées-Salsolées, Salsola soda L. et Salsola kali L., qu'on trouve dans le désert syrien. La cendre de ces plantes contient 20% de soude (carbonate de sodium) et est appelée en arabe littéraire ashnān et en vulgaire kali. Provenant de la Palmyrène et d'ailleurs, elle fut apportée par les Bédouins à Damas et à Tripoli [172]. Or les Mamlouks érigeaient la vente de cet article en monopole. C'est ce qu'on apprend des règlements ottomans qui sans doute étaient copiés des règlements de leurs prédécesseurs. A Damas le kali monopolisé fut distribué en trois parts: une part fut vendue aux savonniers, peintres et dégraisseurs de la ville, un autre tiers appartenait au fisc et un troisième fut vendu aux «Francs». A Tripoli deux tiers étaient destinés au fisc et un tiers à la vente aux marchands (par les Bédouins qui l'apportaient) [173]. Il est clair que les autorités mamloukes et ottomanes vendaient aux marchands étrangers (européens) plus qu'il ne leur était destiné. C'était un moyen d'extorquer de l'argent ou d'obtenir par troc ces textiles dont les Orientaux étaient si avides, les draps écarlates par exemple. Bon nombre de documents vénitiens se réfère en effet à ces transactions avec le gouverneur de Tripoli (v. ci-dessous). La conséquence de cette méthode de l'administration fiscale était le renchérissement de cette autre matière première et le déclin des savonneries [174].

Par contre, les marchands européens pouvaient de cette façon acquérir une matière première qui rendait possible le développement in-

[170] V. le passage du AL-MUSTA'ĪNĪ cité par DOZY, *Supplément* I, p. 817 et cf. SINGER-HOLMYARD-HALL-WILLIAMS, *A History of technology* II, Oxford 1956, p. 354 et s.

[171] C. DEITE, *Die Herstellung der Seifen, Parfümerien und Cosmetica,* dans P. BOLLEY, *Handbuch der chemischen Technologie* VI, 2, Braunschweig 1867, p. 21, 25 et s.; v. aussi *Deite's Handbuch der Seifenfabrikation,* éd. W. Schrauth, I, 4e éd., Berlin 1917, p. 247, 253 et s.

[172] A. DE BOUCHEMAN, *Une petite cité caravanière - Suhné,* Damas s. d., p. 77 et ss.; J. CANTINEAU, *Le dialecte arabe de Palmyre,* II, Beyrouth 1935, p. 70 et ss. Cf. sur l'exploitation au XVIe siècle: L. RAUWOLF, *Aigentlich beschreibung der Reiss,* Lavingen 1583, p. 37 et ss.

[173] MANTRAN-SAUVAGET, *Règlements fiscaux ottomans,* p. 22 et ss., 69. Selon ces documents il y avait, au milieu du XVIe siècle, à Tripoli des savonneries royales, ce qui était apparemment une innovation.

[174] V. par exemple B. LEWIS, *Studies in the Ottoman archives,* dans BSOAS, XVI, p. 493.

dustriel de leurs pays. Au lieu de servir de matière première pour les industries indigènes, la cendre fut exportée en Europe. Autre trait de sous-développement.

Il va sans dire que les marchands italiens ne laissaient pas échapper l'occasion et commençaient à exporter de grandes quantités de cet article qui était appelé par eux cenere [175], lume (le nom le plus commun) [176], lume catina [177], lume de savon [178], allume [179], botassa [180] et portait d'autres noms encore (v. ci-dessous). L'exportation de la cendre syrienne devenait une branche importante du commerce levantin. Les Génois transportaient souvent cet article directement à Gaëte, alors connue pour son industrie du savon [181] ou en Flandre et Angleterre [182]. Mais des quantités considérables furent apportées à Gênes elle-même [183]. Les Vénitiens et les Génois exportaient de la cendre aussi de l'Egypte, bien qu'elle était moins appréciée que la syrienne [184]. Les Gé-

[175] G. P., *Sent.* 30, f. 74b et s. 53, f. 23a 140, f. 58b 187, f. 101a et ss.; Cristoforo del Fiore VI, f. [5b, 17b et s.].

[176] G. P., *Sent.* 54, f. 40a et s. 84, f. 136b et ss. 97, f. 116b et ss. 99, f. 26a et ss. 123, f. 53b et ss. 124, f. 63b et ss.

[177] Zibaldone da Canal, éd. A. Stussi, Venise 1967, p. 66.

[178] G. P., *Sent.* 79, f. 118 b et ss. et aussi cenere ad saponem G. P., *Sent.* 20, f. 122a 71, f. 55a et ss.

[179] G. P., *Sent.* 18, f. 85b et ss. 23, f. 75b et ss.

[180] G. P., *Sent.* 95, f. 75b et s.

[181] ASG, *Carat.* Vet. 1552, f. 125a (a. 1446) transport à Gaëte et à Savone.

[182] *Ibidem*, f. 127a (a. 1446).

[183] V. ASP, *Archives Datini*, 1171; ASG, Carat. Vet. 1453, f. 23b (a. 1458) et v. aussi l'inventaire du bateau de Nic. Grimaldi publié comme appendice à mon article dans le *volume II del commercio levantino di Genova nel secondo Trecento.*

[184] V. Vénitiens: ASV, *Senato*, *Misti* 23, f. 23b, 58a 24, f. 20b et s. 26, f. 89a etc.; Génois: *Datini* 1171: inventaire du bateau de Polo Lercaro, arrivé à Gênes le 6 janvier 1397 («lume di pietra»); bateau d'Oberto di Ruscio, arrivant à Gênes d'Alexandrie, apporte 1500 quintaux de lume; ceux de Benedetto de Fresco (publié dans ledit Appendice), Ottaviano Lercaro et la galée de ... de Negro (tous sans date) apportent «allume»; enfin, le bateau de M... Luziano qui vint à Marseille le 28 avril 1397, avec une cargaison de lume chargé à Alexandrie. Il n'y a pas de doute que toutes ces indications se rapportent à la cendre égyptienne, cf. Pegolotti, p. 380 et Zibaldone da Canal l.c. Il paraît qu'on n'exportait plus à cette époque d'alun d'Egypte, comme l'a justement relevé C. Cahen, *L'alun avant Phocée,* dans «Revue d'Histoire économique et sociale», (1963), p. 444 et ss. La mention de l'alun parmi les articles vendus à Alexandrie, v. Pegolotti, p. 70, est apparemment un anachronisme, car il ne parle pas de l'alun égyptien dans le long chapitre dans lequel il traite des diverses espèces de cette matière, v. p. 367 et ss. C'est pourquoi on doit

nois en achetaient aussi en Syrie, mais l'exportation de la cendre syrienne était, comme celle du coton, à peu près une affaire de Vénitiens. Les bateaux vénitiens exportaient de lourdes cargaisons de «lume» syrien, surtout de Tripoli [185]. Mais les Vénitiens acquéraient cet article aussi à Lattakie [186], à Beyrouth [187] et à Ramla [188]. Le grand rôle que jouaient les autorités mamloukes en Syrie dans ce commerce ressort avec netteté des documents vénitiens. Dans plusieurs actes il est dit expressément qu'on achetait le lume au gouverneur de Tripoli [189], ou qu'on ne pouvait l'exporter sans son autorisation [190]. Comme la plupart des autres cargaisons chargées par les bateaux vénitiens, la plus grande part de la cendre syrienne fut transportée à Venise. Mais on repère aussi quelques envois directs à Gaëte [191]. Pourtant l'exportation de la cendre syrienne n'était pas un monopole vénitien. Des marchands florentins et ancônitains s'adonnaient eux-aussi à ce commerce [192].

La cendre était une matière première lourde et bon marché. Voici quelques indications sur le prix d'un ḳinṭār syrien (de 180 kg) [193]:

modifier l'interprétation des documents datiniens qu'on trouve dans l'article excellent de J. Heers, *Il commercio nel Mediterraneo alla fine del sec. XIV e nei primi anni del XV,* dans «Archivio Storico Italiano», CXIII (1955), p. 171, 172 (c'est certainement lume appelé cette fois allume, car le bateau venait de la Syrie), 196.

[185] G. P. *Sent.* 18, f. 85b et ss. (avant 1408) 54, f. 40a (a. 1425) 71, f. 55a et ss. (a. 1412) 79, f. 118b et ss. (a. 1437) 84, f. 136b et ss. (a. 1436) 95, f. 75b et s. (a. 1442 environ) 97, f. 116b et ss. (a. 1441) 99, f. 26a et ss. (a. 1442 environ) 123, f. 53b et ss. (a. 1443) 140, f. 58b (a. 1462) 187, f. 101a et ss. (a. 1484).

[186] *Cron. Dolfin* f. 378a: une coque transporte en 1437 du coton et 600 sacs de lume de Lattakie; ibidem f. 400a une autre coque y charge en 1444 1200 sacs.

[187] G. P. *Sent.* 20, f. 122a (a. 1411) 30, f. 74b et s. (a. 1412) 53, f. 23a (a. 1428) 124, f. 63b et ss. (a. 1450); Cristoforo del Fiore VI, f. [5b]; G. P. *Terminazioni* III, f. 82a (a. 1477); Marino Sanuto, *Diarii* I, col 404.

[188] G. P., *Sent.* 23, f. 75b et ss. (a. 1412 environ); «de Syrie», sans spécification: ASV, *Senato,* Secreta I, f. 81a et ss.

[189] G. P., *Sent.* 54, f. 40a et s. (a. 1425) 71, f. 55a et ss. (a. 1412).

[190] G. P., *Sent.* 124, f. 63b et ss.

[191] G. P., *Sent.* 20, f. 122a 71, f. 55a et ss.

[192] J. Wansbrough, *A Mamluk commercial treaty concluded with the Republic of Florence, Documents from Islamic Chanceries,* éd. S. M. Stern, Oxford 1965, p. 56, trad. p. 65; F. Melis, *Documenti per la storia economica dei secoli XIII-XVI,* Florence 1972, p. 144 (un bateau apporte à Ancône, en 1379, 650 quintaux de cendre de Tripoli).

[193] Bartolomeo de Paxi, *Tariffa de pesi e mesure,* c. 5b: 600 livres vénitiennes. De même d'après Pegolotti p. 90, 91; le ḳinṭār de Tripoli égait égal au ḳinṭār de Damas, v. note 131 ci-dessus (tandis que le ḳiinḳār de la Syrie septentrional était plus lourd).

PRIX DE LA CENDRE SYRIENNE

Date	Lieu	Prix	Source
avant 1408	Tripoli	4,4 ducats (110 dirhams) [194]	G. P., Sent 18, f. 85b et s.
1411	Beyrouth	2,22 ducats	même série 20, f. 122a
1412	Beyrouth	2,5 ducats	même série 30, f. 74b et s.
1441	Tripoli	1,7-1,87 ducats	même série 97, f. 116b et ss.
1450	Beyrouth	2,3 ducats	même série 124, f. 63b et ss.
1477	Beyrouth	1,7 ducats	G. P., Terminazioni III, f. 82a
1479	Damas	1,8 ducats	G. P., Sent. 188, f. 206a et ss.

Le volume de l'exportation de la soude de Syrie était grand si l'on considère les cargaisons. On en chargeait les bateaux bien qu'elle ait été un produit bon marché. Car les industries européennes les exigeaient. Des commerçants vénitiens achetaient parfois dans une année 450 ḳinṭārs valant 1000 ducats, 600-900 ḳinṭārs valant 1300-1900 ducats ou même 2184 ḳinṭārs, comme Luca et Andrea Vendramin en 1441 [195]. Deux bateaux génois, le bateau de Giovanni Maruffo et de ... Doria apportaient à Gênes, à une date non précisée à la fin du XIVe siècle, selon les rapports des facteurs de Francesco Datini, pas moins de 12,500 quintaux de cendre (alume de rocca) de la Syrie [196]. C'étaient certainement des quintaux génois, donc 3125 ḳinṭārs de Tripoli. Des bateaux vénitiens chargeaient souvent 1000 ḳinṭārs [197].

L'oppression fiscale et l'exportation de la cendre n'amenaient pas la ruine totale de l'industrie du savon en Syrie. Quoique la production ait diminué on produisait du savon aussi au Bas Moyen Age dans plusieurs villes et bourgades. L'historien libanais Ṣāliḥ b. Yaḥyā raconte que son père Saif ad-dīn Yaḥyā avait une savonnerie près de Beyrouth. Cette relation se réfère à la fin du XIVe siècle [198]. Un riche marchand de

[194] V. mon article *Etudes sur le système monétaire des Mamluks circassiens,* dans «Israel Oriental Studies», VI (1976), p. 277.

[195] V. dans mon article *The Venetian supremacy in Levantine trade* et JEEH, III (1974), p. 45 (où on doit corriger l'indication touchant l'achat de Michiel et Lorenzo Barbaro en 1412: il était de 450 ḳinṭārs).

[196] S. HEERS, *Il commercio levantino,* cit., p. 172.

[197] V. dans mon article cité ci-avant 1. c.

[198] *Ta'rīkh Beirūt,* Beyrouth 1927, p. 181 (cf. p. 179 sur la date).

Damas Shihāb ad-dīn Aḥmad b. Sulaimān al-Bakrī, qui achevait en 1464 la construction d'une Maison d'enseignement du Coran, était connu sous le nom d'aṣ-Ṣabūnī – le savonnier. Par conséquent on appelait aussi son établissement aṣ-Ṣabūnīya. C'est au maintien des maîtres de l'école, qu'il destina les revenus de plusieurs villages près de Beyrouth appelés eux aussi aṣ-Ṣabūnīya. Ces villages étaient administrés par la famille dudit historien Ṣāliḥ b. Yaḥyā, des féodaux du district d'al-Gharb [199]. Les savonneries de Damas et de Nābulus existent jusqu'à nos jours [200]. Mais depuis que les savonneries d'Italie étaient approvisionnées par de grandes quantités de soude syrienne, elles développaient considérablement leur production et commençaient à exporter leurs produits en d'autres pays, en Grèce, en Turquie et dans le Proche-Orient. Le Proche-Orient achetait donc un article produit d'une matière première qu'il fournissait...

Les grands centres de l'industrie du savon en Italie étaient les Marches (Ancône et d'autres villes), les Pouilles, Gaëte, Naples et Venise elle-même [201]. On exportait déjà au XIVe siècle des quantités considérables de savon en tous les pays de l'Europe occidentale [202] et aussi en Crète [203], à Chypre [204], à Rhodes [205], à Constantinople [206] et en Turquie [207]. De même les Vénitiens exportaient déjà au milieu du XIVe siècle du savon en Egypte [208]. Les Génois étaient eux-aussi très actifs dans cette branche. On apprend des registres de la douane de Gênes

[199] H. SAUVAIRE, *Description de Damas,* JA, 1894, I, p. 264 et s. et v. aussi JA, 1895, II, p. 224 sur une mosquée construite par le même marchand.

[200] V. Z. AL-ḲĀSIMĪ, -K. AL-AZEM, *Dictionnaire des métiers damascains,* II, Paris 1960, p. 268 et s.

[201] PEGOLOTTI, p. 318 et s.; J. DAY, *Les douanes de Gênes 1376-1377,* Paris 1963, p. 238, 360, 380, 381, 399, 412, 815, 816 (exportation à Gênes) et v. mon article *Il commercio levantino di Ancona,* dans RSI, LXXXVIII (1976), p. 217, 219.

[202] F. MELIS, *Documenti,* cit., p. 312.

[203] *Lettere a Pignol Zucchello,* p. 22 (a. 1344), 37, 38, 41, 42, 43, 45 (a. 1345).

[204] *Ibidem,* p. 125 (a. 1349); PEGOLOTTI, p. 158, 318 et s.

[205] PEGOLOTTI, p. 318 et s. Mais on produisait aussi du savon à Chypre et à Rhodes, v. *Ibidem,* p. 33, 103 et s.

[206] *Ibidem,* p. 33.

[207] *Ibidem,* p. 56. On importait aussi du savon espagnol en Italie, v. *Ibidem,* p. 207; J. DAY, *Les douanes,* cit., p. 485.

[208] V. sur la fixation du fret par le Sénat, à plusieurs reprises, dans mon article *Observations on Venetian trade in the Levant in the XIVth century,* dans JEEH, V (1976), p. 579 note 211.

qu'ils exportaient en 1377 de grandes quantités de savon de Naples et de Gaëte en Egypte [209], ainsi que du savon espagnol [210]. L'Espagne produisait en effet beaucoup de savon qu'on exportait en d'autres pays [211]. Puis, au XVe siècle, le volume de l'exportation de savon européen en Egypte et aussi en Syrie augmentait beaucoup. Les bateaux des Vénitiens apportaient à Alexandrie de lourdes cargaisons [212]. Une part consistait en savon de Gaëte [213]. Quelques marchands s'étaient spécialisés dans cette branche du commerce du Levant. Un tel marchand était, au début du XVe siècle, Carlo Contarini. Plusieurs documents ont trait aux cargaisons de savon qu'il apportait à Alexandrie [214]. C'était un grand marchand. En effet en novembre 1419 le consul vénitien à Alexandrie l'obligea à un payement de droits pour l'achat de poivre valant 13.500 dinars [215]. Il va sans dire que les marchands de Gaëte elle-même exportaient du savon en Egypte [216]. Au même moment les Vénitiens exportaient du savon à Chypre [217]. Les Génois, les Florentins, les Ancônitains et les Français s'adonnaient eux-aussi à l'exportation de cet article dans le Proche-Orient et surtout en Egypte [218]. Mais on importait en Egypte et en Syrie aussi du savon de Chypre et de Chios [219]. L'importation de savon italien dans le Proche-Orient prit un essor encore plus grand au milieu du XVe siècle. Tandis que le prix de cet article ne figure pas sur les listes de prix qu'ont dressées les facteurs d'une grande firme vénitienne (Antonio Zane) dans la deuxième décennie du XVe siècle à Damas, il ne manque pas dans les listes pareilles datant

[209] J. Day, *Les douanes,* cit., p. 268, 351, 527.

[210] *Ibidem,* p. 490.

[211] F. Melis, *Documenti,* cit., p. 314.

[212] G. P., *Sent.* 48, f. 132a et s. (a. 1426) 73, f 94b et ss. (a. 1432) 129, f. 153a et ss. (a. 1457-58); Piloti, p. 150.

[213] ASV, *Proc. di S. Marco,* Comm. miste, Ba 180, Comm. Biegio Dolfin, fasc. 15 (a. 1418).

[214] V. F. Melis, *Documenti,* cit., p. 328 un document de l'an 1419 et dans mon article *Observations on Venice's Levant trade in the fourteenth century,* dans JEEH, V (1976), p. 579 un document de 1418.

[215] Com. Biegio Dolfin, Ba 181, fasc. 23.

[216] Vat. sub 18 juillet 1406; Cron. Morosini c. 340 (a. 1417).

[217] Nic. Turiano IV, f. 18b (le roi achète du savon pour 3000 ducats).

[218] Nicolo Venier B, 2, f. 32a et ss. (a. 1421); J. Wansbrough, *A Mamluk commercial treaty concluded with the Republic of Florence 894/1489*, p. 62.

[219] *Ṣubḥ al-a'shā* VIII, p. 124 et s.; Nic. Venier, B, 2, f. 18b et s. (a. 1419); J. Heers, *Gênes au XVe siècle,* Paris 1961, p. 377 (savon de Chios).

d'une époque postérieure. A la fin du XVe siècle, les marchands vénitiens commençaient à investir dans les savonneries de Gaëte et des Pouilles et en d'autres lieux aussi, en les approvisionnant de combustibles, pour écouler le savon produit aux échelles du Levant. Les défenses du Sénat vénitien étaient vaines [220]. En effet Venise devait mener une lutte difficile avec les savonneries des Marches et de Chios, qui lui faisaient concurrence, pour les marchés du Proche-Orient et dans la «Romanie» [221]. A cette époque la Méditerranée orientale était donc un grand marché où les Vénitiens et les autres marchands italiens vendaient de grandes quantités de leur savon. C'était le dumping dans des régions sous-développées [222]. Que le volume de l'exportation du savon en Egypte du moins, n'était pas petit, on l'apprend d'une relation de Marino Sanuto: en 1496 après le départ des galées d'Alexandrie, il y restait 200.000 miers de savon qu'on n'avait pas vendu [223]. C'est probablement une erreur, car cette quantité aurait été l'équivalent de 6.000 t. Pourtant le volume de ce commerce d'exportation devait être considérable.

Les sources italiennes et des sources arabes contiennent bon nombre de renseignements sur les diverses espèces de savon qu'on offrait à Alexandrie et sur leurs prix. Qu'on veuille considérer le tableau suivant comme supplément aux documents que nous venons de citer touchant l'importation de savon de l'Europe en Egypte.

[220] ASV, *Senato,* Terra X, f. 170a et s. (9 oct. 1489); *Senato*, Mar 13, f. 92b (17 juillet 1492). (Selon les lois vénitiennes toutes les marchandises devaient être d'abord transportées à Venise pour être ensuite exportées).

[221] V. *Il libro di conti di Giacomo Badoer,* éd. V. Dorini - T. Bertele, Rome 1956, cc. 43, 97 (exportation de savon d'Ancône et de Messine à Constantinople en 1436, 1437); ASG, *Notai,* Tommaso Riccio II, no. 56 (14 juillet 1456, exportation de savon de Chios en Turquie); mon article *Il commercio levantino di Ancona,* cit., pp. 228 (a. 1436, 1434), 235 (a. 1459) 236 (a. 1461, 1468, 1469) (exportation de savon d'Ancône en «Romania»). Sur l'exportation de savon en Turquie par des Vénitiens v. G. P., *Sent.* 19, f. 45a et ss. (a. 1410 environ).

[222] Des actes notariés datant de 1428 qui ont trait à l'exportation, par des Vénitiens, de savon d'Alep et des autres villes de la Syrie à Chypre se rapportent probablement à la réexpédition de savon italien qui y était importé, v. Nic. Turiano IV, f. 58b et ss.

[223] *Diarii* I, col, 380.

PRIX DU SAVON EN EGYPTE [224]

Date	Prix d'un ḳinṭār djarwī	Source
26 fév. 1396	savon de Gaëte 7,5 dinars de Raguse 7	Listes de prix Datini
19 oct. 1396	blanc 6 din.	*Ibidem*
février 1403	indigène 8,3 din., autrefois 4	JESHO IV, p. 34 [225]; Sulūk III, p. 1100 et s.
juillet 1403	indigène 8,7 din.	Sulūk III, p. 1107
août 1403	indigène 11,2 din.	JESHO IV, p. 34
juin 1410	indigène 5 din.	*Ibidem*
avril 1413	indigène jusqu'à 4 din.	*Ibidem*
avril 1414	indigène 6 din.	*Ibidem*
avril 1415	indigène 6,4 din.	*Ibidem*
22 fév. 1418	de Venise 6,25 din., de Naples 6,5	Listes de prix L. Dolfin [226]
23 fev. 1418	de Venise 6,25 din., de Naples 6,5	Melis, Doc., p. 320
1418	de Gaëte 6,5 din.	B. Dolfin Ba 180, fasc. 15
19 fév. 1422	de Venise 7 din., de Naples 7,5	Listes des prix L. Dolfin
2 mai 1422	de Venise 6,75 din., de Naples 7,5	Lettre de Nic. Bernardo, Arch. L. Dolfin
13 mai 1422	de Venise 6, 75 din., de Naples 7,25	Listes des prix L. Dolfin
2 fév. 1423	de Venise 6,75 din., de Naples 7,25	*Ibidem*
12 avril 1423	de Venise 7,5 din., de Naples 8,25	Lettre Nic. Bernardo, Arch. L. Dolfin
17 juillet 1423	de Venise 8 din., s'il y en avait, de Naples 9	Lettre du même
31 juillet 1423	de Venise 7,5 din., de Naples 8	Lettre du même
21 août 1423	de Venise 7,25 din., de Naples 8,5	Listes de prix L. Dolfin
22 août 1423	de Venise 7,5 din., de Naples 8	*Ibidem* et lettre de Nic. Bernardo
16 mars 1424	de Venise 6,75 din., de Naples 7,25	Melis, Doc., p. 190
1426	de Venise 6 ducats [227]	G. P., Sent. 48, f. 132a et s.
mai 1427	de Venise 8 ducats [228]	Nic. Turiano IV, f. 18b
avant 1440	de Venise 6 din., de Gênes 7, de Pise 7, de Gaëte 7, de Tripoli 7	Ussano, p. 112
sept. 1501	au Caire 40 duc.	Marino Sanuto, Diarii IV, col. 167 et s.

[224] Faute d'autres indications ce sont les prix à Alexandrie.

[225] E. ASHTOR, *L'évolution des prix dans le Proche-Orient à la basse époque,* dans JESHO, IV (1961), d'après AL-'AINĪ, *'Iḳd al-djumān* (avec quelques corrections).

[226] ASV, *Procuratori di S. Marco,* Commissarie di citra, Ba 282, Comm. Lorenzo Dolfin.

[227] La provenance du savon n'est pas indiquée.

[228] «ad pondum carabatanum», cf. PEGOLOTTI, p. 78 (apparemment le prix fut payé en besants «blancs» de Chypre, bien qu'il fût indiqué en ducats).

On constatera en étudiant ces données que le prix du savon indigène (c'est-à-dire syrien) avait monté de 3-4 dinars (le ḳinṭār djarwī) à l'époque des Croisades et de 2-2,5 dinars au XIVe siècle à 6 dinars au début du XVe siècle. Le prix en 1403, quand la crise économique arriva à son apogée, était tout-à-fait excessif. Le savon importé de l'Europe était toujours plus cher. Mais il se vendait parce qu'il était meilleur et peut-être aussi, quelquefois, parce que l'offre du savon syrien n'était pas suffisante.

Il va sans dire que l'importation du savon européen dans le Proche-Orient était une bonne affaire. Voici quelques renseignements sur le prix du savon dans les grandes villes d'Italie d'où on l'exportait:

Prix du savon en Italie

	Date		Source
Venise		Prix d'un migliaio sottile (301 kg)	
	31 mai 1393	blanc 21 ducats noir 13 ducats	Melis, Doc., p. 302
	1426	16 ducats	G. P., Sent. 48, f. 132a et s.
Gênes		Prix d'un cantaro (47,5 kg)	
	1396	dur 5 duc.	Melis, Doc., p. 304
Ancône		Prix d'un migliaio (346 kg)	
	1459	14 duc.	ASAn, Notai, Ang. di Domenico II, f. 143a et s., 180 a
		14,2 duc.	même notaire II, f. 78a et s.
	1461	13,33 duc.	même notaire IV, f. 102b et s.
	1489	6,2 duc.	ASAn, Notai, Giacomo Alberici VI, f. 56b
	1492	11 duc.	même notaire VIII, f. 116b
		9 duc.	*Ibidem,* f. 118a

Forcément on déduira de ces données, peu nombreuses, il est vrai, que les marchands italiens offraient aux échelles d'Orient surtout les espèces moins chères de savon, en réalisant un profit de 50%. Les Ancônitains, auxquels le savon coûtait moins, réalisaient même des profits de 100%.

f) *La verrerie - un autre secteur industriel en déclin*

La verrerie n'était pas dans l'Orient médiéval seulement un métier touchant à l'art, elle était plutôt une industrie produisant des objets pour l'exportation en d'autres pays. Son évolution était semblable à celle des autres secteurs industriels qui déclinaient au Bas Moyen Age.

C'était un métier d'abord développé en Syrie, d'où il s'était répandu dans l'antiquité dans les pays voisins [229]. Le soufflage était certainement une invention syrienne [230]. Transmis de génération en génération pendant de longs siècles le métier fleurissait en Syrie et en Egypte à l'époque des califes et puis à l'époque des Croisades. Un auteur arabe, écrivant au début du XIe siècle, vante la qualité du verre syrien et dit que sa minceur et sa transparence étaient proverbiales [231]. D'autres auteurs font eux aussi l'éloge de la qualité du verre syrien, surtout de sa transparence [232]. On les peignait aussi en diverses couleurs [233]. La verrerie fleurissait, à l'époque des Fatimides, en Egypte aussi. Des objets de verre produits à cette époque en Egypte on été découverts en plusieurs pays d'Orient et aussi dans la Russie méridionale [234]. C'était donc une industrie d'exportation. Le lustrage était déjà une technique bien connue, dans laquelle les verriers égyptiens et syriens excellaient [235]. Les objets de verre étaient le décor des palais et des bâtiments publics. Le voyageur andalous Ibn Djubair, qui visita Damas en 1184, vante la

[229] A. Leo Oppenheim, *Towards a history of glass in the Ancient Near East,* Presidential address given at the 182th meeting of the American Oriental Society, 1972, dans JAOS, XCIII (1973), p. 259.

[230] D. B. Harden dans Singer-Holmyard-Hall-Williams, II, *A history of technology,* Oxford 1956, p. 232.

[231] ath-Tha'ālibī, *Thimār al-ḳulūb,* Le Caire 1965, p. 532; Idem, *Laṭā'if al-ma'ā-rif,* éd. de Jong, Leiden 1867, p. 95; trad. anglaise par C. E. Bosworth, Edinburgh 1968, p. 118.

[232] J. Ruska, *Übersetzungen und Bearbeitungen von al-Rāzī's Buch Geheimnis der Geheimnisse, Quellen u. Studien zur Geschichte der Naturwissenschaften* VI, p. 22.

[233] J. Ruska, *Das Steinbuch aus der Kosmographie des al-Ḳazwīnī,* dans Jahresbericht der Oberrealschule Heidelberg 1895/96, p. 24.

[234] C. J. Lamm, *Mittelalterliche Gläser und Steinschnittarbeiten aus dem Nahen Osten,* Berlin 1930, p. 15.

[235] C. J. Lamm, *Oriental glass of medieval date found in Sweden and the early history of lustre-painting,* Stockholm 1941, p. 29, 47 et ss.

splendeur de la Grande Mosquée, relevant la beauté de ses soixante-quatorze fenêtres en verre doré et polychrome [236].

La verrerie fleurissait dans plusieurs villes de la Syrie et de la Palestine, mais c'était surtout la ville de Tyr qui était connue pour la bonne qualité de son verre. Un géographe arabe, écrivant à la fin du Xe siècle, parle de l'exportation des objets de verre produits à Tyr, du verre poli, des boules et d'autres encore [237]. Plusieurs auteurs de l'époque des Croisades relèvent l'importance de la verrerie tyrienne [238]. Son grand développement était, non pas en dernière ligne, due à la qualité excellente du sable qu'on trouvait dans les environs de la ville. Un voyageur européen, qui parcourut les pays d'Orient dans la première moitié du XIVe siècle, raconte encore que le sable de Tyr fut exporté en des pays lointains [239]. En effet on l'employait aussi en d'autres villes sur la côte méditerranéenne. Dans un document de la gueniza il est parlé du verre rouge de Beyrouth [240].

Dans ce contexte on doit relever le rôle des Juifs tyriens. Or les Juifs orientaux avaient un penchant pour la verrerie. Dans les documents judéo-arabes de la gueniza, datant pour la plupart du XIe, du XIIe et de la première moitié du XIIIe siècle, mention est faite de nombreux verriers juifs. On a trouvé aussi dans la gueniza des contrats rédigés lors de la fondation de manufactures de verre [241]. Parmi les Juifs de Tyr il y avait bon nombre de verriers. Citons une autorisation donnée à Tyr en 1011: un Juif tyrien autorise un autre à réclamer au Caire

[236] *Riḥla,* Leyden 1907, p. 264; trad. M. Gaudefroy-Demombynes, Paris 1949, p. 305.

[237] AL-MUḲADDASĪ, p. 180; la traduction d'A. Miquel, p. 219, doit être corrigée, v. sur makhrūṭ DOZY, *Supplément* I, p. 362) et v. aussi AL-MAS'ŪDĪ, *Les Prairies d'or VIII,* p. 80.

[238] AL-IDRĪSĪ, *Palästina u. Syrien,* p. 12; Guillaume de Tyr et Jacques de Vitry cités par C. J. LAMM, *Mittelalterl. Gläser,* cit., p. 491.

[239] L. DE SUCHEM, *De itinere Terrae Sanctae,* p. 48.

[240] S. D. GOITEIN, *A Mediterranean Society,* I, p. 421 note 65.

[241] J. MANN, *The Jews in Egypt and in Palestine under the Fatimid caliphs,* II, Oxford 1922, p. 355 (a. 1060); R. GOTTHEIL - W. H. WORRELL, *Fragments from the Cairo Genizah in the Freer Gallery,* New York 1927, p. 70; S. D. GOITEIN, *A Mediterranean Society,* cit., p. 109 et s., 363 et s., 365, 428; E. STRAUSS-ASHTOR, *Documents pour l'histoire économique et sociale des Juifs dans le Proche-Orient* (en hébreu), Zion VII (1941/42), p. 143 (a. 1230 environ); IDEM, *Histoire des Juifs en Egypte et en Syrie sous la domination des Mamlouks* (en hébreu), I, Jérusalem 1944, p. 180 (documents du XIe, du XIIe et du XIIIe siècle); IDEM, *Histoire des prix et des salaires dans l'Orient médiéval,* p. 197, 203 (la maison du verrier, loyers payés en 1182/83 et dans la première moitié du XIIIe siècle).

le prix de 37 vaisselles de verre qu'il y avait envoyées [242]. La voyageur Benjamin de Tudèle, qui parcourut les pays d'Orient en 1160-1170, raconte qu'à Tyr «il y a des verriers juifs produisant le bon verre, appelé verre tyrien, un article apprécié en tous les pays» [243]. Or, une part des juifs tyriens habitait, d'après un rapport datant de l'an 1243, à l'époque de la domination franque le quartier vénitien [244]. C'est pourquoi plusieurs savants ont conclu que les Vénitiens ont appris ce métier chez leurs sujets juifs à Tyr [245]. Les historiens de la verrerie sont enclins à croire que les Vénitiens imitaient surtout la production de verre transparent, tel que produit en Syrie et surtout à Tyr. C'est là aussi qu'ils auraient appris le soufflage [246]. En effet, le verre transparent était au Moyen Age en Europe connu comme «verre juif» [247].

Dans les pays du Proche-Orient eux-mêmes il y avait, au XIIIe et dans la première moitié du XIVe siècle, un nouvel essor de la verrerie. Alep, Damas et Le Caire étaient alors les foyers principaux de ce métier florissant. Les verriers proche-orientaux influencés par des artisans de la ville de Raḳḳa (et d'autres villes de la Haute-Mésopotamie, sans doute), qui s'étaient enfuis devant les Mongols, produisaient d'élégants et précieux objets en verre émaillé et doré, dont les décors avaient des contours en rouge. Cette nouvelle verrerie commençait à fleurir à Alep dans la première moitié du XIIIe siècle et à Damas plus tard, au milieu du siècle. Les objets damascènes se caractérisent, comme les alépins, par les contours fins. Ceux qui datent du XIVe siècle ont une décoration qui est très influencée par l'art chinois. L'influence chinoise, par suite de l'expansion mongole, se manifeste dans des ornements naturalistes et calligraphiques et dans plusieurs autres détails de la décoration. Les objets fabriqués au Caire au XIVe siècle se caractérisent par une

[242] S. Assaf, *Des anciens documents de la gueniza de la Palestine, de l'Egypte et de l'Afrique septentrionale* (en hébreu), Tarbiz IX (1938), p. 196 et s.

[243] *The Itinerary of Benjamin of Tudela,* éd. M. N. Adler (Londres 1907), p. 20 et v. p. 18 sur la ville d'Antioche: il y a (sc. en tout) dix Juifs et ils sont des verriers.

[244] Tafel-Thomas, *Urkunden zur älteren Handels- u. Staatsgeschichte der Republik Venedig,* II, p. 358 et s., cf. J. Prawer, *The Crusaders, a colonial society* (en hébreu), Jérusalem 1975, p. 319.

[245] Heyd, *Histoire du commerce du Levant,* II, p. 710 et s.

[246] R. W. Douglas - S. Frank, *A History of glassmaking,* Hanley-on-Thann 1972, p. 7.

[247] C. J. Lamm, *Mittelalterl. Gläser,* p. 45.

décoration tout à fait singulière – par des inscriptions entrelacées avec des dessins des armoiries mamloukes et des médailles [248]. Tandis que les contours des ornements sur les objets fabriqués à Alep et à Damas sont fins, ceux des objets égyptiens sont plutôt forts [249].

La verrerie d'Alep avait son foyer dans le faubourg d'Armanāz et elle employait le sable blanc du Mont Bishr, dans les environs de la ville [250]. Les produits de la verrerie alépine étaient très appréciés et on les exportait, dans la première moitié du XIIIe siècle, jusqu'en Chine [251]. La conquête d'Alep par les Tartares en 1260 ne porta pas, paraît-il, préjudice à sa verrerie, car il y a plusieurs témoignages de sa survivance jusqu'à la première moitié du XIVe siècle [252]. La verrerie mamlouke de Damas fleurissait dans la première moitié du XIVe siècle et jusqu'à sa fin. Plusieurs relations de voyageurs occidentaux y ont trait [253]. Un autre centre de la verrerie dans cette région était la petite ville de Hébron. Les pèlerins occidentaux qui visitaient la Palestine au XIVe et au milieu du XVe siècle vantent la qualité des objets en verre qu'on y produisait [254]. Les objets de la verrerie syrienne et palestinienne furent alors exportés en de nombreux pays d'Orient et d'Occident, en Arabie, en Chine et en Allemagne [255].

La rapacité des féodaux mamlouks ne laissait échapper aucune

[248] *Ibidem*, p. 247 et v. G. Wiet, *Les lampes en verre de la collection Gulbenkian,* dans «Annales de l'Institut d'Etudes Orientales» (Alger), III (1937), p. 19 et s.

[249] C. J. Lamm, *Oriental glass of medieval date found in Sweden,* p. 60 et s.

[250] V. Yāḳūt I, p. 217, 631; Kāmil al-Ghazzī, *Nahr adh-dhahab,* I, p. 493; J. Gaulmier, *Note sur la fabrication de verre à Armanaz,* dans BEO, VI (1936), p. 53 et ss. La provenance des verriers d'Armanāz d'une localité qui portait le même nom et se trouvait près de Tyr est plus que douteuse, v. C. J. Lamm, *Mittelalterl. Gläser,* p. 491 et note 98. Il s'agit apparemment d'une conjecture que Yāḳūt cite d'après un autre savant arabe.

[251] Ibn Kathīr, *al-Bidāya wa'n-nihāya* 13, p. 120. V. aussi Kāmil al-Ghazzī I, p. 113.

[252] al-Ḳazwīnī, *Āthār al-bilād,* éd. Wüstenfeld, II, p. 123; Ḥamdallāh Mustaufī, cit., p. 205; et v. aussi le texte cité par C. J. Lamm, *Oriental glass,* cit., p. 62 et s.

[253] Ibn Baṭṭūṭa I, p. 208 (cet auteur visita Damas en 1326, v. I, p. 254); *Itinerarium Symonis Semeonis ab Hybernia ad Terram Sanctam,* p. 74 (a. 1323); Fra N. da Poggibonsi, *Libro di Oltramare (1348-1350),* Jérusalem 1945, p. 92; G. Gucci, *Visit to the Holy Places of Egypt, Sinai, Palestine and Syria in 1384 by Frescobaldi,* Gucci, Sigoli, Jérusalem 1948, p. 143.

[254] *Liber peregrinationis di* Jacopo da Verona, éd. Ugo Monneret de Villard, Rome 1950, p. 95 (a. 1335); N. da Poggibonsi, *Libro di Oltramare,* cit., p. 68; *Viaggio in Terrasanta di Lionardo di N. Frescobaldi, Viaggi in Terrasanta,* ed. C. Angelini, Florence 1944, p. 123; S. v. Gumpenberg, dans *Reyssbuch dess heyligen Lands,* Francfort 1609, p. 445.

[255] C. J. Lamm, *Mittelalterl. Gläser,* cit., p. 246, 259, 483; idem, *Oriental glass,* p. 73; W. Pfeiffer, *Acrische Gläser,* dans «Journal of Glass Studies» XII (1970), p. 67 et ss.

source de revenu, l'industrie syro-palestinienne de verre n'en était pas la moindre. Comme dans les autres secteurs industriels, le sultan participait lui-même à la production: il avait ses manufactures de verre [256]. Mais le gouvernement mamlouk ne faisait pas seulement la concurrence à l'industrie privée (car les manufactures royales vendaient une part de leurs produits...), il l'opprimait aussi par des mesures fiscales. Des inscriptions annonçant l'abolition de taxes prélevées sur les fonderies de verre, comme une inscription damascène de 1453, en portent témoignage [257]. On aura aussi raison de croire que l'invasion de la Syrie par Timur porta un coup funeste à la verrerie de ce pays. Le conquérant mongol emmena un grand nombre d'artisans à sa capitale Samarcande [258]. L'appauvrissement général du Proche-Orient en bonnes monnaies était un autre facteur qui nécessairement amenait la décadence de cette industrie. Les émirs et vizirs, les bourgeois et les hauts-fonctionnaires ne pouvaient pas se permettre de payer des objets si coûteux comme autrefois dans le premier siècle du règne mamlouk. Il y avait, enfin, la difficulté d'obtenir des matières premières à bon marché. Avec le kali on employait dans les fonderies du tartre [259] et pour colorer le verre on avait besoin d'oxyde cuivrique («ferretto») qu'on trouvait en Espagne dans les mines de fer [260], de vert-de-gris («verderame») et de réalgar [261]. Or les verriers orientaux devaient acheter toutes ces matières aux marchands italiens qui les importaient de l'Europe. Le prix du tartre figure sur plusieurs bulletins que les agents de Francesco Datini lui envoyaient d'Alexandrie et de Damas [262]. Bon nombre de documents se rapportent à son importation à Alexandrie par des marchands vénitiens [263], génois [264] et florentins [265]. L'oxyde cuivrique ne manque

[256] *Ṣubḥ al-a'shā* IV, p. 188; tr. Gaudefroy-Demombynes, *La Syrie*, p. 151.

[257] J. Sauvaget, *Décrets mamlouks de Syrie*, dans BEO, II, no. 11 (p. 32 et ss.).

[258] V. la relation de Clavijo citée par C. J. Lamm, *Mittelalterl. Gläser*, cit., p. 494.

[259] W. Ganzmüller, *Hüttengeheimnisse der italienischen Glasmacher des Mittelalters*, (dans son recueil) *Beiträge zur Geschichte der Technologie und der Alchemie*, Weinheim 1956, p. 74.

[260] V. H. Blancourt, *De l'art. de la verrerie*, Paris 1697, p. 104; W. Ganzmüller, *Hüttengeheimnisse*, p. 76.

[261] *Ibidem*, p. 76 et s.

[262] ASP., *Archivio Datini*, 1171, listes de prix à Damas du 6 nov. 1379, 2 août 1395; à Alexandrie du 26 fév. 1396.

[263] G. P., *Sent.* 70, f. [entre 11 et 12] (a. 1412, de valeur de 500 dinars), 141b et ss. (a. 1428).

[264] Nic. Venier B, 2, f. 32a (a. 1419).

[265] Vat. sub 8 nov. 1404 (importé de la Provence).

pas non plus sur les listes de prix que dressaient les facteurs des grandes firmes italiennes aux échelles du Levant [266], de même que le vert-de-gris [267]. Le réalgar était en Orient un article très cher. Selon Giovanni da Uzzano 100 manns (81 kg en Egypte) coûtaient, vers l'an 1420, 30 dinars [268]. Les Vénitiens l'offraient toujours à Alexandrie et aux échelles de Syrie [269]. L'importation de ces matières premières se continuait en Syrie au XVIe siècle, comme on l'apprend des règlements de l'administration ottomane [270].

On ne s'étonnera donc pas du déclin de cette industrie orientale à la fin du Moyen Age. Des voyageurs européens qui parcouraient les pays du Levant au XVe siècle s'en rendaient compte. Les recherches des historiens des arts ont abouti au même résultat. Le dominicain bavarois Felix Fabri, qui visita Hébron en 1483, constate que le verre produit n'est pas transparent, mais plutôt noir et les couleurs de moyenne qualité [271]. Les savants qui ont étudié les lampes en verre, les gobelets et les autres objets produits pour le sultan du Caire et les aristocrates mamlouks se sont aperçus de la détérioration considérable de la décoration à la fin du XIVe siècle [272].

A la même époque la verrerie connut un grand essor en plusieurs villes d'Italie, à Pise, à Florence et surtout à Venise. Bien qu'on ait fait de grands efforts pour garder les secrets industriels, il n'y a pas de doute que cet essor était la conséquence d'un grand progrès technologique. Les verriers italiens apprenaient comment ajouter aux matières premières du pyrobusite pour améliorer la transparence et la couleur de leurs produits. On l'appelait «le savon du verrier» [273]. Dans la deuxième moitié du XIIIe siècle, les Vénitiens devaient encore imiter les

[266] ASP, *Archivio Datini,* 1171, liste de prix à Damas du 6 nov. 1379.

[267] Même série, liste de prix à Alexandrie du 29 oct. 1396; N. DA UZZANO, p. 112.

[268] N. DA UZZANO 1. c.; v. aussi les listes de prix Datini, 1171, de Damas du 8 avril et 1 sept. 1386.

[269] *Lettere a Pignol Zucchello,* p. 87, 110 (la même qualité 18 din.); G. P., *Sent.* 123, f. 80b et ss. (réalgar blanc et jaune importé en 1454 à Tripoli).

[270] MANTRAN-SAUVAGET, cit., p. 26, 62 et s.

[271] *Evagatorium in Terram Sanctam, Arabiae et Egypti peregrinationes,* éd. C. D. Hassler (Stuttgart 1842-49) II, p. 341 (Lamm ne connaît pas ce passage et cite son livre allemand qui est plus court et où cette observation manque!).

[272] C. J. LAMM, *Oriental glass,* cit., p. 72.

[273] R. W. DOUGLAS - S. FRANK, *A History of glassmaking,* p. 7.

techniques des verriers proche-orientaux. Quand Venise conclut, en 1277, un contrat avec Boemond VI, prince d'Antioche, on stipulait qu'il fût permis aux Vénitiens d'exporter de Tripoli des tessons de verre [274]. Mais à la même époque on développait et améliorait à Venise les techniques de la production qui étaient employées en Orient. On apprenait la décoration de verre par le lustrage et la production de verre émaillé [275]. On employait des matières premières meilleures et nouvelles. Pour la production du «cristallo», le fameux produit vénitien, on employait des matières qu'on trouvait dans les Alpes, au Tessin et près du col de Saint-Bernard [276]. Pour colorer le verre en bleu on employait du cobalt importé de l'Allemagne [277]. D'autre part on avait recours à la cendre syrienne, employée aussi dans l'industrie du savon. Dans les recettes pour la fabrication du verre, qui datent du XIVe et du XVe siècle, il est toujours parlé d'allume de Soria [278], d'allume catina de Soria [279], d'allume de rocca [280] et de soda de Soria [281]. La verrerie vénitienne arriva à son apogée au milieu du XVe siècle quand la famille des Barovier produisait ses merveilleux objets en cristallo [282]. Dans le dernier quart du XVe siècle, le verre vénitien appelé lattimo était renommé dans le monde entier. C'était une espèce de verre blanc comme le lait.

[274] E.-G. REY, *Recherches géographiques et historiques sur la domination des Latins en Orient,* Paris 1877, p. 42; cité par C. J. LAMM, *Mittelalterl. Gläser,* cit., p. 491.

[275] L. ZECCHIN, *Un decoratore di vetri a Murano alla fine del Duecento,* dans «Journal of Glass Studies», XI (1969), p. 41; IDEM, *Fornaci muranesi fra il 1279 ed il 1290,* dans «Journal of Glass Studies», XII (1970), p. 79 et ss. V. aussi R. SCHMIDT, *Das Glas,* Berlin 1912, p. 62 (un peu exagéré).

[276] W. GANZMÜLLER, *Hüttengeheimnisse,* cit., p. 73.

[277] W. GANZMÜLLER, *Über die Verwendung von Kobalt bei den Glasmachern des Mittelalters,* dans son recueil cité ci-avant, p. 171.

[278] *Dell'arte del vetro per musaico tre trattatelli,* II, éd. G. Milanesi, Bologne 1864, p. 1, 2.

[279] *Ibidem,* II, p. 4, 5, 10, 11, 12 et cf. Zibaldone da Canal p. 66: la lume gatina che si è cenere.

[280] *Ibidem,* III, p. 18.

[281] *Ibidem,* III, p. 65 et v. aussi H. BLANCOURT, *De l'art de la verrerie,* p. 49 et s. et cf. GANZMÜLLER, cit., p. 73 et s. Les verriers de Venise employaient la cendre syrienne depuis longtemps. Un document qui date de 1290 et se rapporte au payement pour «lumine de Soria» en porte témoignage, v. ASV, *Podestà di Murano,* Ba 3, fasc. 1, c 17b (Je suis reconnaissant à M. L. Zecchin pour cette indication).

[282] O. N. WILKINSON, *Old Glass,* Londres 1968, p. 48.

On le fabriquait en ajoutant aux matières premières employées autrefois d'autres matières qui le rendaient opaque [283].

Les objets de verre fabriqués à Murano, le fameux foyer de la verrerie vénitienne, devenaient un article d'exportation qui s'écoulait en Occident et en Orient [284]. Le Proche-Orient musulman, où jadis les Vénitiens avaient appris le métier, commençait lui aussi à acheter du verre de Murano. Des orientalistes, en s'appuyant sur des sources arabes, ont mis en doute ce fait qui est attesté par plusieurs documents vénitiens [285]. Il vaut la peine de citer ces documents qui sont si éloquents quant à la décadence industrielle du Proche-Orient au Bas Moyen Age.

Un acte notarié à Alexandrie, en 1434, se rapporte à l'importation de trois caisses de verre par deux Vénitiens [286]. Selon un acte judiciaire, le marchand vénitien Benedetto Longo importa à Alexandrie, vers l'an 1440 (les actes du procès datent de 1444) des objets en verre émaillé et doré (certi lavori de cristallo rearnidi darzento doradi e smaltadi), qui furent donnés à un marchand musulman, Aḥmad b. Ṣāliḥ, contre 12 ḳinṭārs et 87 raṭls de gingembre beledi valant 18 ducats (le ḳinṭār), 23 ḳinṭārs de bois de Brésil et 800 manns de noix de muscade [287]. Ces objets en verre représentaient donc la valeur de 1000-1100 ducats [288]. Un autre acte judiciaire a trait à une transaction des bien connus fabricants de verre Marco et Johan Barovier. Ils envoyèrent en 1459, à Tripoli 97 kg de verre émaillé, qui furent vendus par Marco Rosso, pour 70 ducats [289].

Les ambassadeurs de la Sérenissime allant chez le sultan du Caire

[283] *Ibidem*, p. 50; T. H. CLARKS, *Lattimo - a group of Venetian glass enamelled on an opaque-white ground*, dans «Journal of Glass Studies», XVI (1974), p. 22 et ss.

[284] V. SCHMIDT, *Das Glas*, p. 63, 65; *Lettere a Pignol Zucchello*, p. 38.

[285] VAN BERCHEM, *Matériaux pour un Corpus Inscriptionum Arabicarum*, I, Paris 1903, p. 679 et par contre YACOUB ARTIN PACHA, *Description de six lampes de mosquées en verre émaillé*, dans «Bulletin de l'Institut d'Egypte», IIe série, VII (1886), p. 230 et ss., M. GAYET, *L'art arabe*, Paris 1893, p. 243; G. WIET, *L'Egypte arabe* (dans) G. HANOTAUX, *Histoire de la nation égyptienne*, IV, Paris 1937, p. 607.

[286] NIC. TURIANO V, f. 8a et s.

[287] G. P., *Sent.* 96, f. 151a.

[288] V. *Histoire des prix et des salaires*, p. 336, 342.

[289] G. P., *Sent.* 130, f. 45b et ss. et v. sur ces fabricants de verre: C. A. LEVI, *L'arte del vetro in Murano nel rinascimento e i Berroviero*, Venise 1895, p. 18 (où il est toutefois parlé de Joh. et Marino Barovier!).

n'oubliaient pas qu'il désirait des objets en verre de Murano. Un ambassadeur partant en 1442 pour le Caire lui apporta «nobili lavori de cristallo vernidi darzento piu belli che fussero mai visti» [290]. Parfois le sultan s'adressa lui-même au gouvernement de Venise avec la demande de lui envoyer du verre. En 1466 le Sénat vénitien délibérait sur la demande du sultan de lui envoyer du verre pour des fenêtres [291]. Citons enfin la relation d'un chroniqueur arabe, Ibn Iyās. Cet auteur raconte qu'un ambassadeur vénitien – c'est Domenico Trevisan – apporta, en 1512, au sultan des cadeaux comprenant des objets de cristal [292]. Il va sans dire que d'autres Occidentaux aussi qui cherchaient l'amitié des musulmans ou avaient recours à leur bienveillance leur donnaient en cadeau du verre vénitien. Le pèlerin milanais Santo Brasca, qui s'embarqua en 1480 sur un bateau vénitien pour aller visiter la Palestine, raconte que le capitaine en arrivant à Jaffa envoya au gouverneur mamlouk de Damas «presenti di certi vasi christalini adciò ne fosse propitio con li altri signori al nostro viagio» [293].

L'importation de verre vénitien se continuait au XVIe siècle d'après ce qu'on apprend des règlements de l'administration ottomane [294].

g) *Balance commerciale déficitaire*

Avant d'essayer de dresser une balance du commerce proche-oriental avec l'Europe méridionale au Bas Moyen Age, on doit mettre en relief les dépenses pour des services dont on avait besoin après la décadence de la flotte mercantile musulmane. Quant au fait de son déclin formidable, au cours du XIVe et du XVe siècle, il n'y a pas de doute. Outre le témoignage explicite d'un auteur arabe [295] on peut évoquer des contrats conclus entre les souverains musulmans de la Tunisie et la

[290] *Cron. Dolfin*, f. 294 a.

[291] *Senato*, Mar VIII, f. 97b. et cf. f. 103b.

[292] Ibn Iyās, éd. Kahle-Mustafa IV, p. 259. Les objets en verre ne sont pas mentionnés dans la relation de l'ambassadeur, v. J. Thenaud, *Le voyage d'outremer* v., Paris 1884, p. 186 et ss. (et non plus dans les inventaires des cadeaux donnés à d'autres personnalités au Caire, p. 191 et s.).

[293] S. Brasca, *Viaggio in Terrasanta,* Milan 1966, p. 63.

[294] Mantran-Sauvaget, p. 26, 27, 62.

[295] V. ma *Social and economic history of the Near East in the Middle Ages,* p. 309.

république de Pise en 1313 et en 1353. On en apprend que le gouvernement tunisien encourageait les Pisans, en renonçant au droit dû pour des transactions commerciales, à la vente de bateaux et, deuxièmement, qu'il avait besoin de leurs services de transport ainsi que parfois il eut recours au séquestre temporaire de leurs navires [296].

La déclin de la navigation musulmane dans la Méditerranée au Bas Moyen Age était progressif. En effet, le transport de passagers et de marchandises était, au XVe siècle, dans une grande mesure passé aux mains des Italiens. La riche documentation qui témoigne de ce fait, indique la grande importance que le payement de ces services avait pour la balance commerciale du Proche-Orient.

Les marchands italiens expédiaient sur leurs bateaux des épices d'Egypte en Tunisie et en d'autres pays de l'Afrique septentrionale [297]. Le gouvernement de la Sérenissime décréta, fidèle à sa politique de concentration de tout le commerce vénitien dans la capitale, qu'on les envoyât d'abord à Venise, mais ces décrets ne furent apparemment pas obtempérés [298]. De même on transportait des marchands musulmans avec leurs marchandises du Maghreb en Egypte et en Syrie. Le gouvernement génois imposa, en 1496, un droit de 3% au transport de passagers vers l'Egypte et un droit d'1% au transport en Syrie. Le transport de marchandises restait exempt de ce droit [299]. En d'autres mots, on voulait favoriser le négoce du transport. Le service de transport était en effet un secteur important de l'économie génoise. Déjà dans le dernier tiers du XIVe siècle les bateaux génois transportaient de grandes quantités d'huile d'olive de l'Espagne en Egypte [300]. Il va sans dire que les nombreux bateaux des villes de l'Italie méridionale participaient au service du transport entre les pays du Maghreb et le Proche-Orient. Des bateaux napolitains desservaient cette ligne, en transportant de l'huile en Egypte [301]. Même constatation quant aux Catalans: eux aussi ex-

[296] M. Amari, *I diplomi arabi del R. archivio fiorentino,* Florence 1863, p. 91, 104.

[297] *Senato,* Mar VII, f. 41a.

[298] Même série VI, f. 206b. (a. 1460) VII, f. 147a (a. 1464).

[299] ASG, *Primi Cancellieri di S. Giorgio,* Ba 88, c. 314-318 (c. 324-328 en latin).

[300] V. J. Day, *Les Douanes,* cit., pp. 469, 470, 531 (a. 1376, valant 6044 duc.), 251, 269, 358, 412, 464, 488, 518 (a. 1377, valant 5124 duc.).

[301] Vat. sub 22 mai 1400.

portaient sur leurs navires de l'huile tunisienne en Egypte [302] et des bateaux catalans sont nolisés par des musulmans pour le transport de leurs marchandises d'Alexandrie à Tripoli [303]. Un bateau de Marseille transporte des marchands tunisiens avec leurs marchandises dans leur pays [304]. Les Vénitiens eux aussi transportaient sur leurs bateaux de l'huile de marchands musulmans en Egypte [305] et de même des textiles produits dans la Tripolitaine et expédiés par des marchands musulmans. Ils louaient aussi leurs bateaux aux musulmans pour des voyages de l'Egypte au Maghreb [306]. Mais, cela se comprend, ils écartaient aussi les commerçants musulmans et achetaient eux-mêmes l'huile maghrébine sur place et l'exportaient sur leurs bateaux en Egypte [307]. Des bateaux vénitiens allaient, dans la première moitié du XVe siècle, très souvent en Tunisie et dans la Tripolitaine pour transporter de là des marchandises en Egypte et pour rentrer à Venise avec les cargaisons acquises à Alexandrie [308]. On appelait cette ligne «viazo de Berberia». Parfois on emmenait de Venise les barils pour charger l'huile à Tunis [309]. Depuis 1461 c'était un service régulier de galées, appelé «galee de trafego». Ces galées chargeaient en Tunisie des articles africains, comme l'ivoire, les plumes d'autruche et la poudre d'or et ayant fait la route d'Alexandrie elles rentraient à Tunis pour y transporter des marchands vénitiens et musulmans et leurs marchandises. Après une deuxième visite à Alexandrie et souvent un détour à Beyrouth elles faisaient le voyage de retour à Venise [310]. Après une fâcheuse affaire à Rhodes où les chevaliers avaient fait prisonniers un grand nombre de passagers musulmans, le gouvernement vénitien décréta, en 1468, que dorénavant il fût défendu de transporter sur des bateaux vénitiens des musulmans et leurs marchandises de l'Egypte vers la Berbérie, sous peine de 1000

[302] Vat. sub 10 mars 1400.
[303] Vat. sub 13 janvier 1406.
[304] Vat. sub 1 avril 1401.
[305] G. P., *Sent.* 74, f. 9b et ss. (a. 1434 environ).
[306] Même série 48, f. 102a et ss.; Vat. sub. 2 sept. 1404.
[307] G. P., *Sent.* 34, f. 11a et ss. (a. 1422) 48, f. 85a et ss. (a. 1427 environ).
[308] Même série 48, f. 85a et ss. 52, f 8b et s. 74, f. 9b et ss.
[309] Même série 48, 1. 85a et ss.
[310] J. Sottas, *Les messageries maritimes de Venise aux XIVe et XVe siècles,* Paris 1938, p. 111 et ss.

ducats. On proposait de défendre aussi le transport de musulmans des pays du Maghreb vers l'Egypte, mais cette proposition ne fut pas acceptée par le Sénat [311]. L'appât du profit était trop grand... Quant au transport de voyageurs musulmans, des marchands et des autres, par les Vénitiens et les Génois, on peut aussi évoquer la relation d'un écrivain arabe. 'Abdalbāsiṭ b. Khalīl raconte qu'il s'embarqua à Tunis, en mai 1463, sur une galée vénitienne pour se rendre en Egypte, avec des commerçants, sans doute des musulmans. A Djerba ils chargeaient d'huile et d'étoffes. Lui-même voyagea jusqu'à Tripoli [312]. Puis en 1466 il s'embarqua à Oran sur une grosse galée génoise venant de la Flandre. Beaucoup de marchands d'Oran et de Tlemcen s'apprêtaient à s'y embarquer en direction de Tunis. Le bateau faisait voile via Bougie et Tripoli vers Alexandrie [313].

Les marchands italiens ne renonçaient pas à ce grand négoce qui était aussi à cette époque tardive du Moyen Age le commerce d'esclaves. Ils exportaient un grand nombre d'esclaves de la Tripolitaine et d'autres pays du Maghreb vers l'Egypte [314]. Parfois le sultan et les autorités mamloukes elles-mêmes avaient recours au service des bateaux italiens pour transporter des hommes et des marchandises. Les actes d'un notaire vénitien qui exerçait son métier à Alexandrie au tournant du XIVe siècle démontrent que les Mamlouks exigeaient ces services déjà à cette époque. En 1399 le gouverneur d'Alexandrie nolisa un bateau ancônitain pour le transport de sel à Tripoli [315]. Un bateau vénitien devait, en 1456, transporter du bois de construction de Tripoli à Damiette [316]. Une année plus tard on craint à Venise qu'une coque envoyée à Lattakie pour charger du coton ne soit employée par les auto-

[311] Senato, Mar VIII, f 150b.

[312] R. Brunschwig, *Deux récits de voyage inédits en Afrique du Nord au XVe siècle,* Paris 1936, p. 95, 96.

[313] *Ibidem,* p. 135. En effet l'auteur ne dit pas explicitement que c'était une galée génoise, mais il n'y en a pas de doute, v. *Ibidem,* note 1.

[314] V. un acte vénitien: G. P., *Sent.* 180, f. 103b (a. 1485). Il paraît toutefois que la conclusion de F. C. Lane (de la bien connue relation de Piloti) touchant le transport (par les Vénitiens) de 1000-2000 esclaves par an est exagérée, v. *Venice, a maritime republic,* John Hopkins University Press 1973, p. 349 et s.

[315] Vat. sub 13 jan. 1400.

[316] *Senato,* Mar V, f. 172a.

rités mamloukes pour leurs besoins [317]. Il paraît toutefois que la part des Génois dans ce négoce ait été beaucoup plus grand que la part des Vénitiens. Car Venise souffrait dans la deuxième moitié du XVe siècle d'une pénurie de bateaux, par suite d'une crise de l'armement. Le gouvernement de la Sérénissime devait encourager les armateurs, en leur promettant des subsides, surtout à la construction de grands bateaux [318]. D'autre part, on défendit aux Vénitiens et aux sujets de Venise de noliser des bateaux arborant un autre pavillon [319].

Mais, pour évaluer l'importance qu'avait le recours au service de bateaux européens pour la balance des payements du Proche-Orient on voudrait avoir des indications précises sur le volume de ce secteur. Hélas, nous ne pouvons pas citer des données statistiques. Toutefois il y a des indices. Le nombre des bateaux européens qui desservaient la communication entre les pays du Maghreb et l'Egypte ne pouvait pas être petit. Dans les cahiers d'Antoniello de Vataciis, notaire vénitien à Alexandrie, on trouve bon nombre d'actes qui se réfèrent aux patrons et à leurs bateaux. Voici un résumé [320]:

Nombre de bateaux européens ancrant à Alexandrie

1400	1401	Juillet-déc. 1404	1405
13	14	14	24

Pourtant, cela se comprend, ces données ne sont pas une liste complète des bateaux européens qui fréquentaient le port d'Alexandrie, car on ne croirait pas que tous les patrons s'adressaient au dit notaire. On peut supposer que du moins 20-30 bateaux européens cinglaient à cette époque chaque année le long des côtes nord-africaines et jusqu'à Alexan-

[317] *Ibidem,* f. 186a.

[318] *Senato,* Mar 12, f. 157a (a. 1488) cf. 13, f. 27a.

[319] *Senato,* Mar 12, f. 148a (a. 1488). En effet on apprend des délibérations du Sénat que des sujets vénitiens avaient vendu à des étrangers des bateaux ainsi qu'on eût difficulté à approvisionner Venise en froment, v. Senato, Mar 14 f. 103b et ss. et cf. F. C. Lane, *Venetian shipping during the commercial revolution,* (dans son recueil) *Venice and history,* John Hopkins University Press 1966, p. 8, 10.

[320] V. mes articles *The Venetian supremacy in the Levantine trade - monopoly or procolonialism?,* dans JEEH, III (1974), p. 7; *Observations on Venetian trade in the Levant in the XIVth century,* dans JEEH, V (1976), p. 565.

drie. Mais combien payait-on pour le frêt? Selon un acte du même notaire on nolisa, en 1404, à Tunis un bateau pour le voyage à Alexandrie pour 1800 doblas, ce qui aurait été l'équivalent de 1666 dinars [321]. En 1405 on paya pour le transport de 2790 jarres d'huile, par un bateau génois, de Séville à Alexandrie, 1400 dinars [302]. Est-ce qu'on se trompe en supposant que le service des bateaux européens coûtait aux Proche-Orientaux à peu près 100.000 ducats par an? En prenant en considération les nombreux bateaux jetant l'ancre à Beyrouth et dans d'autres ports syro-palestiniens cette somme ne semble pas être exagérée. Peut-être est-elle sous-estimée.

Si les capitalistes proche-orientaux avaient investi l'argent, au lieu de l'employer pour l'armement, en d'autres entreprises, les dépenses pour le service des flottes mercantiles étrangères n'auraient pas été nécessairement une perte pour l'économie nationale. Mais ils les thésaurisaient. Plusieurs relations dans les chroniques arabes démontrent que la thésaurisation était aussi à cette époque tardive un phénomène important de la vie économique du Proche-Orient, bien que les trésors cachés et puis découverts aient été plus petits qu'autrefois [323].

En modifiant un tableau equissé ailleurs [324] on pourrait considérer les sommes indiquées ci-dessous comme pas improbables.

Cette esquisse, hypothétique qu'elle soit, démontre encore une fois que la balance des payements du Proche-Orient en ce qui concerne les échanges avec les nations marchandes de l'Europe méridionale était favorable, tandis que la balance commerciale était nettement déficitaire. Nous ne connaissons pas le volume de l'importation des épices destinées à la consommation dans les pays du Proche-Orient eux-mêmes, mais à en juger d'après un budget de famille esquissé par al-Maḳrīzī, il devait être considérable [325]. Quoiqu'il en soit, nos conjectures s'accordent assez bien avec le renseignement fourni par un voyageur français

[321] Vat. sub 18 août 1404 et cf. sub 22 mai 1400: i dobla - 23 carats (23/24) d'un dinar.

[322] Vat. sub 3 nov. 1405.

[323] *Mais voyez Sulūk* IV, p. 113: on trouve chez un haut fonctionnaire 964,000 dinars (en 1409).

[324] V. ma monographie *Les métaux précieux et la balance des payements du Proche-Orient à la basse époque,* Paris 1971, p. 96.

[325] Quant à la consommation des épices v. AL-MAḲRĪZĪ, *Le traité des famines,* trad. G. WIET, Paris 1962, p. 83: un riche bourgeois dépense 1/5 de son budget d'alimentation pour des épices.

Essai d'une balance commerciale du Proche-Orient au XVe siècle

a) *Echanges avec les nations marchandes de l'Europe méridionale (commerce des produits du Proche-Orient et de l'Extrême-Orient)*

Apport des Européens		Contre-valeur remise par les Orientaux	
apport des Vénitiens:		épices pour	350.000 ducats
en espèces	400.000 ducats	coton	150.000 ducats
marchandises (huile, miel, draps) valant	250.000 ducats	autres produits proche-orientaux	100.000 ducats
apport des autres Européens:		en espèces	50.000 ducats
en espèces	150.000 ducats	épices pour	150.000 ducats
marchandises valant	100.000 ducats	produits proche-orientaux	80.000 ducats
		en espèces	20.000 ducats
	900.000 ducats		900.000 ducats
services (navigation)	100.000 ducats		

a) *Balance commerciale de ces échanges*

Importation		Exportation	
marchandises importées par les Vénitiens	250.000 ducats	épices	470.000 ducats
marchandises importées par d'autres Européens	100.000 ducats	coton	150.000 ducats
services	100.000 ducats	autres produits proche-orientaux	110.000 ducats
	450.000 ducats		730.000 ducats

surplus de l'exportation 280.000 ducats

c) *Achats aux Européens, dans d'autres régions euro-asiatiques et dans l'Afrique septentrionale*

Importation		Exportation	
épices pour réexportation en Europe	235.000 ducats	marchandises exportées en Inde	60.000 duc.
épices pour consommation locale	150.000 ducats		
huile maghrébine	50.000 ducats		
esclaves	65.000 ducats		
bois	20.000 ducats		
fer	60.000 ducats		
cuivre	60.000 ducats		
	640.000 ducats		

surplus de l'importation 580.000 ducats

d'après lequel la douane d'Alexandrie était affermée, au début du XVIe siècle, pour 250.000 ashrafīs (ducats) par an [326]. Or ce renseignement indique un volume de 1,25 millions de ducats pour les exportations et les importations [327] (on doit y ajouter au moins 10% pour le profit du fermier) [328]. Nous ne pouvons évaluer le volume des échanges avec le Maghreb et la Turquie où on exportait des produits proche-orientaux et des épices indiennes, mais on ne croira pas qu'ils changeaient la balance totale de façon qu'elle fut favorable aux Proche-Orientaux. L'opinion que la découverte de la voie maritime aux Indes par Vasco de Gama coupa l'artère principale de l'organisme économique du Proche-Orient est erronée [329]. Certainement le commerce des épices indiennes rapportait au Trésor mamlouk et à la classe marchande de gros revenus, mais la source principale de la richesse des pays proche-orientaux était le commerce avec le Soudan occidental d'où on obtenait l'or. La diminution des apports d'or, par suite de l'expansion portugaise dans l'Afrique occidentale, et les dépenses toujours augmentant pour l'armée étaient beaucoup plus préjudicieuses pour l'économie mamlouke que l'entreprise de Vasco de Gama.

L'appauvrissement progressif du Proche-Orient à la fin du Moyen Age ressort clairement des renseignements que nous fournissent les chroniqueurs arabes. Qu'on regarde les relations sur les sommes qu'extorquait le gouvernement mamlouk à peu près périodiquement aux riches par la « muṣādara », la contribution arbitraire imposée en lieu de taxes régulières. A la fin du XIVe siècle et dans la première moitié du XVe siècle le sultan du Caire n'imposa à un haut fonctionnaire, à un officier ou à un riche marchand, la plupart des cas, pas plus de 10.000-20.000 dinars (puis ashrafīs) [330], tandis que des contributions se montant à plus que 100.000 ashrafīs sont rarement mentionnées [331]. Mais on imposait aussi des contributions plus modiques, se montant à quel-

[326] J. Thenaud, *Le voyage d'outremer,* cit., p. 27.

[327] V. mon article *The volume of Levantine trade in the later Middle Ages,* dans JEEH, IV (1975), p. 610.

[328] Pour l'achat des esclaves v. *Métaux précieux,* cit., p. 94, pour l'achat de fer p. 95 et pour le cuivre p. 83.

[329] V. ci-dessus note 29.

[330] *Sulūk* III, p. 965 IV, pp. 19, 116, 645, 767, 868 et s., 934, 938, 1091, 1099.

[331] Ibn Ḥadjar, *Inbā al-ghumr III,* p. 92; Sulūk IV, p. 1169.

ques milliers de dinars, par exemple 6000 dinars imposés à un riche marchand [332] ou 2000-5000 dinars à un haut fonctionnaire [333]. Cent ans plus tôt il s'agissait de sommes fabuleuses [334].

Le revenu per capita avait sans doute diminué. Car la diminution de la terre cultivée était probablement plus grande que la dépopulation. Il semble que les maladies endémiques et les épidémies aient fait de plus grands ravages dans les régions rurales que dans les centres urbains, dont les habitants étaient mieux nourris et plus résistants. Al-Maḳrīzī, un auteur bien informé, relate que les habitants de l'Egypte succombaient facilement aux épidémies parce que leur alimentation était malsaine [335]. Les paysans, dit-il, s'alimentent principalement de pain. Mais on abandonnait aussi les terres pour échapper à l'exploitation fiscale et le dépeuplement de divers districts s'ensuivit. Le même auteur raconte que déjà à la fin du XIVe siècle la population de villages entiers émigrait [336]. Au début du XVe siècle, dit l'auteur arabe, tous les villages tombèrent en ruines et la majeure part des terres resta en jachère [337]. Or la plupart des paysans qui abandonnaient les villages et allaient vivre dans les villes étaient voués à la misère, ils étaient certainement les premiers qui succombaient aux épidémies. Par suite de la famine et des épidémies plusieurs villages en Haute-Egypte restaient sans habitants [338]. Dans un passage de son traité sur la crise économique au début du XVe siècle, al-Maḳrīzī dit que «la plupart des paysans ont péri» [339]. Ces passages se rapportent à la population agraire de l'Egypte. Mais, toujours d'après cet auteur, qui nous a laissé la chronique la plus détaillée de cette époque, les épidémies sévissaient aussi dans les régions rurales de la Syrie, dans le Ḥaurān, la Transjordanie et la Palestine [340]. On conclura des relations d'auteurs postérieurs que ce phéno-

[332] *Sulūk* IV, p. 1157.
[333] *Ibidem,* pp. 5, 931.
[334] V. WEIL, *Geschichte der Chalifen,* IV, p. 392; ST. LANE-POOLE, *A history of Egypt,* New York 1969, p. 307; *Sulūk* II, p. 243 et s., 367, 481, 507 et s.
[335] Al-Khiṭaṭ I, p. 44.
[336] *Traité des famines,* p. 47.
[337] *Ibidem,* p. 49.
[338] *Sulūk* IV, p. 19 et s.
[339] *Traité des famines,* p. 74.
[340] *Sulūk* IV, p. 132, 165.

mène, la plus grande dépopulation des villages, se produisait aussi dans la deuxième moitié du XVe siècle [341]. Pourtant la décadence de l'agriculture et l'abandon des terres était aussi la conséquence de la rapacité des féodaux qui prélevaient des impôts en lieu de la corvée pour le maintien des digues [342]. Le pourcentage de la population urbaine aurait donc été plus grand à la fin du Moyen Age, du moins en Egypte. On se tromperait toutefois en supposant que la plus grande productivité de la population urbaine aurait élevé le revenu per capita. Car la proportion du déclin démographique et du déclin de la production était semblable dans le secteur agraire et dans la ville. Le déclin des industries était plus grand que la diminution de la population urbaine. Tandis que la population du Caire diminuait, selon Clerget, de 600.000 habitants au début du XIVe siècle à 430.000 au milieu du XVIe siècle [343], c'est-à-dire de 30% en deux cents ans, la diminution des raffineries de sucre était déjà au début du XVe siècle de 42% [344]. On aura sans doute raison de croire que le revenu per capita diminua progressivement, comme le déclin industriel était progressif. Voilà un phénomène de sous-développement, bien connu des économistes qui se sont occupés de l'économie des régions sous-développées à notre époque. («the widening gap») [345]. La grande majorité de la population devait dépenser la plus grande part de son revenu pour l'alimentation et celle-ci devenait plus mauvaise. L'augmentation de la culture de l'orge, aux dépens de la culture du blé, en porte témoignage. Citons encore une fois les résumés que B. Lewis a fait des cadastres dressés dans la première moitié du XVIe siècle par les Turcs en Palestine et en Syrie. On constate que dans plusieurs districts les taxes prélevées, selon un taux d'1/3 ou d'1/4 de l'orge, l'emportaient sur l'impôt prélevé sur le blé, ou étaient égales.

[341] *Ḥawādith,* p. 204.

[342] *Sulūk* IV, p. 874.

[343] M. Clerget, *Le Caire,* I, Le Caire 1934, p. 240. On attribuera une plus grande importance aux résultats de la recherche de ce savant qu'à l'évaluation d'un auteur arabe cité dans ma *Social and economic history,* p. 304. Mais celle-ci démontre qu'on se rendait compte du fait que le déclin démographique était formidable.

[344] V. mon article *Levantine sugar industry in the later Middle Ages - an example of technological decline*, dans «Israel Oriental Studies», VII (1977), tableau III.

[345] Baldwin, *Economic development and growth*, p. 6.

PROPORTION DU BLÉ ET DE L'ORGE EN PALESTINE EN 1525/26 [346]

Sandjak Jérusalem

District de Bethlehem	blé	5 ghirāras
	orge	5 ghirāras

Sandjak Ghaza

District d'Ashdod	blé	10 ghirāras
	orge	12 ghirāras
Disctrict de Jaffa	blé	6 ghirāras
	orge	7 ghirāras
District de Tell aṣ-Ṣāfiya	blé	10 ghirāras
	orge	15 ghirāras

Il y aussi d'autres indices de l'appauvrissement. On apprend des sources arabes qu'à la fin du XVe siècle les habitants du Caire commençaient à manger du pain de millet et de dhura, en lieu du bon pain de blé [347].

* * *

Arrivé au bout de cette recherche on posera la question: y a-t-il donc eu, au Bas Moyen Age, dans le Proche-Orient une domination étrangère sur l'économie nationale?

La réponse à cette question doit être négative. Car le secteur agricole qui produisait pour l'exportation n'était pas si grand comme dans les régions sous-développées à notre époque. Les marchands vénitiens qui exportaient le coton et le «lume» étaient pour la plupart des commerçants moyens. Il n'y avait pas à Venise de grands trusts tels qu'à notre époque. Par conséquent leur emprise sur l'économie procheorientale n'était pas totale.

Bref, il y avait, dans le Proche-Orient, à la fin du Moyen Age, beaucoup de phénomènes qui sont caractéristiques du sous-développement. Mais ce n'était pas encore une véritable domination étrangère.

[346] B. LEWIS, *Studies in the Ottoman archives*, dans BSOAS, XVI, p. 490. La ghirāra de Bethlehem était sans doute égale à celle de Jérusalem, voire trois fois autant la ghirāra damascène, v. ci-dessus note 133: celle de Ghaza équivalait à 1 1/2 ghirāras de Damas, v. HINZ, *Islamische Masse u. Gewichte*, p. 38.

[347] *Social and economic history*, p. 319.

II

THE ECONOMIC DECLINE OF THE MIDDLE EAST DURING THE LATER MIDDLE AGES AN OUTLINE*

Some Persian and Arab authors of the fourteenth and fifteenth centuries dwell on the great economic decline of Persia, Iraq, Syria, and Egypt during their days. Although these authors also cite official documents, such as accounts of tax revenues, their testimony is essentially a literary one, and statements of contemporary writers about misery and distress are not always trustworthy. These may be substantiated, however, by documents in the archives of south European countries which contain a wealth of information about the economic life of the Levant during that period. The purpose of this paper is to verify the statements of these Oriental writers by comparing them to the documentary evidence. Do these documents bear out the supposition of a general decline of the Oriental economies in the later Middle Ages? Using terms such as Levant and Orient, we have in mind countries whose agricultural and industrial structures and produce were very different. Hence, another question arises: is it possible to sketch a general pattern of the development of countries so different as Persia and Egypt? Finally, the reasons for their decline should be sought.[1]

Depopulation

The writings of Arab and Persian authors of the later Middle Ages comprise many passages dealing with the decline in the number of local inhabitants. Although these accounts are often considerably exaggerated, as are those of other medieval authors, in essence they are in accordance with fact.

The Mongol conquest of Iran and Iraq, accompanied by massacre and devastation, wrought havoc upon the populations of these countries. Although

* Paper presented at the International Conference on The Economic History of the Middle East, 1800–1914: A Comparative Approach, Haifa, December 1980.

1 I have dealt with these problems in several papers, and in my book, *A Social and Economic History of the Near East in the Middle Ages*, London 1976, to which I refer in the text.

Khurasan suffered more than other regions, the populations of Tabaristan and Iraq also must have decreased greatly. There followed other invasions and wars with neighboring states, which brought yet more destruction and further depopulation. Some towns of Persia remained in ruins for a long time. A Persian author writing 100 years after the Mongol conquest of Iran names more than 30 towns which were still in ruins and others which had deteriorated into mere villages. Moreover, he cites data indicating a sharp decline in the number of villages in several provinces of Persia.[2] At the end of the fourteenth century the wars of Timur Lenk had similar consequences, while the misrule of some Turcoman rulers of the fifteenth century must also have been disastrous for the demographic development of both Iran and Iraq. Although these are *a priori* suppositions and literary accounts, they are substantiated by reliable evidence.

A surface survey made by an archaeological expedition of the University of Chicago in the province of Diyala, east of Baghdad, indicates the tremendous decrease of the built-up area and points to a great de-population. According to the conclusions of this expedition, about half of the built-up area was abandoned during the period of the Īl-Khāns. The population appears to have numbered 870, 000 at the peak of Abbasid rule (about 800 C.E.), 400,000 in 1100 C.E., and only 60,000 after the Mongol conquest.[3] These estimates include the town of Baghdad. The development of grain prices is certainly a clear indicator of population trends, as it reflects the oscillations of supply and demand. Although available data concerning grain prices in Iraq during the later Middle Ages are scanty, they are sufficient to show the progressive decline from the tenth century onwards. During the first half of the fourteenth century grain prices were apparently 17 per cent lower than they had been 200 years previously.[4] The price of bread declined much less, no doubt due to the fact that bakers' wages had increased.[5] A lessened demand for cereals and increased wages owing to a shortage of workers are clear signs of depopulation.

Syria also suffered from the Mongol invasions, although much less than Persia and Iraq. The invasions, together with rumors of impending ones, caused many Syrians to flee to Egypt, and certainly a not inconsiderable number of them remained there. Hence, the population of Syria can hardly have increased very much during the second half of the thirteenth century. According to the

2 L.P. Petrushevsky, 'The Socio-economic Condition of Iran under the Īl-Khāns,' *Cambridge History of Iran*, V, pp. 483ff., 497; see also my *Social and Economic History*, p. 252.

3 R. MacAdams, *Land behind Baghdad*, Chicago 1965, pp. 108, 115.

4 E. Ashtor, *Histoire des prix et des salaires dans l'Orient Médiéval*, Paris 1969, p. 451.

5 Ibid., p. 452.

estimates of an Orientalist, the whole of Syria and Palestine may have comprised 900 thousand–1.2 million inhabitants prior to the Black Death, which reduced the population by a third.[6] The Black Death was followed by 15 heavy epidemics from the mid-fourteenth to the end of the fifteenth century,[7] so that population numbers undoubtedly decreased further. Moreover, it was not only pestilence and disease which decimated the population. Inter-tribal Bedouin warfare resulted in the destruction and abandonment of hundreds of villages.[8] The population decline in Syria during the fifteenth century must have been noticeable, as is clearly shown by the census taken by the Ottomans when they had conquered the country. From the registers of this census the Turkish scholar Barkan has concluded that Syria, including Palestine and some provinces of southern Asia Minor, comprised 571,360 inhabitants at that time.[9] The demographic decline of Palestine was certainly not of more limited scope than in other provinces of Syria. In a book published some years ago the demographer Bachi calculated the population of Palestine prior to 1348 at 225,000 and after that at 150,000. He believes that on the eve of the Turkish conquest it numbered no more than 140,000–150,000 inhabitants, with Jerusalem comprising only 2,000. The number of villages in Palestine also must have decreased greatly. A comparison of census figures with the number listed in a treaty between the Mamlūk sultan Qalā'ūn and the Crusader principality in Acre in 1283 is revealing. Out of 63 places listed in the treaty in the district of Acre, only 20 appear in the census records taken by the Turks in 1595/96. Of the 7 listed in the district of Haifa and the 12 on the Carmel, none are mentioned in the Turkish records. According to a Latin source, the Crusader principality of Safed comprised 260 villages, and at the beginning of Mamlūk rule their number may have been even greater, for Sultan Baibars settled Muslims there who had been expelled by the Crusaders. The Arab author Khalīl al-Ẓāhirī (d. 1468), who held an administrative post in Safed for some time, recounts that in his days the province (which included the districts of Tyre, Acre, and Tiberias) comprised 1,200 villages. In contrast, the Turkish census of 1525/26 mentioned only 231 villages in this province.[10]

6 A.W. Poliak, 'The Demographic Evolution of the Middle East,' *Palestine and the Middle East* 10 (1938): 201.

7 Ashtor, *Social and Economic History*, p. 302.

8 I.M. Lapidus, *Muslim Cities in the Later Middle Ages*, Harvard 1967, pp. 39, 254.

9 'Essai sur les données statistiques des registres de recensement dans l'Empire Ottoman aux XVe et XVIe siècles,' *Journal of the Economic and Social History of the Orient* 1 (1958): 20, 27.

10 R. Bachi, *The Population of Israel*, Jerusalem 1978, pp. 23, 362; D. Barag, 'A New Source

Egypt of the later Middle Ages had a different demographic history insofar as it witnessed a population increase during the second half of the thirteenth and the first half of the fourteenth century. Egypt was never invaded by the Mongols, nor did it suffer many epidemics during that period. The great pestilence of the mid-fourtenth century proved to be a turning point. According to a contemporary writer, Ibn Ḥabīb, both Egypt and Syria lost a third of their population, that of Egypt amounting to perhaps to 3–4 million inhabitants.[11] Cairo alone, which comprised 450,000–600,000 inhabitants, probably lost 200,000.[12] After the Black Death the country suffered from a series of epidemics which impeded a demographic recovery.[13] In addition to the literary accounts, data are available from excerpts of official documents concerning the number of villages in Egypt. Discounting data which are altogether unreliable, perhaps the following are acceptable:[14]

656	2,395
996–1020 (al-Ḥākim)	2,340
1035–1094 (al-Mustanṣir)	2,186
1210	2,071
1315	2,284
1375	2,163
1434	2,170
1460	2,365
1477	2,121

Concerning the Ultimate Borders of the Latin Kingdom of Jerusalem,' *Israel Exploration Journal* 29 (1979): 213; M.L. Favreau-Lilie, 'Landesausbau und Burg während der Kreuzfahrerzeit, Safad in Obergaliläa,' *Zeitschrift des Deutschen Palestina-Vereins* 96 (1980): 84; Ashtor, *Social and Economic History*, p. 316; Khalīl al-Ẓāhirī, *Zubdat Kashf al-Mamālik*, Ravaisse (ed.), p. 44; B. Lewis, 'Studies in the Ottoman Archives,' *Bulletin of the School of Oriental and African Studies* 16 (1954): 475.

11 Poliak, 'Demographic Evolution'; J.C. Russell, 'The Population of Medieval Egypt,' *Journal of the American Research Center in Egypt* 5 (1966): 76; Ibn Ḥabīb, 'Durrat al-aslāk,' in Juynboll, Roorda, and Weijers (eds.), *Orientalia*, II, Amsterdam 1840–1846, p. 388.

12 M.W. Dols, *The Black Death in the Middle East*, Princeton 1977, pp. 198, 202, 215. But A. Raymond believes that during the Middle Ages Cairo never comprised more than 200,000 inhabitants; see his paper, 'Les populations du Caire de Maqrizi à la description d'Égypte,' *Bulletin d'Etudes Orientales* 28 (1975): 205f.

13 Ashtor, *Social and Economic History*, p. 302.

14 For the sources, see my review of Dols in *Bibliotheca Orientalis* 35 (1978): 273.

Since, the datum for 1460 may be incorrect, it is preferable not to take it into account. From the remaining data it can be concluded that, during the period subsequent to the Black Death, Egypt comprised 200 villages less than during the Fāṭimid period.

That there was an increase in the population of Egypt under the first Baḥrī Mamlūks and a decline from the middle of the fourteenth century is borne out by a weath of data in various sources about changes in grain and bread prices. The price of wheat, which had been 1.07 dinars per 100 kg at the end of the thirteenth and the beginning of the fourteenth century, fell to 0.56 dinars during the second half of the fifteenth century.[15] This surely was the result of a smaller demand. However, the price of bread, which was lower at the end than during the first half of the thirteenth century, rose after the Black Death.[16] Obviously, the shortage of manpower in Egypt brought about the rise of real wages.

The accounts of travellers who visited Egypt and Syria and the end of the Middle Ages corroborate the conclusion of a general population decline.[17] Their tales of uninhabited districts and towns in ruins brings home most poignantly the fact that depopulation was the most important feature of both Egypt's and Syria's social and economic history during the later Middle Ages, one which had far-reaching consequences for all sectors of the respective, national economies. This entailed the fall of grain prices, on the one hand, and the rise of industrial production costs, on the other. Agricultural production had to be adapted to the new conditions, and the industries were forced to either concentrate on certain articles or cease production altogether.

Whereas depopulation in Persia and Iraq was greatly the result of military invasions, in Syria and Egypt the epidemics were mainly responsible. But the underlying cause seems to have been misrule, i.e., heedless exploitation of the population by the Mongol, Turkish, and Circassian invaders. Many inhabitants fell victim to the epidemics because of malnutrition. Villages were wholly or partly abandoned by peasants incapable of bearing the tax burden, and those who fled led a wretched life in the suburbs of the large towns, ultimately succumbing to the periodically returning pest. Hence, impoverishment and depopulation went hand in hand.

15 Ashtor, *Histoire des prix et des salaires*, pp. 394, 455; idem, 'Quelques problèmes que soulève l'histoire des prix dans l'Orient médiéval,' in *Studies in Memory of G. Wiet*, Jerusalem 1977, pp. 207 ff., 212.

16 Ashtor, *Histoire des prix et des salaires*, pp. 131, 309 f., 310, 313.

17 Idem, *Social and Economic History*, pp. 303 f.

Agricultural Decline

In most regions of the Middle East the area under cultivation must have diminished from the middle of the thirteenth century onwards. Undoubtedly, the fertile soil of these subtropic countries still yielded rich harvests. Ḥamdallāh Qazwīnī, writing at the end of the 1330, expatiates on the variegated production of fruits and grains in Iran during his day. However, Rashīd al-Din, whose testimony is undisputed, asserts that only a tenth of the area of the Īl-Khānid kingdom was cultivated.[18] The measures taken by Īl-Khān Gāzān (1295–1304) to foster agriculture probably brought only temporary relief. Even under his rule agricultural production did not approach the level it had reached before the Mongol conquest.[19] This is clearly evident from data cited by Hamdallāh Qazwīnī concerning the tax revenue of Persia and Iraq. These indicate that the taxes collected by the Īl-Khāns from Media, Azarbaydjan, and Iraq amounted to no more than 10 per cent of what the Seljuks had levied there. On the average, the Mongol rulers collected 19 per cent of what their predecessors had cashed in from these countries.[20] Furthermore, the area under cultivation had greatly diminished in those villages which were still inhabited. Accordingly, provinces in which a great number of villages still existed yielded a relatively small amount of taxes.[21]

Egypt, the granary of Rome and Byzantium, continued to, produce sufficient cereals for its population. During normal years it was even capable of exporting great quantities of grain to other countries. However, other sectors of both Egypt's and Syria's agriculture greatly declined. This emerges clearly from a wealth of information drawn from documents preserved in the archives of Italy, southern France, and Catalonia. A study of these documents, which deal with commercial relations with the Muslim Levant, reveals the great volume of foodstuffs imported from southern Europe into Egypt and Syria during the fourteenth and fifteenth centuries, whereas in previous periods the local supply had sufficed.

Olive oil was the most prominent among the list of imported goods. In earlier centuries Egypt had imported it from Syria and Tunisia. During the Mamlūk period, however, its production in Syria must have declined to such an extent that the south European trading nations could export great quantities to these regions. While the import of European olive oil into Egypt had begun a long

18 Ibid., p. 260.
19 Petrushevsky, p. 500.
20 Ibid., p. 498.
21 See Ashtor, *Social and Economic History*, p. 259.

time before, at least as early as the end of the thirteenth century,[22] it seems to have increased even more at the end of the fourteenth and during the fifteenth century. The Cretan Emmanuel Piloti, writing during the third decade of the fifteenth century, dwells upon the voluminous shipments of olive oil to Egypt from Andalusia and Majorca. He also mentions the import of Greek olive oil.[23] Olive oil to sustain regular trade was also imported into Egypt from southern Italy, both from Apulia and the Campania. Merchants from Apulia marketed Italian oil in Egypt through agents,[24] but Venetians also exported it to the Muslim Levant.[25] The olive oil of the Campania was shipped to Egypt by the merchants of Naples, Amalfi, and Gaeta.[26] While the Genoese exported the oil to Egypt from Naples and the Provence,[27] it goes without saying that the merchants of southern France themselves also engaged in this trade.[28] Enough olive oil was even imported into Syria from southern Europe.[29]

Among the various kinds of olive oil shipped to the Muslim Levant from southern Europe, that of southern Italy (both Apulia and the Campania) and Spain ranked first; they fetched higher prices than the Greek variety.[30] The difference in price between local Syrian olive oil and that of Europe (or Tunisia) was very great, ranging from 50 to 100 per cent.[31] This implies that the European olive oil was destined for the upper classes of society, who lived at a higher economic level. This is a clear sign of the existence of a dual economy, so characteristic of underdeveloped countries. The volume of this import trade must have been considerable. A Venetian ship carried olive oil to Syria in 1406 for not less than 25,000 ducats.[32] Furthermore, in negotiations with a Venetian embassy, the Mamlūk sultan could maintain in 1512 that in previous times the

22 Marino Sanuto (the Elder), *Secreta Fidelium Crucis,* Hannover 1611, p. 24.

23 *Traité d'Emmanuel Piloti sur le passage en Terre Sainte* (1420), H.P. Dopp (ed.), Louvain 1958, pp. 146, 154.

24 Archivio di Stato, Venice (hereafter ASV) *Giudici di Petizion, Sentenze a Giustizia* (hereafter *G.P.*), pp. 150 f., 71b ff.; Christoforo del Fiore, published in my paper, 'New Data for the History of Levantine Jewries in the Fifteenth Century,' *Bulletin of the Institute of Jewish Studies* 3 (1975): 97 ff.

25 *G.P.*, 58 f., 57b.

26 ASV, Cancellaria Inferiore, Notai, Ba 222, Antoniello de Vataciis (hereafter Vataciis), 2 July 1404, 28 December 1405; Ba 211, Nicolo Turiano (hereafter Turiano), V, fols. 8b ff.

27 Vataciis, 1 September 1401, 28 February 1405.

28 ASV, Cancellaria Inferiore, Notai, Ba 229, fasc. V, Leonardo de Valle, 24 March 1403.

29 ASV, Senato, *Misti* 35, fol. 159b.

30 See Ashtor, 'Quelques problèmes,' p. 220.

31 Ibid.

32 ASV, *G.P.*, Sentenze e Interdetti VIII, fols. 24b ff.

Venetians had exported 3,000–4,000 butts of olive oil to Egypt every year.[33]

Another European commodity of which considerable quantities were imported during that period into the Middle East was honey. Both Marino Sanuto[34] and Emmanuel Piloti dwell on its import into Egypt. The latter author mentions many countries from which it was shipped. According to him, honey in Egypt was marketed from Salonica, Euboea, Morea, the Greek archipelago, Rhodes, Crete, Corfu, Lombardy, and Catalonia.[35] The export of honey from Greece to the dominions of the Mamlūk sultan is also dealt with in the registers of the Venetian Senate.[36] The Venetians, of course, exported to Egypt great quantities of honey from Apulia, a region where they engaged in extensive commercial activities.[37] From Catalonia various kinds of honey were exported to the Muslim Levant, that of Mequinanza having an especially high value. However, the other kinds of Catalan honey also fetched higher prices in the Muslim Levant than those of Italy and Greece.[38] The export of honey from Catalonia was obviously in the hands of Catalan merchants.[39] Southern France also supplied the Muslim Levant with honey, which was exported by merchants of Montpellier[40] and Narbonne,[41] and also by the Genoese.[42] It is noteworthy that even this was exported from all countries of southern Europe not only to Egypt, but also to Syria.[43] The obvious conclusion is that agriculture had declined in the latter country as well.

The list of foodstuffs exported from southern Europe into the Muslim Levant is varied. The Venetian merchants marketed Apulian almonds there,[44] the Catalans those of their own country.[45] Even greater quantities of chestnuts were

33 M. Reinaud, 'Traités de commerce entre la république de Venise et les derniers sultans d'Égypte,' Journal Asiatique 2 (1829): 32, and cf. 28. A butt contained 540, 71; see U. Tucci, 'Un problema di metrologia navale: la botta veneziana,' *Studi Veneziani* 9 (1967): 215 f., and cf. Ashtor, 'Quelques problèmes,' p. 221. On the volume of European olive oil exported to the Middle East, see Ashtor, 'Quelques problèmes,' pp. 226 f.

34 Sanuto, *Secreta Fidelium Crucis.*

35 Piloti, *Traité,* pp. 143, 147, 150, 151, 154, 156, 157, 158.

36 ASV, Senato, *Misti,* 56, fols. 104a ff.

37 *Misti* 34, fol. 47b.

38 Piloti, *Traité,* p. 147; Ashtor, 'Quelques problèmes,' pp. 224 f.

39 Leonardo de Valle, 22 December 1401.

40 Vataciis, 9 December 1399, 20 May 1401, 9 December 1405.

41 Vataciis, 4 October 1404.

42 ASV, Cancellaria Inferiore, Notai, Ba 230, Nicolo Venier (hereafter, Venier) B, 2, fols. 42b ff.

43 *Misti* 55, fol. 92a.

44 *G.P.* 59, fols. 190b ff.; 184, fols. 206b ff.; *Misti* 41, fol. 92b; ASV, Collegio, Notatorio VIII, fol. 106a.

45 Piloti, p. 148.

exported by the Venetians to Egypt[46] and Syria,[47] a portion of these coming from Crete.[48] As chestnuts had become an important article in Egypt, a decision of the Venetian Senate establishes the *consolazium* to be paid to the Venetian consul in Alexandria for this commodity.[49] The import of hazelnuts was even more voluminous. From the end of the thirteenth century large shiploads were exported to the Muslim Levant by merchants from all the countries of southern Europe.[50] Hazelnuts were shipped to Egypt from Rhodes,[51] from the Campania by merchants of Naples and Amalfi,[52] from Liguria ('hazelnuts of Ventimiglia'),[53] from southern France by merchants from Montpellier,[54] and from Catalonia.[55] The Venetians engaged widely in this trade, as is borne out by a great number of documents.[56] The import of hazelnuts into the Middle East became a very profitable trade in the course of time, so that whole ships were chartered for this purpose.[57] During the fifteenth century agriculture had declined so greatly in the Levant that even figs had to be imported from Greece,[58] the Greek islands, Rhodes,[59] Chios,[60] and Crete.[61]

Among the various fruits marketed by European merchants in the Muslim Levant during the later Middle Ages, dried raisins were popular. These came mostly from Rhodes.[62] While most documents refer to the import of raisins into Egypt,[63] they were imported into Syria as well.[64]

46 *G.P.*, IX, fols. 23b f.
47 Same series V, fols. 84a f.
48 ASV, Cancellaria Inferiore, Notai, Ba 229, fasc. V, Verb. Cons. XII (the protocol of the Council of the Venetian colony in Alexandria), 25 August 1402.
49 *Misti* 46, fol. 94a (1403). On the import of chestnuts by Venetians into the dominions of the Mamlūks, see also *G.P.*, VIII, fols. 47b. ff.
50 Sanuto, *Secreta Fidelium Crucis.*
51 Turiano, IV, fols. 9a ff.; V, fols. 43b f.
52 Vataciis, 2 July 1404, 19 August 1405.
53 Piloti, p. 149.
54 Leonardo de Valle, 24 March, 5 September 1403.
55 Piloti, p. 148; Turiano, II, fols. 51a f.; V, fols. 30b, 35a.
56 *G.P.*, Interdetti VII, fols. 76b ff.; *Misti* 53, fol. 210b; Turiano, II, fol. 54a; V, fol. 1a. On the *consolazium* to be paid by Venetians in Alexandria, see *Misti* 41, fol. 92b; 46, fol. 94a.
57 Felix Fabri, *Evagatorium in Terram Sanctam, Arabiae et Aegypti Peregrinationes,* III, C.D. Hassler (ed.), Stuttgart 1843–1849, p. 153.
58 Piloti, p. 154 (from Morea).
59 Vataciis, 16 June 1400, 22 August 1405.
60 Verb. Cons. XII, 9 March 1402.
61 Turiano, IV, fol. 7a.
62 Vataciis, 22 August, 7 September 1405; Venier, B, 2, fols. 16a ff., 43b ff. (a very large quantity), 50b, 55a; *G.P.* 187, fols. 75a ff.
63 Turiano, II, fols. 8a f., 51b; *G.P.* 167, fols. 135a ff.
64 *G.P.* 165, fols. 93b ff. (import by Venetians).

The above data leave no doubt as to the great agricultural decline of Egypt and Syria during the later Middle Ages. This is highlighted by some documents mentioning the import of dairy products into the dominions of the Mamlūk sultan. Piloti reports that butter was imported into Egypt from Sicily,[65] and cheese both from Sicily and Crete.[66] The import of cheese from Crete into Egypt is also mentioned in the registers of the Venetian Senate and in judicial acts.[67] Notarial acts drawn up in Alexandria refer to the export of cheese from Rhodes to Egypt,[68] whereas decisions of the Venetian Senate refer to its export to Egypt from the Greek mainland.[69]

Raw Material Supplies to European Industry

A change in crop production was even more characteristic of the Middle East during the later Middle Ages. When the demand for cereals decreased considerably, the peasants were forced to replace the cultivation of wheat and barley by other crops. Consequently, there was an upswing of cotton planting in several regions. A portion of the cotton was processed in local industries, but in those cotton-growing regions having commercial relations with the European trading nations the greater part of the produce was apparently exported and served as a raw material for the textile industries of several European countries.

Ḥamdallāh Qazwīnī mentions the cotton plantations in his description of almost all the provinces of Persia. According to his accounts, much cotton was grown not only in Khorastan and in Fars, where cotton planting had been an important sector of agriculture during the period of the caliphs, but also in Media, Azarbaydjan, Arran, Kurdistan, in the Shabānkāra province, in the Great Desert, and in Kirman.[70] Upper Mesopotamia must have seen a spectacular increase in cotton plantations. During earlier periods that area had exported great quantities of wheat to Iraq, but when the demand for cereals diminished owing to depopulation, cotton plantations had to be extended. Ḥamdallāh Qazwīnī mentions the plantations of the districts of Irbil, Bāsabda,

65 Piloti, p. 147.

66 Ibid., pp. 147, 158.

67 *Misti* 37, fol. 99b; *G.P.* 56, fols. 78b ff.

68 Turiano, V, fols. 43b f.

69 *Misti* 56, fols. 104a ff. On the *consolazium* to be paid by Venetian merchants in Alexandria for the import of cheese, see *Misti* 41, fol. 92b.

70 The geographical part of the *Nuzhat al-qulūb,* Guy Le Strange (trans.), Leyden 1919, pp. 60, 66, 72, 76, 77, 86, 88, 89, 90, 92, 108, 109, 137, 140, 141.

Arzan, Rās al-ʿAyn, Barṭallā, and Mārdīn.[71] Undoubtedly much cotton was also grown in other provinces of Upper Mesopotamia.

Cotton planting increased greatly in Syria and Palestine as well. Here it was a consequence not only of depopulation and a lesser demand for cereals, but perhaps much more of the loss of markets, resulting from the destruction of Crusader towns by the Mamlūk sultans. This increase in cotton planting is revealed by the descriptions of Arab and European authors dating from the period before the fall of Acre and that subsequent to it.[72] This was especially the case in northern Syria and the Galilee, the surroundings of Acre, and the Plain of Esdraelon. In 1304 a Venetian embassy made a first visit to the Mamlūk governor of Safed, who ruled over that region.[73] There can be no doubt that the greater part of the cotton produced in Syria and Palestine was exported to Europe. There were three major centers of cotton planting in Syria and Palestine: the province of Aleppo, where Sarmīn was a great cotton market, the province of Hama, and northern Palestine. Italian traders strictly distinguished between the different kinds of Syro-Palestinian cotton. According to Pegolotti, the cotton of Hama was the best; that of Sarmīn ranked next; and that of Acre (i.e., the Palestinian) was of poorest quality.[74] This statement is not substantiated, however, by Venetian documents, which, together with judicial acts and price lists (including those in the Datini archives), indicate that Palestinian cotton was sold on the European markets at the same price as the Sarmīn cotton and sometimes even at a higher price. However that may be, all kinds of Syro-Palestinian cotton, considered superior to the cotton of Turkey and other countries, were highly valued in Europe. Their fibers were longer and the cotton was more pliant. Hence the great demand. Doubtless, a small portion of the Syrian cotton was processed by local manufacturers, who produced the *bocasine* exported to Europe. During the Mamlūk period Baalbek was an industrial town marketing cotton stuffs in Egypt and other countries. Nor was it the only town or village in Syria where cotton stuffs were produced.[75] Nevertheless, much more cotton than that destined for the local industries was shipped to Europe, a great part of it serving as raw material for the fustian industry of Lombardy. The Venetians supplied cotton to the manufacturers of

71 Ibid., pp. 102 ff.

72 See E. Ashtor, 'The Venetian Cotton Trade in Syria in the Later Middle Ages,' *Studi Medievali*, 3rd series, 17 (1976): 680 f.

73 Th. Predelli, *Diplomatarium Veneto-Levantinum*, I, Venice 1880–1899, no. 17.

74 *Pratica della mercatura*, Evans (ed.), p. 366.

75 Ashtor, 'The Venetian Cotton Trade,' pp. 682 ff.

Ravenna, Padua, and Verona; the Genoese supplied it to southern France and Tuscany; Piacenza and Cremona obtained it from both Venice and Genoa.[76] During that period Egypt also produced cotton which was exported to Europe.[77] Nevertheless, the bulk of the Middle Eastern cotton shipped to southern Europe came from Syria, and in the course of time its purchase and shipping became a Venetian business. As a consequence, Venetian colonies came into being in Hama, Sarmīn, and Lattakia.[78] When fustian industries were founded in several towns of southern Germany during the 1370s, the export of Syrian cotton increased greatly. These new German manufacturers were wholly dependent upon the Syrian cotton, with which they were supplied by the Venetians. Venice organized a shipping line which served the cotton trade. In February and August convoys of licensed cogs departed for Syria to load cotton in Lattakie. Tripoli, and Acre. Altogether there were about ten to twelve such convoys a year.

During the 1370s the volume of the cotton export from Syria and Palestine must already have been great, for according to the account of a contemporary Arab author, the port taxes of Acre were farmed for 50,000 dirhams a year.[79] This points to a revenue of 70,000 ducats from import and export taxes. As the import was undoubtedly much smaller than the export, it may be assumed that the value of the cotton exported from Palestine amounted to 50,000 ducats. At the end of the fourteenth century the export of cotton from Syria probably increased. During the 1390s the Venetians alone exported about 8,000 sacks of raw cotton yearly as well as small quantities of spun cotton. As prices were low during that period (a north Syrian qinṭār amounting to 25 ducats), the total value of the cotton exported by the Venetians from Syria and Palestine may have been 150,000 ducats. It is possible, however, that a part of these shipments came from Cyprus.[80]

This growing supply of Levantine raw materials to the European textiles industries was a sign that the Middle Eastern countries had begun to fill the role of an underdeveloped region. In fact, several other materials were shipped from the Levant to southern Europe.

76 Ibid., p. 694.
77 Ibid., pp. 685 f.
78 Ibid., pp. 692 f.
79 B. Lewis, 'An Arabic Account of the Province of Safed,' *Bulletin of the School of Oriental and African Studies* 15 (1953): 483; cf. Ashtor, 'The Venetian Cotton Trade,' p. 708.
80 See Ashtor, 'The Venetian Cotton Trade,' pp. 701 f. On the volume of cotton exported from Syria by the Venetians, see the many accounts in letters written to the Datini firm by its agents and friends in Venice.

An important example was the supply of silk. It should be stressed that during that period some regions of southern Europe produced silk considered of excellent quality. Price lists dating from the fifteenth century reveal that the silk of southern Spain ('of Almeria') and the Abruzzi was valued as highly as the best Persian silk. But perhaps these regions simply did not produce enough. Moreover, the silk of Persia was considered much better than that of Calabria and Sicily.[81]

Several kinds of Persian silk were shipped to Europe during the later Middle Ages. The highest value was set upon the so-called *legi* (or *lezi*) silk, named after Lāhidjān, once the chief town of Gīlān.[82] A Merchant Guide dating from the middle of the fifteenth century states that this kind of silk should be thick and white or pink.[83] The *ghella* (from Gīlān) silk was apparently of the same quality.[84] The term '*leggibonte* silk' is also often found. This is no doubt another name for Gīlān silk.[85] Also mentioned often is *talani* silk,[86] probably named after the district of Tālish, a strip of land on the shores of the Caspian Sea running north from its southwestern corner,[87] or perhaps after the country of Dailam.[88] The silk called *massándroni* in the Italian sources was obviously from Mazandaran, the expansive country on the southern shores of the Caspian Sea;[89] *amali* silk was named after Amol, the well-known town in that country.[90]

81 G. Gargiolli (ed.), *L'arte della seta in Firenze, trattato del secolo,* XV, Florence 1868, p. 108.

82 See Uzzano, 'Pratica della mercatura,' in Pagnini, *Della decima,* IV, Lisbon-Lucca 1765–1769, p. 192. Giosafa Barbaro speaks about silk 'of Azi'; see Lockhart, Morozzo della Rocca, and Tiepolo (eds.), *I viaggi in Persia degli ambasciatori veneti Barbaro e Contarini,* Rome 1973 (Il nuovo Ramusio VII), p. 140 (cf. Lockhart's mistaken comment, p. 286); see further the commentary of Evans to Pegolotti, p. 430. On Lāhidjān, see Guy Le Strange, *The Lands of the Eastern Caliphate,* Cambridge 1905, p. 174; on the production of silk in this district, see Ḥamdallāh Qazwīnī, p. 159. So the doubts of R.H. Bautier are unjustified; see his paper, 'Les relations économiques des Occidentaux avec les pays d'Orient au Moyen Age,' in *Sociétés et compagnies de commerce en Orient et dans l'Océan Indien,* Actes du VIII Colloque Int. d'Histoire Maritime, Paris 1970, p. 291.

83 *El libro di mercatantie et usanze de' paesi,* Fr. Borlandi (ed.), Turin 1936, p. 164.

84 Pegolotti, pp. 297, 300, and see p. 208 about its sale in Pisa; cf. W. Heyd, *Histoire du commerce du Levant,* II, p. 671; commentary of Evans to Pegolotti, p. 430.

85 Gargiolli, p. 108; cf. G. Barbaro, p. 151. On Lahazibenth, a region on the shore of the Caspian Sea, cf. Lockhart, p. 293.

86 Pegolotti, pp. 298, 300, and cf. p. 208; Uzzano, p. 192.

87 Heyd, II, p. 672; cf. Le Strange, p. 173.

88 This is a hypothesis of Petrushevsky, p. 505.

89 Uzzano, p. 192, and see Pegolotti, p. 297: *masseria*; cf. Heyd, II, p. 671. The pistachio also came from the southern shore of the Caspian Sea; see Heyd, II, p. 671.

90 Uzzano, p. 192; Heyd, II, p. 671.

Countries west of the Caspian Sea also produced and exported silk to Europe. One kind from this region was the *canari,* named after a place on the plain of Karabagh in the country of Arran.[91] Another was *sicchi* or *sacchi,* named after Shaki, also in Arran.[92] The silk of Gandja in Azarbaydjan was highly favored by the silkweavers of Lucca.[93] The country of Shirwan also exported silk to Europe, such as that of Shamākha.[94] Much silk was also produced in the countries east of the Caspian, and even this was exported to Europe. Very high value was set upon the *stravai* silk (or *stavagi, stanai,* etc.), named after Astarabad, a town in Djurdjan.[95] The *mordascascia* silk was named after the town of Merw Shāhidjān, one of the capitals of Khurasan.[96] The *taracheze* silk, mentioned more than once in Venetian documents of the fifteenth century was perhaps named after Tarkus, a trading town of Central Asia.[97] Syrian silk was also bought by Venetian merchants in the Levant, but the most expensive kind of silk and that exported in greatest quantities was always the *legi.*[99] In price lists drawn up in Venice, London, and Bruges, and in letters written from London to Venice at the end of the fourteenth and during the fifteenth century, two kinds of Persian silk are mentioned most often: the *legi* and the *talani.*[100]

Documents from the Italian archives show convincingly that the export of Persian silk through Syria to Europe was enhanced increasingly from the end of the fourteenth until the beginning of the sixteenth century. The prices of various kinds of Persian silk are rarely cited in the price lists drawn up by the agents and friends of Fr. Datini and those sent to Venetian firms by their agents in Syria

91 Pegolotti, pp. 298, 300, and cf. p. 208; Uzzano, p. 192.

92 Uzzano, p. 192; cf. Heyd, II, p. 672. See also *Ḥudūd al-'ālam,* Minorsky (trans.), p. 77. But Shakki is also a province west of Shirwan; see *Ḥudūd al-'ālam,* pp. 144, 398.

93 Heyd, II, p. 672.

94 Sanuto, *Diarii* IV; col. 192; cf. Heyd, II, p. 672; Le Strange, p. 179.

95 Uzzano, p. 192; G. Barbaro, p. 140; cf. Heyd, II, pp. 671 f. Also sometimes mentioned in the documents is *giorgiana* silk; see Bautier, pp. 291 f.

96 Pegolotti, pp. 298, 300, and cf. p. 208; cf. Heyd, II, p. 673; Beautier, p. 291, n. 1. On other kinds of silk, see Pegolotti, pp. 287 f.; Bautier, p. 292.

97 *G.P.* 156, fols. 86b ff., 88a ff.; Sanuto, *Diarii* V, col. 943; see further *Ḥudūd al-'ālam,* p. 118. But Tarkus was a small town north of Soghd in a region unknown as a silk producer. So it may be that this name is not a geographical one, as all the others, and is derived from *tār-e ghoze,* a Persian word meaning 'silkworm's cone'; see Steingass, *Persian-English Dictionary.*

98 'Del paese' in a price list; ASV, Procuratori di S. Marco, Commissarie Miste, Ba 128a, Com. Antonio Zane, price lists of 1413, 22 March, 8 June, 14 and 19 September 1413.

99 Rarely was its price lower than that of other Persian silk; see, for instance, a price list of Alexandria dated 23 February 1419 and printed by F. Melis in *Documenti per la storia economica dei secoli XIII–XVI,* Florence 1972, p. 320, where the price of *stravai* is higher.

100 Ibid., pp. 188, 302, 314, 316.

during the first half of the fifteenth century. During that period the Italian merchants acquired much Persian silk in Caffa, Tana, and Trebizond. At the end of the fourteenth century the galleys of the Venetian Romania line annually carried large loads of Persian silk to Italy. The increase in the purchase of Persian silk in Syria was, however, not simply the consequence of a change in trade routes. It was certainly more the result of the great upswing of the silk industry in Europe. During the second half of the fifteenth century the Venetians purchased great quantities of Persian silk in Syria. They bought a great deal of it in Aleppo, the first Syrian town in which the silk caravans from Persia arrived.[101] There they purchased *legi* silk,[102] as well as *stravai,* [103] *talani* and *canari.*[104] They also bought Persian (and Syrian) silk in Tripoli, in whose surroundings silk was grown.[105] Even Damascus was a market for Persian silk.[106] Being a precious article, the shipment of silk from Syria by cogs was forbidden by Venetian law. Thus the silk had to be loaded on Beirut galleys. The increased shipment of Persian silk in Venetian galleys to Italy was of course due to the greater demand by the fast developping European silk industries. However, it also seems to have been connected with a fall in prices owing to deflationary conditions in Iran. A Syrian raṭl (either of north Syria or Damascus) of *legi* silk cost ten to twelve ducats at the end of the fourteenth and the beginning of the fifteenth century;[107] at the end of the fifteenth century it cost only eight to nine ducats. The price of *talani* silk fell from nine to five or six ducats.[108]

The account books of some Venetian merchants and companies preserved in the archives of Venice shed light on the great volume of Persian silk exported to

101 Sanuto, *Diarii* V, cols. 339, 779, and cf. col. 821; ASV, Cancellaria Inferiore, Notai, Ba 83, Cristoforo del Fiore V, fol. 1a (1453); *G.P.* 186, fol. 27b. On the shipments of Perisian silk by the Venetian Romania galleys, see J. Heers, 'Il commercio nel Mediterraneo alla fine del sec. XIV e nei primi anni del sec. XV,' *Archivio Storico Italiano* 113 (1955): 169, 186, 187.

102 Giudici di Petizion, Terminazioni IX, fol. 13a.

103 Same series IV, fol. 8b. (1472).

104 *G.P.* 175, fols. 36b f., 46a (1480); Sanuto, *Diarii* VI; col. 69.

105 *G.P.* 121, fols. 60a ff. On Syrian silk and especially that of Tripoli, see Pegolotti, p. 209; cf. Heyd, II, p. 674; Bautier, p. 291, n. 1. See also the accounts of the Malipieros below.

106 Cristoforo del Fiore VI, fol. 3b (*talani* silk); *G.P.* 180, fols. 31 b ff. The export of silk from Damascus is also mentioned in some Merchant Guides; see, for instance, an anonymous Merchant Guide, MS British Museum, Egerton 73, fol. 59b (first half of the fifteenth century).

107 See price lists of Damascus dated 1 September 1386 in Melis, *Documenti,* p. 318; dated 1413 in Com. Antonio Zane (see note 98 above).

108 See price list of Damascus dated 21 August 1484 in Melis, *Documenti,* p. 186; see also accounts of the Malipiero family.

Table 1 *Silk purchases of the Malipiero family*

	Ducats	*Dirhams*
Lunardo, 1475 in Damascus		
Syrian silk	88	6
legi silk, 21 sacks being 776 rațls	7,381	
pink silk, 2 sacks being 73 rațls	621	4
stravai silk, 6 sacks being 199 rațls	1,901	
	9,991	10
Lunardo, 1476 in Damascus		
legi and *stravai* silk, 20 sacks being 1,818 rațls	16,362	
'low *stravai* silk,' 1 sack	184	
....silk	864	
silk of Tripoli, 11.9 rațls	84	
	17,494	
Anzolo, 1478		
legi silk, 175.21 rațls	4,116	31
talani silk, 45 rațls	234	16
canari silk, 81 rațls	365	
	4,715	47
Anzolo, 1479 in Aleppo		
legi silk	3,924	45
talani silk	241	32
canari silk	181	49
	4,348	26
Anzolo, 1485		
legi silk, 1,257 rațls (Aleppo)	9,804	30
legi silk, 1,277 rațls (Damascus)	9,557	25
	19,362	5
Tomaso, 1479		
canari silk	93	35
legi silk	2,785	4
talani silk	277	29
	3,156	18
Tomaso, 1482		
legi silk	8,573	
Tomaso, 1483 in Aleppo		
legi silk, 477 rațls	356	4

Europe during the fifteenth century. During the 1450s the firm of Francesco Contarini yearly bought in Syria some sacks of *canari, stavai, talani, legi, taracheze* and *legibente.*[109] The firm of Alvise Baseggio-Polo Caroldo purchased silk in Damascus during the 1470s and 1480s.[110] The Malipieros were a family of rich merchants who separately or jointly engaged in business in Syria and bought much Persian silk. Some data concerning their purchases is presented in Table 1.[111] Such accounts are no more than random examples; many others could be cited. They show how voluminous the export of silk to Europe had become during the second half of the fifteenth century.

Persia and Syria supplied the European industries not only with cotton and silk, but also with alkali ashes. In Syria it was obtained from two plants, *Salsola soda L.* and *Salsola kali L.*, which grew in the desert. These contain 45 per cent sodium carbonate and the substance yielded by burning them to ashes was called *ushnān* in the Arabic literary tongue and *kali* in the vernacular. It was brought by the Bedouins to Tripoli and Damascus. Because the Mamlūks had established a monopoly over the trade, two thirds of the alkali had to be handed over to the authorities in Tripoli and one third in Damascus.[112] Egypt also produced alkali, but it was considered of lower quality. A great portion of the Syrian alkali was acquired by Venetian merchants, either from private merchants or the Mamlūk authorities. It served as raw material for the European soap industries and also for the production of glass. The so-called 'hard soap' (or soap of Marseilles or Venice) was made from olive oil and alkali. The great centers of the European soap industry in those days vere Gaeta, the Marches of Ancona, and Venice. The Venetians of course supplied alkali to their hometown, but it was also shipped to Gaeta.[113] The Genoese supplied the workshops of Gaeta with Syrian alkali[114] and also shipped it to Flanders and

109 Museo Correr (Venice), PD 911/I, fols. 5a, 14a, 16a, 25b, 26a, 27a, 40a, 41a, 42a, 87a, 88a; 912/I, fols. 73a, 117a.

110 ASV, Procuratori di S. Marco, Commissarie Miste, Ba 117, fasc. 16.

111 Ibid., Ba 161, fasc. 1. The prices comprise all the expenses in Syria. There is some difficulty as to the genealogy of the Malipieros because the same names were borne by persons belonging to different branches of the family living at the same time. However, it seems that Tomaso (di Nicolo) was the father of Lunardo and Anzolo. Tomaso married in 1451, Anzolo died in 1520 and Lunardo in 1490. See M. Barbaro, 'Arbori dei Patritii Veneti,' MS, in ASV IV, p. 420; 'Genealogy of the Zusto Family,' MS, in possession of the Zusti del Giardino, p. 758. (I am thankful to Avv. Lanfranchi for the data from the latter MS.)

112 R. Mantran and J. Sauvaget, *Règlements fiscaux Ottomans, la Syrie,* Beirut 1951, pp. 22 ff., 69.

113 *G.P.* 20, fol. 122a; 71, fols. 55a ff.

114 Archivio di Stato Genoa, Carat. veterum 1552, fol. 125a.

England. It was a cheap article, a Damascene kintār (of 180 kg) being worth two ducats in Syria, and it could also serve as a ballast on the ships. The volume of the alkali exported from Syria was not insignificant. Many judicial acts of the Venetian tribunal of the *Giudici di petizion* refer to the great quantities of Syrian alkali purchased by Venetian merchants in Syria.[115]

In addition to cotton, silk, and alkali, the Middle East exported some dyeing materials produced in Iraq, Palestine, and elsewhere. One of these was indigo, used for blue dyes; it was an important commodity on the European market.

The above bits of information piece together to produce a clear picture of the economic relations between the Levantine countries and the nations of southern and western Europe. The economic historian is interested in how such relations came about. Were they the consequence of an internal development, independent of the activities of the European merchants, or were they perhaps conditioned by their intervention? The answer seems to be that both factors had great impact. The increase in the production of Levantine raw materials was undoubtedly the consequence of a lesser demand for cereals. Moreover, local industries would have been incapable of absorbing the great supply of cotton and silk. Only exports to Europe made cotton and silk production profitable.

The Decay of Middle Eastern Industries

During the time in which the Middle Eastern countries began supplying European industries with large quantities of various raw materials, local industries declined greatly. Consequently, the Levant began importing industrial products from Europe on a large scale. This is another aspect of the relationship between underdeveloped and industrialized regions. The decay of the Oriental industries was to a great extent the result of technological backwardness; but whatever its cause, it had a major impact upon the economic and political history of the Middle East. Ultimately, it paved the way for the imperialist expansion of the European powers.

Evidence in Arab sources points to a decline in the Levantine textile industries, textiles being the most important sector of medieval industry in both the East and West. According to such sources the once famous textile manufacturers of Tinnīs, Dabīk, and other towns in lower Egypt were closed

115 See E. Ashtor, 'The Venetian Supremacy in Levantine Trade,' *Journal of European Economic History* 3 (1974): 45.

down at the end of the twelfth and during the first third of the thirteenth century.[116]

European documents preserved in the archives of Italy, southern France, and Catalonia also offer data alluding to the decay of the Levantine textile industries. Notarial acts drawn up in Genoa indicate that a large quantity of Flemish, French, and north Italian cloth was exported from the 1180s onwards.[117] A great portion of this was destined for Sicily, Muslim Syria, and Egypt. Similar conclusions may be drawn from notarial acts in Marseilles. Beginning at the end of the twelfth century Provençal merchants paid for a great portion of the merchandise bought in Acre by French and other cloth. The Manduels, a family of great merchants from Marseilles who carried on a lively trade with Acre during the first half of the thirteenth century, exported much cloth of Chalons, Arras, Douai, and other French towns to this area.[118] The supposition that Egypt had imported much cloth from Flanders as early as the Ayyubid period is borne out by an Arab work on administration dating from the reign of Saladin. Cl. Cahen has correctly interpreted the word *bazz* — used for textiles imported, according to this source, into Egypt by sea (via the ports of Alexandria, Tinnīs, and Damietta) — as meaning cloth from Flanders.[119]

The import of European cloth and linen into Egypt increased throughout the thirteenth and fourteenth centuries. In his account of Sultan Baibars' voyage to Alexandria in 1263, Ibn Wāṣil relates that his vizier went there first and collected (as a contribution) 95,000 pieces of cloth from Yemen and Venice, as well as *djūkh.*[120] 'Venetian cloth' (*bunduqī*) in this context obviously refers to various kinds of textiles imported by the Venetians; *djūkh* refers to European cloth in general. This account clearly shows that the import of European cloth into the Middle East was already of great volume during the second half of the thirteenth century. During the first half of the fourteenth century the Baḥrī Mamlūks flourished, and Egypt and Syria knew some economic expansion. Yet, notarial acts from Genoa testify to the fact that even then European textiles were

116 See idem, 'Aspetti della espansione italiana nel basso medioevo,' *Revista Storica Italiana* (hereafter *RSI*) 90 (1978): 7.

117 D. Abulafia, *The Two Italies,* Cambridge 1977, pp. 261, 263.

118 Idem, 'Marseilles, Acre and the Mediterranean, 1200–1291,' in P.W. Edbury and M. Metcalf (eds.), *Coinage in the Latin East, The Fourth Oxford Symposium on Coinage and Monetary History,* Oxford 1980, p. 26.

119 Cl. Cahen, 'Douanes et commerce dans les Ports Méditerranéens de l'Égypte médiévale d'après le Minhādj d'al-Makhzūmī,' *Journal of the Economic and Social History of the Orient* 7 (1964): 288.

120 Quatremère, *Histoire des sultans mamlouks,* I, pt. 1, p. 252.

imported into the dominions of the Mamlūks. In 1312 Nicolo di Fossatello, a cloth merchant, left Genoa for Syria with scarlet cloth from Brussels as well as cloth from Malines.[121] In 1313 another merchant received in Genoa a *commenda*'s consisting of cloth from Chalons-sur-Marne to be sold in Syria.[122] A year later a certain Barnaba Bernus received a *commenda* consisting of French cloth for Syria.[123] Additional *commenda*'s of this type given in Genoa are also documented.[124] Other eloquent testimony to the import of European textiles into the Muslim Levant is found in a late fourteenth-century travelogue; the Florentine Leonardo Frescobaldi, who in 1384 embarked on a pilgrimage to Jerusalem via Egypt and visited Cairo, recounts that the women of this town wore garments of Reims linen.[125]

The great economic crisis which Egypt underwent during the first years of the fifteenth century accelerated the decline of its textile industries and was responsible for the increase in the import of European cloth and linen. The contemporary Arab author al-Maqrīzī speaks about a drastic change in dress which he witnessed in Egypt: local textiles were replaced by European products.[126] This statement, although perhaps somewhat exaggerated, is basically true.

Of course, various kinds of textiles continued to be produced in Egypt, Syria, Iraq and Persia. Alexandria could export precious silken stuffs to Europe even at that late period.[127] In Syria cotton industries existed not only in Baalbek, but in other towns and villages as well. In Upper Mesopotamia, too, cotton was woven in several towns, especially Mosul. Mārdīn was also a textile center; cotton fabrics and woolen cloth manufactured from goathair were produced there. A cotton industry also existed in Ḥiṣn Kaifā, and in Baghdad silk stuffs were manufactured.[128] Textile manufacturers existed in Persia, in neighboring

121 R. Doehaerd, *Les relations commerciales entre Gênes, la Belgique et l'Outremont, d'après les archives notariales génoises aux XIIIe et XIVe siècles,* III, Brussels 1941, no. 1753.

122 Ibid., no. 1809.

123 Ibid., no. 1820.

124 Ibid., no. 1847.

125 *Viaggi in Terrasanta,* C. Angelini (ed.), Florence 1944, p. 48.

126 *Al-Khiṭaṭ* II, p. 98, R. Dozy (trans.); *Dictionnaire détaillé des noms des vêtements chez les Arabes,* Amsterdam 1845, p. 128.

127 Turiano, V, fols. 40a f. (1435).

128 Sulūk IV, pp. 792, 800; Ibn Baṭṭūṭa II, pp. 143, 311; G. Barbaro, pp. 114, 116, 117; Ashtor, *Social and Economic History,* p. 262. Serjeant's doubts as to the reading of *kudsī* in Ibn Baṭṭūṭa's text (see *Bulletin of the School of Oriental and African Studies* 26: 656) are unjustified, as the export of this cotton product is mentioned by the Arab author in accounts of his travels in other regions.

countries, and in many towns. In fact, Khiyār in Azarbaydjan and Kāzerūn in Fars were genuine industrial centers.[129] Linen was woven in Rīshah.[130] Kāshān was reknowned for its silk fabrics, made from *legi* and *stravai*, which were exported to India and Turkey. Velvet was produced in Tibriz and Nishapur and exported to India and elsewhere. Shiraz and Yazd also produced silken stuffs, white Isfahan was known for its cotton veils.[131]

Nevertheless, the great change which occurred about the year 1400 is evident from cargo inventories found in the Datini archives and other documents referring to the convoys of European ships returning from the Levantine ports. Some documents dated prior to 1400 comprise data about silken stuffs shipped from Syria and Egypt to Sicily[132] and Barcelona.[133] The registers of the Venetian Senate contain data on the import of Oriental silken fabrics to Venice.[134] Price lists drawn up by the friends and agents of Fr. Datini in the 1370s and 1390s in Syria indicate the cost of several silk fabrics and brocades.[135] During the fifteenth century, however, European ships seldom loaded silk fabrics in Levantine ports.

Al-Maqrīzī himself alludes to the causes underlying the great transition. He recounts that the big factories, run by the state and called *ṭirāz*, were closed in his days.[136] In the *Muqaddima* of Ibn Khaldūn a similar statement can be found.[137] The small workshops obviously could not afford to experiment with technological improvements of production methods, whereas in Europe the textile industries had altered their methods altogether. Two important innovations had been made: the use of looms put into gear by a pedal, and fulling by automatic engines, operated by water power. These new production methods were not introduced in the Middle East.[138] At the same time the

129 Hamdallāh Ḳazwīnī, pp. 85, 125.

130 Ibid., p. 129.

131 G. Barbaro, p. 140; Ibn Baṭṭūṭa II, p. 311; III, p. 81; R.B. Serjeant, 'Material for a History of Islamic Text up to the Mongol Conquest,' *Ars Islamica* 10 (1943): 88, 11/12 (1946): 108; *The Travels of Marco Polo*, Yule (ed.), London 1904, vol. I, p. 88.

132 *Misti* 42, fol. 111b (1392).

133 See the inventories published by M. Spallanzani, *Ceramiche orientali a Firenze nel rinascimento*, Florence 1978, pp. 145 ff.

134 *Misti* 35, fol. 2a (1375); 40, fol. 72a (1387); 42, fol. 69b.

135 Archivio di Stato, Prato, Datini (hereafter Datini) 1171; price lists of Damascus dated 1379, 30 May 1395.

136 *al-Khiṭaṭ* II, pp. 98 f.

137 Fr. Rosenthal (trans.), vol. II, p. 67.

138 See E. Ashtor, 'Les lainages dans l'Orient Médiéval, emploi, production, commerce,' in *Atti della 2a settimana di studi, Istituto Datini*, Florence 1978, pp. 684 f.; *Aspetti della espansione italiana*, pp. 9 f.

growing shortage of workhands resulted in a steep rise of production costs and prices.[139]

As the Levantine manufacturers were incapable of competing with the cheaper and better products coming from the textile industries of Italy, France, Catalonia, and Flanders, the import of European cloth and linen became a real dumping. Many documents testify to this, including judicial acts, notarial acts, and decrees of the Venetian Senate. The numerous data in these documents leave no doubt as to the volume of European textiles exported to the Levant.[140] A letter written by a merchant from Gaeta to the Datini firm in Florence in 1391 states that 'the galleys of the Genoese which sail to Syria (and anchor in Gaeta) carry mostly cloth.'[141] Another letter, written from Gaeta to the Datini firm in Genoa in 1399, relates that the ship of the Genoese Novello Lercaro, which arrived from Spain and sailed to Alexandria, carried 400 bales of cloth from Valencia and Languedoc.[142] As a bale usually contained ten pieces of cloth, and even the cheap Catalan cloth was sold in the Muslim Levant for ten to twelve ducats, this shipment had the value of at least 50,000 ducats. At the end of the fourteenth and during the first third of the fifteenth century Catalan cloth was apparently the European textile imported in greatest quantities into the Muslim Levant. During the middle and the second half of the fifteenth century there was a great upswing in the import of English cloth. A Venetian who compiled a Merchant Guide at the end of the fifteenth century compares the cloth measures used in London with those used in Damascus, Aleppo, Tripoli, and Alexandria. A great portion of the English cloth exported to the Middle East consisted of the coarse but strong *kerseys*. The author also compares the measures used for this fabric.[143] The account books of some Venetian firms, such as the Priuli family, dating from the beginning of the sixteenth century, contain much data concerning the export of *kersey* to Alexandria.

139 See idem, 'L'évolution des prix dans le Proche-Orient à la basse-époque,' *Journal of the Economic and Social History of the Orient* 4 (1961): 34 f.

140 See the documents cited in my 'Les lainages,' pp. 673 ff., 'L'exportation de textiles occidentaux dans le Proche Orient musulman au bas Moyen Age, 1370–1517,' in *Studi in memoria di Federigo Melis*, II, Naples 1978, pp. 303 ff.

141 Datini, 649, letter of Antonio e Doffo degli Spini, 26 October 1397.

142 Datini, 777, letter of Agnolo di Ser Pino e Giuliano di Giovanni, 16 July 1399.

143 Bartolomeo Paxi (de Pasi) compares the measures of *kersey* with those of cloth used in Damascus, Beirut, Aleppo, Tripoli, and Alexandria, see *Tariffa di pexi e mexure*, fols. 276, 28a, 28b, 29b. On the term *kersey*, see N. Beldiceanu, 'Recherches autour de Qars, nom d'une étoffe de poil,' *Bulletin of the School of Oriental and African Studies* 31 (1968): 330 ff., 341 ff.; J. Wansbrough in D. Dalby (ed.), *Language and History in Africa*, London 1970, p. 95; cf. accounts of the Priuli MS, Museo Correr PD 911/I, 5 and 18 March, 17 June 1511; 5 August 1512.

It is worth noting that much of the various kinds of European cloth shipped to the Muslim Levant was destined for Aleppo. During the second half of the fifteenth century this town had a very active colony of Venetian traders who imported much European cloth. It does not appear to be an error in judgement when one assumes that a great deal of this cloth was sold in Iraq and Persia. The caravans carrying Persian silk to Aleppo probably returned with heavy loads of European cloth. This assumption is backed by written evidence. A letter written in Damascus on 15 May 1504 and destined for Venice states that, with the silk caravan, many merchants came to Aleppo with a great sum of money in order to buy 'red cloth' for the 'Sophi' (i.e., Ismā'īl I, founder of the Safawid dynasty).[144] Possibly this 'red cloth' was the scarlet cloth of which the Orientals were known to be so fond.

Another Levantine industry which declined greatly at the end of the fourteenth and the beginning of the fifteenth century was the sugar industry. This had flourished in Persia (especially Khuzistan), Syria, and Egypt from the eleventh century onwards. Many new factories appear to have been founded in Egypt during the second half of the thirteenth century. Accounts of extensive sugar consumption in Egypt during the rule of al-Malik an-Nāṣir Muḥammad (1309–1341) confirm the large volume of sugar production at that time.[145] Under the Baḥrī Mamlūks Egypt and Syria were able to export considerable quantities to Italy, southern France, and Catalonia.[146] The export of sugar continued until the great economic crisis which shook the economy of the Mamlūk kingdom at the beginning of the fifteenth century. From Venetian sources it becomes evident that the Levantine countries exported both lump sugar[147] and powdered sugar.[148] Under Venetian law fine sugar had to be shipped on galleys; powdered sugar could be shipped on cogs. Both kinds were bought in several Syrian towns, in Tripoli, a major center of the sugar industry,[149] and elsewhere. Sometimes the Mamlūk authorities sold it to the

144 Sanuto, *Diarii* VI, cols. 57 f.

145 E. Ashtor, 'Levantine Sugar Industry in the Later Middle Ages: An Example of Technological Decline,' *Israel Oriental Studies* 7 (1977): 231–232.

146 Ibid., pp. 235–236.

147 On the sugar export from Egypt in that period, see also *Misti* 34, fol. 109a (1374); 38, fol. 132b (1384); 42 fol. 63b (1392). On its export from Syria, see *Misti* 40, fols. 30b (1386), 48a, 72b, 119a (1387); 42, fol. 63a (1392): 44, fols. 5a (1397), 47a (1398).

148 On Egypt, see *Misti* 23, fols. 23b (1345), 58a (1346); 24, fols. 20b f. (1347); 26, fol. 89a (1352); 34, fol. 8a (1372). On Syria, see *Misti* 34, fols. 76b f., 110a (freight tariffs).

149 *Misti* 40, fol. 117b (1388).

Italian merchants or compelled them to buy it.[150] Up to the beginning of the fifteenth century Egypt and Syria also exported sugar to Sicily.[151]

By the end of the fourteenth century, however, many Egyptian sugar factories had been closed down. Many more probably had to stop production during the great crisis of the first decade of the fifteenth century.[152] At the same time the sugar industries of Cyprus and Sicily began to flourish. Of course, Egypt, Syria, and Persia still produced and sometimes even exported sugar, especially the fine thrice-boiled sugar, in demand by European merchants. But Europeans also purchased Egyptian Damietta sugar[153] and candy,[154] as well as Syrian sugar,[155] and the Venetians continued to export powdered sugar from the dominions of the Mamlūks.[156] Sugar production in the Muslim Levant cannot have been insignificant during the fifteenth century, since the Mamlūk authorities imposed compulsory purchases of sugar upon the European merchants from time to time.[157] Even pilgrims bound for Jerusalem were sometimes compelled to buy certain quantities.[158] Merchant Guides, compiled in Venice at the end of the fifteenth century, indicate sugar exports from Fūwa[159] and Damietta, the latter noted for its sugar plantations and production. From Damietta sugar was exported to Rhodes, Chios, and the fairs of Lanciano (in the kingdom of Naples).[160] Even Persia continued to produce much sugar, especially in Khuzistan.[161]

Nevertheless, the production of sugar in the Middle East and its export to European countries must have declined greatly. In letters written by Pere Tequin, a great merchant of Perpignan, to the Datini firm in Barcelona in the last years of the fourteenth and at the beginning of the fifteenth century, the

150 On the purchase of sugar from the governor of Aleppo (about 1390), see *Misti* 43, fol. 17b.

151 Vataciis, 22 August 1405; to Ancona, Leonardo de Valle, 19 August 1405.

152 Ashtor, 'Levantine Sugar Industry, ' pp. 239 f.

153 *G.P.* 151b, fols. 161a f. (about 1470).

154 Turiano, II, fol. 10a (1455).

155 *Misti* 52, fol. 68a; 56, fols. 104a ff. (1427); 57, fol. 220a (1417); 58, fols. 10a ff., 62a, 63a f. (1431). On candy, see *G.P.* 34, fols. 4a f. (1404). Some of the sugar shipped by the Venetians from Syria may have been from Cyprus; see *Misti* 58, fols. 159a ff.

156 On Syria, see *Misti* 52, fols. 24a f. (1417); 53, fols. 158b ff. (1421); 54, fols. 116b ff. (1423); 55, fol. 31a (1424); 57, fol. 117a (1429); 58, fols. 62a, 70a f. (1431). On Egypt, see Turiano, II, fols. 63a f. (1456).

157 *Misti* 52, fols. 76a (1417), 119a; 58, fols. 23a ff. (1430).

158 *Misti* 52, fol. 133a (1418).

159 'Tariffa di pexi e spese' (1493), MS Marciana, It. VII, 384 (7531), fols. 36a f.

160 Pasi, fols. 43b, 45b, 46a.

161 Ḥamdallāh Qazwīnī, pp. 109, 140.

prices of Damascene sugar are often quoted; yet another merchant of this town, Jean Fabre, writes to the same firm in 1406 that a Catalan ship has brought Sicilian sugar.[162] Meanwhile, important technological innovations had been made in the sugar industries of Cyprus and Sicily, such as trituration of the sugar cane by cylinders thrown into gear by water-driven mills. This kind of pounding was both much more effective and much cheaper than that by wooden pestles or by rammers operated by oxen, and output was greater.[163] On the other hand, the price of Levantine sugar rose due to a considerable increase in labor costs following the great epidemics.[164] Hence the decline of the Middle Eastern sugar industry was mainly due to technological stagnation.

As the Levantine economies declined during the later Middle Ages, the Middle Eastern countries began to import considerable quantities of molasses, mainly from Sicily. Notarial acts drawn up in Palermo and Alexandria bear witness to this important trade.[165] An act dated 1450 in Palermo refers to the charter of a Venetian ship for the export of a great quantity of molasses to Alexandria.[166] However, molasses were also shipped to Egypt from Cyprus and Rhodes.[167]

The soap industry of Syria had a long history, and in the first half of the fourteenth century it was still flourishing. In several towns of Syria and Palestine soap was produced in different colors, and the produce of the Syrian soap factories had a good market in Egypt.[168] However, the high taxes imposed by the Mamlūk government on the sale of olive oil, a basic ingredient in soap, had disastrous effects, as did the compulsory purchase of oil imposed time and again on the soap manufacturers.[169] These decrees were not maintained for long, however. Several inscriptions found on gates of mosques and elsewhere testify to the fact that forced purchases of olive oil and soap were later abolished.[170] While soap production did not halt altogether in Syria, the Syrians

162 See Datini 906, letters of Pere Tequin, 22 November 1395, 8 August 1396, 9 May 1397, 5 July 1397, 17 August 1400, 19 April 1400; Datini 907, letter of Jean Fabre, 15 May 1406. (Pere Tequin must have died before 1406; see Datini 907, letter of Jean Fabre, 27 July 1406.)

163 See Ashtor, 'Levantine Sugar Industry,' pp. 244 f.

164 Ibid., pp. 248 ff., 254, 255 f.

165 Turiano, IV; fols. 22b, 23b ff. See also Pasi, fols. 47b, 49b.

166 Archivio di Stato, Palermo, Notai, Giacomo Comito 850, 5 September 1498.

167 Turiano, V, fols. 43b f.; Pasi, fol. 45b.

168 Ad-Dimishkī, *Nukhbat ad-dahr*, Mehren (ed.), p. 200 (trans., p. 270); Ibn Baṭṭūṭa I, p. 145.

169 Mudjīr al-Din al-'Ulaimī, *al-Uns al-Jalil*, pp. 694 f.

170 M. Sobernheim, *Matériaux pour un Corpus Inscriptionum Arabicarum*, II, pt. 1, Cairo 1909, nos. 25, 32.

could not compete with their European couterparts. The decline, however, was gradual, and during the fifteenth century soap was still exported from Syria to Egypt.[171] At the same time the Mamlūk authorities sold Syrian alkali ashes to the Italian merchants or even compelled them to buy it. It follows that European soap factories were will supplied with raw materials; in fact, during that period the soap industry developed greatly in several provinces of Italy, which began exporting its products to the Levant on a grand scale. As early as the first half of the fourteenth century soap had been exported from southern Europe to the Muslim Levant, and for the Venetians it was an extremely profitable business. An anonymous Merchant Guide, dating from the beginning of the fourteenth century, lists soap as one of the articles marketed by European merchants in Alexandria. When in 1345 the Venetians resumed transport of their galleys to Alexandria, so much soap was loaded on them that a great deal of it had to be unloaded.[172]

During the fifteenth century the export of soap to the Muslim Levant increased greatly. Some Venetian merchants marketed considerable quantities,[173] which they exported to Egypt and Syria.[174] During this period Gaeta was a great center of the soap industry, and its merchants exported the produce on their ships to Alexandria.[175] Genoese traders also sold Gaetan soap in the Muslim Levant.[176] The soap which Provençal merchants sold in Egypt was probably produced in Marseilles, another center of this industry.[177] The Anconitans exported soap produced in the Marches.[178] Even the Florentines engaged in this trade.[179]

171 *G.P.* 151, fols. 161a f.

172 Anonymous Merchant Guide, MS Marucelliana (Florence) C 226, fol. 10a; F.C. Lane, 'The Venetian Galleys to Alexandria, 1344,' in *Wirtschaftskräfte und Wirtschaftswege, Festschrift H. Kellenbenz,* I, Nuremberg 1978, p. 136; *Misti* 23, fols. 24b, 32b (1345); 24, fol. 21a (1347); 30, fol. 17a (1361); 46, fol. 94a.

173 S. Morosini shipped (about) 1,425 boxes of soap for 1,450 ducats to Egypt; see *G.P.* 65, fols. 105a ff.

174 *G.P.* 152, fols. 72b ff.

175 Turiano, V, fols. 8b ff. (1434).

176 Datini, 504, letter of Sandro Mazzetti e Guido Pilestri & Cie from Gaeta to the Datini firm in Pisa, 23 April 1388; see further Datini, 876, letter of Antonio e Doffo degli Spini & Cie from Gaeta to the Datini firm in Barcelona, 16 April 1400.

177 Leonardo de Valle, 7 February 1403.

178 E. Ashtor, 'Il commercio levantino di Ancona,' *RSI* 88 (1976): 217, 228, 240 f.

179 J. Wansbrough, 'A Mamluk Commercial Treaty with the Republic of Florence,' in S.M. Stern (ed.), *Documents from Islamic Chanceries,* Oxford 1965, p. 62. For more information on the export of soap from southern Europe to the Middle East, see my 'Le Proche-Orient au bas Moyen Age: une région sousdévelopée, une économie en déclin,' in *Atti della Xa settimana di studi, Istituto Datini* (forthcoming).

Whether the great development of the European soap industry was connected with technological innovations unknown to the Levant is an unanswered question. This does, however, seem to have been the cause of the decline in the Levantine paper industry during the later Middle Ages. The Muslims, first the Persians and then the Arabs, had learnt to make paper from rags during the middle of the eighth century. The rags of linen fabrics first underwent a process of fermentation after which the material was pounded to a pulp by wooden pestles in mortars. This process, however, could not remove long fibers. Although in Morocco this operation came to be performed by water-driven mills, in the Middle East the old methods were adhered to. The pulp thus obtained was subsequently put into a vat made of reed. Finally, the paper was bonded with starch.[180] The manufacturers using these methods were unable to triturate the fibers sufficiently, and the chains of the paper were irregular. In 1270 a new paper industry developed in Fabriano, in the Marches of Ancona, where great innovations were made. The most important was the use of water-driven batteries of iron hammers for the pounding. The batteries operated alternately and regularly, so that the rags were better and more equally stamped. Furthermore, metal wire was used for the mold, so that the transparent lines of the paper were much more regular. Another important innovation was the replacement of vegetable starch by animal glue, such as gelatin prepared from animal skins. This material did not contain the destructive germs found in the vegetable starch.[181] The paper produced by these new methods was both better and cheaper than the old Arab paper, and of course it had great commercial success. Before long, paper manufactures employing the methods of Fabriano were founded in other towns of Italy and also in the countries beyond the Alps, and their produce began to be exported to the Muslim Levant. Copious information is found in the Italian and Catalan archives concerning the export of the new kind of paper to the Muslim Levant;[182] both the registers of the Venetian Senate[183] and judicial and notarial acts testify to the sale of European paper by Venetians in Syria and Egypt at the

180 J. Karabacek, 'Das arabische Papier,' *MPER* 2/3 (1887): 318 ff.; 'Neue Quellen zur Papiergeschichte,' *Mittheilungen aus der Sammlulng der Papyrus Erzherzog Rainer* 4 (1888): 84, 88, 93.

181 A.F. Gasparinetti, 'Paper, Paper-Making and Paper Mills of Fabriano,' in *Zonghi's Water Marks*, Hilversum 1953 (Monumenta Chartae Papyraceae Historiam Illustrantia, III), pp. 69, 701.

182 Se Ashtor, 'Le Proche-Orient au bas Moyen Age.'

183 On the *consolazium* to be paid by Venetians in Alexandria for the import of paper, See *Misti* 46, fol. 94a (1483). On exports to Syria, see ibid, 60, fol. 47b (1436).

end of the fourteenth and during the fifteenth century.[184] Notarial acts drawn up in Barcelona deal with consignments of paper exported by Catalans to Egypt.[185] It should be stressed, however, that the paper marketed in the Levant by the south European merchants was mostly cheap and not of high quality. Paper of local (Levantine) manufacture continued to be used for official documents. Thus, paper production, like that of other industries, was not entirely discontinued in the Muslim Levant despite the technological stagnation.

Lastly, the decline of the Levantine glass industry should be mentioned. Glassmaking had been from time immemorial one of the famous crafts of Syria, and so much of its products had been exported to Eastern and Western countries that one has cause to speak of an industry. However, in the course of the fifteenth century it declined considerably. A German traveller who spent a long time in the Levant at the end of the fifteenth century and left a comprehensive account of his travels, stated that the glass produced in Hebron was rather black and that the colors with which it was painted were of poor quality.[186] At the same time the Mamlūk authorities supplied the glassmakers of Italy with Syrian alkali ashes, an important raw material for its production. Glassmaking in Italy and especially Murano made great progress during that period, not least because raw materials from the Alps and Germany began to be used. There is also clear evidence of new methods of production.[187] As had been the case with other industries, the export of Italian glass to Egypt and Syria ensued, and during the second half of the fifteenth century even the sultan of Cairo ordered glass from Murano.[188]

From the numerous documents, of which only some examples have been cited here, a clear picture emerges: the countries of the Middle East had become underdeveloped as compared with those of Christian Europe. The Middle East supplied Europe with raw materials and bought industrial products from them. However, this was a case of underdevelopment wholly different from such as modern economists have in mind. Modern economists have built up a pattern of underdeveloped former colonies which had never had a highly developed

184 *G.P.* 66, fols. 57b ff.; Giudici di Petizion, Terminazioni IV; fol. 180a; Turiano, II, fol. 54b (1455). Much of the paper was certainly Fabriano paper; for inexplicit, but sufficiently clear evidence of the import of Fabriano paper to Venice, see *Misti* 42, fol. 93b (1392).

185 *Archivo Historico de Protocolos,* Barcelona, Tomas de Bellmunt, *Quartus Liber Manualis Comendarum,* fols. 8b f., 16b (1414).

186 F. Fabri, *Evagatorium in Terram Sanctam,* II, p. 341.

187 Ashtor, 'Le Proche-Orient au bas Moyen Age.'

188 See ASV, Senato Mar VIII, fol. 97b, and cf. fol. 103b.

monetary economy. Such a pattern does not fit the case of the late medieval Muslim Levant. What we are dealing with here is a previously industrialized and monetary economy which, having declined, became dependent upon a swiftly progressing and more modern economy.

Recourse to European Shipping

Another aspect of the process of Levantine underdevelopment during the later Middle Ages was the necessity to use European shipping for traffic within the Levant itself. This is indeed a striking feature of underdeveloped countries according to the notions economists have of this stage of economic life. Even this aspect of Levantine economic life has been documented in Arab and especially European sources.

Ibn Khaldūn, an excellent observer, includes in his famous *Prolegomena* a chapter about the decline of Muslim shipping. He says quite clearly that in his days the Muslims were no longer capable of building seaworthy vessels and had lost much of their nautical aptitude. He maintains that they were dependent upon European Christians for shipbuilding and navigation.[189] As far as the Muslims of the Mediterranean countries of his period are concerned, his statement is borne out by much evidence, including that found in many documents in European archives.[190]

The third Lateran Council in 1179 was already forbidding Christians to serve as helmsmen on Muslim ships; transgressors were to be excommunicated.[191] This decision was renewed at the fourth ecumenical council held in the Lateran in 1215, with the additional stipulation in effect for four years, that it was forbidden to send ships to the Muslim Levant.[192] This decree was certainly issued in connection with preparations for a new Crusade. However, perhaps it was also meant to impede the sale of ships to the Muslims. During the thirteenth ecumenical council, held in Lyon in 1245, it was again forbidden to serve the Muslims as helmsmen or to render them other services on ships. Those who sold ships to the Muslims were also subject to excommunication.[193] Similar decrees were enacted by provincial councils. A council held in Montpellier in 1195

189 *Muqaddima,* Fr. Rosenthal (trans.), vol. II, p. 46.

190 The following information is supplemented by data cited in my 'Le Proche-Orient au bas Moyen Age' and my 'L'artiglieria veneziana e il commercio di Levante' in *Armi e cultura nel Bresciano 1420–1870,* Brescia 1981, pp. 141 ff.

191 H. Hefele, *Histoire des Conciles,* V; pt. 2, Paris 1913, p. 1104.

192 Ibid., p. 1390.

193 Ibid., p. 1656.

forbade the sale to Muslims of timber for the construction of ships; the goods of transgressors were to be confiscated and they themselves were to become slaves.[194] After the fall of Acre in 1291 the popes took up the matter and issued bulls against those Christians who granted the Muslims help for maintaining their shipping. However, it is obvious that many greedy merchants and mariners paid no heed to the prohibition. This can be concluded from the fact that in 1297 Pope Boniface VIII authorized the bishops of Barcelona and Tortosa to grant absolution to transgressors.[195] Very interesting is a bull of this pope issued in 1299. It is directed against those who sold galleys and other ships to the Muslims, served them as helmsmen or granted them technical help (*vel in machinis aut quibuslibet aliis aliquod eis impenderent auxilium*).[196] Documents found in the archives of almost all south European countries show that the measures taken by the Church were justified, since many Christians rendered various services to the Muslims concerning their shipping.

The 1272 Statutes of Ragusa forbid the sale of ships to the Muslims.[197] A Venetian decree of 1358 refers to Genoese who served on Muslim ships as mariners,[198] while another dated 1368 forbids the subjects of the Serenissima to work on Muslim ships as oarsmen and helmsmen.[199] These and many other documents show how dependent the Muslims were upon the shipping of the south European trading nations. The traffic between Tunisia and other Maghrebin countries, on the one hand, and Egypt, on the other, was almost entirely in the hands of the European trading nations. Instructions to a Catalan embassy, which reached the Muslim ruler of Tunis in 1444, are revealing. They ensure the Muslim king that if his subjects charter ships of Castillians, Venetians, Florentines, and Rhodisians, they will be secure as long as these nations do not become enemies of the king of Aragon.[200] This indicates that all these nations chartered whole ships to the Tunisian merchants. However, the most active in the transport business along the shores of North Africa, an extremely profitable venture, were the Genoese. In 1470 the Flemish pilgrim Anselme Adorno (who was of course of Genoese origin) arrived in Tunis on a Genoese ship and then left on another for Alexandria. There were a hundred

194 St. Baluze, *Concilia Galliae Narbonnensis,* Paris 1668, p. 30.
195 *Les registres de Boniface,* VIII, Paris 1884, vol. I, p. 926, no. 1233.
196 Ibid., vol. II, pp. 557 ff., no. 1354.
197 Krekic, *Dubrovnik, Raguse et le Levant au Moyen Age,* Paris 1961, p. 113.
198 *Libri Commemoriali,* II, Predelli (ed.), lib. VI, no. 22.
199 Ibid., lib. VII, no. 479.
200 Archivo de la Corona de Aragon, Barcelona, Cancilleria Real, Reg. 2698, fol. 39b.

Muslims, male and female, on this latter ship. Some of them, as recounted by the pilgrim, were merchants who carried olive oil with them; others were pilgrims bound for Mecca.[201] In the course of time the traffic between Tunisia and Egypt, as well as the transport of Muslim merchants who engaged in trade between these countries, became an important sector of Venetian shipping. Venice established a State line of galleys to serve this purpose, the so-called *galee de trafego.* These visited Tunis, then sailed to Tripoli and Alexandria and, finally, either returned to Tunis or travelled to Beirut before returning to Venice. This galley line, however, did not function regularly. It was established in 1461, discontinued in 1466, reestablished in 1474, and again halted in 1485 and 1490. It functioned from 1493 to 1498, as well as from 1500 to 1506. In 1507 Venice sent its State galleys to Tunis and Alexandria.[202]

During that period the decay of Muslim navigation was so extensive that the rulers of the Levantine countries were sometimes compelled to requisition European trading ships for the transport of goods they needed. In 1422 Sultan Barsbay promised a Florentine embassy that the ships of Florence would not be employed by force by the Mamlūk authorities.[203] Such promises were of course forgotten when the Muslim authorities urgently needed ships. A Ragusan ship, for instance, was compelled in 1450 by the governor of Alexandria to carry an Egyptian ambassador to Cyprus and to transport to Alexandria wheat to be bought in Cyprus and Asia Minor. As the wheat could not be found there, the captain lost much time.[204] In 1474 Genoese ships were requisitioned by the sultan of Cairo.[205]

Conclusion

It can be safely maintained that the wealth of data in the European sources, and especially the documents in the archives, bear out the statements which Oriental authors made concerning the general decline of the Middle Eastern economies during the later Middle Ages.

It seems that in spite of the differences between the structures of the various

201 *Itinéraire d'Anselme Adorno en Terre Sainte (1470–1471),* J. Heers and G. de Groer (eds.), Paris 1978, pp. 54, 140.

202 A. Tenenti and C. Vivanti, 'Le film d'un grand système de navigation: les galères marchandes vénitiennes, XIVe–XVIe siècles,' *Annales E.S.C.* 16 (1961): 83 ff.

203 M. Amari, *I diplomi arabi dell 'Archivio Fiorentino,* Florence 1863, p. 342.

204 Krekić, no. 1258.

205 ASV, Secreta 26, fol. 138; cited by Magnante in *Archivio Veneto,* Va seria, 11–12 (1929), p. 21.

Levantine countries their economic development had much in common. Depopulation was found everywhere, creating high production costs of industrial goods. Technological stagnation, too, was a common feature. Independent of one another, these two factors were responsible for the decline of several industries in each of the Middle Eastern countries. In fact, the technological decline had begun a long time before the later Middle Ages. The closure of the textile centers in lower Egypt during the late twelfth and throughout the first third of the thirteenth century was undoubtedly the result and not the cause of a long decline. The Arab geographer Ibn Ḥauḳal, writing at the end of the tenth century, complains that many water mills on the banks of the Tigris no longer functioned in his day.[206] Consequently, the technological decline had begun in Upper Mesopotamia even earlier than in Egypt. The relative decline in grain growing and the increase of the export of raw materials to the European countries was the consequence both of depopulation and of the decay of the local industries. On the one hand, the Levantine cotton and silk industries needed less raw materials than before (and much less than was produced) and, on the other, the swiftly developing European industries could probably afford to pay higher prices. However, let us beware of exaggeration. During the fifteenth century the countries of the Middle East were an underdeveloped region as compared with Western Europe. Yet they had not declined to such a degree of economic underdevelopment as that of some former European colonies during the twentieth century. The production of the raw materials was not organized by the foreign merchant-exporters, nor were local industries put wholly out of existence; all of them continued production, although on a smaller scale than before.

Even the reasons underlying the economic decline were similar in all Middle Eastern countries. The general and almost progressive depopulation was the effect of epidemics to which many fell victim because malnutrition had weakened their power of resistance. Another cause of depopulation were the frequent wars, accompanied by devastation and the abandonment of whole districts. A third reason was misrule, prevalent throughout the Levant. The hopeless plight of people is sometimes the main factor underlying depopulation. This was certainly true for the Oriental populations during the later Middle Ages. The heedless exploitation of the peasants resulted in their fleeing the land. The runaway peasants, who led a miserable life in the suburbs of towns with mainly proletarian inhabitants, were probably those most terribly hurt by the

206 *Ṣūrat al-arḍ*, Kramers (ed.), pp. 219 f.

epidemics. The decay of industries was also largely the result of misrule. Within the Muslim feudal system many industries, such as the sugar factories of Egypt, were appropriated by various methods. An analysis of the data in Arabic sources shows that the sugar boileries owned by the Muslim upper classes destroyed their bourgeois competitors.[207] In control of the industries, the feudal lords marketed their products by forced purchases. Hence they had no need of technological improvements. However, the misrule and exploitation inherent in such a feudal system cannot have been the only reasons for the technological backwardness. The almost natural opposition to innovation certainly constituted another factor. There is good reason to believe that such resistance was stronger in Muslim countries than in Christian Europe. For instance, had the populations of Persia and Iraq not been opposed to the use of paper money and had they accepted the banknotes issued by Il-Khān Gaikhātū, (Chinese) printing would have spread in the Muslim countries of the Middle East 200 years before Gutenberg.[208] This is, however, only a hypothesis. The supposition that technological stagnation is a concomitant phenomenon of depopulation is another.

However, if it is maintained that the misrule of the feudal lords and a strong conservatism opposing technological progress had a much greater impact in the Muslim countries than in Christian Europe, one is on firm ground. In the Muslim world these factors were much more powerful, as they were felt in all sectors of life. They brought about the downfall of the splendid civilizations of the caliphs, and, soon after the Ottoman Turks built up another great Muslim empire, their destructive power was felt again. A recently published book about towns in sixteenth-century Palestine shows that the demographic upsurge following the Ottoman conquest of Palestine was of short duration. Within a rather short period of time population figures in these towns began to drop once more.[209] The same probably happened, although somewhat later, in the countryside. Henceforth the population remained more or less stable. The opposition to technological innovations was as strong then as during the later Middle Ages, and when the Spanish Jews who had settled in Safed began to full

207 See Ashtor, 'Levantine Sugar Industry,' pp. 236 ff.

208 K. Jahn, 'Das iranische Papiergeld,' *Archiv Orientalni* 10 (1938): 308 ff.

209 A. Cohen and B. Lewis, *Population and Revenue in the Towns of Palestine in the Sixteenth Century*, Princeton 1978, pp. 25 f.

cloth by water-driven mills, the Muslims were loathe to accept the new method.[210]

210 S. Avitzur, 'Safed, Center of the Manufactures of Woven Woollens in the Fifteenth Century' (in Hebrew), in I. Ben-Zvi and M. Benayahu (eds.), *Studies and Texts in the History of the Jewish Community of Safed,* Sefunoth VI, Jerusalem 1962, pp. 46, 56 ff.

III

LEVANTINE SUGAR INDUSTRY IN THE LATER MIDDLE AGES—AN EXAMPLE OF TECHNOLOGICAL DECLINE

The decline of the Near Eastern sugar industry at the end of the Middle Ages is well known, but the explanations that have been given of this phenomenon are hardly satisfactory. On the other hand, an attempt to find a new analysis is a promising inquiry for several reasons. A correct interpretation of this case of industrial decline might enable us to elucidate similar phenomena. Further, in various sources there is relatively rich information on the development of the Levantine sugar industry. The works of chroniclers, geographers and other Arabic writers contain plenty of records on sugar production. They are supplemented by numerous data in the Italian Merchants' Guides and in mostly unpublished documents in Italian archives.[1] The confrontation of all these source materials makes it possible to shed light on the interdependence of industrial structures and technological decline, a major problem of the economic history of the Near East in the waning Middle Ages. Perhaps comparison with the data concerning other Near Eastern industries will point to a pattern of technological and industrial decline.

[1] The most important sources for this research are:

Balducci Pegolotti, Fr.: *La pratica della mercatura*, ed. A. Evans, Cambridge, Mass. 1936. — Pegolotti.

Uzzano, Giovanni da: 'La pratica della mercatura', (in) Pagnini, *Della decima* IV, Lisbon-Lucca 1766. — Uzzano.

El libro di mercatantie et usanze de' paesi, ed. Fr. Borlandi, Torino 1936. — *Libro di mercatantie.*

Melis, F.: *Documenti per la storia economica dei secoli XIII–XVI*, Firenze 1972 — Melis, *Documenti.*

ASV (Archivio di Stato, Venice); Giudici di petiziòn, *Sentenze a giustizia.* — G.d. P., *Sent.*

" Procuratori di S. Marco, Commissarie di citra, Ba 282, Commissaria Lorenzo Dolfin. — Arch. L. Dolfin.

" Procuratori di S. Marco, Commissarie miste, Ba. 180, 181, Comissaria Biegio Dolfin. — Arch. B. Dolfin.

" Cancelleria inferiore, Notai, Ba 211, Nicolo Turiano. — Nicolo Turiano.

ASG (Archivio di Stato, Genoa): *Caratorum Veterum*, no. 1552, 1553, 1556. — *Car. Vet.*

ASF (Archivio di Stato, Prato): *Quaderni di carichi e prezzi* 1171, 1175. — Datini.

Levantine Sugar Industry in the Later Middle Ages

a) PLANTATIONS FROM 1250 TO 1400, GEOGRAPHICAL DISTRIBUTION

Many data, found in various sources, leave no doubt that in the period stretching from the middle of the thirteenth century to the end of the fourteenth century sugar planting was still a flourishing sector of the economies of several Oriental contries.

The geographer Šams al-dīn al-Dimišqī who wrote at the beginning of the fourteenth century, says that in several towns on the coast of Makran and its hinterland fānīd sugar was produced. He reports that this kind of unrefined sugar was exported to Khurāsān and Iraq.[2]

The Mediterranean coast of Syria for a long time had a very prominent place among the sugar producing regions of the Near East. As at the end of the thirteenth century the Mamluks had destroyed the towns formerly occupied by the Crusaders and even laid waste the surrounding districts, the question arises as to whether or not sugar plantations remained there after this fateful change. There can be no doubt as to the continuity of sugar planting in the area around Tripoli. There is evidence of it both in literary and documentary sources.[3] But there are also records on sugar plantations in other districts of the Syrian coast. The Veronese pilgrim Giacomo da Verona (a. 1335) mentions coastal sugar plantations in the plain near Beirut. Also the Florentine Giorgio Gucci, who returned in 1385 via Beirut from his pilgrimage to Jerusalem, saw sugar plantations in the areas surrounding the town.[4] Johannes Poloner, writing in 1422, dwells on the excellent quality of the sugar cane grown in the district of Sidon.[5] Both an Arabic author writing in the 1370's and the Flemish pilgrim Ioos van Ghistele (a. 1485) say that sugar is grown in the surroundings of Tyre.[6] Finally, there is a passage in the Arabic encyclopaedia of al-Nuwayrī in which the sugar plantations of Acre and Beirut are mentioned.[7] However, these texts should be considered with a great deal of discretion. Johannes Poloner certainly copied the *Description of the Holy Land* written

[2] *Nuxbat al-dahr*, ed. Mehren, p. 176 (transl. p. 238); cf. E. Wiedemann, *Aufsätze zur arabischen Wissenschaftsgeschichte* (Hildesheim 1970) II, p. 411 note 1.

[3] al-Dimišqī, op. cit., p. 207 (transl. p. 282); *Géographie d'Aboulféda*, éd. Reinaud - de Slane (Paris 1840), p. 253 (transl. pt. 2, p. 30). M. Gaudefroy-Demombynes, *La Syrie à l'époque des Mamelouks* (Paris 1923), p. 112.

[4] *Liber peregrinationis di Jacopo da Verona*, ed. U. Monneret de Villard (Rome 1950), p. 139; *Visit to the Holy Places of Egypt, Sinai, Palestine and Syria in* 1384, transl. Bellorini-Hoade (Jerusalem 1948), p. 147.

[5] 'Descriptio Terrae Sanctae' (in) T. Tobler, *Descriptiones Terrae Sanctae ex saeculo VIII, IX, XII et XV* (Leipzig 1874), p. 262.

[6] B. Lewis, An Arabic account of the province of Safed, *BSOAS* 15 (1963), p. 482; *Tvoyage* (Ghendt 1572), p. 63.

[7] *Nihāyat al-'arab fī funūn al-adab* VIII (Cairo 1931), p. 271f.

by Burcardus de Monte Sion in 1283.[8] The account given by al-Nuwayrī clearly refers to the period preceding the destruction of the Crusader towns, as is borne out by the mention of sugar plantations in the neighbourhood of Acre, not recorded in any other source. Even what Abu-l-Fidā says about sugar planting in the district of Marqab is not above suspicion.[9] As long as there is no other explicit witness to the survival of the sugar plantations after the conquest of Marqab by the Mamluks, the testimony is somewhat dubious. One should not forget that after the downfall of the Crusader towns the agriculture of the surrounding districts lost their markets and that at the same time the commercial relations with the Christian Occident declined as a consequence of the measures taken by the Papacy. Probably crops had to be changed in some districts.[10]

Al-Qalqašandī speaks about sugar plantations in the "*aġwār*", the "deep valleys", by which he means the districts on the banks of the Jordan. In addition he says that in his day sugar was less plentiful in Syria, and, in another passage, he states that it was more expensive than in Egypt.[11] The statements of this Arabic writer are fully borne out by other evidence. Arabic texts and accounts of European travellers testify to the existence of sugar plantations in the plain of Baysān, in the district of Jericho and in the area of the Dead Sea. Since a trip to Jericho and on to the Jordan valley beyond it was part of the normal "tour" of Western pilgrims, several travelogues of the fourteenth century mention the sugar plantations in these districts.[12] Jacob of Verona also mentions plantations east and south of the Dead Sea.[13] This statement is surely correct, as it is supported by both archeological and literary evidence. On one hand, remnants of sugar mills have been found in the neighbourhood of the Dead Sea[14] and, on the other hand, sugar "of Karak" (or Monreal) is mentioned by Pegolotti.[15] Ancient sugar mills (or their remnants) have also been found in the Wādī Far'a, between Nabulus and the Jordan bridge of

8 'Descriptio Terrae Sanctae', (in) J. C. M. Laurent, *Peregrinationum medii aevi quatuor* (Lipsia 1864), p. 26.

9 P. 255 (transl. pt. 2, p. 32).

10 What al-Maqrīzī says about sugar growing in the district of al-'Arīš, s. al-*Xiṭaṭ* I, p. 189, undoubtedly refers to the remote past.

11 *Ṣubḥ al-a'šā* IV, p. 87, 182.

12 'Riccoldo de Monte Crucis', (in) Laurent, op. cit., p. 109; *Liber peregrinationis di Jacopo da Verona*, p. 51; Fra Niccolò da Poggibonsi, *Libro d'oltramare* (Jerusalem 1945), p. 87; Giorgio Gucci, p. 134; Lionardo Frescobaldi, (in) *Viaggi in Terrasanta*, ed. C. Angelini (Florence 1944), p. 145. On the remnants of sugar mills in 'Ayn al-sulṭān, near Jericho, s. Ritter, *Erdkunde von Asien* XV, p. 512, 525f.

13 P. 53.

14 F.-M. Abel, Mélanges, *Revue Biblique*, n. s. VII (1910), p. 553.

15 P. 296, 363f.

Damiya and near the village of Qarāwā, west of it. Indeed, Yāqūt mentions the sugar plantations of Qarāwā, probably the village now called Qarāwāt al-Mas'ūdī, northeast of the mountain Sarṭaba.[16] Since the region of *al-aġwār* also included the plain of Baysān, and the Mamluk sultans had big estates in the region, there is good reason to believe that even in this district in the second half of the thirteenth century and in the fourteenth century considerable quantities of sugar were produced.[17]

One may sum up the information on Syria's (and Palestine's) sugar production in the said period by stating that although it was probably smaller than in the days of the Crusaders the country still produced sugar in such quantities that some of it could be exported to other regions.

In Egypt sugar was planted in almost all provinces. The data that can be gleaned from the travelogues of the Western pilgrims refer to the plantations in the Delta, which they visited on their travel to Cairo. Arabic sources contain rich information on sugar growing in Upper Egypt.

The Irish monk Symon Semeonis, who visited Egypt in 1323, saw sugar plantations in the neighbourhood of Fūwa.[18] Lionardo Frescobaldi, sixty years later, saw plantations near Rosetta, whereas his travel-companion Simone Sigoli makes a broader statement, saying that sugar is grown on the banks of the Nile from Alexandria to Fūwa.[19]

Al-Maqrīzī recounts that at the beginning of the fourteenth century there were sugar plantations opposite Būlāq, a suburb of Cairo.[20] This author also gives some information about sugar growing in Upper Egypt. It is supplemented by Ibn Duqmāq and other Arabic writers. There were indeed sugar plantations in almost all the provinces of Upper Egypt. But from a passage in the chronicle of al-Maqrīzī one learns that there were also plantations in Middle Egypt in the Fayyum.[21] Ibn Duqmāq's *Topography of Egypt*, written at the end of the fourteenth century, abounds in data concerning the sugar production in Upper Egypt.[22] As the sugar factories were usually in the same

16 Abel, ibidem; Yāqūt IV, p. 51.

17 S. A. N. Poliak, *Feudalism in Egypt, Syria, Palestine and the Lebanon* 1250–199 (London 1939), p. 46 note 4.

18 *Itinerarium Symonis Semeonis ab Hybernia ad Terram Sanctam* (Dublin 1960), p. 65.

19 *Viaggi in Terrasanta*, ed. Angelini, p. 86, 184. The travelogue of Giorgo Gucci, p. 97, contains an even more general statement. He says that on the land between the two branches of the Nile much sugar is produced.

20 *al-Xiṭaṭ* II, p. 131.

21 *Sulūk* II, p. 419.

22 He mentions in his *al-Intiṣār* (Cairo 1893) V, 32 l. 7 Kemišboġā al-Ḥamawī as being "at present" atābek. This emir was appointed to the post of atābek when Barqūq returned to Cairo in 1391 and became sultan again. In 1397 Kemišboġā was imprisoned, s. Ibn Ḥaǧar, *Inbā al-ġumr* II, p. 81. But the work of Ibn Duqmāq (who died in 1407) shows clearly that he collected his materials and compiled them over a period of many years.

area where the sugar was grown, one may unhesitatingly assume that there were plantatations in the neighbourhood of towns and villages where such factories are listed by Ibn Duqmāq. According to these authors there were sugar factories in Mīr, al-Qūṣiya and Maysāra (now Messir), villages north of Manfalūṭ and west of the Nile.[23] Manfalūṭ itself,[24] Ṭahanhūr, Saqalqīl, and Būtīğ (now Abūtīğ) in the province of Asyūṭ,[25] Sūhāğ (or Sūhay), southwest of Ixmīm, were all towns in which there were sugar factories. The sugar produced in Sūhāğ was known for its excellent quality.[26] In the small townlet of al-Bulġanā, south of Guerga, there were several sugar factories, if one is to believe Kamāl al-dīn al-Adfuwī (d. 1347).[27] In the province of Qūṣ, sugar planting was a very important part of agriculture. There were sugar factories in Naqāda, west of the Nile,[28] Qamūla, south of Qūṣ,[29] and probably in many other villages.

So it would seem that in this period Upper Egypt was the foremost among the sugar producing regions of the Levantine countries. This conclusion is corroborated by the reports of the Arabic authors who say that the sugar refineries of the sultan were in Upper Egypt.[30]

b) THE VOLUME OF SUGAR PRODUCTION

It is clear that any attempt to estimate the sugar production of Syria and Egypt in this period will remain a mere conjecture. But the particulars found in the archives of Italian merchants may perhaps make it possible to evaluate the role of sugar in the exports of these countries. Further it seems that the information available is sufficient to draw some conclusions concerning the development of the sugar industry in this period.

At the beginning of the fourteenth century an Arabic writer, Muḥammad Ibn al-Mutawwağ, drew up a list of the sugar factories of Old Cairo: it contained the names of 66 factories.[31] This is certainly a very impressive

[23] *al-Intiṣār* V. p. 22 l. 9, 13.

[24] V, p. 22 l. 20.

[25] V, p. 24 l. 8; 25, l. 2.

[26] V, p. 27 l. 22.

[27] *al-Ṭāli' al-sa'īd al-ğāmi' li-asmā' nuğabā' al-Ṣa'īd* (Cairo 1966), p. 39, copied by al-Maqrīzī, *al-Xiṭaṭ* I, p. 203.

[28] Ibn Duqmāq V, p. 33 l. 21–25.

[29] *Géographie d'Aboulféda* p. 104 (transl. pt. 1, p. 140).

[30] *Sulūk* II, p. 431.

[31] *al-Xiṭaṭ* II, p. 342/3; cf. on this author who finished his work in 1325 (and died five years later) A. R. Guest, "A list of writers, books and other authorities mentioned by El Maqrīzi in his Khiṭaṭ", *JRAS* 1902, p. 116 and cf. Fr. Rosenthal, *A History of Muslim Historiography*, 2nd ed. (London 1968), p. 427.

account. But Cairo was by no means the town where the majority of the Egyptian sugar factories had been established. In fact, as has already been said, most of them were on or near the estates where sugar was grown. In the writings of the Arabic authors of the fourteenth and fifteenth centuries there is abundant evidence of this fact. Some small towns in sugar growing districts of Upper Egypt even had many sugar factories. The townlet of Mallawī, on the west bank of the Nile, between Minya and Manfalūṭ, in this period had no fewer than 11 sugar-presses.[32] In Samhūd, a small town south of Guerga, at the beginning of the fourteenth century there were 17 sugar-presses.[33] Qift, the ancient Koptos, was another great centre of the sugar industry. According to the Arabic writers it then had no less than 40 sugar refineries and 6 sugar-presses. Its sugar was known for its good quality.[34]

The author who supplies most particulars concerning the sugar industry in Upper Egypt unfortunately does not say when the factories were founded. But Ibn Duqmāq, who copied and elaborated Ibn al-Mutawwağ's list of the factories in Old Cairo, added a note on the history of some of them. As the Arabic dictionaries of biographies and the chronicles seldom contain data concerning businessmen (besides the great capitalists who were also well known philanthropists), it is difficult to establish the period of many owners (or founders) of sugar factories listed by these authors. With some degree of probability we can guess the time in which 29 factories were founded. They are to be found in the following table.

TABLE 1:

Foundation of sugar factories in Fusṭāṭ

before 1250	2nd half of 13th cent.	beginning of 14th cent.	2nd half of 14th cent.	end of 14th cent.
8	13	2	3	3

Compared with the whole list, our table comprises poor data. It does not make it possible to draw conclusions that could be considered as sure. But it points to the fact that in the second half of the thirteenth century there was a real boom in the Egyptian sugar industry. It was the time when the Mamluk emirs began to invest money in this profitable sector of Egypt's economy.

32 Ibn Baṭṭūṭa I, p. 101.

33 al-Adfuwī, *al-Ṭāli' al-sa'īd*, p. 18; copied by Ibn Duqmāq V, p. 32 l. 10–11 and in *al-Xiṭaṭ* I, p. 203.

34 al-Adfuwī, op. cit., p. 13; Ibn Duqmāq V, p. 33 l. 4/5; *al-Xiṭaṭ* I p. 232.

Not only was the number of the sugar factories of the Near Eastern countries in the first hundred years of Mamluk rule considerable, but the output was likewise. The accounts one finds in Arabic chronicles of the great public banquets in the thirteenth and the fourteenth centuries shed light on the enormous quantities of sugar stored by the princes of Mesopotamia, Syria and Egypt. We are told that al-Malik al-Muẓaffar Gökböri, prince of Irbil (1190–1232), gave a banquet every year on the birthday of Mohammed distributing 10,000 chickens, 5000 roasted lambs, 100,000 dishes of other food and 30,000 of sweetmeats.[35] When in 1239 the Ayyubid sultan of Egypt, al-Malik al-ʿĀdil II, heard that his brother al-Malik al-Ṣāliḥ Naǧm al-dīn had been caught and imprisoned in Karak, he gave a great banquet in Cairo and offered his guests 1500 sugar-loaves.[36] This quantity corresponds to 1215 t.[37] At the wedding of Emir Qawṣūn and the daughter of the Mamluk sultan al-Malik al-Nāṣir Muḥammad, in 1327, the latter presented the guests sweetmeats for which 11,000 sugar-loaves had been used (8910 t).[38] Five years later Ānūk, a son of the sultan, married. On this occasion 18,000 qinṭār of sugar (1620 t) were used for the preparation of halva and syrup for the banquet.[39] In the days of al-Malik al-Nāṣir Muḥammad (third reign: 1309-1341), in the month of Ramaḍān the Royal court of Cairo consumed 1000 qinṭār sugar (90 t) and later, in 1344, 3000 qinṭār.[40]

These data must not necessarily be considered exaggerated. They are supplemented by other reports.

In an account of the confiscation of the goods of Karīm al-dīn al-kabīr, nāẓir al-xāṣṣ of al-Malik al-Nāṣir Muḥammad, in the year 1323, al-Maqrīzī narrates in this chronicle that sugar and candy valued at 80,000 dinars were found.[41] In another work he says that he remembers the days when in the month of Raǧab, the confectioners of Cairo sold shaped sweets, such as figures of horses and other animals, made of sugar and weighing from a quarter of a raṭl to 10 raṭls (0,22 to 9 kg).[42]

[35] Sibṭ Ibn al-Ǧawzī, *Mir'āt al-zamān*, ed. Jewett, p. 451.

[36] *Sulūk* I, p. 290.

[37] A loaf (*ablūǧ*) was equal to about 9 qinṭārs, s. *al-Xiṭaṭ* I, p. 102/3 and, on the other hand, sugar was weighed by *qinṭār ǧarwī* (of 90 kg, below, note 110).

[38] *Sulūk* II, p. 288.

[39] Op. cit. II, p. 346.

[40] *al-Xiṭaṭ* II, p. 231.

[41] *Sulūk* II, p. 243. Similar data could be quoted from inventories of the property left by prominent men. A vizier who died in 1387, for instance, left 1000 qinṭār sugar, s. al-Ǧawharī, *Nuzhat al-nufūs* I (Cairo 1970), p. 161.

[42] *al-Xiṭaṭ* II, p. 100; cf. E. W. Lane, *Manners and Customs of the Modern Egyptians* (London 1954), p. 472 ff.; M. J. Kister, Rajab is the month of God, *Israel Oriental Studies* I (Tel Aviv 1971), p. 220f.

Notwithstanding the great quantities of sugar consumed by the court and the well-to-do, Egypt like Syria in this period could still export a part of the produce to other countries. The sugar produced in these countries was renowned everywhere, both in the Muslim and the Christian world. For instance, in Morocco, the sugar cane was grown and in some towns there were many sugar boileries. Marrakesh had 40 in a certain period. But Egyptian sugar was considered to be better than that produced in Morocco.[43]

As to the export of sugar from Syria and Egypt in that period, the historian finds plenty of records in various sources.

Just at the beginning of the Mamluk period, in 1252, the Mongols intercepted a caravan near Harran transporting 600 loads of Egyptian sugar to Baghdad.[44] An Arabic author, who wrote in the first half of the fourteenth century, dwells on the export of Egyptian sugar to Bahrain.[45] The Venetian Marino Sanudo Torsello, writing in the first decade of the fourteenth century, speaks about the export of Egyptian sugar to the ports of Cilicia (then the kingdom of Little Armenia), from where it was sent to the Turkish hinterland.[46] He also asserts that sugar was exported from Egypt to Western Europe via North African ports.[47]

These authors speak of Egyptian sugar without specifying what kind. But in the Italian merchants' archives and in other European sources, which are based on the latter, there is an exact specification of the various kinds of Levantine sugar exported to European countries. Pegolotti gives a description of the most important kinds of sugar: the best is the *muccaro*, then follow, in descending order, *caffettino*, *babilonio* (or *bambillonio*), *musciatto*, *domaschino* and powdered sugar.[48] Clearly, *muccaro* (or *mucchero*) is the transcription of the Arabic "*mukarrar*" — refined sugar, and *babilonio* means Cairene sugar whereas "*caffettino*" has been explained as meaning "basket" sugar (from Arabic *quffa*).[49] On the other hand, one finds in al-Qalqašandī's *Ṣubḥ al-aʿšā* the following list of the various kinds of Egyptian sugar: *mukarrar*, *tabaʿ*, *wasaṭ*, *nabat*.[50] In a manuscript used by Wüstenfeld there was an additional kind, inserted in this list after *tabaʿ*: *ʿāl*. Moreover, this manuscript reads

[43] Ibn Faḍlallāh al-ʿUmarī, *Masālik al-abṣār fī mamālik al-amṣār* I, trad. Gaudefroy-Demombynes (Paris 1927), p. 176 (where l. 9 qand has been erroneously translated to candy; it should be raw sugar, s. below note 110).

[44] *Sulūk* I, p. 383f.

[45] Ibn Faḍlallāh al-ʿUmarī, quoted in *Ṣubḥ* VII, p. 370.

[46] *Secreta fidelium crucis*, p. 29.

[47] Op. cit., p. 28.

[48] P. 362ff.

[49] E. O. v. Lippmann, *Geschichte des Zuckers*, 2nd ed. (Berlin 1929), p. 344; Evans in his glossary to Pegolotti, p. 434.

[50] III, p. 313.

instead of *nabat* — *nabāt*.[51] This latter word, transcribed in European Merchant Guides as *naibet* (or *nebec*)[52], means "candy sugar".[53] So we have the three kinds of Egyptian sugar corresponding to those mentioned by Pegolotti (besides the *mukarrar*, the thrice-boiled finest kind, and the *domaschino*, the Damascene sugar), viz. *caffettino*, *babilonio*, and *musciatto*. From this fact one may also infer the meaning of *musciatto*, a denomination that has remained incomprehensible to the scholars interested in this field of economic history. Perhaps we are not mistaken in surmising that *musciatto* is nothing else than a transcription of *muwassaṭ*.[54] These three kinds of sugar were boiled twice (*di due cotte*), but there was also another kind that was only boiled once (*di una cotta*). As this kind of sugar was mainly destined for the home market and seldom exported to European countries, it did not figure on the price lists (and the Merchant Guides). In Syria, too, such a sugar was produced.

The price lists of the Italian merchants contradict Pegolotti's classification of the various kinds of sugar in so far as, according to most of them, the *domaschino* is more expensive than the *babilonio* and the *musciatto*.[55] But other than this, they substantiate his information.

Accordingly the main kinds of Levantine sugar may be classified as follows:

TABLE 2:
Main Types of Levantine Sugar

	Egyptian (according Qalqašandī)	Syrian	Pegolotti's list
Thrice boiled (*tre cotte*)	*mukarrar*	*mukarrar*	*muccaro*
Twice boiled (*due cotte*)	*taba'*		*caffettino*
	'āl	*domaschino*	*babilonio*
	muwassaṭ	*tripolino*[56]	*musciatto*
Once boiled (*una cotta*)	Egyptian	simple	
	Powdered sugar	Powdered sugar	*polvere*
	nabat	*nabat*	candy

[51] Wüstenfeld, *Geographie und Verwaltung von Ägypten* (Göttingen 1879) (*Abhdl. der Königl. Ges. der Wiss. zu Gött.* 25), p. 34.

[52] *Zibaldone da Canal*, ed. A. Stussi (Venice 1967), p. 57, 66.

[53] Dozy, *Suppl.* II, p. 633.

[54] S. Lippmann p. 344 (who concludes that it meant the same as the later *moscobado*, *moschiado*, the meanest kind of sugar!); Evans p. 435.

[55] S. below Table 11. However, it is true that according to al-Qalqašandī, s. note 11, the price of Syrian sugar was higher. But the difference between the prices of Damascene sugar and twice-boiled Egyptian sugar in these price lists is considerable.

[56] In a price list (in the Datini archives 1171) of Venice, dated December 31, 1393, the price of Tripoli sugar is lower than that of Damascus sugar.

Some of these types of sugar are again subdivided according to their origin.[57] In some sources other kinds of sugar are also mentioned. Pegolotti speaks of *rosato* (sugar mixed with rose water) and *violato* (mixed with essence of violets).[58]

All these products of the Levantine sugar industry were exported to Italy, Southern France and Catalonia, and from there some was shipped to Flanders and England or transported by land to Germany and other countries of Central Europe. The Datini archives contain many cargo lists in which Syrian and Egyptian sugar is mentioned, like those of the Venetian galleys coming from Beirut in 1393, 1394, 1395, 1399, 1404, 1405 and 1406 (some of them partially loaded in Tripoli), or from Alexandria in 1382 and 1399; of a Venetian cog coming from Alexandria in 1404; of Genoese cogs coming from Beirut and Alexandria, some of them sailing to Aigues-Mortes; of Catalan galleys and cogs sailing from Beirut and Alexandria to Barcelona, in 1371, 1383, 1384, and 1391, or to Aigues-Mortes and Marseilles, in 1399 and 1400. It was not only the major South-European trading nations that were engaged in the Levantine sugar trade, there are also freight lists of cogs transporting sugar from Tripoli and from Alexandria to Ancona (a. 1379). Those accounts are supplemented and confirmed by the Genoese custom registers.[59]

57 The price lists and tariffs (of duties, freights) distinguish between candy and powdered sugar of Syria and Egypt and sometimes even between "*polvere domaschino*" and "*polvere di Cracco*" (of Karak in Transjordan) and, on the other hand, between powdered sugar of Alexandria and of Cairo. Sometimes powder of thrice-boiled, twice-boiled, once-boiled, and candy are separately listed, s. Pegolotti p. 296.

58 P. 297 cf. Evans' glossary p. 435. An anonymous German pilgrim of the first half of the fourteenth century says that there are three kinds of sugar in the Near East: black sugar used in the pharmacy, red used in the kitchen, and white sugar, s. "Ein niederrheinischer Bericht über den Orient", ed. Röhricht-Meissner, *Zeitschrift für Deutsche Philologie* 19, p. 83f. What the author says of black and red sugar refers perhaps to molasses, s. below, or to once-boiled sugar.

59 J. Heers, 'Il commercio mediterraneo alla fine del sec. XIV e nei primi anni del XV', *Archivio Storico Italiano* 113 (1955), p. 171f., 174.; F. Melis, *Aspetti della vita economica medievale* I (Siena 1962), p. 383; id., *Documenti*, p. 144, 324; E. Ashtor, *Les métaux précieux et la balance des payements du Proche-Orient à la basse époque* (Paris 1971), p. 121. All these authors quote documents of the Datini archives. In our text reference is made to other documents belonging to these archives. On the export of sugar from Egypt s. also *Histoire du commerce de Marseille II* (par E. Baratier-F. Reynaud), p. 248. See further a summary of data in the Genoese custom registers of 1376/7, published by J. Day, in my paper 'Il volume del commercio levantino di Genova nel secondo Trecento', (in) *Miscelanea di storia ligure* (Genova 1977) (in press). The value of the cargoes was calculated according to the price lists in the same archives, s. below. Conjectural though these estimates are they contradict the supposition that Oriental industries did not produce (or usually did not produce) for export, s. Cahen "Quelques mots sur le déclin commercial du monde musulman à la fin du moyen âge", (in) M. A. Cook, *Studies in the economic history of the Middle East* (London 1970), p. 35.

What was the value of these shipments and, accordingly, what was the place of sugar in the export trade of Syria and Egypt at the end of the fourteenth century, a period for which we have relatively rich information?

Since the price lists found in the Datini archives and in some Arabic chronicicles are incomplete, we can only make some conjectures as to the value of the sugar shipments. However, it seems probable that, on the average, a convoy of Venetian galleys shipped sugar from Beirut or Alexandria worth 2000–3000 dinars. But the galleys were mainly intended for the transport of spices. On the other hand, a cog of the Catalans or another trading nation often loaded sugar of the value of 2000–4000 or even 6000 ducats. And there were instances of a convoy of Venetian galleys carrying sugar worth 10,000-20,000 dinars, e.g. the Alexandria galleys in 1382 and the Beirut galleys in 1394, 1395. So one may surmise that the value of the sugar Syria and Egypt exported to Europe at the end of the fourteenth century amounted to 30,000–50,000 dinars a year. Compared with the shipments of spices the value of these cargoes looks insignificant. But one should not forget that sugar was also exported by land and by sea to other Near Eastern countries and to North Africa and, secondly, that sugar was not goods in a transit like the spices, but a home-grown product. Consequently, the export of sugar was by no means without importance for the balance of payments of Syria and Egypt.

c) THE STRUCTURE OF THE SUGAR INDUSTRY

The flourishing of the Levantine sugar industry and the export of substantial quantities to Southern Europe came to an end at the beginning of the fifteenth century. It is no exaggeration to speak of a breakdown. The number of factories diminished considerably, the output even more so. Some scholars have expressed the opinion that this change was the consequence of the wrong policy of the sultans, of Barsbay and others.[60] This interpretation of the facts is true to some extent, but it cannot explain the phenomenon as a whole.

The closing of sugar factories had begun a long time before the economic crisis of the Mamluk kingdom at the beginning of the fifteenth century. The number of factories in Upper Egypt had begun to diminish from the beginning of the fourteenth century, as is explicitly stated by al-Adfuwī.[61] Ibn Duqmāq and al-Maqrīzī testify to the reduction in the number of sugar factories in Upper Egypt, the main centre of Egypt's sugar industry, in the fourteenth century. Speaking of several towns, these authors say that there "were" many

60 L. Hautecoeur-G. Wiet, *Les mosquées du Caire* (Paris 1932) I, p. 97; A. Darrag, *L'Egypte sous le règne de Barsbay* (Damascus 1961), p. 57ff.

61 *al-Ṭāli' al-sa'īd*, p. 18, 19.

sugar factories.[62] Al-Maqrīzī also mentions, in another chapter of this *Topography of Egypt*, the ruin of the sugar factories in Fusṭāṭ. He says that the rubbish-heaps were used for making a dam, in the days of sultan al-Malik al-Kāmil Šaʿbān (1345–46)[63]. The decline in the number of sugar factories was probably the result of the pressure brought upon the private enterprises by the emirs and the sultans.

The sugar industry of Egypt (and probably that of Syria) was a true capitalistic enterprise, with big trusts which systematically pushed the small enterprises aside. The sugar centre of Mallawī, for instance, in the first half of the fourteenth century was dominated by the Banū Fuḍayl family, which planted 1500 feddan sugar cane a year.[64] This was, judging from the name, a bourgeois family. But the great sugar industrialists were first of all the Mamluk emirs and the directors of the sultan's financial administration. The Arabic chronicles with their interesting and detailed information on the structure of the Egyptian sugar industry leave no doubt about this fact. Al-Maqrīzī reports that in 1298 emir Sayf al-dīn Mankūtimur received a new fief, comprising 27 sugar-presses destined for himself (that means without the obligation to share the output, or the income from the sale, with his mamluks).[65] Emir Qawṣūn was a great sugar industrialist. In 1327 the director of his sugar factory was fined 100,000 dirhams.[66] The vizier ʿAlā al-dīn Ibn Zunbūr, deposed in 1352, had 25 sugar-presses.[67] Emirs of lower rank and their families were also engaged in this business, Tankizboġā al-Māridīnī had a sugar factory in Fusṭāṭ, a son of his had one in Maysāra, in Upper Egypt.[68]

The sons of sultan al-Malik al-Nāṣir Ḥasan (1347–51, 1354–61) were true sugar barons. In Upper Egypt, they had:

3	sugar	factories	in	Mīr
4	"	"	"	Būtīğ
2	"	"	"	Ṭahanhūr

and other in Fusṭāṭ.[69] The sons of other sultans were also great sugar producers. The chronicle of ʿAbdalbāsiṭ b. Xalīl contains, under the year 1447, an

[62] Ibn Duqmāq V, p. 32 l. 10/11; *al-Xiṭaṭ* II, p. 99, 203, 204, 232.

[63] *al-Xiṭaṭ* II, p. 167.

[64] *Sulūk* II, p. 431; *al-Xiṭaṭ* II, p. 204; Ibn Baṭṭūṭa I, p. 101.

[65] *Sulūk* I, p. 841.

[66] Op. cit. II, p. 419. He was surely one of the richest men of Egypt in his day. The result of the plundering of his treasures was the fall of the exchange rate of the dinar, s. *Les métaux précieux*, p. 48.

[67] Ibn Iyās I, p. 198.

[68] Ibn Duqmāq IV, p. 46 l. 7/8 V, p. 22 l. 13.

[69] Op. cit. V, p. 22 l. 9, 24 l. 8, 25 l. 2, and see below note 81.

account of a litigation between 'Uṯmān, son (and later successor) of sultan Ǧaqmaq,and a bourgeois merchant. They had a sugar factory in partnership.[70]

The sultans themselves were very much engaged in the sugar industry. According to Ibn Duqmāq the sultan in his days had seven sugar factories in Manfalūṭ and several in Sūhāǧ.[71] As there was a special department of the sultan's sugar industry in Syria, its volume cannot have been insignificant. At least some of the sugar presses in the Jordan valley belonged to it, and there were also sultan's sugar factories in Damascus itself.[72] The same is true for the sugar plantations in the district of Tripoli: at least some of them belonged to the sultan.[73]

It is not very difficult to understand why the emirs and the sultan himself had so great an interest in the sugar plantations and in the sugar industry. Indeed, they enjoyed some privileges that enabled them to outstrip the competition of the civilian sugar producers.

The raw material they used was cheaper, for the peasant who grew sugar had to pay a special tax from which feudal lords were exempted.[74] Also, the peasants in the districts where the sultan had sugar plantations were liable to corvée.[75] And last but not least, the emirs who held high posts in the administration and other rich industrialists had special "arrangements" with the tax-collectors. The Banū Fuḍayl, for instance, paid taxes for a produce of 1000 qinṭār of raw sugar a year,[76] although it amounted to 540,000 at least!

That the competition between the emirs (viziers, sons of sultans etc.), who ran sugar factories, and the burgeois industrials was unequal was noted by such an experienced scholar as the late A. N. Poliak.[77] But he did not thoroughly analyse the very interesting data collected by Ibn Duqmāq concerning the development of the sugar factories in Fusṭāṭ. The analysis of this survey sheds bright light on the history of the Egyptian sugar industry and will perhaps make it possible to give a more satisfactory explanation of its breakdown.

The survey given by Ibn Duqmāq is not complete. He tried to provide information on the past and the present state of the factories listed by Ibn

70 *al-Rawḍ al-bāsim*, MS. Vaticana 728, f. 49a.

71 Ibn Duqmāq V, p. 22 l. 20, 27 l. 22.

72 *Ṣubḥ* IV, p. 183 cf. 188, 190, and see note 17 and *Sulūk* I, p. 576; E. Ashtor, Etudes sur quelques chroniques mamloukes, *Isr. Or. Studies* I (1971), p. 281 (the sultan buys, in 1359, estates in the Baysān valley).

73 *Ṣubḥ* 13, p. 34.

74 al-Nuwayrī VIII, p. 254, 261.

75 See the passage quoted in note 73, further *Ṣubḥ* 14, p. 33 and cf. note 9; see also Poliak in *REI* 1936, p. 262.

76 *Sulūk* II, p. 431.

77 Les révoltes populaires en Egypte à l'époque des Mamelouks, *REI* 1934, p. 253, 254.

al-Mutawwağ, but often he did not succeed in obtaining details concerning the actual conditions, so that he left the question open saying "and now...". Apparently he hoped to get the information later. Several passages of his book show, indeed, that the text is a draft, successively changed and corrected.

In classifying the particulars collected by Ibn Duqmāq, one cannot be sure. In the following table those factories whose rubrics in Ibn Duqmāq's text do not contain a remark concerning the suspension of sugar production have been classified as "working". It may be however that some no longer served this purpose. On the other hand, one may be mistaken in classifying as ex-factories all those Ibn Duqmāq describes as living-houses. For it seems that often the manager of a sugar factory lived in the factory.[78]

TABLE 3:

Sugar Factories in Fusṭāṭ according to Ibn Duqmāq IV, p. 41–46

	Working	Work suspended	Unknown
a) Factories of the sultan and the royal princes:			
State factory[79]	1		
Factories of the sultan[80]	4	1	
Factories of the royal princes[81]	6		
b) Factories of emirs and viziers			
Factories of emirs	6[82]	6	4
Factories of viziers		2	
c) Factories of bourgeois and others:			
Factories of bourgeois	7	16	7
Factories of waqf	1	1	7
Unknown proprietor		2	1

78 S. IV, p. 42 l. 7ff. about *Maṭbax al-Ğalāl al-kabīr*; IV, p. 42f. what is said about the "Maṭbax known as sakn Tāğ al-dīn Ibn al-Naxīf"; p. 43 l. 5–7 about *Maṭbax Ibn al-Muḥtasib.*

79 *Maṭbax al-dawla.* Formerly there had been two such factories, one had been given over to royal princes.

80 Three at all times assigned to the "*xāṣṣ*", one acquired by sultan Barqūq. Formerly the *xāṣṣ* (domain of the sultan) had six factories, but three were later given to the royal princes.

81 Five were in the possession of the sons of al-Malik al-Nāṣir Ḥasan; as to four, the author says that they are of "the sons" of the said sultan, whereas one was, according to him, in the possession of his son Ismā'īl. One factory had been managed by the sons of sultan al-Malik al-Ašraf Ša'bān (1363–76) and after his death it had been rented by Barqūq, while he was still an emir, and upon his accession to the throne it was managed by al-Malik al-Ṣāliḥ Ḥāǧǧī, son of al-Malik al-Ašraf Ša'bān and himself a dethroned sultan.

82 Listing nine of them, the author does not make any statement as to the actual situation. Of two only he expressly says that they were still producing sugar.

Summing up these data one finds that the sultan and the royal princes had 12 factories, the emirs and the viziers 18, and the burgeois 30.

Who were the burgeois sugar industrialists? Most of them were themselves very rich men and established true sugar trusts. Out of 30 factories, half belonged to five families:

a) 3 factories to the al-Xarrūbī
 two to the brothers Nūr al-dīn (d. 1400) and
 Sirāǧ al-dīn (d. 1422), sons of ʿIzz al-dīn ʿAbdalʿazīz,
 one to Zaki al-dīn al-Xarrūbī[83]

b) 4 factories to the family Ibn Marzūq

c) 4 " " " " al-Qaṭrawānī

d) 4 " " " " Ibn aṣ-Ṣawwāf

Even some of the remaining 15 factories were surely in the possession of great capitalists, such as Kārimī merchants.[84] The Xarrūbīs, who had 3 factories, were one of the richest families of Kārimī merchants and connected by marriage with another rich family of Kārimīs, the Ibn Musallam. They were surely great sugar industrialists. Al-Maqrīzi narrates that Badr al-dīn Muḥammad b. Muḥammad b. ʿAlī al-Xarrūbī (d. 1361), a great sugar industrialist who had some factories (*al-tāǧir fī maṭābix al-sukkar*), founded a college in Cairo extra muros.[85]

But under the rule of the Mamluks dynasties of rich merchants could not develop. Before long their riches were squeezed by the "*muṣādara*". In 1338 al-Našw, director of the sultan's private revenue, confiscated 14,000 qinṭār of sugar found in the stores of the Banū Fuḍayl and imposed on them as a fine the payment of the value of 8000 qinṭār.[86] Surely this is only one sample of the *muṣādara* fines. The history of the sugar industry in mediaeval Egypt is characteristic of the unequal competition between bourgeois and feudal (royal) industrialists. The bourgeois succumbed under the pressure of fines and other oppressive methods used by the Mamluks. Calculating the percentage of the factories that belonged to the different classes of owners and were no longer operating one finds:

[83] S. my paper "The Kārimī merchants", *JRAS* 1956, p. 48/49, and see now *Inbā* III, p. 289.

[84] S. IV, p. 44 l. 12–15 on *Maṭbax ʿaqabat al-milḥ*.

[85] *al-Xiṭaṭ* II, p. 369.

[86] *Sulūk* II, p. 431; *al-Xiṭaṭ* II, p. 204.

TABLE 4:
Fusṭāṭ sugar factories whose production was suspended according to Ibn Duqmāq

Sultan-royal princes	Emirs-viziers	Bourgeois
9%	33%	53%

The number of the factories of the bourgeois that had to suspend production is much greater than that of the factories of the emirs-viziers. The latter group is incomparably greater than that of the factories of the sultan and the royal princes that no longer functioned. In other words: the emirs pushed aside the bourgeois capitalists, surely with the help of the sultan's government, and the sultan and the royal princes suppressed the industry of the aristocrats.

The gradual suppression of the burgeois capitalists also emerges from another analysis of Ibn Duqmāq's survey. The Arabic historian provides many particulars concerning the successive changes of the ownership of factories. They are summed up in the following table:

TABLE 5:
Change of ownership of Fusṭāṭ sugar factories according to Ibn Duqmāq

To emirs		To bourgeois	
from bourgeois	5	from emirs	6
from waqf	3	from waqf	1
			7
To royal princes			
from bourgeois	2		
To the sultan			
from bourgeois	1		
from waqf	1		
	12		

For a just estimate of these data one should take into account that according to Ibn Duqmāq's survey the appropriations of bourgeois factories by an emir started from the beginning of Mamluk rule, whereas the changes from aristocratic to bourgeois ownership occurred mostly towards the end of the fourteenth century, when the grip of feudal rule began to give way.

The Arabic chronicles and other sources leave no doubt as to the methods used by the emirs and the sultans to suppress free competition. Although they had cheaper raw material and enjoyed reduction of taxes or tax exemption, they used violent methods to get competition out of the way. The most usual method used to ruin the bourgeois competitors was to impose on the merchants the acquisition of the sultan's or the emirs' sugar by forced purchase, the so-called *ṭarḥ* system.

Al-Našw had been known for his uncouth methods of extorting money from all classes of the population. One of them was the *ṭarḥ*.[87] His successor did the same. He even sold the sugar of the sultan to the merchants forcibly but at a cheaper price than al-Našw.[88] The opposition of various classes of the population to these compulsory purchases was so strong that the sultan had to abolish them. But there can be no doubt that the *ṭarḥ* system was soon re-established. In fact, one reads in a chronicle that emir Tenem, the rebellious governor of Damascus, in 1399 sold sugar and other commodities by force to the inhabitants of the town.[89] The Arabic chronicler, whom we quote, emphasizes that the governor compelled all classes of the population to buy his products, even the theologians. This report is borne out by a Venetian document, according to which the Venetian merchants had to buy a certain quantity of sugar for the high price of 90 ducats a qinṭār.[90] The Arabic chroniclers mention the compulsory purchases usually in connexion with extraordinary occasions, such as festivities for which great sums of money were needed or revolts and other cases of emergency. But their accounts should not mislead us. The *ṭarḥ* system was surely a method rather regularly employed by the government in Cairo and the provincial governors to obtain money. But sometimes the pressure brought upon the merchants was so great that it aroused bitter opposition and on these occasions the chroniclers found it necessary to mention the matter.

One of the most cruel and greedy of the Mamluk sultans was surely Barsbay (1422–38), even taking into consideration that the progressive economic decline of Egypt and Syria compelled him to take severe measures to balance his budget. He was not content with the *ṭarḥ* method, but tried to make the sugar production altogether a state monopoly. In the years 1423–1433 he proclaimed several times that sugar should only be sold by his agents. These successive decrees, all of them abolished a short time after their promulgation, were to establish different degrees of monopoly. In 1423, the sultan proclaimed that all the sugar factories besides his own should suspend production. Two years later he decreed that the produce of the factories should be delivered to his agents who would sell it. The decree promulgated at the end of 1427 was

87 *Sulūk* II, p. 460; *al-Xiṭaṭ* II, p. 107.
88 *Sulūk* II, p. 488.
89 Ibn Ḥağar, *Inbā* II, p. 92.
90 N. Jorga, "Notes et extraits", *Revue de l'Orient latin* IV, p. 228.

the most rigorous, for the sultan forbade even the planting of sugar cane anywhere but on his estates. A year later, in January 1429, the more lenient policy of 1425 was adopted: it was permitted to produce sugar, but it had to be sold to the sultan. At the beginning of the year 1430 the government again established this monopoly and, by the *ṭarḥ* method, required the merchants to buy sugar from it at a high price. Some time later Barsbay once more established the monopoly of 1427, i.e. forbade growing sugar except on his estates. The opposition these measures aroused was so strong that Barsbay had to abolish them time and again.[91] But each time, shortly after the abolition, he had recourse to other methods of extortion.

One of them was the *ṭarḥ* system. In the year 1433 the forced purchase of the sultan's sugar was once more abolished in Damascus, as is indicated by an inscription and the report of a chronicler.[92] It is almost superfluous, however, to say that the solemn abolition of the *ṭarḥ* of sugar was soon forgotten. An anonymous chronicler of Damascus recounts that in 1435 the confectioners were forcibly transferred to a market within the town walls "in order to make the *ṭarḥ* of sugar easier, as all of them would be in one place".[93] At the beginning of the ninth decade of the fifteenth century there was once more great excitement in Damascus because of the forced purchase of sugar. A contemporary chronicler narrates how the inhabitants of Damascus put forth strenuous opposition to the authorities, who imposed on them the purchase of the sultan's sugar at double the market price.[94] But even when the sultan abstained from monopolizing the sugar production altogether or using the *ṭarḥ* method, he imposed imposts on the sugar trade that had a similar effect: the competition was strangled, since the sultan's agents were exempted from the taxes.

91 S. M. Sobernheim, "Das Zuckermonopol unter Sultan Barsbai", *Ztschrft f. Assyriologie* 27 (1912), p. 75–84. As to the measures taken by the government in 1430 Sobernheim quotes a passage in the *Sulūk* where the establishment of the monopoly of the sugar trade in Ǧumādā I (February 1430) is reported. Then he refers to a report about the prohibition of sugar planting (other than on the estates of the sultan) in Šaʿbān (May, 1430). He does not quote the passages and in fact they are not contained in the Paris MS. of al-Maqrīzī's *Sulūk*. But since Ibn Ḥaǧar says that this year the said prohibition was enacted, the two authors supplement one another.

92 Sobernheim p. 78ff.; this abolition was considered as a very solemn act and therefore the inscription announcing it was engraved, as one did on such occasions in several places s. G. Wiet, "Notes d'épigraphie syromusulmane", *Syria VI* (1925), p. 165; *Ḥawliyyāt dimišqiyya* 834–839 h., ed. Ḥ. Ḥabašī (Cairo 1968), p. 79. Sobernheim believed that the decree abolished the monopoly established in 1430, but neither the inscription nor the anonymous chronicler's report refer to a general prohibition of sugar growing. So perhaps it is more probable that it abolished the *ṭarḥ* only.

93 *Ḥawliyyāt dimišqiyya*, p. 142.

94 Ibn Ṭūlūn, *Mufākahat al-xillān* I (Cairo 1962), p. 41, 42.

An undated inscription in Damascus announces the abolishment of such a tax by sultan Barsbay.[95]

The management of the sugar factories of the emirs and of the sultan was apparently very corrupt. The Arabic sources do not contain many accounts of the management of these enterprises, since the managers did their best to avoid exposing their activities. But there are in the chronicles accounts from which one must draw conclusions as to the corruption of the sugar industry and there are even some that are explicit.

In some passages of his great chronicle al-Maqrīzī mentions the fines imposed in the first half of the fourteenth century on the managers of the sugar factories of the emirs and the sultan. In 1337, al-Našw imprisoned all the managers of the sugar industry in Upper Egypt in order to extort fines from them. Ibn al-Mušanqaṣ, director of the sugar factory of Emir Qawṣūn, was fined 100,000 dirhams. He was accused of adulterating the sugar, and, despite the protest of Qawṣūn, the sultan's finance director confiscated the property al-Mušanqaṣ had inherited from his father.[96] Some months later, al-Našw imposed a fine of 160,000 dirhams on the inspector of the sultan's sugar factories in Upper Egypt.[97] We are probably not wrong in supposing that these stories testify not only to the greediness of the sultan's finance director.

A text in the *Collection of biographies* of Ibn al-Suqā'ī is more explicit. From this long story there emerges the image of terrible corruption. A Samaritan manager of the sultan's sugar production in Damascus and his assistants, under the reign of sultan Baybars, had embezzled 300,000 dirhams from the net proceeds of the sugar sale. When the embezzlement was discovered in 1269, Baybars himself came to Damascus to give instructions on how to proceed. From the long story told by the Arabic author one learns that a whole group of Muslim and Jewish managers and clerks were mixed up with this affair.[98] A passage in the chronicle of al-Ğawharī sheds light on the corruption in the sultan's sugar factories in the eighth decade of the fourteenth century. It appears that matters were much worse than in the days of Baybars. In the biography (obituary notice) of Šams al-dīn Ibrāhīm Ibn Kātib Arlān

[95] G. Wiet, "Répertoire des décrets mamlouks de Syrie", (in) *Mélanges syriens offerts à R. Dussaud* (Paris 1939) II, p. 526 no. 45.

[96] *Sulūk* II, p. 419. Characteristically enough the name of this manager figures among the proprietors of sugar factories in Fusṭāṭ in the list of Ibn Duqmāq IV, p. 41 ultima 44 l. 5. where one reads that he was a Jew (should be son of a Jew).

[97] *Sulūk* II, p. 431.

[98] Faḍlallāh Ibn al-Suqā'ī, *Tālī Kitāb Wafayāt al-'a'yān*, ed. J. Sublet (Damascus 1974) p. 62 ff. I gave a translation of this text in my *History of the Jews in Egypt and in Syria under the Mamluks III* (Jerusalem, 1970), p. 149f. The date given there should be corrected, as from *Sulūk* I, p. 585 it is seen that the sultan came to Damascus on Rabī' II 668 (December 23, 1269) (and not in 1270).

(d. 1387) one reads that the government had no more sugar factories and that the latter restored them to it.[99] That means that in the years before Barqūq's accession to the throne the factories of the sultan had been sold or rented, fully or partly. The author of the chronicle speaks indirectly in the passage preceding this statement about the farming out of the sultan's revenues according to certain percentages, fifty fifty etc., and goes on to say that in the days of this vizier all these arrangements were abolished. Sapienti sat.

Corruption was one consequence of the suppression of free competition; the aversion to technological innovations was another. When there was no more free competition, or the competition had been very much weakened, there was indeed no need to improve production methods. The managers did not feel that it was necessary to invest money in experiments, when the confectioners and other retailers were forced to buy the products of a more or less monopolistic industry.

d) TECHNOLOGICAL STAGNATION

In the second half of the thirteenth century and until the end of the fourteenth century, the technological level of the Near Eastern sugar industry was relatively high. It was by no means lower than that of the sugar industries in South European countries. Syrian specialists were renowned and taught their methods in Cyprus until the second half of the fifteenth century.[100] That the Syrian sugar production served as a model for the sugar industry of Cyprus is borne out by the fact that some of its products were offered as "Damascus sugar made in Cyprus" (*domaschini di Cipri*).[101] Then, there is the well known story told by Marco Polo about Egyptian sugar refiners who taught their methods in China in the second half of the thirteenth century.[102]

When the pressure brought upon the bourgeois-owned sugar industry in Egypt and in Syria became really crushing, certain technological innovations were made by sugar-makers in Cyprus, in Sicily, and perhaps in Spain. Of course, it is almost impossible to establish the date of these innovations. The date of inventions has seldom come down to us. Often one must be content with circumstantial evidence.

There is good reason to believe that at the beginning of the fifteenth century oxen were no longer used for operating the sugar mills in Christian countries. Probably they had already been replaced by horses and water-power in the

[99] *Nuzhat al-nufūs* I, p. 161.

[100] J.M.-J.-L. de Mas Latrie, *Histoire de l'île de Chypre sous le règne des princes de la maison de Lusignan* (Paris 1855–61) III, p. 219.

[101] Uzzano, p. 101 (chapter on Genoa).

[102] *The Book of Ser Marco Polo*, transl. H. Yule (London 1920/21) II, p. 226.

sugar mills of Sicily and Cyprus. The substitution of horses for oxen, which was made possible by the introduction of the new stiff collar, was one of the major innovations in the history of mediaeval agriculture of Europe and meant great progress. The mediaeval horse was stronger than ours, it could work more in a day and moved more rapidly than oxen. French writers of the sixteenth century reckoned that a horse did as much work in one day as three or four oxen.[103] As far as the sugar mills of Palermo are concerned it is explicitely said in a 1418 travelogue that horses were used.[104] Another important innovation was the introduction of the so-called "*trappeto*". This innovation is ascribed to Pietro Speciale who supposedly made it in the year 1449, in Ficarazzi, Sicily. The *trappeto* was an adaptation of an ancient Roman press. It consisted of three cylinders, lying or standing, with a small intervening space. The sugar cane was pushed between the first and the second cylinders in one direction and between the second and the third cylinders in the opposite direction. The cylinders themselves were thrown into gear by a water-wheel. Compared with the old sugar mills the rolling by the *trappeto*, whose pressure was lighter, was more effective and cheaper. It is, however, certain that even before Speciale the Sicilian sugar producers used a press of this kind or a press of wood whose pressure was lighter. A notarial act drawn up in Palermo on December 5, 1427, reads as follows: *Faryonus Malti iudeus locavit operas suas... Philippo de Nuglacio. ...eius trappetto... coquendi zuccarum... ad faciendum ignem... tornelli trappetto...* .[105] This innovation was surely one of the reasons for the great upsurge of Sicily's sugar industry in the fifteenth century. Whereas Pegolotti, writing in the middle of the fourteenth century, does not mention Sicilian sugar, Giovanni da Uzzano, a hundred years later, included in his Merchants' Guide a special chapter about the export of sugar from Sicily to Venice.[106]

[103] Lynn White, *Medieval technology and social change* (Oxford 1965), p. 59ff.; B. H. Slicher van Bath, *The Agrarian History of Western Europe A. D.* 500–1850 (London 1963), p. 63f.; Ch. Parain, "The evolution of agricultural techniques", *Cambridge Econ. Hist. of Europe I* (Cambridge 1966), p. 144.

[104] *Voyaige d'oultremer en Ihérusalem par le Seigneur de Caumont*, ed. Marquis de la Grange (Paris 1858), p. 117.

[105] Lippmann, p. 338;F. M. Feldhaus, *Die Maschine im Leben der Völker* (Basel 1954) f. 44a. Pietro Speciale was a high ranking official in Palermo in the middle of the fifteenth century, see Vincenzo di Giovanni, *La topografia antica di Palermo* (Palermo 1889/90) I, p. 327. Perhaps it was he who introduced the invention made by another sugar producer in the sugar presses of Palermo and other towns. p. 186 f.; Arch. di Stato Palermo, Notai 823, Aprea, Nicolo. See also C. Trasselli. La canna da zucchero nell'agro palermitano nel sec. XV, (in) *Annali della acoltà di economia e commercio*, Univ. di Palermo VII (1953), no. 1, p. 120ff.

[106] Uzzano, p. 195 (chapter 82); C. Trasselli, "Produzione e commercio dello zucchero dal XIII al XIX secolo", (in) *Economia e storia III* (1955), p. 333f.

But the Egyptian and Syrian sugar industries were sticking to their old methods. Al-Nuwayrī says that sugar mills in Syria were operated by water or oxen. Sometimes, according to him, wooden stamps were used. Speaking of the Egyptian sugar-presses, he mentions only oxen as driving power.[107] So most of the cane produce was pressed by mills put into gear by oxen. This is a conclusion borne out by other reliable evidence. Both an Arabic writer of the end of the twelfth century and two Western pilgrims who visited Egypt at the end of the fifteenth century bear witness to it.[108] The conservatism of the Levantine sugar makers was in keeping with the attitude of the agriculturists who likewise did not change the ox for the horse; as in the many centuries before, they ploughed with oxen.[109]

The difference between the old methods used in Syria and Egypt and, on the other hand, the new methods used in Christian (or semi-Christian) countries emerges clearly from some figures given in texts and documents, which contain data about the output of the sugar production in Egypt, Syria, and Cyprus.

Al-Nuwayrī says in one passage that in Egypt 24,000 raṭl *layṭī* juice of the sugar cane yield 15–25 qinṭār "*qand*" (raw sugar) and 8–12 qinṭār syrup (*'asal*).[110] That would mean that 14,400 kg juice yielded 1350–2250 kg raw

[107] VIII, p. 268, 271 (translated by Wiedemann, *Aufsätze II*, p. 140, 143).

[108] Ibn Mammātī, K. *Qawānīn al-dawāwīn* (Cairo 1943), p. 367 l. 3; Ioos van Ghistele, *Tvoyage*, p. 150; *Pilgerfahrt des Ritters Arnold von Harff* (Köln 1860), p. 83. Cf. however below p. 96 and note 266.

[109] *al-Xiṭaṭ* I, p. 42.

[110] P. 271. *Qand* sometimes means candy, but in other passages (like this one) — raw sugar; s. Ibn Sīda, *al-Muxaṣṣaṣ* (Cairo 1316–21) V, p. 3: *al-qand 'aṣīr qaṣab al-sukkar*. A *raṭl layṭī* (not "*Latin*" *raṭl* as translated Wiedemann II, p. 142) corresponds according to Hinz, *Islamische Masse u. Gewichte*, p. 29, to 620 gr. The equivalents given in the various Italian Merchants' Guides differ very much. Pegolotti p. 74 has the equation 1 *raṭl layṭī* — 193 *libbre sottili* of Venice (0,581 kg), Zibaldone da Canal p. 69: 1 *qinṭār ǧarwī* — 156 *raṭl layṭī* (0,577 kg), Uzzano p. 110: 1 *raṭl layṭī* — 170 *libbre sottili* of Venice (0,512 kg) and *Libro di mercatantie*, p. 101 contradictory equations, which point to an equivalent of 203 *libbre sottili* of Venice (0,611 kg) and others indicating 0,621 and 0,558 kg. So one would probably not be wrong in concluding that this raṭl was equal to 0,6 kg. The sugar was weighed in *qinṭār ǧarwī*, s. Ibn Mammātī, p. 361. This qinṭār was according to Hinz ibid. the equivalent of 96,7 kg (100 *raṭl ǧarwī*, cf. op. cit. p. 25). This equation is borne out by a price list in the Datini archives, dated Alexandria, July 24, 1386. There one reads that a *qinṭār ǧarwī* is the equivalent of 322 *libbre sottili* of Venice. But Pegolotti l.c. says that it was equal to 300–301 *libbre sottili* of Venice that means about 90 kg. The same equation (300 *libbre sottili*) is to be found in Zibaldone da Canal p. 69 and in G. d. P., *Sent*. 129, f. 153a ff. The indications of Uzzano p. 110 (318 *libbre sottili*), *Libro di mercatantie* p. 99 (316 *libbre sottili*) p. 141 (300 pounds Genoa) and Tariffa (Venice 1925), p. 28, 61 (312 *libbre sottili* of Venice) would however indicate 0.95 kg for the *raṭl ǧarwī*. Apparently most Italian sources give us information about the real equivalent, whereas the Arabic sources (quoted by Hinz) give the equation according to Muslim law.

sugar and 720–1080 kg syrup. From another passage in al-Nuwayrī's work we learn that in Syria a qinṭār of raw sugar yielded 5/12 boiled sugar and 7/12 molasses (*quṭāra*).[111] This was a very small output, as compared with the white sugar obtained in the sugar factories of Cyprus at the end of the fifteenth century. There, 2000 quintals of white sugar had as a by-product 250 quintals "*zamburri*" (waste-material) and 250 quintals molasses.[112] Surely there is no reason to believe that from the days of al-Nuwayrī till the end of the fifteenth century the output of Levantine sugar boilers had increased. A statement of al-Maqrīzī tallies very well with another account of al-Nuwayrī. For al-Nuwayrī reports that a feddan yields 600 qinṭār *qand* and molasses and 120 qinṭār syrup.[113] Al-Maqrīzī, on the other hand, says that a feddan yields 40–80 sugar loaves, each of 9 qinṭārs approximately.[114] So the average output would have been 60 loaves, corresponding to 540 qinṭārs (against the 600 indicated by al-Nuwayrī).

e) SUGAR PRICES

Whereas neither the production methods nor the quality improved, the prices of Levantine sugar rose considerably from the end of the fourteenth century. This rise of the sugar prices was the consequence of the general rise in wages, itself a result of the shortage of labour subsequent to the Black Death and other epidemics in the second half of the fourteenth century. The development of sugar prices is clearly indicated by the data found in Arabic and in Italian sources, scarce though they are. As we have found many more notes about the prices of sugar in Egypt, a table comprising these data will be given first.[115]

111 P. 272.

112 De Mas Latrie p. 297.

113 P. 271. In order to make this passage agree with what the author had said before about the proportion of sugar (*qand*) and syrup, viz. 2: 1, one must suppose that in this latter passage (which is in fact in the text the preceding one) he has reckoned the molasses to the syrup. That he speaks in one passage of *raṭl layṭī* and in the other (dealing with the yield of a feddan) of *raṭl miṣrī* (of 450 g) must not be considered as a contradiction. The juice of the sugar cane was weighed in *raṭl layṭī*, the sugar itself in *raṭl ğarwī* (to be corrected from *miṣrī*).

114 *al-Xiṭaṭ* I, p. 102f.

115 The prices of candy are those of a so-called "Egyptian" qinṭār (of 45 kg), the other — of the *qinṭār ğarwī*, s. note 113. The indication of Ibn Mammātī saying that sugar is weighed in *qinṭār ğarwī* is corroborated by the price lists in the Datini archives where all kinds of sugar besides candy are enumerated under the heading of Merchandise weighed in *qinṭār ğarwī*.

The sources most often quoted and abbreviated are the following: *Lettere di mercanti a Pignol Zucchello* (1336–1350), ed. R. Morozzo della Rocca (Venice 1957); Badr al-dīn al-'Aynī, *'Iqd al-ğumān*, MS. Istanbul Čarullah 1591; Ibn Qāḍī Šuhba, *al-I'lām bi-ta'rīx al-islām*, MS. Paris 1599; al-Maqrīzī, *Iğāṭat al-umma* (Cairo 1940).

When the kind of sugar is not specified in the source (and we have classified it by conjecture according to the prices) a small circle has been added before the figure (both in this and in the following table).

If there is no other indication, the prices in Cairo are given.

Among the prices listed in this table those quoted from al-Maqrīzī's works are perhaps the most characteristic of the general development. They show that the prices of sugar went down in the middle and the second half of the fourteenth century. The data in the letters to Pignol Zucchello refer to a period of dearth. The same is true for the report in a Venetian source about the sugar price in 1394: it was a year in which Egypt suffered from a dearth and the prices of all victuals were exceptionally high. In the first two decades of the fifteenth century, prices rose again and even much more than in 1345–1347. The reports of al-Maqrīzī about living cost in 1405 and that of al-ʿAynī about prices in the year 1415 show that sugar prices were very high at the beginning of the fifteenth century. They had risen from the end of the thirteenth century by 200 % and even more. The prices noted in Italian sources from the years 1418, 1422–24, 1435 and before 1440 are in keeping with these data. If Barsbay forcibly bought the sugar at 16 2/3 dinars a qinṭār, he sold it at 18 or 20 at least. The price at which it was sold by the retailers was certainly higher.

The information on the development of sugar prices in Mamluk Syria points to the same trend. (See table 7 on page 252.)

As far as the price of sugar in Syria under the first Mamluks is concerned, unfortunately we have no exact information. Ibn Faḍlallāh al-ʿUmarī says simply that sugar "is more expensive in Syria".[116] Probably this statement does not imply a very great difference. So one is perhaps not mistaken in supposing that in the second half of the thirteenth century a Damascus qinṭār of simple sugar cost 18–20 dinars, twice-boiled sugar (*domaschino*) 22–25 dinars, and refined sugar — about 30 dinars. The data we have collected from the price lists in the Datini archives show that in the first twenty years of the fifteenth century a qinṭār of *domaschino* cost 90–120 ducats (i.e. 75–100 dinars) and later 50 ašrafīs. So the price had been doubled at least. The data from the middle and the second half of the fifteenth century point clearly to the fact that in this period sugar was cheaper in Syria than in Egypt. Whereas according to Giovanni da Uzzano, twice-boiled sugar cost 35 ašrafīs[117] in Egypt, the same quality cost only 25 in Syria. This difference in prices probably shows that the economic decline in Syria was greater than in Egypt. Wages were lower and accordingly so were prices. This conclusion would be in keeping with other facts, which point to the same phenomenon.[118]

116 *Ṣubḥ* IV, p. 182.

117 He gives this figure as the average price of sugar and, on the other hand, the price of "*babilonio*" lies in the middle between the prices of refined and "Egyptian" sugar. If the data in Uzzano's price list from Alexandria are really given in canonical dinars (and not in ašrafīs because dating from the years before 1425) the difference would have been much greater.

118 S. *Histoire des prix et des salaires*, p. 400.

TABLE 6:
Sugar prices in Mamluk Egypt

Date	Refined (*Mukarrar*)	*Caffettino*	*Babilonio*	*Musciatto*	Egypt.	Candy	Source
Second half of 13th cent.[119] 1301	12,5 din.				7,5 din.		Ibn Faḍlallāh in *Ṣubḥ* III. p. 447
						Cattle plague:10 din.	Baybars al-Manṣūrī, Br. Mus. 1233 f. 233a
1344	°10 din.						*Xiṭaṭ* II, p. 231
Feb. 1345, Alexandria		40 din.					Zucchello p. 33
Aug. 1347 "		24–27 din.					Op. cit. p. 87
Sept. 1347 "		27 din.	23 din.				Op. cit. p. 88
Sept. 1347 "			24 din.[120]				Op. cit. p. 104
Nov. 1347 "		25–26 din.	23 "				Op. cit. p. 109
Dec. 1347 "		26 din.	23 "				Op. cit. p. 110
Dec. 1347 "		26 "	23 "				Op. cit. p. 111
Second half of 14th cent.[121] 1384	12 din.				°6,4 din.		*Sulūk* III, p. 1104;
						40 duc.	*Xiṭaṭ* II, p. 99
							Gucci p. 153
24 July 1386 Alexandria			50 "	40 din.			Melis, Doc., p. 320[122]
1394 "	°65 duc.						Cecchetti, Arch. Ven. 30, p. 75ff.
Sept. 1394 "					°24 din.		Ibn al-Furāt IX p. 399[123]
Sept. 1395 "					°20 "		Op. cit. p. 416
Feb. 1396 "			55 "	55 "			Datini 1175
Feb. 1403 "	33 din.						al-ʿAynī f. 669b
							Sulūk III, p. 1104
March 1404 "	Dearth, 55 din.						Op. cit. f. 674b
15 April 1404 "	°60 din.						*Sulūk* III, p. 1123
Spring 1404	°70 "						Ibn Qāḍī *Šuhba* f. 216a
June 1404	°80 din.[124]						Ibidem

1405	°46,6 din.				*Iġāṯa* p. 78[125]
March 1414 ”		40 ”	35 ”		Arch. B. Dolfin 180, fasc. 14
April 1415 ”	38 ”				al-ʿAynī f. 736b
Jan. 1418 ”		40 ”	28 ”		Arch. L. Dolfin
Febr. 1418 ”		40 ”	30 ”		Melis, Doc., p. 320
Febr. 1422 ”		40 ”	30 ”		Arch. L. Dolfin
May 1422 ”		40 ”	30 ”		Ibidem
Febr. 1423 ”		40 ”	35 ”		Ibidem
July 1423 ”		40 ”	30 ”		Ibidem
Aug. 1423 ”		40 ”	30 ”		Ibidem
Dec. 1423 ”				Barsbay buys at 16.6 din.	*Sulūk* IV, p. 654[126]
March 1424 ”		40 ”	30 ”		Arch. L. Dolfin
Aug. 1435 ”				°17,75 duc.[127]	Nic. Turiano V. f. 61b.
before 1440[128] ”		35 din.[129]			Uzzano p. 111
1492				Low prices: 9 ašr.	Saxāwī, *Ḏayl*, Bodl. 853, f. 207a

119 Ibn Faḍlallāh al-ʿUmarī (d. 1349) wrote his *al-Taʿrīf* in 1340, s. Brockelmann *GAL*[2] II, p. 178, but what he says about prices probably refers to the second half of the thirteenth century.

120 The writer of this letter gives the price of sugar as half *caffetino* half *babilonio*.

121 al-Maqrīzī says in the passage quoted from *al-Xiṭaṭ*: when I was young, sugar cost 170 dirhams, and he was born in 1364; in the other passage (in the *Sulūk*) he says that before the great crisis at the beginning of the fifteenth century refined sugar cost 309 dirhams.

122 From Datini 1171.

123 For this and the following prices quoted from Arabic sources s. my paper "L'évolution des prix dans le Proche-Orient à la basse-époque," *JESHO* IV (1961) p. 32, where the items are given as found in the sources.

124 The Arabic author says: Egyptian sugar (1 raṭl) 80 dirh., Syrian 55. But there can be little doubt that he means "refined sugar".

125 French translation: G. Wiet, *Le traité des famines de Maqrīzī* (Leiden 1962), p. 78.

126 The quotation of this text by Darrag p. 147 is mistaken. One reads there: *wa maʿa ḏālika fa al-nās fī ḍīq min al-ḥaǧr ʿala al-sukkar wa al-imtināʿ min bayʿihi ʾillā li-l-sulṭān bi-arbaʿat ālāf dirham al-qinṭār*.

127 "White sugar of Egypt" sold by a Christian merchant to the chemist Bernardus Rochalonza of Rhodes.

128 This year is given at the end of the book, but many of the prices and other data given in some chapters are undoubtedly those of an earlier date.

129 "*di piú sorte*". The author says "bis." (*bisanti*, i.e. dinars).

TABLE 7:

Sugar prices in Mamluk Syria[130]

Date	Refined	Damascus	Simple Candy	Source
Nov. 1379	1800 dirh.	1250 dirh.	2000 dirh.	Datini 1171
		30–32 duc.		Melis, Doc., p. 111
8 April 1386		°2000 dirh.	3600 ”	Datini 1175
1 Sept. 1386		1300 ”	2400 ”	Melis, Doc., p. 318
Aug. 1394		°1800 ”	3400 ”	Datini 1171
23 Oct. 1394		2200 ”	2300 ”	Melis, *Aspetti*, p. 384
30 May 1395	2300 ”	2000 ”	4200 ”	Datini 1171
2 Aug. 1395		1800–2000 dirh.	3500–4000 dirh.	Melis, Doc., p. 184
		°1800 dirh.	3500 dirh.	Datini 1171
8 April 1396		2000 ”		Ibidem
15 Aug. 1398	2700 ”	2350 ”	3000 ”	Ibidem
15 Sept. 1398		1700 ”		Ibidem
14 Febr. 1399		°1400 ”	3000 ”	Ibidem
1399	°90 duc.			ROL IV, p. 228[131]
Febr. 1402		dearth: 3000 dirh.		Ibn Qāḍī *Šuhba* f. 196b
Jan. 1405	5500 dirh.			Op. cit. f. 216a
Nov. 1406, Beirut		°3200 dirh.	6000–7000 dirh.	Datini 1171[132]
26 March 1411		°4000 ”	6000 dirh.	Arch. A. Zane[133]
30 April 1411		°4300 ”	7000 ”	Ibidem
24 July 1411		90 duc.	200 duc.	Ibidem
14 April 1412		100 ”	150 ”	Ibidem
14 April 1413		110 ”	250 ”	Ibidem
8 June 1413		130 ”	200–250 duc.	Ibidem
16 Aug. 1413		110 ”	250 duc.	Ibidem
19 Oct. 1413		120 ”		Ibidem
14 April 1417		120 ”	250 ”	Ibidem
Without date (1420?)		80 ”	200 ”	Arch. L. Dolfin
Before 1440		50 ”	130 ”	Uzzano p. 114
Without date (1442 ?)			60 ”	L. Dolfin
(About) 1444,[134] Tripoli	°60 duc.			G. P., Sent. 106, f. 15b ff.
1459, Tripoli	70 duc. (approximately)			Same series 130, f. 45b ff.
June 1481		°25 ashr.		Ibn Ṭūlūn, *Mufākaha* I p. 41

130 All prices are those of a Damascus qinṭār, equal, according to Hinz, p. 30, to 185 kg. But in many Italian sources one finds the equation 1 Damascene qinṭār — 600 *libbre sottili* of Venice, s. Tariffa p. 26, 64; G. d. P., Sent. 19, f. 66a f., 114, f. 75a 181, f. 123a, 186, f. 75b f. Often even smaller quantities of Venetian pounds are indicated as its equivalent, see Sami-

To estimate the impact of the technological innovations it would be useful to know how they influenced the prices of Cyprus and Sicilian sugar, as compared with Levantine sugar.

TABLE 8:

Prices of Cyprus sugar[135]

Date	Thrice-boiled	Twice-boiled	Once-boiled	Powdered	Source
Nov. 1404			45 duc.		ASV Notai 222, Ant. de Vataciis sub 12 Nov. 1404
26 Aug. 1428			21.4 duc.		Nicolo Turiano IV, f. 75a[136]
1445–1448				18 duc., 16 asp. of Rhodes	de Mas Latrie III, p. 27
26 Apr. 1464				25–35 duc.	Op. cit. III, p. 88ff.
13 Aug. 1464	100–120 duc.				Op. cit. III, p. 220
3 March 1468		70 duc.			Op. cit. III, p. 248f.
5 Oct. 1468			36 duc.		Op. cit. III, p. 231f.
1476		100 duc.			Röhricht, *Deutsche Pilgerreisen*, p. 170[137]

niato de' Ricci, *Il manuale di mercatura* (Genoa 1963), p. 120; *Libro di mercatantie*, p. 147. So it must have been 180 kg.

Some items listed in my *Histoire des prix et des salaires dans l'Orient médiéval*, (Paris 1969) p. 405 have been omitted here as they refer to dates close to those for which information is given here and there were no great changes in the prices. Further I abstain from quoting here some sugar prices in Northern Syria, s. in my book p. 404.

131 S. supra note 90.

132 Another copy of this document has for the candy 6000–7500.

133 ASV Procuratori di S. Marco, Commissarie miste, Ba 128a.

134 The item is quoted in a lawsuit of 1447.

135 The ducats, which are not specified, seem to be Venetian sequins.

136 The notorial act refers to Cyprus sugar sold by the ambassador of the king of Cyprus in Alexandria (as his commercial agent).

137 This item is quoted from the account presented to duke Albrecht of Saxony, who visited Jerusalem in 1476, by the patron of the pilgrim's galley Andrea Contarini. It has been published by R. Röhricht in his *Deutsche Pilgerreisen nach dem Heiligen Lande* (Gotha 1889), p. 170, where the price has been misunderstood. The text reads: *Item propter damnum zuchar-*

From this table it can be seen that once-boiled sugar of Cyprus was cheaper than Egyptian and Syrian, while twice-boiled, and probably thrice-boiled, fetched the same price as Egyptian, but it cost more than in Syria.

TABLE 9:

Prices of Sicilian sugar[138]

Date	Twice-boiled	Once-boiled	Source
1413–1424		17.5 fl.	Trasselli, art. cit., p. 334
Before 1440	25–30 fl.	16–18 fl.	Uzzano, p. 165
		17 fl.	Op. cit. p.195
		15–17.5 fl.	Op. cit. p. 94
1425–1441		sold in Genoa: more than 20 fl.	Trasselli l. c.
1481		more than 20 fl.	Ibidem

These data show that the price of Sicilian sugar, both once-boiled and twice-boiled, was the same as that of Egyptian sugar, but higher than Syrian.

orum candium et zucharorum duarum cotarum..., cantara sex, constat quoddam cantarium ducatos centum, quod ascendit unum cantarium ad libras octingentas ex nostris libris ad subtile, que constant dictae duc. duodecim pro centenario et simul cum expensis plus quam ducati XVII, et faciunt revendita Venetiis ducatos XI pro centenario et passus sum in damno ducatos 5 pro centenario quod ascendens dictum damnum in ducatis trecentis.

The content of the account is clear, but it may be that the text which Röhricht used was faulty (besides the passage which he has misinterpreted).

The patron claims the loss sustained from the purchase of 6 quintals of sugar bought in Cyprus and later sold in Venice. That the sugar was bought in Cyprus results from the equation 1 quintal — 800 *libbre sottili.* The equivalent of the quintal of Famagusta was indeed, according to the Merchants' Guides 750–775 *libbre sottili,* s. Pegolotti p. 97, *Libro di mercatantie* p. 67, Zibaldone da Canal p. 555 (this latter has 496 *libbre grosse* of Venice). The patron had paid for 100 Venetian pounds 12 ducats and with "expense" 17. But Röhricht has read instead of "*que constant... ex primo* (when bought) *ducatos duodecim*" — *ducentos duodecim*! As the patron has sold them in Venice for 11 ducats the 100 pounds, he had lost 6 and accordingly for 6 quintals, according to the equation 1 quintal — 800 libbre, 6×48=288 ducats. So he claims 300. The passage where one reads "*et passus sum in damno ducatos* 5" must be faulty and probably be corrected to "*ducatos* 6"!

However that may be, the text refers to the price of Cyprus sugar and not to Syrian sugar, as Lippmann believed, op. cit., p. 714.

138 In quintals of Palermo, which were equal to 230 pounds of Florence, s. Uzzano p. 94. Therefore 1 quintal corresponded to 78 kg. (Trasselli p. 341 calculates, however, according to an equivalent of 80 kg.)

The following table sums up the comparison of sugar prices in these four countries.

TABLE 10:
Average prices of sugar produced in Egypt and Syria, compared with Cyprus and Sicilan sugar

	Cyprus sugar (quintal of 226 kg)	Sicilian sugar (quintal of 78 kg)	Egypt. sugar (qinṭār of 90 kg)	Syrian sugar (qinṭār of 180 kg)
Once-boiled	30 duc.	16.25 duc.		
	Egypt. qinṭār at this price: 12 duc.	Egypt. qinṭār at this price: 18.9 duc.	18 duc.	
	Damas. qinṭār at this price: 24 duc.	Damas. qinṭār at this price: 37.8 duc.		25 duc.
Twice-boiled	85 duc.	27.5 duc.		
	Egypt. qinṭār at this price: 33.8 duc.	Egypt qinṭār at this price: 31.68 duc.	35 duc.	
	Damas. qinṭār at this price: 67.6 duc.	Damas. qinṭār at this price: 63.36 duc.		50 duc.
Thrice-boiled	110 duc.			
	Egypt. qinṭār at this price: 43.74 duc.		45 duc.	
	Damas. qinṭār at this price: 87.5 duc.			

The consequences of the development of production prices in these and other regions which produced sugar are even more convincingly shown by the comparison of the prices they fetched on the international market (see table 11).

The archives of Francesco Datini contain many price lists from the great Western emporia and in some of them the prices of Levantine sugar appear together with those of Cyprus, Sicilian, and Spanish sugar. These data are compiled in Table 11. They show clearly, although the data are not numerous, that Cyprus sugar (see prices in Avignon in 1392), Sicilian sugar (s. prices in Pisa in 1405) and Spanish sugar were cheaper than Syrian sugar of all kinds (s. prices in Avignon in 1392, Paris 1395, Pisa in 1405). Even if a particular kind of Levantine sugar was a bit cheaper, the costs of transport (and the

TABLE 11:

Prices on the international sugar market at the end of the 14th and the beginning of the 15th century

Date	Ref. Lev. sugar (*muccaro*)	Dam.	*babil.*	*musciatto*	Malaga sugar 3 boil.	Malaga sugar 2 boil.	Malaga sugar 1 boil.	Sicilian sugar 3 boil.	Sicilian sugar 2 boil.	Lump sugar 1 boil.	Lump sugar Dam.	Lump sugar Mal.	Powdered sugar Dam.	Powdered sugar Mal.	Powdered sugar Cyp.	Source
Barcelona Dec. 1383 1 carrega[a]	80 liv.	65 liv.[b]	70 liv.							52	1				25–30 liv.	Melis, Doc., p. 312,
Avignon Aug. 1392 1 quintal[c]	180 fl.[d]	166–170 fl.	125–130 fl.	120 fl.									80 fl.		45–72 fl.	Heers, Com., p. 162
Paris 29 Dec. 1395 1 lb.[e]		9 s.	7 s.		7 s.	6 s.					7 s.	5 s. 2 d.				Melis, Doc., p. 312
Genoa 1396 100 lb.		45 liv.[f]		34 liv.												Op. cit., p. 304
Pisa 27 Aug. 1405 100 lib.[g]		26–28 fl.			24–26 fl.	23–24 fl.	17–18 fl.	24–27 fl.	13–15 fl.							Op. cit., p. 306

a) According to Pegolotti p. 224, 416 Genoese pounds, but Uzzano p. 108, and *Libro di mercatantie* p. 112f. have 390. So a carrega would be about 126,7 kg. Cl. Carrère, Barcelone (Paris 1967) I, p. 95 has 123 kg.
b) 11 shilling were equal to 1 fl. of Aragon, s. Carrere II, p. 705. So a carrega *damaschino* amounted to 118 fl. of Aragon (1/5 less than the gold coin of Florence).
c) A quintal of Avignon corresponded to 120 pounds of Pisa, this latter being equal to that of Florence i.e. 339 gr. s. *Libro di mercatantie*, p. 105. Thus 3 quintals were 122 kg.
d) The French fl. was worth 1/7 less than the Florentine gold piece.
e) S. *Libro di mercatantie* p. 131.
f) 1.25 Genoese pounds were equal to a gold piece (Genovino) or a ducat, s. C. M. Cipolla, *Studi di storia della moneta* (Pavia 1948), p. 42. So 45 pounds — 36 Genovini.
g) S. note c.

greater profits of the merchants) raised its price so much that it was more expensive than Cyprus, Sicilian, or Spanish sugar. Secondly, these price lists belong to the period preceding the technological innovations of the fifteenth century and the great economic crisis in Egypt and Syria at its beginning. So there can be little doubt that in this later period the Levantine industries could no longer compete on the international market with the European sugar. Consequently Cyprus could export considerable quantities of its sugar to Venice, Florence, Ancona, and other Western emporia. At the beginning of the fifteenth century there was a sugar fair in Cyprus every year in the fall.[139] Sicily supplied sugar to all trading towns of Italy[140] and even Spanish sugar was exported from Cadiz, Malaga, and Majorca to Genoa, Pisa (s. Table 11), and France.[141] From the great commercial centres of Italy all these different kinds of sugar were shipped to Flanders and to England or sent by land to Germany.[142]

f) DECLINE OF LEVANTINE SUGAR PRODUCTION IN THE FIFTEENTH CENTURY

Everyone who studies documents in Italian archives concerning the Levantine sugar trade in the fifteenth century will be a bit confused at first. There are many documents that refer to the import of European sugar to the Near East, while others speak of the export of Levantine sugar to Europe. But in fact different kinds of sugar are spoken of.

The production of sugar in the Near East was not suspended altogether by the end of the Middle Ages. Its volume had diminished very greatly, but in several regions the sugar cane was still grown and good sugar produced.

The Venetian ambassador Giosafat Barbaro, who visited Iraq and Persia in

139 ASV Senato, Mar IV, f. 118b V, f. 43b, 91a; G. d. P., *Sent.* 28, f. 26b f. 142, f. 43a 180, f. 171a; Giudici di petiziòn, *Terminazioni* VII, f. 71a; C. Müller, *Documenti sulle relazioni delle città toscane coll'Oriente cristiano e coi Turchi* (Florence 1879) p. 359; Archivio di Stato, Florence, Mar, fasc. V, f. 63a; Statutes "del mar, del tersenale e della dogana" of Ancona of the fourteenth century, (in) E. Spadolini, *Il Commercio, le arti e la loggia de' mercanti in Ancona* (Portocivitanova 1904), p. 16f. At least a part of the sugar bought by the Genoese in Chios was probably Cyprus sugar, s. ASG *Car. vet.* 1552, f. 49b, 132b f.; Melis, *Documenti*, p. 312; Uzzano p. 23, 82, 95; *Libro di mercatantie*, p. 142. Jorga, Notes et extraits, *ROL* V (1897), p. 327.

140 Du Cange VIII, 434b; G. d. P., *Sent.* 90, f. 130b 126, f. 81b; ASG *Car. Vet.* 1553, f. 60a, 60b, 67b; M. E. Mallett, *The Florentine galleys* (Oxford 1967) p. 119, 120 cp. p. 71; Uzzano p. 95, 191; *Libro di mercatantie* p. 113.

141 Uzzano p. 191; Melis, *Documenti*, p. 306, 312, ASG *Car. vet.* 1556 f. 27a, 28a, 47a ff.

142 Melis, *Documenti*, p. 314; K.O.Müller, *Welthandelsbräuche* (1480–1540) (Wiesbaden 1962), p. 35, 38, 183; ASV Senato, Mar V, f. 129b, 134b; ASG *Car. Vet.* 1552, f. 61a.

1473–79, praises the sugar of Baghdad and the products made of it. He says that they are exported to Persia and elsewhere.[143] In the Jordan valley, near Jericho, sugar was grown at the end of the fifteenth century as before.[144] In the fifteenth century sugar growing was even developed in some districts of Egypt where plantations had not existed before. That happened in the province of Guerga, where Barqūq had settled Beduins of the Hawwāra tribe. According to al-Maqrīzī, the second successor of the chieftain who had been sent there by Barqūq planted sugar cane and founded factories. So it must have been in the first half of the fifteenth century.[145] Both in the Western and the Eastern provinces of the Delta there were extensive sugar plantations in the fifteenth century. Several European travellers and other authors mention the plantations on the banks of the Western arm of the Nile, near Rosetta and Fūwa.[146] That Fūwa was a centre of sugar production is also known from an Arabic inscription, dating from the year 1413. Its subject is the abolishment of a tax that had been imposed on the sugar factories.[147] The sugar plantations in the district of Damietta, at the mouth of Eastern branch of the Nile, are mentioned in several Arabic sources of the fifteenth century,[148] as well as by the Spanish traveller Pero Tafur.[149] An Arabic writer of this period says that in Damietta a great quantity of sugar is produced and that it is exported to many countries.[150] A Christian author, Emanuel Piloti of Crete, who wrote in 1420, speaks of the sugar cane grown on the land between the two branches of the Nile.[151]

But all these accounts of sugar plantations and factories should not mislead us. The sugar production of Syria and of Egypt had considerably

[143] *I viaggi in Persia degli ambasciatori veneti Barbaro e Contarini*, ed. Lockhart-Morozzo della Rocca-Tiepolo (Rome 1973), p. 148.

[144] F. Fabri, *Evagatorium in Terram Sanctam, Arabiae et Aegypti peregrinationes*, ed. Hassler (Stuttgart 1843–49) II, p. 50.

[145] *El-Macrizi's Abhandlung über die in Aegypten eingewanderten arabischen Stämme*, ed. Wüstenfeld (Göttingen 1847), p. 36.

[146] *Travel of Meshullam of Volterra* (in Hebrew), ed. A. Ya'arī (Jerusalem 1949), Joos Van Ghistele, *Tvoyage*, p. 205; *Pilgerfahrt des Ritters Arnold von Harff*, p. 83; Leo Africanus, *Description de l'Afrique* (Lyon 1556), p. 343, 344; Jean Thenaud, *Le voyage d'outremer*, ed. Schefer (Paris 1884) p. 33.

[147] G. Wiet, "Décrets mamlouks d'Egypte", (in) *L. A. Mayer Memorial Volume* (Jerusalem 1964), p. 134.

[148] Ibn Ḥağar, *Inbā'* III, p. 512, 514; Abū Bakr al-Badrī, *Rāḥat al-arwāḥ*, quoted by Fr. Rosenthal, *The Herb* (Leiden 1971), p; 79.

[149] *Travels and adventures* 1435–1439, transl. M. Letts (London 1926), p. 68.

[150] Xalīl al-Ẓāhirī, *Zubdat kašf al-mamālik*, ed. Ravaisse (Paris 1894), p. 35 cf. p. 108.

[151] *Traité d'Emmanuel Piloti sur le passage en Terre Sainte*, ed. P. H. Dopp (Louvain 1958), p. 69.

declined by the beginning of the fifteenth century, or more exactly the diminution of factories had become much more sizable. In this period the factories of the bourgeois were not absorbed by those of emirs and sultans. So there was a total decrease in the production of sugar. In the chapter of his *Topography* that deals with the markets of Cairo, al-Maqrīzī speaks woefully of the sweetmeats' market in days bygone, when he was a child. "When these tribulations happened to us and the dearth of sugar owing to the ruin of the presses in Upper Egypt and the abandonment of the refineries in Fusṭāṭ, the confectionery diminished very much and those engaged in it passed away".[152] In a manuscript of the work, al-Maqrīzī has added the following remark to the passage dealing with the sugar boileries of Fusṭāṭ: "I have still seen a great number of these factories. They existed till the year 806 h. (1403/4) when these fateful events and civil wars began and they (the factories) were closed because of the deterioration of the government. There still remained eight. Then, in the year 1418, even these factories were destroyed and their untwisted parts were taken away under the management of Badr al-dīn Ḥasan b. Naṣrallāh, the director of the sultan's domain."[153] The sugar production in Syria must have declined too. For it is surely not by chance that al-Qalqašandī speaking of the sultan's sugar factories in Damascus uses the past tense.[154]

There is good reason to believe that those factories not closed in the fifteenth century produced mostly refined sugar and, though less, simple sugar. The production of simple (once-boiled) sugar had probably much decreased and that of twice-boiled even more, because the demand for these articles had become smaller both in Syria and Egypt. Just as few people belonging to the bourgeois classes could afford çostly textiles for their clothes, the number of the customers who bought these kinds of sugar had considerably diminished. The expensive "*mukarrar*" (thrice-boiled sugar), on the other hand, had never been intended for export, or at least only a very small part of the production had. A long time before the economic crisis of the Mamluk kingdom at the beginning of the fifteenth century Pegolotti writes that this expensive sugar is seldom exported to European countries: *del muccharo poco ne viene verso il Ponente, che quasi tutto si ritiene per la bocca, e per l'ostello del soldano.*[155] In the price lists of the Datini firm the rubrics of *mucchari* are mostly empty. It was not offered on the markets of Alexandria and Damascus. But when the Italian merchants succeeded in obtaining it, they bought it readily. For it

[152] *al-Xiṭaṭ* II, p. 99.

[153] P. Casanova, *Description historique et topographique de l'Egypte III* (Cairo 1906), p. 299 note 2.

[154] *Ṣubḥ* IV, p. 183.

[155] P. 362.

was still much esteemed by the Europeans and given to their rulers and ambassadors as gifts.[156]

So Levantine sugar still figures on the tariffs fixed by the Italian towns for the freights and the customs.[157] The proceedings of several litigations brought before the Giudici di petiziòn in Venice prove that these tariffs were established for practical purposes, they show that through the fifteenth century Venetian merchants exported sugar from Syria and from Egypt. [158] The Genoese too exported sugar from these countries in the fifteenth century. A document in the archives of Biegio Dolfin, Venetian consul in Alexandria, refers to such a transaction in the year 1418.[159] The records of Genoa's customs services comprise data concerning the export of sugar from Beirut via Chios to Genoa by several Genoese merchants, who transported their merchandise on the same ship. That shows that these records refer to quite normal shipments.[160]

But from some of the documents dealing with the export of sugar from Syria and Egypt to European countries in the fifteenth century, one must conclude that the quantities spoken of were very small.

On the other hand, one finds in the Italian archives not a few references to the import of sugar into the Muslim Near East. Italian merchants and others imported sugar into Egypt and Syria from Cyprus, Sicily, and perhaps from Spain. These documents leave no doubt as to the quality of the sugar: it was mostly cheap sugar, once-boiled sugar, powdered sugar, and molasses. These kinds of sugar were indeed cheaper in Southern Europe, because of the technological superiority of its industry, and, on the other hand, there were in the Muslim Near East many customers who could not afford refined sugar. So the import of European sugar to the Near East was the consequence of technological inferiority and impoverishment in the area.

156 S. Lippmann, op. cit., p. 324ff. and J. Wansbrough, "A Mamluk letter of 877/1473", *BSOAS* 24 (1961), p. 209 and Thenaud p. 181.

157 Venice: *Ordo navigii Sirie*, a. 1427 ASV Senato, Miste 56, f. 105a; duties to be paid to Piero Quirino appointed consul of Tripoli, a. 1442, Senato, Mar I, f. 125b; Florence: *Trattato di mercatura d'incerto*, MS. Laurenziana, *Acq. e doni* 13, a. 1422 p. 80. This text, which also contains dates of the fourteenth century, and the *Libro di gabelle* at the beginning of Uzzano's work supplement one another; see further the tariff of freights in Müller, *Documenti*, p. 358 f. (a document dating apparently from 1442, as in this year the tariff for freights to the West was also established).

158 G. d. P., *Sent.* 19, f. 56b ff cf. 32, f. 30b f. (a lawsuit in 1413) 106, f. 15b ff (export from Tripoli, a lawsuit in 1447) 121, f. 98a ff. (export from Tripoli, a lawsuit in 1456) 129, f. 153a ff. (export of sugar and candy from Alexandria in 1456–58) 137, 1 50b f. (candy from Damascus, a lawsuit in 1462) (neither in this text nor in that quoted in the first place is it clearly stated that the sugar was exported) 130, f. 45b ff. (export of thrice-boiled sugar from Tripoli in 1459).

159 Ba 181, fasc. 23 sub January 22, 1418.

160 ASG *Car. Vet.* 1553, f. 23a cf. 74a.

Venetian documents mention the import of molasses in Egypt in the years 1418, 1419, 1426, and 1427. In the documents from the year 1426 it is explicitely stated that the molasses came from Palermo.[161] A deed drawn up by a Venetian notary in Alexandria in 1428 deals with the import of sugar from Cyprus, sold for 8400 ducats, a very substantial sum.[162] The import of molasses into Alexandria in 1443 was the subject of a litigation brought before the Giudici di petiziòn in Venice. It was exchanged for spices.[163] The exchange of molasses imported by Venetians to Alexandria for pepper is dealt with in a law-suit before the same tribunal in 1445.[164] It should be emphasized that in several of these documents great quantities of sugar are spoken of. Sometimes Venetian merchants even imported refined sugar into Egypt. Such a case, probably rather exceptional in this period, is the subject of a law-suit in 1409.[165] The import of sugar to Syria in time became a matter the Venetian government had to deal with. In 1477, it decreed that every year a galley of the Beirut convoy, before going to Syria, should visit Tunisia to charge coral and then proceed to Cyprus and there charge sugar and powdered sugar.[166] Obviously, the Florentine and Genoese merchants shared in this profitable trade. They too imported sugar to Egypt and Syria.[167] A report quoted by Marino Sanuto mentions the import of 70 casse of sugar by Genoese merchants in Beirut in 1509.[168] The Italian merchants also imported sugar to other Muslim countries, e.g. Tunisia. A law-suit pleaded before the Giudici di petiziòn in Venice in 1458 had as its subject the import of "*zuchari e polvere*" into Tunisia.[169]

So in the second half of the fifteenth century, the revenge of Europe was complete. Those who had learnt from the Orientals the refining of sugar produced it better and cheaper, and the molasses was exported to the im-

161 Archives B. Dolfin, Ba 181, fasc. 23 (consolazi); G. d. P., *Sent.* 34, f. 37a ff. 48, f. 5a f. 54, f. 31b ff. cf. f. 34a ff., 36a ff.; Nicolo Turiano IV, f. 40a. ff. Molasses were cheap, see ibid.: 1 qinṭār 3.75–4.32 duc, and f. 23b ff.: 4.5 duc.

162 Nicolo Turiano IV, f. 74b. Powdered sugar was already being imported from Cyprus in 1394, see F. F. Melis, *Aspetti della vita economica medievale* (Siena 1962), p. 384. On the import of molasses from Cyprus s. also Piloti, op. cit., p. 158.

163 G. d. P., *Sent.* 96, f. 66a.

164 Same series 98 f. 117b ff. See also Piloti, op. cit. p. 147, 158 about the import of molasses from Sicily and Cyprus.

165 Same series 20, f. 20a f.

166 ASV Senato, *Incanti I*, f. 49b; Marino Sanuto, *Diarii V*, col. 944 on sugar and molasses *e altre cose solite a mandare in Soria* (a. 1503) (from Cyprus).

167 G. d. P., *Sent.* 54, f. 36a ff. (a. 1426); G. Müller, *Documenti*, p. 358 (tariff of freights fixed in 1460). M. Amari, *I diplomi arabi del R. archivo fiorentino*, p. 375. Even Ragusan merchants imported sugar into Egypt, s. B. Krekić, *Dubrovnik (Raguse) et le Levant au Moyen Age* (Paris 1961), p. no. 616 (a. 1415).

168 *Diarii X*, col. 95.

169 G. d. P., *Sent.* 129, f. 109a.

poverished Near East. But before the century was over the sugar industry had begun to flourish in Madeira, where the Portuguese had introduced it, and the product was incomparably superior to the Sicilian and Cyprus sugar. A Venetian author narrates how in August 1496 "*vine in questa terra de l'insula de Madera* 4 *caravele grosse di Portogal, con casse* 4000 *di zucari. Et è da saper come, da quatro in cinque anni in qua, ne era venute etiam di le altre caravele predetti, cossa insolita a vegnir di questa sorte, per esser sta nuovamente trovate*".[170] The author goes on relating that the Portuguese "*ne fano tanta quantità e di boni* (*sc. zucari*) *che empieno el levante e ponente, in modo che i zucari di Cipri, Alexandria, Soria, Damiata, Cecilia, Valenza e altri luoghi, sono reduti in vilissimo prezzo. Et in questa terra, da* 8 *in* 10 *anni in qua, ogni anno vien* 5 *over* 6 *nave, caravelle e barze da* 200 *fin* 500 *bote l'una, et fano grande abondantia*".[171] In another chapter the author quotes a letter written in January 1497 in Pera, according to which a Portuguese ship had brought 1700 casse of Madeira sugar.[172] In January 1499 he states that two Portuguese ships came to Venice with Madeira sugar worth 16,000 ducats. He says that as far as he knows it was sugar planted by the king of Portugal and intended for the Florentine merchant Matteo Cini.[173] A German Merchants' Guide from the first half of the sixteenth century confirms these reports: the German merchants bought Madeira sugar in Genoa.[174] The Portuguese even supplied England with their sugar.[175]

g) SOME REMARKS ABOUT THE DECLINE OF LEVANTINE TEXTILE INDUSTRIES[176]

It is a well known fact that there were flourishing textile industries in all Near Eastern countries until the end of the Crusader period and even later. Iraq produced precious silk fabrics, such as *siqlāṭūn* (silk interwoven with gold) and other brocades, filoselle (*xazz*), *'attābī* (a cotton stuff), carpets (in the Maysān province and in Upper Mesopotamia), woollen stuffs (in Takrīt and elsewhere). Syria had a renowned silk industry whose main centres were

170 That means that the islands had been recently discovered.
171 Marino Sanuto, *Diarii I*, col. 270f.
172 Op. cit. I, col. 916.
173 Op. cit. II, col. 333.
174 K. O. Müller, *Welthandelsbräuche*, p. 1777.
175 Op. cit. p. 84.
176 I have dealt with this subject extensively in lecture on "Les lainages dans l'Orient médiéval", published in *Produzione, commercio e consumo dei panni di lana, Atti della seconda settimana di studio*, Istituto Fr. Datini (Firenze 1976) p. 677 ff. In the notes for this lecture copious references to the sources are given.

Damascus, Gaza and Ascalon. Egypt was famous for its linen industry. In many towns and townlets of the Delta various kinds of excellent linen fabrics, such as white and coloured stuff, brocaded linen (*diqq*) and fine linen (*šarb, qaṣab*), embroidered and figured stuffs (*muwašša'*) were manufactured. Upper Egypt produced woolen stuffs, which were exported to other countries.

The flourishing of these industries came to an end in some regions in the first half of the thirteenth century, in others at the turn of the fourteenth century.

Tinnīs, the most important centre of Egypt's textile industry was evacuated and destroyed in 1227, owing to the danger of a Crusader occupation, and the workshops and factories were never opened again. Al-Maqrīzī and Ibn Duqmāq when speaking of Tinnīs and Damietta's industries use the past tense.[177] Other industrial towns of Lower Egypt, Tūna and Šaṭā for example, in the days of al-Maqrīzī were in ruins too.[178] Dabīq had probably ceased to be a centre of the textile industry before the end of the twelfth century, since Yāqūt, writing at the beginning of the thirteenth century, is not sure of its location.[179] Even the industries of Dīfū and Dumayra belonged, according to al-Maqrīzī, to the glories of the remote past.[180]

A second catastrophe befell the industries of Syria and of Egypt at the end of the fourteenth century and at the beginning of the fifteenth century. In the year 1401 Damascus was sacked and ruined by the Mongol invaders under the leadership of Tamerlane and, according to some Oriental chronicles, a great number of skilled workers were deported to Samarkand. Time and again one reads in modern works that a consequence of this deportation was that some industries of Damascus ceased to exist.[181] Al-Maqrīzī, on the other hand, includes in his chapter on the markets of the woolen stuffs in Cairo a very interesting account of the change of the habits of dress that took place in Egypt at the beginning of the fifteenth century. This market, called *al-ǧūxiyyīn*, was the place where *ǧūx*, i.e. European woollen fabric, was sold. The Arabic author says that in bygone days people belonging to the upper classes of society did not wear *ǧūx*. But at the beginning of the fifteenth century, when cloth (sc. Egyptian) became expensive, the Egyptians were compelled to change their habits and to use European woollen fabrics.[182] This account is supplemented by other evidence. Whereas at the end of the fourteenth century

177 *Sulūk* I, p. 224; *al-Xiṭaṭ* I, p. 177 l. 31ff., 181 l. 25ff.; Ibn Duqmāq V, p. 79.

178 *al-Xiṭaṭ* I, p. 181 l. 31f., 226 l. 13.

179 II, p. 548 cf. 546.

180 *al-Xiṭaṭ* I, p. 177 l. 35, 226.

181 Ph. K. Hitti, *History of the Arabs,* 7th ed. (London 1960), p. 701.

182 *al-Xiṭaṭ* II, p. 98.

Alexandria still had 12–14,000 looms, in 1434 there were no more than 800.[183]

But were the Crusader invasion of 1227, the occupation of Damascus by Tamerlane, and the economic crisis in Egypt in 1404 really the reasons for the decline of Levantine textile industries? Is it not reasonable to suppose that the factories of Tinnīs would have been re-opened after the retreat of the Crusaders, perhaps elsewhere, if they had been profitable? Is it not a well documented fact that a massive import of European textiles, mainly woollen fabrics, into the Near East had begun in the thirteenth century, a long time before the crisis of 1404?[184] And is it true that the textile industries of Damascus no longer existed in the fifteenth century? Both the writings of European and Arabic authors of the end of the Middle Ages would contradict such a supposition.

In fact, the decline of the Near Eastern textile industries resulted from a great change in social and economic conditions in this part of the world and, first of all, from the technological stagnation.

In the flourishing period of Oriental textile industries, in the days of the ʿAbbāsid caliphs and also in the two hundred years subsequent to the downfall of their empire, nowhere was there difficulty in obtaining good raw materials. Wool of Armenia and the Maghreb was used in other countries,[186] the various dyes, so important for mediaeval textile industries, were interchanged among several regions. Excellent saffron was grown in some provinces of Media, such as Qumm, Iṣfahān, Hamadān, Rudrāwar, Nihāwend and Barūǧird, and considerable quantities of it were exported to other countries.[187] The Caspian province of Tabaristan, too, exported saffron.[188] The crimson, for which the Armenian carpets were world famous, came from Western Persia and from Iraq.[189] But this colouring matter was also used in Egypt.[190]

Another characteristic feature of industrial life in the Near East in that period was the mutual interchange of techniques. The textile industry of Khuzistan imitated Egyptian fabrics, those of Dabīq and others. Armenian upholstery served as model for the manufactures of al-Ušmunayn in Upper

183 Ibrāhīm al-Ǧazarī, *Ǧawāhir al-sulūk*, MS. Paris 6739, f. 171b; *al-Nuǧūm al-zāhira* VI, p. 714.

184 S. Ibn Wāṣil quoted by Quatremère in his notes to the *Histoire des sultans mamlouks* I, 1, p. 252.

185 *Traité d'Emmanuel Piloti*, p. 136; Ibn Ṭūlūn, *Mufākahat al-xillān* I, p. 146.

186 Ch. Pellat, 'Ǧāḥiẓiana I', *Arabica* I, p. 160.

187 al-Iṣṭaxrī p. 199f.; Ibn Ḥawqal, ed. Kramers, p. 360; al-Muqaddasī, p. 396.

188 S. al-Balāḏurī, *Futūḥ al-buldān*, p. 338; Ibn al-Aṯīr V, p. 22.

189 S. Serjeant, "Materials for a history of Islamic textiles up to the Mongol conquest", (in) *Ars Islamica* I, p. 96.

190 *al-Xiṭaṭ* I, p. 239 l. 13, cf. Serjeant, op. cit., *Ars Islamica* 13/14, p. 96.

Egypt. The silk industry of Iraq was influenced by the methods used in south-western Persia. The textile industries of Upper Mesopotamia, again, imitated Armenian methods of production.[191]

There are reasons to believe that in the late Middle Ages the supply of good raw materials became an arduous problem for the Near Eastern textile industries. After the Mongol conquests, in the middle of the thirteenth century, trade relations between Iraq and Syria-Egypt were cut off for a long time, so that it became difficult or almost impossible to obtain crimson and saffron. This latter article had to be imported from some European countries, from the "Marches" in Italy or from Catalonia; and from Italian documents and Merchants' Guides one learns that exorbitant prices had to be paid for it.[192] The wool industry of the Near East had to use the same wool as before. On the other hand, it is well known that the great growth of Flemish, Florentine, and Catalan wool industries was, to a certain degree, the consequence of the use of English wool, which was of a much better quality than that of the Spanish and other kinds of wool used before.

But the decline of the Near Eastern textile industries was also the result of a technological stagnation.

The massive import of European textiles was possible, because meanwhile three great innovations had been made in the European textile industries. One of them was the introduction of the spinning wheel, which was used in France and Germany from the second half of the thirteenth century, in England at least from the fourteenth century, and in Catalonia from the second half of the century.[193] That was a very important innovation. Adam Smith, the founder of the modern science of economics, emphasized that it made possible double the output with the same effort. Another innovation was the invention of the treadle loom, which was used in England from the end of the twelfth century and in France from the thirteenth century.[194] The third innovation was the use of the automatic fulling mill, operated by water. This innovation was made at the end of the tenth century and the beginning of the eleventh century in Tuscany and in Lombardy and spread in the eleventh and twelfth centuries all over Western Europe.[195] The importance of these technological

[191] A. Mez, *Die Renaissance des Islâm*, p. 434; Serjeant in *Ars Islamica IX*, p. 90, 91, 13/14, p. 109.

[192] S. my *Histoire des prix et des salaires dans l'Orient médiéval*, p. 343, 432.

[193] Lynn White, op. cit., p. 119, 132f.

[194] Op. cit., p. 117.

[195] Op. cit., p. 38f., 89; A.-M. Bautier, "Les plus anciennes mentions de moulins hydrauliques industriels et de moulins à vent", *Bulletin philologique et historique du Comité des ravaux historiques et scientifiques* 1960, vol. II, p. 581ff.

innovations was so great that historians of the European economy called it an industrial revolution.[196]

European textiles in the later Middle Ages were not only better but also cheaper. In fact, the Italian and Catalan merchants imported into all countries of the Near East great quantities of cheap fabrics, such as the *loesti, panni de fontego, de San Matteo* and other Florentine stuffs, the products of Brescia, the Catalan woollen fabrics and even Irish stuffs. This was the reason for the dumping of European textiles and the decline of Near Eastern textile industries.

Once again the question arises of why the Oriental textile industries did not make these innovations. Why did they stick to the old methods of production?

A major factor was probably the great role played by the royal factories, the so-called *ṭirāz*. These factories, which were often farmed out to rich entrepreneurs, were great enterprises. They could afford experimentes that needed much time and money. Along with the royal factories in all countries of the Near East there were private manufactures and as the *ṭirāz* sold their produce (part of it) to private customers,[197] there was a true competition. But in the later Middle Ages the great *ṭirāz* factories were closed. The rich merchants no longer invested their capital in factories that could easily be confiscated. They preferred to hoard the money. On the other hand, labour had become very expensive as a consequence of the great epidemics in the fourteenth century. Al-Maqrīzī complains indeed a great deal of the difficulty of finding a worker.[198] The small workshops could not afford costly experiments. So the technological stagnation resulted from the fiscal policy of the despotic governments.

h) THE CASE OF THE ORIENTAL PAPER INDUSTRY

The development of the paper industry in the Near East was, from several view-points, very similar to that of the sugar and textile industries. It is, mutatis mutandis, the same story.

It seems that this industry flourished in all Near Eastern countries until the end of the fourteenth century.

Persia apparently produced paper fashioned after the Chinese model. At least part of the Persian paper was made from the bast of the paper-mulberry and other vegetable materials. Perhaps the *Güni Tebrizi* and *Xaṭā'ī* were such

[196] E. M. Carus-Wilson, 'An industrial revolution of the thirteenth century' *EHR* 11 (1941), p. 39–60; id., Haberget, "A medieval conundrum", *Medieval Archaelogy* 13 (1969), p. 165f.

[197] al-Idrīsī, *Description de l'Afrique et de l'Espagne* (Leiden 1866), p. 50.

[198] *Le traité des famines*, p. 75.

kinds of paper.[199] The paper produced in Baghdad was renowned for its excellent quality until the end of the Middle Ages.[200] It was thick and soft paper and of a large size. It was on such paper that letters to mighty rulers used to be written.[201] In the second half of the thirteenth century paper was still produced in Karx, north of Baghdad.[202] An anonymous author, who wrote in the first half of the fourteenth century, mentions the paper produced in Dār al-qazz, formerly a quarter of Baghdad itself.[203] As it became more and more difficult to obtain the fine Baghdadi paper in Egypt and Syria, in 1412 people began to imitate its production in Cairo.[204]

Syrian paper was also renowned and exported to other countries. It was considered to be better than Egyptian paper. The main centre of the paper industry in Syria in the late Middle Ages was Damascus.[205] In Egypt various kinds of paper were produced, such as *al-Manṣūrī*, *al-ʿāda* (ordinary paper, also called *maṣlūḥ*, i.e. refined), *ʿāl* (excellent) and *wasaṭ* (medium quality). Further there was "paper for carrier-pigeons" (*waraq al-ṭayr*) and Fūwa paper, i.e. produced in the town of Fūwa (or at least, it was first produced there). This latter paper was of a very small size.[206] Paper of various colours was also produced.[207]

Although there is no explicit evidence from the later Middle Ages, it is very probable that in Egypt and Syria at least a great part of these different kinds of paper was produced in royally owned plants. On the one hand, plenty of paper was needed by the government offices and, on the other hand, it was a writing material that had been introduced by the caliphal government.[208]

199 J. Karabacek, 'Das arabische Papier', *MPER* II/III (1887), p. 127; K. Jahn, 'Das iranische Papiergeld', *Archiv Orientální* X (1938), p. 333f.

200 Karabacek, art. cit., p. 143ff.

201 *Ṣubḥ* II, p. 476.

202 al-Qazwīnī, *ʿAǧāʾib al-maxlūqāt*, ed. Wüstenfeld (Göttingen 1848–49) II, p. 298.

203 *Marāṣid al-iṭṭilāʿ*, ed. Juynboll, I, p. 384 cf. Yāqūt II, p. 522. There is no reason to believe that the writer who compiled the *Marāṣid* would not have copied the passage of Yāqūt if the paper industry had no longer existed. — When in 1294 the attempt was made by the Ilxān to introduce paper money in Persia and Iraq, factories in several towns were producing paper. Mention is made of Mosul, Mayyāfāriqīn and Shiraz, s. Jahn, art. cit., p. 327.

204 Karabacek, art. cit., p. 142.

205 S. the "*Dīwān al-inšā*" quoted by Quatremère in his notes to *Histoire des Mongols de la Perse... par Raschid-Eldin* (Paris 1836), p. CXXXV. On the *Dīwān al-inšā* s. Gaudefroy-Demombynes, *La Syrie à l'époque des Mamelouks*, p. V/VI.

206 *Ṣubḥ* II, p. 476f. VI, p. 189ff.; cf. W. Björkman, *Beiträge zur Geschichte der Staatskanzlei im islamischen Ägypten* (Hamburg 1928), p. 114.

207 Karabacek, art. cit., p. 146f; id., "Neue Quellen zur Papiergeschichte", *MPER* IV (1888), p. 112ff.

208 The fact that in the later Middle Ages the paper industry in these countries was con-

There is no doubt that Near Eastern paper was exported to Europe; the evidence is convincing. The Arabic word *rizma*, meaning a parcel of 20 quires, each of 25 sheets, has been taken over as a loan-word in several European languages. In English it has become ream, in French rame, in German Ries, in Italian risma and in Spanish and Portuguese resma.

The Arabic sources contain a detailed description of the methods of paper production. It is worthwhile, for our purpose, to note some features of it.

The rags of linen fabrics, that were the raw material for its production, first of all underwent a process of fermentation (*taʿṭīn*).[209] Then, with mortars and wooden pestles the material was ponded into a pulp, in which long fibres often remained.[210] In some places this was done more effectively by water-driven mills. At the beginning of the thirteenth century according to a local historian there were 400 paper mills in Fez. They were destroyed or fell into ruins at the end of the rule of the Almohades.[211] Here, the pulp was put into vats made of a kind of reed and then the paper was sized by starch, but sometimes other materials were used for the sizing.[212] In Muslim Spain the same methods were used as in the Near East. The paper of Jativa was wavy, since the fibres were not well triturated. The chain lines were not regularly spaced.

These were the methods used for many centuries, since the production of paper had been introduced in the Near East at the end of the eighth century.

Owing to the methods used, paper had always been expensive in Near Eastern countries. At the beginning of the fifteenth century, when living costs rose considerably it became difficult for many old customers to buy the good Syrian or even Egyptian paper. At the same time the Italian merchants began to import European paper.

What was the reason for their success?

It was the consequence of technological innovations made in Europe.

The Muslim (or Jewish) paper production of Jativa, apparently the first paper manufacture in Europe, was imitated in the twelfth century in several towns of Catalonia, in Gerona, Saint Vicens de Jonqueres, La Riba and others. But the methods used there were the same as those practised in Jativa. The specimens of the Catalan paper that date from the end of the thirteenth

centrated in the capitals is another argument in favour of this supposition. That paper produced by royal manufactures was sold to private customers does not contradict this supposition. On the location of the paper factories in Cairo, s. Karabacek, 'Das arabische Papier', p. 124.

209 *al-Xiṭaṭ* I, p. 481 l. 2.

210 Karabacek, 'Neue Quellen', p. 93.

211 Ibn Abī Zarʿ, *Rawḍ al-qirṭās*, trad. A. Beaumier (Paris 1860), p. 58. The translation "fabriques" (also in the Spanish translation by A. Huici Miranda, Valencia 1964, I, p. 95) is, however, mistaken. In fact, only millstones are spoken of.

212 Karabacek, 'Das arabische Papier', p. 318f.; 'Neue Quellen', p. 84, 88.

century, on the other hand, show a remarkable improvement. The fibres are much shorter and better triturated. The chains have become parallel and regular. This change suggests that the stampers were shod with carefully positioned spikes.[213]

At the same time the paper industry began to flourish in the small town of Fabriano, south-west of Ancona (half-way between this town and Perugia). It may be that paper production had been introduced there by Arab prisoners or other Muslims in an earlier period, but the first documents that refer to it date from the years 1268–1276.[214] The technological improvements made in the paper industry of Fabriano were even greater than those made in Catalonia. The most important innovation was the use of water-wheel driven batteries of iron hammers to pound the rags. As these batteries operated alternately the rags were better and more equally stamped. In addition, the paper was no longer mixed with foreign substances. Another innovation was the use of metal wires for the mould, with the result that the transparent lines of the paper became much more regular. A third innovation was the replacement of vegetable by animal glue. The papermakers of Fabriano used gelatin prepared from scraps of animal skins. This substance did not contain, as the starch used by the Arabs did, the living and active germs of its own destruction. Last but not least, they introduced the water mark[215] into the paper industry. Of course, all these innovations were made over a period of time. The most ancient specimens of Fabriano paper are made of badly pounded rags, are coarse and are mixed with heterogeneous substances, but later specimens are finer and more equally stamped.

The great flourishing of paper-making in Fabriano and in other towns of Italy, however, was not only the result of technological innovations. It was also connected with a change of habits. Just at the time when the paper makers of Fabriano made their experiments and invented new methods of production, people in many regions of Europe began to wear underlinen (instead of wool). So it was much easier to obtain the raw material for paper making.

It is almost superfluous to emphasize that because of the technological innovations and the lower price of the raw material the paper itself became cheaper.[216]

213 O. Valls i Subira, *Paper and watermarks in Catalonia* (Amsterdam 1970) (Monumenta chartae papyraceae historiam illustrantia XII), p. 14f.

214 A. Zonghi, "The ancient papers of Fabriano" (originally published in Italian, Fano 1884), (in) *Zonghi's watermarks* (Hilversum 1953) (Monumenta chartae etc. III), p. 18; A. F. Gasparinetti, "Paper, papermakers and paper-mills of Fabriano", op. cit., p. 68f.

215 A. Zonghi, "The principal watermarks on the papers of Fabriano from 1293 to 1599", (in) *Zonghi's watermarks*, p. 10; Gasparinetti, art. cit. p. 70f.

216 A. Blum, *Les origines du papier, de l'imprimerie et de la gravure* (Paris 1935), p. 35.

Fabriano became a great centre of the paper industry and its skilled workers introduced the new methods in many other towns of Italy and even other countries. Before the end of the thirteenth century they founded paper factories in Bologna and in the course of the fourteenth century in Treviso (a. 1340), Colle Val d'Elsa (province of Siena), Foligno (in Umbria), Padova (a. 1339), and at the beginning of the fifteenth century in Sampierdarena and Voltri, near Genoa. In the middle of the fourteenth century the new paper industry had been introduced into France, and in 1390, the well known Stromer family, with the help of paper makers from the "Marches", brought it to Nuremberg.[217]

The products of the new flourishing industry were exported to many countries. According to accounts found in the records of local notaries and industrialists, Fabriano itself in the fourteenth century exported paper to Venice, Perugia, Genoa, and the Provence,.[218]

Before long the Italian paper was also exported to the Near Eastern countries, which had once supplied Southern Europe with this commodity.

Many Venetian documents bear evidence of the export of Italian paper to the Near East. Most of them refer to the export to Egypt.

The Venetians had already begun to export paper to Egypt at the end of the fourteenth century, as is borne out by the cargo inventories of the Alexandria galleys of a. 1400, preserved in the Datini archives. In a lawsuit between Johann Lio and the widow of Lorenzo Bembo, who had been his agent in Alexandria in 1412, he claims that, among other articles, he had sent him "*carta da scriver*".[219] Also in many other documents good writing paper is explicitly referred to. The said Johann Lio imported much paper into Egypt. After the death of Lorenzo Bembo he entrusted, in 1417–19, Giacomo di Zorzi with the sale of certain shipments of paper in Alexandria.[220] In a lawsuit between Michiel Michiel and the administrators of the property left by the Venetian merchant Nicolo de Nani the plaintiff claims that in 1441 he had sent him "*charte balle* 6 *risme* 68" (six bales containing 68 risme).[221] The subject of a litigation brought before the Giudici di petiziòn in 1448 was the import of "*balla una charta fina*".[222] The paper had been exchanged against spices. Apparently that was done very often, as one learns from a lawsuit concerning transactions in Alexandria in 1456–58.[223]

217 Op. cit., p. 32f.; Gasparinetti p. 74f; A. Zonghi, "The ancient papers of Fabriano"p. 19.

218 A. Zonghi, art. cit., p. 19, 22, 27.

219 G. d. P., *Sent.* 70, folio between f. 11 and 12.

220 Same series 45, f. 33a ff. cf. 52, f. 6a ff.

221 Same series 96, f. 81a ff. A bale of simple paper contained 10 rismas, whereas a bale of "royal paper" had only 5, Uzzano p. 173; *Libro di mercatantie*, p. 45.

222 G. d. P., *Sent.* 108, f. 68a ff.

223 Same series 129, f. 153b. Other records concerning the import of paper into Egypt by Venetians s. Archives B. Dolfin Ba 181, fasc. 23 sub February 8, 1418: carte bale 9.

Other Venetian documents refer to the import of paper into Syria. In Tripoli, a great centre of the cotton trade, Venetian merchants exchanged paper against cotton, as is borne out, for example, by the pleadings in a litigation in Venice in 1458.[224] In most of the documents quoted so far rather small shipments of paper are dealt with. But in a protest lodged in 1460 before a Venetian notary in Damascus the import of 100 bales is referred to.[225] The Venetians sold paper in all provinces of Syria. In a lawsuit in 1461, reference is made to the export of paper to Aleppo.[226]

They exported it also to Turkey, to Bursa and other towns, at least from the end of the fourteenth century.[227] Similar records from the middle of the fifteenth century refer to the export of "*chartae fine*" to Salonica and Constantinople.[228] The importation of Italian paper into Turkey by the Venetians probably increased very much after the conquest of Constantinople by the Ottomans, for it is a well established fact that there was no paper industry in the town (or its surroundings) before the seventeenth century.[229] Needless to say, they also supplied the countries of North Africa, Tunisia and others, with this commodity.[230]

The Genoese and Florentine merchants also took part in this trade. The inventory of the property left by a Genoese merchant, Johannes de Chorfogeo, dated August 10, 1421, in Alexandria, comprises "*balle 5 de cartis ad scribendum, balle sex de cartis p lazerrando*"[231]. The import of paper by the Genoese went on till the end of the Mamluk reign. A report of Marino Sanuto contains the notice that a Genoese ship brought 20 bales of paper to Beirut in 1509.[232] The fact that paper is included in the tariffs fixed by the Florentine authorities for the freight on travel to the Near East in the middle of the fifteenth century is a clear proof that Florence participated in the export of this product to the Levant.[233]

224 G. d. P., *Sent.* 129, f. 27b ff.

225 ASV Cancelleria inferiore, Notai, Ba 83, Cristoforo del Fiore VI, f. [4a].

226 G. d. P., *Sent.* 132, f. 166b ff.; see also Marino Sanuto III, col. 1188 inventory of the cargo of the galleys of Beirut in 1500.

227 G. d. P., *Sent.* 37, s. d. August 24, 1402.

228 Same series 102, f. 82a 112, f. 121a.

229 F. Babinger, "Appunti sulle cartiere e sull 'importazione di carta nell' Impero Ottomano specialmente da Venezia", *Oriente Moderno* 11 (1931), p. 406 ff.

230 G. d. P., *Sent.* 55, f. 16b.

231 ASV Cancelleria inferiore, Notai, Ba 230, Nicolo Venier, fasc. II, pt. 2, f. 32a/b. p *lazerrando* probably means the same as *carta da macero* or *carta-straccia*, used paper, s. Battaglia II, s. v.; the Florentine tariff of 1460/61 (s. below note 233) has indeed *charte da stracci* (beside writing paper).

232 *Diarii* X, col. 95.

233 See G. Müller, *Documenti*, p. 357 (dating apparently from 1442), 358 (1460/61) (this text with some different readings also in ASF Mar IV, 4) and cf. M. E. Mallett, *The Florentine*

What kind of paper was in these bales mentioned in so many documents? The answer to this question is very important for the understanding of our problem: the decay of Oriental industries and all the economic questions connected with it.

The Venetians surely exported Treviso and Fabriano paper.[234] The Genoese had their paper industry in Sampierdarena and in Voltri, but even they traded a good deal in paper produced in Fabriano and Foligno. A Merchants' Guide written in 1396 in Genoa contains passages about "*charti che vanghano da Perugia e da Fulingno... Genova*" and "*mandando charte da Pisa a Vingnone, e non chomperalle in Pisa, ma farlle venire da Fabriano*".[235]

Neither the good Fabriano paper nor other European paper of good quality was cheaper than that produced in Syria and Egypt. According to a document from the year 1438, Italian paper imported into Barcelona cost 0,018 duc. a sheet.[236] The price of good "Syrian" paper in Egypt at the beginning of the fifteenth century was only 0,01 dinar (worth perhaps 0.012 duc.).[237] But it seems that the Italian merchants imported mostly cheap paper into the Muslim countries. Paper imported by Venetians in Tunisia about 1420 cost 0.0021 duc. a sheet.[238] Al-Qalqašandī classifies the European paper (and that of the Maghreb) as the worst kind: *radī ǧiddan sarīʿ al-bilā qalīl al-makṯ*.[239] In those regions of the Near East where paper was not produced the South European merchants also imported better kinds.[240] In other words, the import of European paper into the Near East was essentially a true dumping of cheap manufactured products, just like that of sugar and textiles.

The role of the paper import in the Levantine trade of the late Middle Ages should not be underestimated. Surely paper was not a major item on the list of the European articles imported in the Near East. Certainly the import of textiles and metals was much more substantial.[241] But paper was only one of

galleys, p. 115. See also Marino Sanuto, *Diarii* III, col. 1199 on the import of paper from France (a. 1500).

234 S. supra p. 270 and note 217.

235 *Il manuale di mercatura di Saminiato de' Ricci*, p. 76, 84.

236 Valls i Subira, *Paper and watermarks in Catalonia*, p. 19. On the high prices of European paper in the fourteenth century see A. Blum, *La route du papier* (Grenoble 1946), p. 15.

237 E. Ashtor, "L'évolution des prix dans le Proche-Orient à la basse-époque", *JESHO* IV (1961), p. 35 (*manṣūrī* and Egyptian paper were cheaper).

238 G. d. P., *Sent.* 55, f. 16b.

239 *Ṣubḥ* III, p. 477.

240 See Ibn Taġrībirdī, *Ḥawādiṯ al-duhūr*, p. 686: In the fall of 1468 Sultan Qā'itbay received a copy of a letter written by Shāh Suwār to the inhabitants of Syria on *xāṣṣ waraq al-firanǧī*, cf. the notes of the editor p. XXIX saying that it should be *waraq firanǧī xāṣṣ*.

241 S. my *Les métaux précieux et la balance des payements du Proche-Orient à la basse époque*, p. 82ff., 95.

several products of the European industries that were imported. Soap of Gaeta, Naples, Pisa, Venice (partly from Apulia), Tripolitania, and elsewhere was another.[242] Altogether the sale (exchange) of all these products enabled the Italian merchants to acquire great quantities of spices, and, on the other hand, diminished the amount of good coins which the Levantine economies received for their merchandise.

i) A PATTERN OF TECHNOLOGICAL DECLINE

The historian who has shown that technological stagnation had a tremendous impact on the economic development of the Near East at the end of the Middle Ages cannot have the feeling that he has accomplished his task. His conclusions raise other questions: Were this phenomenon and the industrial decline closely connected with it the consequences of the invasions of foreign armies? Were the Near Easterners in the later Middle Ages less enterprising than they had been before? Or did they, perhaps, abstain from making innovations just because they were conservative?

The invasion of Syria by the army of Tamerlane, in 1400/01 was a true catastrophe, and the devastations caused by it were perceptible even half a century later. But it cannot be maintained that the decline of Syrian industries was the direct result of this fateful event. For there were some flourishing industries in Damascus even after the occupation by Tamerlane. The great quantities of bocassin the European merchants exported from Damascus in the fifteenth century bear evidence of it. The archives of the Venetian firm Antonio Zane contain the reports of its agent in Damascus on the purchases of the Venetian merchants in some years, from the departure of the galleys in fall. They include the following items:[243]

Purchases of the Venetians in Damascus

	up to Oct. 8, 1411	up to Sept. 14, 1413	up to Sept. 24, 1416
bocassin, pieces	8000	7500	5000

242 Import in Egypt by Venetians: G. d. P., *Sent.* 48, f. 132a f. 73, f. 94b ff. 129, f. 153a ff. (exchanged against pepper); Archives B. Dolfin Ba 180, fasc. 13, a. 1418:

cargo de la galia Patro' Piero Michiel al viazo d'Alexandria

Carlo Contarini	*savoni s*[i] *(acchi)*	156
Sebastian Ruzier	.	20
Piero Bernardo	*savoni s*[i]	196

and Ba 181, fasc. 23 in the folder *Note e conti senza data,* a scrap of paper beginning with *per stagni coli* 7 the third item: *savoni*; by Genoese: Nicolo Venier fasc. II, pt. 2, f. 32b f.; in Syria (from Cyprus) by Venetians: Nicolo Venier fasc. II, pt. 2, f. 18b f.; in Satalia: G. de P., *Sent.* 19, f. 45a ff.; see also Uzzano p. 112.

243 ASV Procurat. di S. Marco, Commissarie miste, Ba 128a A. Zane.

Many other documents referring to the acquisition of Damascene bocassin by Italian merchants in the fifteenth century could be quoted.[244] This textile, a product of cotton, was also exported to Genoa.[245] The town of Baalbek, which had also been occupied by the Mongols, still had a flourishing cotton fabric industry in the fifteenth century.[246] Certainly this industry had connexions with the textile manufactures in Damascus.[247] The Syrian capital itself still produced its *camocato*, a precious silk fabric, and it was exported to the great European emporia.[248] The number of people employed in this industry cannot have been insignificant, since Ibn Ṭūlūn reports on a demonstration made by the silk workers of all quarters of the town, who came with their banners on November 22, 1491 to the Great Mosque to protest against a new impost.[249] So the calamity that befell Syria at the time of the Mongol invasion cannot have been the reason for the decay of its industries and the dumping of European manufactured goods.

But aversion to innovation is a well known phenomenon in the history of technology. New methods of production often encounter opposition, because people believe that the standard will be lowered. It was for this reason that the introduction of fulling-mills in several provinces of France where fine textiles were produced occurred later than their spread elsewhere.[250] The water-driven mill itself spread only very slowly over the countries of Europe and reached Scandinavia not before the second half of the twelfth century. It was generally accepted in this part of Europe only in the fourteenth century.[251] For a long time many people in Europe, and above all the princely courts and their chanceries, refused to use paper, which was considered to be a writing material of inferior quality.

Some time people refuse to introduce innovations for specific reasons, and sometimes without reason. The general opposition that the issue of paper

[244] Melis, *Documenti*, p. 318 (a similar report, but from the winter only). Cf. on the bocassin Heyd II p. 702f., who was probably not aware of the fact that it was also produced in Syria, a cotton producing country par excellence.

[245] Melis, *Documenti*, p. 306, ASG Car. Vet. 1552, f. 132b f. (via Chios a. 1448) 1553, f. 23b (from Beirut a. 1458) 1556, f. 13a (from Chios, a. 1507) f. 36a ff. (from Beirut, a. 1507).

[246] S. Dozy, *Dictionnaire des vêtements*, p. 82f. and especially H. Zayyat, "Baalbek et ses caractéristiques autrefois" (in Arabic) *al-Mašriq* 41 p. 157ff; cf. also my paper "L'évolution des prix", *JESHO* IV, p. 38f.

[247] On cotton weaving in Damascus at the beginning of the sixteenth century see Ibn Ṭūlūn, *Mufākahat al-xillān* I, p. 363.

[248] See Melis, *Documenti*, p. 306; *Libro di mercatantie*, p. 47.

[249] Ibn Ṭūlūn op. cit., I, p. 146 cf. 156.

[250] A.-M. Bautier, *Les plus anciennes mentions de moulins etc.*, p. 591.

[251] M. Bloch, "Avènement et conquête du moulin à eau", (in his) *Mélanges historiques* (Paris 1963) II, p. 801.

money in Persia in 1294 met belongs perhaps to this second kind of aversion against innovation. It was a fateful contest. If this experiment made by the Īlxān Gayxātū had been successful, a probable consequence might have been the introduction of printing in the Near East 150 years earlier than in Europe. That conservatism is a basic attitude of Orientals is surely true. The fact that the Mamluks refused almost until the end of their rule to use fire-weapons, which they considered as not decent for noble knights, is a clear proof of this presumption. In so far as they were used by their army, they were assigned to socially inferior units.[252]

For a long time it has been maintained that cheap manpower, such as the existence of massive slavery, is an impediment to innovation. M. Bloch concluded that the automatic mill did not spread in the Roman empire because there was an abundance of manpower (slaves). The Germans too, he explained, had many slaves and, in addition, there was their conservatism. Weighty arguments have been put forth against the opinion that slavery and cheap manpower in general impeded innovation. Rightly, it has been maintained that the output of slaves is smaller than that of free, hired workers, and thus production costs are the same.[254] However that may be, there is not the slightest doubt that at the end of the Middle Ages the Near East suffered from chronic and progressive depopulation. Slaves were employed in the domestic services.

Technological innovations sometimes need a long series of experiments, which can be very costly. Often considerable investment is also required for the introduction of new production methods. It is well known that wealthy and enterprising public bodies, such as the order of the Cistercians and other orders, built many of the new industrial mills in Europe.[255] There were no such bodies in the Muslim Near East, but the high ranking emirs and the rich merchants had enough money to embark on such activites. However, the fiscal system of the Mamluks, which was based on almost periodical expropriations, kept them from doing it. This may have been another reason for the technological stagnation.

For the foundation of new industries or for the reconstruction of old ones, besides capital, plenty of good raw material and certain facilities were needed. It has already been said that the great growth of the wool industries in Western and Southern Europe was connected with the import of high quality

252 S. the monograph of D. Ayalon, *Gunpowder and Firearms in the Mamluk Kingdom* (London 1956), p. 46ff., 107f.

253 Art. cit., p. 807f., 811.

254 B. Gille, "Lent progrès de la technique", *Revue de synthèse* n. s., 32 (1953), p. 72.

255 Ch. Singer, E. J. Holmyard, A. R. Hall, Tr. I. Williams, *A History of Technology*, 2nd ed., II (Oxford 1957), p. 610.

English wool and that the Oriental wool industry used the same kind as before. Further in this period there was a dearth of good dyes in the Near East. Owing to the progressive decline of the middle classes (which wore underlinen) and the decay of the textile industries, the quantity of rags for the paper production was limited.

It is true that the Muslim countries east and south of the Mediterranean have fewer rivers and brooks that could be used for operating grinding and industrial mills. Where such streams existed, mills were built. There were once water-driven mills on the Euphrates and on the Tigris[256] and in the province of al-Ahwāz in South-Western Persia.[257] Tlemcen, Fez, Marrakesh, and Cordova had a great number of water-driven grinding-mills.[258] On the Wadi Fez, west of the capital, there were 3000 mills, if we are to believe Ibn Sa'īd, an author of the thirteenth century.[259] Also in the Near East springs and brooks were used for operating mills.[260]

But certainly the quantity of flowing bodies of water which the Near Easterners could use cannot be compared with that available in European countries. According to the Domesday Book, England had 5624 mills at the end of the eleventh century.

A factor which certainly must be taken into account in an inquiry about technological stagnation is the attitude of the government. The government could either foster technological progress or put obstacles in the way. The system of government as it had been developed in the Near East undoubtedly created conditions that were very unfavourable to technological innovations. The feudals did not keep their fiefs for all their lives, as changes were very often made. So they frequently had no interest in building new factories. The *muṣādara* system was a sword of Damocles hanging above the heads of all rich and supposedly rich people. The *mukūs*, the commercial taxes, were another check to technological development. The State, which had not succeeded in establishing a system of general taxes, imposed all kinds of duties on the crafts and branches of commerce. From time to time they were abolished and then reestablished, but they were altogether very cumbersome. As the bourgeois classes enjoyed neither political nor economic liberty and were oppressed by taxes, and as people were never sure that their property would

256 See below.

257 Yāqūt I, p. 411.

258 Al-Bakrī, *Description de l'Afrique septentrionale*, éd. revue (Paris 1965), p. 76 (transl. p. 156); Ibn Faḍlallāh al-'Umarī, op. cit., p. 157, 192; *Rawḍ al-qirṭās*, transl. Beaumier, p. 57; al-Idrīsī,, *Description de l'Afrique et de l'Espagne*, p. 212.

259 S. Ibn Faḍlallāh al-'Umarī, p. 160f.

260 See Burcardus de Monte Sion, op. cit., p. 58 on the surroundings of Jericho: *fons Helisei... fluit iuxta locum Galgale a parte australi et impellit magna molendina.*

not be seized the next day, technological progress was, from the outset, unlikely.

Technological progress also depended, to a certain degree, on the structure of industry. The great share the government and the upper strata of the army had in various industries was indeed another aspect of the feudal regime as built up by the Turkish knights who ruled over the Near East from the second half of the ninth century. Both in the textile and the sugar industry the factories which were in the possession of the sultan and the emirs (their sons, the viziers etc.) were probably more numerous and bigger than those run by bourgeois. The paper industry was perhaps a government enterprise (monopoly) as a whole. The consequences of the lack of equilibrium and of freedom of enterprise was the want of competition, corruption in the monopolized industries, and lack of incentives for innovations. Here we have a pattern of the development of industries and its impact on the methods of production.

But although all these factors must have been very detrimental to technological progress, they cannot explain why the Near Eastern industries did not introduce new methods of production. Attributing the lack of innovations to these environmental factors alone would not be a fully satisfactory explanation of the decline of Oriental industries in the late Middle Ages, for sometimes great inventions have been made by individuals without the help of big enterprises or public bodies.

Carefully reading the Arabic chronicles of the twelfth century, one indeed becomes aware of the fact that even in that early period there had begun a general technological decline of the Muslim Near East, as compared with the Christian world.

The introduction of the fulling-mill in the textile industry and the use of batteries of iron hammers in the paper factories were innovations in Western Europe that took place in stages in a long and slow development whose real accomplishment was the great success of transferring the energy created by the wheel into horizontal power, that is, rotary motion into reciprocal motion. In the middle of the fifteenth century the use of water-wheels for operating cranks and connecting-rods had begun.[261] The introduction of fulling-mills was surely a very important step in this development. It brought about a great change in various crafts and industries. Once people had learnt to use water-power for operating fulling-mills they also began to use it for trip-hammers in forges, wood-saws, tanning mills, grinding machines and for other purposes.[262]

Whereas the use of water-driven mills increased so much in the Western

261 Lynn White, p. 113.
262 Op. cit., p. 83f., 89.

world, a contrary development characterised the technological history of the Near East in the Middle Ages. In the tenth century there were many ship-mills on the rivers of Mesopotamia and of Near Eastern countries. Abū ʿAbdallāh Muḥammad al-Xwārizmī, an Arabic author who wrote in the second half of the tenth century, mentions the ship-mills, undoubtedly on the Tigris.[263] The geographer Ibn Ḥawqal, who wrote at the same time, gives precious information about these mills called *ʿaraba*. He narrates that once there were many of them on the Tigris near Mosul. They were to be found in mid river, where the stream is strong, and were tightened by iron chains. Every ship had four mill-stones. In the town of Balad, not far from Mosul, there had also been, according to Ibn Ḥawqal, many ship-mills which had been working for export (sc. of flour) to Iraq. But all of them in the days of the author had disappeared. On the other hand, some of them remained in the town of al-Ḥadīṯa (on the Tigris). Ibn Ḥawqal continues his account saying that there had also been such mills on the Euphrates in ar-Raqqa and Qalʿat Ǧaʿbar, but that these had been incomparably inferior and their number had been smaller. He also says that some had remained on the Tigris in Takrīt, ʿUkbarā, and Baradān (a suburb of Baghdad). In Baghdad itself there were no ship-mills at all. Tiflis, the capital of Georgia, had many of these mills on the river Kur. But in Mosul, the capital of Ibn Ḥawqal's native country, only six or seven had been spared, owing "to the blessing of the Banū Ḥamdān".[264]

The modern historian will not easily accept Ibn Ḥawqal's explanation. From the bottom of his heart he hated the Banū Ḥamdān, who then ruled over Upper Mesopotamia, and he held them responsible for many shortages and accused them of unbearable tyranny. But in fact the decrease in the number of water-driven grinding mills was in keeping with the technological decline of the Near East in the period subsequent to the decline of the caliphal empire. Al-Qazwīnī, who wrote in the second half of the thirteenth century, still mentions the ship-mills of Mosul,[265] but, generally speaking, there is no doubt as to the progressive decrease of the number of water-driven mills in the Near East. One may quote in this context Domenico Trevisan, a Venetian ambassador and a very keen observer. Trevisan, who came to Egypt in 1512, says bluntly that in this country "there are neither water-driven mills nor wind mills". The Egyptian mills are operated by horses and by oxen according to the travelogue.[266] Several European travellers who visited the Near East

[263] *Mafātīḥ al-ʿulūm*, ed. Van Vloten (Leiden 1895), p. 71.

[264] P. 219f.

[265] II, p. 309.

[266] *Le Voyage d'outremer de Jean Thenaud*, p. 209. What this author says about the use of horses is contradicted by statements in other sources, see above notes 107, 108.

in later periods noticed time and again the scarcity of mills operated by water.[267]

The Muslim engineers knew how to operate contrivances by putting stagnant water into motion. The fourteenth century geographer al-Dimišqī gives a detailed account of such a mill in the town of Merend in Azerbaijan.[268] It seems that such mills had been invented in this region or elsewhere in Persia and that they were therefore called "Persian mills" (*ṭawāḥīn fārisiyya*). Al-Bakrī, writing in the eleventh century, mentions such mills in Monastir, in Tunisia.[269] A "Persian mill" is also spoken of in the biography of a mamluk who lived in the fifteenth century. Xayrbay al-Ašrafī (d. 1482) had an estate in the Fayyūm where he had planted sugar cane, established a sugar press, and built — a Persian mill.[270] There were probably other mills of this kind in Egypt and Syria.[271] But most mills were driven by animals, whereas the devices for using stagnant water or water taken from a river and conducted elsewhere served other purposes, such as constructing clocks or other automatic devices.[272] Apparently they were not used for industrial purposes. That was due to lack of enterprise, and it is characteristic of the technological stagnation of the Near East in the late Middle Ages.

The technological stagnation, or even decline, had, however, begun a long time before the end of the Middle Ages. Many reports about dams that burst or were swept away by floods and about building activities that failed shed light on this phenomenon. Detailed chronicles of the twelfth century contain accounts of strenuous efforts made by the Selǧukid governor of Iraq, Bihrūz, to rebuild the big dam of Nahrawān. The old bed of the Nahrawān canal was dug out and made deeper and a high dam was constructed in order to divert the water from it. On the other hand, a loop canal from the Diyālā was dug so that more water should flow to the Nahrawān. But all these construction activities to which six years (1140–46) were dedicated, were in vain. The big dam broke down and remained amidst dry land.[273]

Although the conscientious historian will include in his explanation of

[267] E. Graf v. Mülinen, "Beiträge zur Kenntnis des Karmels", *ZDPV* 30 (1907), p. 155.

[268] *Nuxbat al-dahr*, p. 188 (transl. p. 254), German translation in Wiedemann, *Aufsätze* I, p. 214ff.

[269] *Description de l'Afrique septentrionale*, p. 26 (transl. p. 79).

[270] Al-Saxāwī, *al-Ḍaw al-lāmi'* III, p. 208.

[271] The engineer and mathematician, 'Alam al-dīn Qaysar, called Ta'āsīf, perhaps built such a mill on the banks of the Orontes, s. Abul-Fidā, *al-Muxtaṣar*, ed. Reiske-Adler, IV, p. 479 and cf. *Bibl. Geogr. Arab. Gloss.* p. 375 s.v.

[272] Wiedemann I, p. 72, 75 note a, 100ff., 185 II, p. 48ff., 471ff., cf. 478; F. M. Feldhaus, *Die Maschine im Leben der Völker*, p. 167; cf. Brockelmann, *GAL Suppl.*, I, p. 902f.

[273] Ibn al-Ǧawzī, *al-Muntaẓam X*, p. 84, 95; Ibn al-Aṯīr 11, p. 43, 41.

technological decline and similar phenomena a good deal of "we do not know", it seems that usually such a trend is concomitant with demographic decline just as growth of population is often accompanied by technological progress.

Roman civilization made great progress in technology in the first century of the Christian era, as did Western Europe from the eleventh to the thirteenth century and once again in the fifteenth century. These were indeed periods of population growth. The history of technology in the Near East is fully in keeping with this pattern, conceived by a French historian.[274] Great progress was made in the eighth and ninth centuries and, on the other hand, the first signs of stagnation were perceptible in the second half of the tenth century, when Ibn Ḥawqal wrote his *Geography*. That was exactly the time when the population of the central provinces of the caliphal empire began to decrease. The decline of the Egyptian textile industry began in the first half of the thirteenth century, when Egypt suffered from tremendous depopulation, as is borne out by the development of prices and wages.[275] Some industries of Egypt flourished again under the reign of the first Baḥrī sultans, when the country recovered and the population increased once more. The industries of Egypt collapsed under the Circassians, a period of considerable demographic decline.

But even the demographic downward trend was not the last reason for the technological decline. It was probably the general impoverishment. In fact both phenomena, technological decline and depopulation, are interwoven; they are part of a much greater and more general phenomenon of economic retrogression.

This paper is an elaboration of a lecture given at the Conference on the economic history of Near East held in Princeton in June 1974 and to be printed in its Proceedings.

274 B. Gille, *Lent progrès de la technique*, p. 78f.
275 See my *Histoire des prix et des salaires*, p. 128f., 224, 455, 458f., 465.

IV

L'ASCENDANT TECHNOLOGIQUE DE L'OCCIDENT MÉDIÉVAL

Introduction

Les sources historiques du bas Moyen Age, sources documentaires et littéraires en diverses langues, contiennent de nombreuses relations qui sont de clairs indices d'une dichotomie éclatante qui s'est produite dans le développement technologique des grandes civilisations du Vieux-Monde. L'évolution industrielle des pays chrétiens de l'Europe centrale et occidentale est caractérisée depuis l'époque des Croisades par un progrès presque continu des techniques, par des innovations importantes amenant des changements fondamentaux dans les méthodes de production et aboutissant à un nouvel essor économique. Les économies des pays musulmans au sud de la Méditerranée souffrent en revanche d'une stagnation technologique et on peut affirmer que, pour quelques secteurs de leur production industrielle, il s'agit plutôt de déclin, si on les compare avec leur niveau d'autrefois.

En mettant en relief la relation entre le déclin technologique des pays orientaux et l'expansion européenne et en recueillant des données y relatives on rendrait possible une meilleure compréhension de ce dernier phénomène, considéré longtemps comme expression de la vitalité occidentale. Il ne l'était que partiellement. Il n'y aurait pas eu en effet d'expansion économique de l'Occident sans le déclin des civilisations sur les autres bords de la Méditerranée.

Le recul économique de ces pays et leur déclin industriel ont pour conséquence l'importation massive en Orient de produits manufacturés en Occident alors qu'à la même époque l'Europe occidentale voit affluer des matières premières. L'importance du volume de ce commerce ressort avec netteté des recherches faites dans les archives d'Italie, de la France méridionale et de la Catalogne après la publication par W. Heyd de son œuvre classique sur l'histoire du commerce du Levant. Ayant commencé le dépouillement systématique de ces archives, on s'est rendu compte que, à la fin du Moyen Age déjà, s'était établi un rapport pays développés – pays sous-développés entre l'Occident chrétien et les pays orientaux et maghrébins. L'emprise économique a précédé la domination politique.

Après avoir traité dans plusieurs études de ce phénomène et de ses effets économiques, on voudrait dans le présent essai élargir le tableau selon deux points de vue: on montrera d'une part que cette évolution continue se dessine aussi dans d'autres secteurs de la production industrielle et, que d'autre part, elle caractérise non seulement les rapports entre la civilisation chrétienne-occidentale et le monde musulman proche-oriental, mais aussi les rapports entre l'Europe occidentale et les pays de l'Afrique septentrionale et les territoires qui faisaient autrefois partie de l'empire byzantin. On nous permettra aussi de citer des textes se référant à la production industrielle en Turquie, au XVIe siècle. Ils jettent une vive lumière sur les rapports qui sont le sujet de cette analyse. En effet, les méthodes de production dans le nouvel empire se caractérisent par leur empreinte médiévale et la mentalité typique du Proche-Orient. On ajoutera dans cet essai des matériaux nouveaux, fruits de recherches récentes faites en ce domaine. On doit avouer qu'il est difficile de trouver des réponses satisfaisantes, - but de cette étude -, à la question des causes décisives de l'ascendant européen et du déclin des autres civilisations, issues elles aussi de la même civilisation gréco-romaine. Il est probable que de grandes innovations se sont faites par hasard et que d'autres furent le résultat de longues, patientes et coûteuses expériences. Il y a des engins qui se sont répandus très lentement et d'autres qui furent introduits en plusieurs pays en quelques années seulement[1]. Il est arrivé que la même innovation a été acceptée dans certains pays et rejetée par d'autres, bien que leur milieu culturel et social n'ait pas été très différent. Les données rassemblées dans cet essai aideront, peut-être, des chercheurs plus capables à dégager des conclusions convaincantes. C'est ce qu'espère, sincèrement, l'auteur en les soumettant à la bienveillance du lecteur.

L'industrie lainière

Les grandes innovations qui ont vraiment bouleversé les méthodes de production dans les industries textiles de l'Occident, - les plus importantes des industries médiévales dans toutes les autres régions du Vieux-Monde à l'époque médiévale - sont bien connues: ce sont la diffusion du rouet, au XIIIe siècle, l'emploi du métier à marche et surtout l'introduction du moulin à eau pour le foulage, qui se répandit dès le XIe siècle. La productivité du rouet était le double de celle du fuseau. Le foulage par le moulin mécanique opérée par la force hydraulique économisait considérablement l'emploi de main-d'œuvre. Il révolutionnait l'industrie drapière.

1 V. par exemple M. Bloch, «Avènement et conquête du moulin à eau», dans ses *Mélanges historiques*, Paris 1963, II, p. 800 et ss.

Ce qui importe pour l'esquisse des rapports entre la civilisation occidentale et les civilisations d'outre-mer à la fin du Moyen Age, c'est la constatation que tous ces engins ont subi en Occident, au cours de cette époque, un processus d'amélioration presque continu. Un grand nombre d'innovations étaient certainement considérées comme des secrets industriels, ce qui explique qu'on trouve rarement des témoignages s'y rapportant. Mais le fait lui-même ne peut être mis en doute, comme le montrent certaines sources. En 1416, par exemple, Francesco Petri de Rhodes obtint à Venise les droits de brevet pour le moulin à eau qu'il avait inventé. Le brevet était valable pour 50 ans[2].

En Orient ces innovations ne furent pas introduites, ou, du moins, ne furent pas employées dans la production industrielle jusqu'à la fin du Moyen Age. Ce furent les juifs espagnols qui y introduisirent le foulage mécanique. S'étant établis dans l'empire ottoman ils y fondèrent dans plusieurs villes de florissantes industries lainières qui employaient des moulins à eau pour le foulage. L'emploi de ces moulins était la raison principale de leur succès. Safed, en Galilée, devint au XVIe siècle un centre de production de lainages. Les juifs espagnols qui habitaient la ville avaient transformé des moulins employés pour la mouture à l'usage du foulage et les appelaient de leur nom espagnol «batan». Fait caractéristique, après le déclin de l'industrie lainière de Safed, les Arabes, en Palestine, foulaient les draps avec les pieds, sur la côte de la mer[3]. Salonique, où un grand nombre de réfugiés espagnols s'étaient établis, devint, elle aussi, un foyer bien connu de l'industrie lainière. Peut-être n'exagère-t-on pas en soutenant que c'était la ville drapière par excellence dans l'empire ottoman entier. L'«abba» (ou en turc «Selanik čohasi», c'est-à-dire tissu de Salonique), un lainage plutôt grossier produit par les manufactures des juifs à Salonique, était employé pour les uniformes des janissaires. Il était vendu aux foires tenues en plusieurs villes des Balkans et même exporté jusqu'en Amérique. Presque tous les juifs de Salonique vivaient de cette industrie[4]. Les méthodes de travail étaient espagnoles, tout le vocabulaire en usage, tous les termes techniques, indiquent bien l'origine espagnole de cette industrie[5]. Le foulage était mécanique et les fouleurs étaient appelés bataneros, comme à

2 C. Mandich, «Primi riconoscimenti veneziani di un diritto di privativa agli inventori», in *Rivista di diritto industriale,* VII parte 1, 1958, p. 114 et s.; idem, «Privilegi per novità industriali a Venezia nei secoli XV e XVI», in *Deputazione de storia patria per le Venezie, Atti dell'Assemblea del 8 sett. 1963,* p. 15.

3 S. Avitzur, «Safed - centre de la manufacture de lainages au XVIe siècle» [en hébreu], in *Sefunoth,* VI, 1962, p. 46, 56 et ss.

4 J. Nehama, *Histoire des Israélites de Salonique,* Salonique 1935-36, III, part 2, p. 37 et ss., 42; I.-S. Emmanuel, *L'histoire de l'industrie de tissus des Israélites de Salonique,* Paris 1935, supplément à son *Histoire des Israélites de Salonique,* I, Paris 1936, p. 23 et s.

5 J. Nehama, *op. cit.,* p. 41.

Safed. C'est ce qu'on conclut de nombreuses réponses rabbiniques[6]. Safed et Salonique étaient les foyers les plus connus de cette nouvelle industrie lainière, parce que les communautés juives de ces villes constituaient aussi de grands centres culturels de la diaspora judéo-espagnole. Mais les réfugiés espagnols étaient aussi des manufacturiers de lainages en d'autres lieux. Même les Chevaliers Hospitaliers de Rhodes leur concèdent des moulins pour le foulage des draps[7].

Si l'emploi de ces engins est la raison principale de l'essor des industries lainières en Europe, leur introduction manquée en Orient, mis à part leur emploi par les communautés juives-espagnoles en Turquie au XVIe siècle, peut apparaître comme la cause de leur déclin. Mais il y avait d'autres causes. On sait bien que les Orientaux avaient un fort penchant pour les draps élégants de Florence, de Venise et d'autres lieux encore, qui se distinguaient par leurs belles couleurs, rouges et autres. Or l'art de la teinture s'était considérablement développé en Occident, les méthodes avaient été fortement améliorées à la fin du Moyen Age. C'est ce qu'on infère de plusieurs traités sur la teinture qui datent de cette époque. En étudiant ces manuels, comme la bien connue *Plictho* de Giovanventura Rosetti (imprimée en 1548), on est impressionné surtout par le grand nombre de préceptes visant à produire des variétés nuancées. De tels manuels contiennent des préceptes employés depuis longtemps, ce sont donc des recueils qui rendent possible la connaissance des pratiques du bas Moyen Age. Un phénomène qui se dégage avec netteté de ces préceptes est le grand rôle que jouaient dans la teinture des textiles les matières colorantes importées de l'Orient, surtout le bois de Brésil et l'indigo. Voilà un indice du rapport qui s'était établi entre l'Orient et l'Occident. L'Orient, - comme les autres régions sous-développées à toutes les époques, - fournissait à l'Occident des matières premières. Pourtant, on constate aussi que pour les belles écarlates et en général pour les draps on avait recours à plusieurs matières colorantes produites en Occident: au kermès (provenant en partie de l'Espagne et en partie de l'Asie Mineure), à la garance et au pastel, par exemple. La possibilité d'employer des matières colorantes trouvées sur place et importées de l'Orient était certainement pour les industries drapières de l'Occident un grand avantage. Car les frais de teinture représentaient une part non négligeable dans l'ensemble des frais de production des draps[8].

6 S. A. Rosanes, *Histoire des Israélites de Turquie* [en hébreu], III, Sofia 1938, p. 388 et s.; S. Avitzur, «L'industrie lainière de Salonique» (en hébreu), in *Sefunoth*, 12, 1971-78, p. 153.

7 J. Nehama, *op. cit.*, p. 38.

8 *The Plictho of Gioanventura Rosetti* ... translated by S. M. Edelstein - Hector C. Borghetty, Cambridge Mass. 1969, p. XVI, XVIII; C. Rebora, *Un manuale di tintoria del Quattrocento*, Milan 1970, p. 15, 22, 69, 70, 72, 113 et s., 130 et d'autre part les couleurs occidentales p. 84 et s. 126; Fr. Brunello, *L'arte della tintura nella storia dell'umanità*, Vicenza 1968, p. 162. Quant à l'époque de laquelle datent les préceptes contenus dans la

C'est ainsi que s'explique l'importation massive de draps occidentaux dans les pays orientaux, à partir du XIIIe siècle. Elle revêtait le caractère d'un dumping, donnant le coup de grâce à des industries indigènes languissantes depuis longtemps, et apportait des revenus considérables aux économies de plusieurs pays européens. Ayant déjà traité de ce commerce d'exportation vers l'Egypte et la Syrie en plusieurs autres ouvrages[9], on ne citera ici, pour souligner sa portée économique, que quelques données fournies par les chroniques vénitiennes du début du XVIe siècle[10].

Tableau 1. Exportation de draps par les galères vénitiennes

date	galères d'Alexandrie	galères de Beyrouth	sources
1500	133 balles	400 balles	Marino Sanuto III, col. 1188
1501	-	330 balles	Priuli II, p. 183
1503	127 balles	560 balles	Op. cit. II, p. 254 et s.
1504	-	450 balles	Op. cit. II, p. 335
1510	«merze e panni» de la valeur de 250,000 ducats		Marino Sanuto IX, col. 516
1511	134 balles	-	Op. cit. XII, col. 78

En supposant qu'une balle contenait 10 pièces, valant chacune en moyenne 30 ducats, on obtiendra pour les 130 balles exportées par an à Alexandrie la valeur de 40000 ducats et pour les 430 balles vendues à Beyrouth, 130000 ducats. Mais si la plupart de ces draps avaient été des draps de Brescia ou des créseaux, c'est-à-dire des draps bon marché, la valeur de ces importations n'aurait été que de moitié[11]. Marino Sanuto relate aussi pour l'année 1500 l'arrivée à Alexandrie d'un grand bateau génois qui,

Plictho le langage ne laisse aucun doute, v. par exemple l'emploi prévalent de verzino pour le bois de Brésil, f. B 1a, B 3b, L 3a, tandis qu'on trouve rarement brasilio, v. K 2a. Sur l'importance qu'avaient les dépenses pour la teinture v. H. Hoshino, *L'arte della lana in Firenze nel basso medioevo,* Florence 1980, p. 93.

9 E. Ashtor, «Les lainages dans l'Orient médiéval», in *Atti della II^a settimana di studio,* Istituto Fr. Datini, Prato/Florence 1976, p. 657 et ss. et surtout p. 673 et ss.; «L'exportation de textiles occidentaux dans le Proche-Orient musulman au bas Moyen Age (1350–1517)», in *Studi alla memoria de Federigo Melis,* Naples 1978, II, p. 303 et ss. (quelques données citées dans ces articles sont citées encore une fois et cela pour en tirer des interprétations nouvelles); *Europäische Tuchausfuhr in die Mittelmeerländer im Spätmittelalter (1350–1500),* Nürnberg 1982, p. 5 ss., 13 ss., 25 ss.

10 Cf. «L'exportation de textiles occidentaux», p. 373 (quelques fautes typographiques qui s'étaient glissées dans le texte lors de l'impression ont été corrigées ici).

11 Cf. *art. cit.,* p. 374.

selon un rapport, y apporta 4600 pièces de draps et selon un autre 150 balles, c'est-à-dire 1500 pièces[12]. Le rapport cité en dernier lieu est problablement exact et, selon lui, les draps apportés par ce bateau auraient eu la valeur (de vente) de 45000 ducats (en attribuant à chaque pièce la moyenne de 30 ducats). Trois bateaux français avaient apporté durant le même temps à Alexandrie, à en croire le rapport cité par Marino Sanuto, 13000 pièces de drap[13]. Si cette relation est exacte il devait s'agir de draps ayant une valeur de 200000 ducats au moins.

Au XVe siècle, les marchands italiens (et d'autres) exportaient aussi les produits de leurs industries lainières vers les pays du Maghreb. Ils y étaient très appréciés et étaient écoulés sans difficulté en Tunisie et ailleurs. Quand le gouvernement de Gênes passa, en 1433, un contrat avec le souverain de Tunis pour racheter des prisonniers chrétiens, celui-ci stipula qu'une part de la rançon serait payée en draps florentins de la valeur de 40–50 fl. la pièce[14]. L'exportation de draps florentins vers le Maghreb est aussi attestée par d'autres documents. Quand le gouvernement de Florence établit le tarif du frêt pour l'exportation de marchandises par les galères vers le Maghreb, les draps produits dans la ville elle-même n'y manquaient pas[15]. Comme la Tunisie avait été à l'époque des Croisades un foyer d'industries textiles, ces documents sont des témoignages éloquents. Ils révèlent la décadence des industries indigènes et la supériorité de la production de textiles en Italie. Certainement, l'industrie textile n'était pas éteinte en Tunisie ni dans les pays avoisinants. Mais, leurs produits étaient de qualité inférieure, en comparaison avec les draps fins européens, et les Maghrébins se rendaient compte de ce fait.

Pourtant le grand marché des draps florentins était à cette époque l'empire ottoman. Certes, on ne les écoulait pas sans se heurter à la concurrence d'autres lainages italiens. Mais il semble que dans la deuxième moitié du XVe siècle les draps florentins dits «garbo» y aient joui d'une excellente réputation et qu'on en ait vendu de grandes quantités. Ils étaient écoulés par de nombreux marchands florentins résidant à Constantinople et ailleurs et aussi par des Ragusains et d'autres encore[16]. Selon la relation d'un auteur florentin complétée par une autre source, on exportait de Florence en Turquie à la fin de XVe siècle les quantités suivantes de draps[17].

12 *Diarii,* III, col. 942, 1199.

13 *Loc. cit.*

14 L. de Mas Latrie, *Traités de paix et de commerce et documents divers concernant les relations des Chrétiens avec les Arabes de l'Afrique septentrionale au Moyen Age,* Paris 1866–1872, II, p. 141.

15 A. Amari, *I diplomi arabi del R. Archivio fiorentino,* Florence 1863, appendice, p. 66.

16 H. Hoshino, *L'arte della lana in Firenze,* p. 269; sur la prévalence des draps de «garbo» parmi ceux vendus à la dite époque en Turquie *v. op. cit.*, p. 268, 274.

17 H. Hoshino, *op. cit.*, p. 270.

Si la pièce était vendue 30 fl.[18], 5000 pièces représentaient la valeur de 150 000 fl.

Tableau 2. Exportation de draps florentins en Turquie

année 1470	8000 pièces
1471	7500 pièces
1472	8000 pièces
1474	3300 pièces
1476	3000 pièces
1483	5000 pièces

L'industrie des toiles

Le déclin des manufactures de toiles dans les pays musulmans face à l'essor de cette industrie en Occident est encore plus caractéristique du rapport entre les diverses civilisations méditerranéennes à la fin du Moyen Age. Car c'était là une des plus anciennes industries orientales, l'Egypte surtout avait été célèbre pour ses toiles depuis les temps les plus reculés. Il suffit de jeter un coup d'œil sur les magnifiques objets conservés dans les musées de plusieurs pays pour se rendre compte de leur qualité. De plus, une grande partie des toiles n'étaient pas teintes, on n'utilisait pas de matières colorantes, coûteuses, comme pour la production des draps. Mais en Egypte l'industrie des toiles était en pleine décadence depuis le début du XIIIe siècle[19]. C'est surtout à cette industrie que songeait al-Makrīzī en parlant du cataclysme des industries textiles survenu en Egypte au début du XVe siècle. L'écrivain médiéval était impressionné par la grande crise économique qui donna alors à cette industrie un coup fatal. En fait, le déclin avait commencé longtemps avant cette époque. Etant donné que les produits de cette industrie étaient exportés vers tous les pays voisins (et lointains) et rapportaient aux industriels - et au fisc qui percevait des droits - des revenus considérables, on ne peut douter qu'on avait un grand intérêt à ce qu'elle continuât à fonctionner. Pourtant les efforts entrepris restèrent vains. L'industrie des toiles périclitait aussi dans les autres pays musulmans, bien qu'on ait tenté d'y remédier. Au Xe siècle déjà les musulmans s'aperçurent des progrès réalisés dans les manufactures européennes et tâchèrent d'imiter leurs méthodes et d'employer les mêmes outils. Selon un document vénitien de l'an 971, on exportait alors vers la Tunisie des cardes de tisserands[20]. A cette époque du moins on était donc prêt dans les pays

18 Cf. *op. cit.*, tableaux XLVII, XLIX.

19 V. mon article «Aspetti della espansione italiana nel basso medioevo», in *RSI* 90, 1978, p. 7 et s. (où les sources sont citées).

20 G. L. Fr. Tafel; G. M. Thomas, *Urkunden zur älteren Handels- u. Staatsgeschichte der Republik Venedig*, Vienne 1856-57, I, p. 28.

musulmans à faire des innovations technologiques. Mais au bas Moyen Age la décadence de cette industrie était apparemment générale et irrésistible dans tous les pays orientaux. Elle était surpassée par les manufactures de toiles européennes et ne pouvait plus faire face à l'importation de leurs produits.

Le grand essor des manufactures de toiles en Occident chrétien s'explique à cette époque par plusieurs innovations technologiques. Tandis que les drapiers mettaient à profit le foulage mécanique, la floraison de l'industrie des toiles était dans une grande mesure l'effet de l'emploi de rouets perfectionnés, qui avaient remplacé le fuseau dans la plupart des pays occidentaux au XIIIe siècle. Avec le temps on y apporta des modifications. Les rayons minces furent remplacés par des disques pleins. Puis on monta le rouet sur une banquette, comme le métier à marche, en augmentant considérablement son diamètre et la distance moyeu-broche. En outre, on employait aussi le rouet pour le bobinage[21]. L'introduction du cardage à points métalliques modifia beaucoup les opérations du filage. Il semble que l'aiguille métallique ait été inventée en France ou en Flandre, car elle était inconnue à Florence au XIVe siècle. Or le cardage à points métalliques produisait des voiles régulières[22]. Une autre innovation technologique qui amena le progrès de l'industrie des toiles fut l'introduction de la broie, d'abord dans la transformation du chanvre, puis dans celle du lin. Elle aussi se répandit dans les pays européens au XIIIe siècle[23]. L'emploi de la broie signifiait une économie considérable de main d'œuvre et ses effets pour le développement de l'industrie des toiles sont évidents. Au XIIIe siècle, Reims était le centre le plus fameux de cette industrie, puis Constance et Saint-Gall devinrent de florissants foyers de la production de lin. Dans cette dernière ville on employait l'indigo oriental pour teindre en rouge[24]. La qualité de la teinture des toiles avait aussi une grande importance pour les possibilités d'exportation. Or on les teignait en diverses couleurs, comme on l'apprend dans les manuels de teinture[25]. Trait caractéristique, dans la *Plictho*, le manuel le plus important de cette époque, les préceptes pour teindre des toiles et des cotonnades en rouge mentionnent seulement une matière colorante - le bois de Brésil[26]. Encore une fois, on s'aperçoit du rapport région sous-développée, fournisseur de matières premières, - région industrialisée, qui s'était établi entre les grandes civilisations autour de la Méditerranée.

21 W. Endrei, *L'évolution des techniques de filage et de tissage*, Paris 1968, p. 52 et s.
22 *Op. cit.*, p. 50 et ss.
23 *Op. cit.*, p. 51 et s.; R. J. Forbes, *Studies in ancient technology*, IV, p. 30 suppose que cet engin a été inventé aux Pays-Bas au XIVe siècle, tandis qu'Endrei est enclin à croire qu'il a eu son origine en Hongrie.
24 H. Lüthy, «St. Galler Leinwandindustrie», in *Ciba Rundschau* 89, 1950, p. 3301.
25 *Plictho*, p. 98 et s.
26 S. M. Edelstein, «Dyestuffs and dyeing in the sixteenth century», dans son recueil *Historical notes on the wet-processing industry*, Dexter Corporation 1972, p. 122, 124.

Les toiles manufacturées en plusieurs pays de l'Europe occidentale étaient très appréciées dans le Proche-Orient, au Maghreb et dans les territoires qui appartenaient autrefois à l'empire byzantin. Des marchands génois les importaient en Perse à la fin du XIIIe siècle et dans la première moitié du XIVe siècle. Le voyageur florentin Lionardo Frescobaldi, qui visita l'Egypte en 1381, raconte que les femmes égyptiennes portaient des vêtements faits de toiles de Reims. Des chroniqueurs arabes relatent qu'en 1391 le gouverneur de Caire prit des mesures contre les femmes portant des longues chemises faites de «toiles de Venise». La police reçut l'ordre de couper les manches de ces chemises[27]. Ces témoignages (et d'autres encore) sont une preuve de plus pour soutenir l'interprétation qu'on a faite plus haut du récit d'al-Makrīzī concernant la ruine des industries de textile égyptiennes: elle avait commencé longtemps avant le début du XVe siècle.

De nombreux témoignages, dans des documents conservés dans les archives de l'Europe méridionale et dans des sources littéraires datant du bas Moyen Age, montrent que l'exportation de toiles occidentales vers le pourtour méditerranéen atteignait alors un volume considérable.

Au XIVe siècle, et plus tard aussi, les toiles de la Champagne, comme celles de Reims, étaient très estimées dans tous les pays[28]. Mais on importait aussi dans le Proche-Orient des toiles produites à Noyon (département de l'Oise)[29]. En effet l'industrie des toiles entra en décadence en Champagne à la fin du XIVe siècle tandis qu'elle commençait à fleurir dans le Hainaut, dans les régions de Nivelles, de Cambrai et de Valenciennes, et aussi dans celle de Tournai[30]. Pourtant l'industrie linière de Reims fleurissait encore au XVe siècle[31]. Mais les toiles allemandes tenaient la première place parmi les produits d'exportation de cette industrie. C'est pourquoi les toiles qu'on exportait de Venise vers l'Orient sont si souvent appelées «tele di fontico», c'est-à-dire arrivées au «Fondaco dei Tedeschi»[32]. Les toiles allemandes, produites à Constance et, à une époque postérieure, à Saint-Gall, arrivaient à Venise en juillet ou en août[33], on retardait parfois le départ des galères de Beyrouth afin de les prendre en charge[34]. A Venise, le commerce

27 V. mon article «Observations on Venetian trade in the Levant in the XIVth century», *JEEH,* V, 1976, p. 581 et s. (où les sources sont citées).

28 V. ASV (Archivio di Stato, Venezia), Giudici di petiziòn, Sentenze a giustizia (cité dorénavant G. P., Sent.) 55, f. 100 a et ss. (exportation de toiles de Reims de Rhodes à Chypre).

29 ASV, Senato, Misti (cité dorénavant Misti) 41, f. 29b.

30 Mollat-Johansen-Postan-Sapori-Verlinden, «L'économie européenne aux deux derniers siècles du Moyen Age», *Relazioni del X Congresso int. di scienze storiche,* III, Florence 1955, p. 719 et ss.

31 V. *Les affaires de Jacques Cœur, Journal de procureur Dauvet,* éd. M. Mollat, Paris 1952–53, I, p. 363 II, p. 477.

32 Misti 33, f. 58a, 109b 34, f. 26b.

33 Misti 31, f. 63a 38, f. 156a.

34 Misti 42, f. 4a.

des toiles allemandes fut si volumineux que des agents des manufactures et d'autres marchands devaient y résider pour s'en occuper[35]. Parmi les toiles allemandes vendues au «Fondaco dei Tedeschi» à Venise on distingue entre «tele vetere» et «tele di novo fontico»[36]. Mais les toiles italiennes ne manquaient pas non plus parmi les textiles exportés vers l'Orient. C'étaient des toiles de Lombardie et des Marches[37] et aussi des produits de la Ligurie, de Gênes[38] et de Novi Ligure[39].

Les toiles produites dans les territoires grecs[40], dans le Proche-Orient et aussi au Maghreb[41] ne pouvaient soutenir la concurrence des produits occidentaux. Les bateaux venant d'Europe méridionale en apportaient de lourdes cargaisons[42].

Dans plusieurs chapitres de manuels de commerce qui ont été compilés en Italie dans la première moitié du XIVe siècle, il est parlé de l'exportation de toiles vers Constantinople, dans plusieurs villes de l'Asie-Mineure, La Tana, Trébizonde et Tebriz. Ce sont des toiles de la Champagne et d'Italie[43]. L'exportation de toiles occidentales vers ces pays s'est poursuivie à la fin du XIVe et au début du XVe siècle, comme on l'apprend à travers plusieurs décisions du Sénat vénitien touchant le trafic des galères. Pourtant à cette époque ce sont des toiles allemandes, qui y ont remplacé les produits de la Champagne[44]. Puis, dans la quatrième décennie du XVe siècle, des marchands vénitiens exportent vers Constantinople des grandes quantités de «veli», autre espèce de toiles[45]. Les Vénitiens exportent aussi des toiles en Syrie depuis le début du XIVe siècle, d'après ce qu'on lit dans un autre manuel de commerce compilé à Venise à ladite époque[46]. A la fin du XIVe siècle et au début du XVe siècle ce commerce augmente considéra-

35 H. Simonsfeld, *Der Fondaco dei Tedeschi in Venedig,* Stuttgart 1887, II, p. 65 (et voyez I, no 59 un droit de 2% est imposé en 1494 à l'importation de draps et de toiles de la Suisse à Venise).

36 Misti 26, f. 62b 32, f. 59a.

37 Pegolotti, *La pratica della mercatura,* éd. A. Evans, p. 45.

38 Un vénitien exporte en 1480 à Alep «tela genovexini larghe» G. P., Sent. 178, f. 36b et s.

39 Problablement plusieurs textes où il est parlé de «tela di Novo» se réfèrent en effet à des produits de cette ville, cf. mon article. «L'exportation de textiles occidentaux», p. 357.

40 «Tarifa zoè noticia dy pexi e mesure di luogi e tere che s'adovra marchantia per el mondo», Venise 1925 (cité dorénavent Tarifa), p. 43: «tele grexesche fate in Romania greze e bianchizade».

41 De Mas Latrie, *Traités,* II, p. 275 (où des matières blanchissantes que fournissent les Vénitiens aux Maghrébins pour la production de toiles sont mentionnées).

42 Qu'on veuille considérer les textes cités ci-dessus comme complément à ceux évoqués dans mon article, «L'exportation de textiles occidentaux», p. 354 et s.

43 Pegolotti, p. 24, 27 et cf. 30, 34 et s., 61; Tarifa, p. 16, 43, 45; *Zibaldone da Canal,* éd. A. Stussi, Venise 1967, p. 70.

44. Misti 32, f. 59a 33, f. 58a 45, f. 53a et s.

45 *Il libro dei conti di Giacomo Badoer,* éd. U. Dorini-T. Bertelè, Rome 1966, c. 19, 61, 93, 108, 134. On produisait les voiles de lin et du coton.

46 Ms. Marucelliana (Florence) c. 226, f. 51b et s.

blement[47]. En 1400 une compagnie vénitienne exporte à Damas 42 balles de toiles, valant 4200 ducats[48]. Il paraît qu'elles étaient constituées pour la plupart de toiles allemandes[49]. Il va de soi que des marchands de Gênes et d'Ancône s'adonnaient eux aussi à l'exportation de toiles occidentales vers la Syrie[50]. Les documents qui ont trait à l'importation de toiles dans la Syrie septentrionale durant la deuxième moitié du XVe siècle sont très caractéristiques du nouveau rapport entre l'Occident techniquement développé et l'Orient sous-développé. Car il n'est pas douteux qu'une grande part de ces toiles transportées à Tripoli[51] et surtout à Alep était destinée à l'exportation vers la Perse. Alep était en effet le point d'arrivée des caravanes qui apportaient en Syrie la soie de la Perse, et il va sans dire qu'elles ne repartaient pas sans s'approvisionner en produits occidentaux. Le commerce de toiles occidentales à Alep était d'un volume considérable. Un acte judiciaire dans une série du tribunal vénitien des «Giudici di petiziòn» se réfère aux transactions de Marco Trevisan à Alep. Ce marchand vénitien vendait en 1471 à Alep les quantités de toiles suivantes[52].

Tableau 3. Vente de toiles par Marco Trevisan à Alep

année 1471	ducats	dirhams*
toiles larges et blanchies, 58 pièces, encaissé	432	2
toiles grises, 20 pièces, encaissé	142	24
toiles étroites, 41 pièces, encaissé	108	45

* 50 dirhams équivalent à un ducat.

En Egypte, des marchands européens importaient des toiles depuis le début de cette époque. On les importait de Venise, au milieu du XIVe siècle, via Chypre[53]. Des marchands florentins et provençaux écoulaient au début du XVe siècle des toiles françaises et probablement d'autres encore[54].

Les pays maghrébins constituaient eux aussi depuis le XIIIe siècle un marché pour les toiles européennes. Au XIIIe siècle les Génois y exportent des toiles ligures et françaises[55], au milieu du XVe siècle les Vénitiens et les

47 G. P., Sent. IV, f. 14a; ASV, Giudici di petiziòn, Sentenze e interdetti VIII, f. 49a et ss.; Chronique Morosini, ms. Vienne (copie à la Marciana, Venise, VII, MMIXL = 8331/2), c. 193.
48 G. P., Sent. VII, f. 100a et ss.
49 Misti 38, f. 156a.
50 ASV, Cancelleria inferiore, Notai, Ba 230, Nicolo Venier B, 2, f. 10a/11a; ASV, Notarile, 14832, Giacomo della Torre, no 23.
51 G. P., Sent. 161, f. 181a et s. 163, f. 44b et ss., 46a et ss.,90a et ss., 93a.
52 ASV. Giudici di petiziòn, Terminazioni (cité dorénavant G. P., Ter.) IV, f. 11a.
53 Misti 26, f. 86a.
54 ASV, Cancelleria inferiore, Notai, Ba 229, fasc. V, Leonardo de Valle, sub 5 sept. 1403; Ba 222, Antoniello de Vataciis, sub 8 nov. 1404.
55 M. G. Canale, *Storia civile, commerciale e letteraria dei Genovesi dalle origini all'anno 1797,* Gênes 1844-47, II, p. 552.

Génois offrent à Tunis des toiles de Bourgogne[56]. Mais les Florentins vendaient eux aussi des toiles au Maghreb[57]. Puis, à la fin du XVe siècle et au début du XVIe siècle, ce commerce d'importation constitua pour les Vénitiens un grand négoce. Ils vendaient des toiles européennes à Tripoli, à Oran et au Maroc[58].

Il va de soi que l'exportation massive de toiles en Méditerranée rapportait aux industriels et aux marchands européens des profits non négligeables. A la fin du XVe siècle les 100 aunes («braccia») de toile (large) coûtaient à Venise 10 ducats et se vendaient en Syrie en pièces de 70 aunes à un prix considérablement plus élévé[59].

Autres industries textiles

Tandis que les manufactures de lin avaient décliné dans le Proche-Orient depuis l'époque des Croisades, le grand développement de la culture du coton, conséquence de la baisse de la demande de céréales dans une région en plein déclin démographique, eut pour effet un essor de l'industrie cotonnière. Les produits des manufactures de Baalbek[60] et d'autres villes et bourgades de Syrie, les «boccassins» surtout, étaient écoulées en Egypte et les marchands italiens les exportaient aussi vers l'Europe[61]. Mais on produisait aussi des cotonnades en Haute-Mésopotamie, à Mosul et ailleurs, qui étaient écoulées dans d'autres pays[62].

Dans tout le pourtour méditerranéen les marchands européens pouvaient vendre facilement les produits des industries cotonnières qui fleurissaient en Haute-Italie et dans l'Allemagne méridionale[63]. On exportait les étoffes de coton et les fûtaines vers toutes les échelles du Maghreb, comme Tripoli, Tunis, Bougie et Oran[64].

56 De Mas Latrie, *Traités,* II, p. 141, 249; v. aussi G. P., Sent. 38, f. 120a et s.

57 A. Amari, *I diplomi arabi,* appendice, p. 66.

58 De Mas Latrie, *op. cit.,* II, p. 275, 277 et s.

59 G. P., Sent. 174, f. 74b 177, f. 9a et s.; G. P., Ter. VIII, f. 30a et ss. V. aussi le prix de toiles cités dans «L'exportation de textiles occidentaux», p. 358 (100 pics syriens étaient égaux à environ 85 braccia de Venise, v. Tarifa, p. 84 et Uzzano, apud G. Fr. Pagnini, *Della decima,* Lisbonne-Lucques, 1765-66, IV, p. 114).

60 Ibn Battūta, I, p. 18 186; Ibn Taghrībirdī, *an-Nudjūm az-zāhira,* éd. Popper, VII, p. 501, 760; cf. H. Zayyat, «Baalbek et ses caractéristiques autrefois» [en arabe], *al-Machrique* 41, 1947, p. 157 et ss.; Th. Wiegand, *Baalbek,* Berlin-Leipzig 1921-25, III, no 32; E. Ashtor, «Venetian cotton trade in Syria in the later Middle Ages», *Studi Medievali* 17, 1976, p. 683 et s.

61 «The Venetian cotton trade», p. 710 et s.

62 Al-Makrīzī, *as-Sulūk,* IV, p. 792.

63 V. Les récents livres de M. F. Mazzaouvi, *The italian cotton industry in the later Middle Ages, 1100-1600,* Cambridge 1981; W. v. Stromer, *Die Gründung der Baumwollindustrie in Mitteleuropa,* Stuttgart 1978.

64 Uzzano, p. 193; A. Amari, *I diplomi arabi,* appendice, p. 66; de Mas Latrie, *Traités,* II, p. 277, 278.

De même, diverses soieries européennes étaient à la fin du Moyen Age écoulées en Orient. Le grand essor des manufactures de soie en Europe méridionale, et, d'autre part, leur formidable déclin dans les pays grecs et dans le Proche-Orient est un autre phénomène symptomatique du nouveau rapport Occident-Orient. Au bas Moyen Age on n'avait plus besoin de faire de la contrebande pour obtenir les précieuses soieries de Byzance, comme on s'était accoutumé à le faire aux temps des Carolingiens et de leurs successeurs. Une série d'innovations technologiques avait amené la floraison de manufactures de soie en plusieurs villes d'Italie. La première avait été l'invention du moulin à retordre la soie, le filatoire inventé à Lucques, devenue le premier foyer de cette industrie. Pourtant il ne se passa pas un long temps avant que ce secret industriel fût trahi par un Lucquois exilé. En 1272 (ou 1276) le guelfe Borghesana s'en alla à Bologne et y construisit le même moulin. Qui plus est, il semble qu'on l'y ait considérablement perfectionné. Le moulin employé à Bologne était mû par la force hydraulique, il était doté d'une bobineuse mécanique et le filage se faisait par des bobines (et non pas par des dévidoires)[65]. Tandis que le vieux filatoire lucquois, manuel, sans bobines mécaniques et muni de dévidoires, produisait une soie simple, le nouvel engin rendait possible la production de soie fine[66]. Or, il n'est pas douteux que ces perfectionnements aient été opérés à Bologne longtemps avant la fin du XVe siècle, car en 1538 on y condamna à mort (par contumace) Cesare Dolcini et Vincenzo Giovanni di Fradio pour avoir transmis ces secrets aux manufacturiers d'une autre ville[67]. Répandues en plusieurs villes d'Italie, surtout à Florence et à Venise, ces techniques perfectionnées ne tardèrent pas à amener la floraison d'une nouvelle industrie de la soie. Ses produits jouissaient partout d'une excellente réputation et on commençait à les exporter vers les territoires byzantins et le Proche-Orient musulman, jadis célèbres pour leurs étoffes de soie.

Jusqu'au début du XVe siècle, les marchands italiens (et d'autres, sans doute) achetaient encore des soieries en Orient, comme le montrent les inventaires des cargaisons de galères vénitiennes et d'autres bateaux venant des échelles du Levant[68]. Puis on écoula des soieries de toutes les espèces, surtout des velours, en Egypte et en Syrie[69]. A la fin du XVe siècle et au début du XVIe siècle il n'y avait pas, semble-t-il, de bateaux européens par-

65 C. Poni, «All'origine del sistema de fabbrica, tecnologia e organizzazione produttiva dei mulini di seta nell'Italia settentrionale (sec. XVII-XVIII)», in *RSI* 88, 1976, p. 447. Cet auteur corrige les développements de Fl. Edler de Roover, «Lucchese silks, *Ciba Review* 80, 1950, p. 2915 et ss.

66 Poni, *art. cit.* p. 452.

67 Poni, *art. cit.* p. 455.

68 J. Heers, «Il commercio mediterraneo alla fine del sec. XIV e nei primi anni del XV», *Archivio Storico Italiano* 112, 1955, p. 168, 173.

69 «L'exportation de textiles occidentaux», p. 363 et ss.

tant pour le Proche-Orient qui ne transportaient des étoffes de soie. Voici quelques données tirées des inventaires que nous ont transmis les chroniqueurs des cargaisons de galères vénitiennes.

Les étoffes de soie ne manquaient pas non plus dans les cargaisons des bateaux génois qui cinglaient vers les échelles du Levant. Le bateau Zustignan en apporta à Alexandrie 10 caisses[70] en 1500.

Tableau 4. Exportation de soieries par les galères vénitiennes

année	galères d'Alexandrie	galères de Beyrouth	sources
1500	7 caisses	10 caisses*	Marino Sanuto III, col. 1188; Priuli II, p. 74.
1503	3 caisses	10 caisses	Priuli II, p. 254 et ss.
1511	-	15 caisses	Marino Sanuto XII, col. 78.

* Priuli: 6 caisses.

Les pays maghrébins étaient eux aussi un bon marché pour cet article. On vendait des soieries italiennes partout, en Tunisie, en Algérie, et au Maroc[71].

La production de cuir

En traitant du progrès technologique qui se réalisait dans plusieurs domaines en Europe au bas Moyen Age et de l'expansion économique vers l'outre-mer, on ne doit pas écarter les témoignages touchant le développement de l'industrie du cuir.

Les termes de «cordouan» et de «maroquin» rappellent l'origine de nos cuirs: au haut Moyen Age les pays maghrébins et l'Espagne musulmane étaient les foyers de cette industrie et c'était de ces pays qu'on importait le cuir dans l'Europe chrétienne. En effet le «cordouan» vermeil et le «maroquin» rouge étaient très appréciés en Occident. De nombreux documents révèlent que l'importation des cuirs maghrébins se poursuivit au bas Moyen Age. Au XVe siècle encore on les importait en Italie[72]. Dans tous les traités conclus au Moyen Age entre les nations marchandes et les souverains musulmans du Maghreb, mention est faite de l'exportation de cuirs

70 Marino Sanuto, *Diarii,* III, col. 942.

71 A. Amari. *I diplomi arabi,* appendice, p. 66; de Mas Latrie, *Traités,* II, p. 275, 276 et s.

72 Pegolotti, p. 275; G. P., Sent. 96, f. 53b et ss. 127, f. 51b et ss. 129, f. 109a; A. Amari, *I diplomi arabi,* appendice, p. 67.

vers l'Europe[73]. Mais on acquiert aussi des cuirs en Egypte[74] et surtout dans les échelles de la mer Noire[75]. Certainement, on produisait aussi du cuir en Italie et ailleurs, mais c'était le «cordouan» espagnol-maghrébin qu'on imitait[76].

A la fin de l'époque des Croisades ce secteur de la production industrielle fut lui aussi le théâtre d'un grand progrès technologique. On inventa de nouvelles méthodes qui révolutionnèrent la production du cuir.

A la fin du XIIIe siècle on commença en Toscane, à Pise surtout, à employer une nouvelle méthode de tannage: au lieu de tanner les peaux par de l'eau froide, on employait de l'eau chaude. Si dans l'ancienne méthode les peaux étaient trempées dans l'eau froide et du myrte, avec le nouveau procédé, l'eau bouillie absorbait mieux les acides. On employait d'abord du myrte, puis de la chaux et de l'alun. Le tannage par la nouvelle méthode nécessitait seulement dix jours, alors que selon l'ancienne il exigeait six mois. Grâce au nouveau tannage on pouvait produire du cuir bon marché, tandis que par l'ancien système on produisait du cuir de luxe[77]. Puis avec le temps on améliora la nouvelle méthode de tannage. Pour produire du cuir doux on employa dans les lavages successifs du jaune d'œuf, de la farine et de l'huile. Cette méthode de tannage est décrite dans un manuscrit bolognais datant du XVe siècle et aussi dans la *Plictho* de Giovanventura Rosetti, qui date de la première moitié du XVIe siècle[78]. Des manuels de teinture de cette époque il ressort que la variété des couleurs employées pour teindre le cuir était très grande. Pour le rouge on avait toujours recours au bois de Brésil, importé de l'Extrême-Orient. Pour le bleu, on employait l'indigo, autre matière colorante importée de l'Orient[79].

Ces nouvelles méthodes de tannage connurent un grand succès. Au milieu du XIVe siècle, une nouvelle industrie de cuir se développa dans l'Ile de France[80], puis, au XVe siècle, la Ligurie devint un foyer de cette industrie. Les inventaires de cargaisons des bateaux génois venant du Maghreb et de la Sicile vers la métropole révèlent le changement survenu: tandis que les inventaires et des autres documents se référant à ce trafic et datant de l'époque antérieure indiquent l'importation de cuirs, ce sont maintenant les peaux qui ont pris leur place[81].

73 V. les textes cités par de Mas Latrie, *Traités,* I, p. 216e et s.
74 G. P., Ter. VII, f. 10b.
75 G. P. Sent. 106, f. 40b; J. Heers, *Il commercio,* p. 173.
76 Ch. Singer, *The earlest chemical industry,* Londres 1948, p. 81.
77 D. Herlihy, *Pisa in the early renaissance,* New Haven 1958, p. 140 et ss.
78 S. M. Edelstein-H., C. Borghetty, «Dyeing and tanning leather in the sixteenth century», dans son recueil *Historical notes on the wet-processing industry,* p. 143 et s.
79 *Art. cit.,* p. 145–146.
80 V. l'edict du roi de 1359 en faveur des tanneurs qui teignent le cuir en rouge, en noir et en d'autres couleurs à Paris et dans sa banlieue: *Ordonnances des rois de France,* III, p. 370.
81 C. Trasselli, «Frumento e panni inglesi della Sicilia del XV secolo», (dans son recueil) *Mediterraneo e Sicilia all'inizio dell'epoca moderna,* Cosenza 1977, p. 313.

On peut aussi démontrer comment le changement survenu à cette époque dans les méthodes de production a influencé les rapports économiques entre l'Europe occidentale et le Proche-Orient. Un acte notarié, écrit à Alexandrie en 1434, se réfère explicitement à l'importation de cuir par des marchands vénitiens[82].

Savon, papier, verre

Le clivage entre les civilisations sur les deux rives de la Méditerranée était à la fin du Moyen Age à peu près général. Presque toutes les industries dans les régions d'outre-mer avaient décliné, alors que les mêmes secteurs de la production industrielle jouissaient d'un nouvel élan dans l'Occident chrétien. Autre trait caractéristique de ce développement: il s'agissait d'industries qui avaient leur origine dans le Proche-Orient et avaient été transplantées en Occident.

La décadence de l'industrie du sucre affaiblissait sans doute considérablement les économies du Proche-Orient, car jusqu'à la fin du XIVe siècle, on en exportait de grandes quantités vers les pays européens. Puis, cette source de revenu écartée, on importa de la mélasse de Sicile[83]. Certes, il y avait encore dans les pays orientaux des raffineries de sucre, mais leur production avait diminué de beaucoup et la qualité de leurs produits était plus souvent médiocre.

La même observation est valable quant à une autre ancienne industrie orientale: la savonnerie. Après avoir fleuri pendant de longs siècles en Syrie et ailleurs, cette industrie fut ruinée par le prélèvement de lourds impôts sur la vente de l'huile, sa matière première par excellence, et sur la vente de ses produits eux-mêmes. La monopolisation de la soude et sa vente aux marchands européens privait en outre les savonneries orientales de l'autre matière première principale[84].

Le grand essor des savonneries dans plusieurs régions de l'Europe méridionale, surtout dans la Marche d'Ancône, à Gaëte et à Venise, avait sans doute été rendu possible par l'acquisition de quantités considérables de soude syrienne. Il était dû aussi pourtant au progrès technologique. Le savon qu'on produisait en Italie, en Provence et en Espagne était le même savon «dur» qu'on manufacturait en Orient, à base d'huile et de soude.

82 ASV, Cancelleria inferiore, Notai, Ba 211, Nicolo Turiano V, f. 8a et s.

83 V. E. Ashtor, «Levantine sugar industry in the later Middle Ages, a case of technological decline», *The Islamic Middle East, 700–1900, Studies in economic and social history,* Princeton 1981, p. 91 et ss.

84 Cf. mes développements détaillés: «Le Proche-Orient au bas Moyen Age – une région sous-développée», in *Atti della Xa settimana di studio,* Istituto Fr. Datini, Prato 1978, p. 406 ss.

Mais on y ajoutait diverses autres matières, rares en Orient, comme les cendres de peupliers et de la chaux vive[85]. Pour le nettoyage des vêtements on fabriquait du savon mêlé avec du tartre et de la cendre de vignes[86]. Certaines espèces de savon étaient produites à base de suif, et non d'huile[87]. Le savon à base d'huile était en Europe meilleur marché, parce qu'on employait des presses à huile mécaniques. Mais toutes les espèces de savon qu'on exportait vers l'outre-mer étaient de qualité supérieure au savon oriental.

L'exportation de savon vers l'Orient devint un grand négoce. De nombreux textes en portent témoignage[88]. Quand Venise obtint la permission du Saint-Siège de reprendre le commerce avec les Mamlouks et équipa un convoi de galères pour l'année 1345, les cargaisons de savon étaient si grandes qu'on en laissa une partie[89]. Les marchands vénitiens n'étaient pas hommes à laisser échapper ce commerce et désormais il n'y eut plus de bateau partant pour l'Egypte sans une cargaison de savon. Les décrets du Sénat vénitien qui fixent le frêt le démontrent[90]. De même on exportait du savon vers la Syrie, au moyen de galères et d'autres bateaux[91]. Il va de soi que d'autres marchands, par exemple des Provençaux, exportaient également du savon en Egypte[92]. Les Vénitiens écoulaient le savon aussi bien à Constantinople qu'à La Tana[93]. Pour les marchands d'Ancône c'était l'article d'exportation par excellence, car leur ville était le centre d'une région de grande production de savon[94].

Comme le savon européen, les meilleures espèces de papier qu'on fabriquait à Fabriano, au moyen de moulins mus par la force hydraulique, à partir de 1268, se vendaient dans tous les pays orientaux, bien que, pour les documents importants on ait toujours employé le papier des manufactures locales. Les Génois offraient en Orient du papier manufacturé à Sampierdarna et à Voltri[95], les Vénitiens, pour la plupart, semble-t-il, du papier

85 F. W. Gibbs, «The history of the manufacture of soap», *Annals of Science,* IV, 1939/40, p. 175.
86 S. M. Edelstein, «The secrets of the Reverende Maister Alexis of Piemont», dans son recueil *Historical notes on wet-processing industry,* p. 32.
87 *Ibid.*
88 Les citations suivantes doivent être considérées comme supplémentaires aux textes cités dans ladite conférence à Prato et dans «Aspetti della espansione italiana», p. 17.
89 F. C. Lane, «The Venetian galleys to Alexandria, 1344», in *Wirtschaftskräfte u. Wirtschaftswege, Festschrift H. Kellenbenz,* Nürnberg 1978, I, p. 436.
90 Misti 24, f. 21a 30, f. 17a. V. aussi G. P., Sent. 65, f. 105a et s.
91 Misti 55, f. 123b; G. P., Sent. 79, f. 118b et ss.
92 Leonardo de Valle, sub 7 fév. 1403; Marino Sanuto, *Diarii,* III, col. 1122 et s.
93 Misti 45, f. 53a et s. 55, f. 117b.
94 E. Ashtor, «Il commercio levantino di Ancona», *RSI* 88, 1976, p. 227 et ss., 235 et ss.; *Levant trade in the later Middle Ages,* Princeton University Press 1983, appendice A 5.
95 Marino Sanuto, *Diarii,* III, col. 942.

fabriqué à Fabriano[96]. Les territoires qui avaient appartenu autrefois à l'empire byzantin étaient eux aussi un grand marché pour le papier occidental. Il semble même que l'exportation du papier vers la «Romania» ait commencé plus tôt, car l'auteur d'un manuel italien de commerce datant de la première moitié du XIVe siècle, parle de l'exportation de papier vers Constantinople et La Tana[97], sans le mentionner parmi les articles exportés vers la Syrie et l'Egypte. A la fin du XIVe siècle, les Vénitiens vendaient aussi du papier dans l'arrière-pays de leurs colonies sur la mer Noire. En 1375 Daniele da Molin en exporta vers Astrakhan[98]. Le nouvel empire ottoman ne disposa pas longtemps de papeteries, et eut donc recours au papier fourni par les Italiens[99]. On exportait aussi du papier vers le Maghreb. C'est ce qui ressort du tarif du frêt fixé par le gouvernement de Florence en 1461 pour les galères d'Etat[100].

A en juger d'après les objets conservés dans les musées on supposerait que l'industrie du verre, une des plus anciennes industries du Proche-Orient, surpassait encore au XIVe siècle la production des verreries italiennes. Mais plusieurs sources démontrent que la production de Murano était à cette époque déjà très appréciée en Egypte et ailleurs. Ce phénomène était évidemment la conséquence, d'une part, de la politique erronée des Mamlouks qui fournissaient les verreries italiennes en soude - une importante matière première - et, d'autre part, des innovations technologiques faites à Murano. On sait à partir des registres du Sénat vénitien qu'on permit en 1338 à un ambassadeur de Chine (qui était un Génois!) d'acquérir des «iocalia de cristallo» et de les emmener[101]. Un chroniqueur arabe raconte que des ambassadeurs européens apportèrent en 1366 des objets de cristal, garnis d'or, à la cour du sultan[102]. C'était sans doute des ambassadeurs vénitiens[103]. D'autres textes se rapportent à la vente d'objets en verre par des marchands italiens et provençaux commerçant dans le Proche-Orient. Le Vénitien Antonio Dolfin vend en 1396 à Alexandrie «capsa 13 vitrorum a speculis[104]». Un acte notarié à Alexandrie en 1403 a aussi trait à l'expor-

96 Misti 60, f. 47b; G. P., Sent. 66, f. 57b et ss.; G. P., Ter. IV, f. 180a et cf. Misti 42, f. 39b (sur l'origine du papier vendu par les Vénitiens).

97 Tarifa, p. 47, 63.

98 G. P., Sent. IX, f. 85b.

99 Misti 45, f. 53a et s.; G. P., Sent. 156, f. 13b et ss.

100 A. Amari, *I diplomi arabi.* appendice, p. 66. V. en plus les citations de textes relatifs à ce commerce dans mon article paru dans *Israel Oriental Studies,* VII, 1977, p. 266 et ss. (où on trouve aussi un résumé des innovations technologiques faites à Fabriano); «Aspetti della espansione italiana», p. 17.

101 Misti 17, f. 116b.

102 *Ibn Iyās,* éd. M. Mostafa, I, part. 2, Wiesbaden 1974, p. 36.

103 Cf. al-Makrīzī, as-Sulūk, III, p. 122 et cf. sur l'ambassade génoise venue au Caire dans la même année Heyd, *Histoire du commerce du Levant,* II, p. 53.

104 G. P., Sent. VI, f. 65a.

tation de verre par des Provençaux[105]. Au XVe siècle, quand la verrerie proche-orientale était en pleine décadence, on importa régulièrement en Egypte et en Syrie des produits des manufactures italiennes. En 1471, un Vénitien, appelé Paulus Cristallarius, exporta à Damas «capsam unam de christallo guarnitam et fulcitam argento smaltato due vasa seu botatia magna de christallo laborata a lateribus aparventis more adamantum fulcita argenti cum smalto et navem unam de christalo sup' quattuor rotis de christalo etiam fulcitam et guernitam argenti»[106].

Les données qu'on trouve dans les chroniques touchant les cargaisons des galères vénitiennes qui allaient au début du XVIe siècle en Orient, démontrent que l'exportation des produits de toutes ces industries, certainment moins importantes que celle des textiles, se poursuivait toujours.

Tableau 5. Exportation de savon, de papier et de verre par les Vénitiens

année	galères d'Alexandrie	galères de Beyrouth	sources
1500	savon: 62 sacs cristal: 3 caisses	papier: 42 balles	Marino Sanuto III, col. 1188; Priuli II, p. 74.
1503	savon: 378 caisses papier: 23 balles		Priuli II, p. 253, 255
1511	savon: 602 caisses	cristal: 5 caisses	Marino Sanuto XII, col. 78.

Le déclin de presque toutes les industries orientales face à l'ascendant technologique et économique de l'Occident chrétien ne pouvait pas ne pas avoir de répercussions dans les autres domaines où se faisait fortement sentir l'inégalité des civilisations autour de la Méditerranée. Quoique l'époque dans laquelle la supériorité technologique et économique de l'Occident devait aboutir à la domination politique et militaire eût été encore loin, ce grand progrès technologique assurait aux Occidentaux une place de premier ordre dans des domaines qui ne relevaient pas du tout de l'économie.

La marine

Un effet de leur supériorité technologique était la domination de la mer. Guillaume Adam, archevêque catholique de Perse de 1322 à 1324 et très au fait des conditions du Proche-Orient, écrit en 1317 que des Chrétiens ven-

105 Leonarde de Valle, sub 7 fév. 1403.

106 G. P., Sent. 169, f. 19a; description détaillée dans G. P., Ter. IV, f. 70b. Des autres textes sont cités dans *Le Proche-Orient au bas Moyen Age,* chapitre f; Aspetti della espansione italiana, p. 19.

dent et construisent aux Musulmans des bateaux. Selon ce qu'il raconte, ils auraient appris aux Musulmans à construire des bateaux et même servi dans leurs flottilles pour s'adonner ensemble à la piraterie[107]. On n'acceptera cette relation que cum grano salis, car pour le prélat toute collaboration de Chrétiens et de Musulmans était un péché et équivalait à la piraterie. Mais le fait lui-même ne doit pas être mis en doute. Car cette relation est corroborée par un témoin au-dessus de tout soupçon. C'est le savant arabe Ibn Khaldún, l'auteur d'une œuvre sur la sociologie des peuples musulmans. Dans cette œuvre, écrite à la fin du XIVe siècle, il affirme que les Chrétiens ont retrouvé la pratique de la haute-mer, et battent les Musulmans à chaque rencontre navale. Les Musulmans sont devenus des étrangers à la vie maritime, à l'exception d'un petit nombre d'habitants de la côte[108].

Plusieurs relations dans diverses sources confirment les jugements exprimés par ces auteurs et leurs rapports. Elles révèlent que les flottes des Musulmans, commerciales et militaires, étaient à cette époque en pleine décadence. Les marins arabes et grecs qui dominaient jadis la Méditerranée n'égalaient plus les Occidentaux.

Le chroniqueur arabe al-Makrīzī raconte par exemple que les bateaux de guerre équipés par le sultan mamlouk pour attaquer Chypre en 1425 étaient construits par un Arménien, le raīs Fādil, arrivé en Egypte l'année précédente[109]. L'incapacité des Musulmans à construire des bateaux ressort aussi d'une consultation de Nicolò de Auxino, secrétaire du pape Urbain V. C'est un jugement prononcé lors de la reprise du commerce avec les Musulmans du Proche-Orient après une longue suspension, due à l'embargo du Saint-Siège et à l'expédition du roi de Chypre contre Alexandrie. En 1371 ledit homme d'Eglise maintient qu'il est défendu de se rendre en pays d'Islam aux charpentiers chrétiens qui sont experts dans la construction de galères. Car ils sont susceptibles de rester in partibus infidelium de gré ou de force. Les rameurs, les pilotes et les autres marins également ne doivent plus se rendre en pays d'Islam[110].

Des relations contenues dans les chroniques arabes du bas Moyen Age font aussi conclure à l'inhabilité des marins musulmans. Les chroniqueurs racontent que ces marins ne savaient pas bien manœuvrer en haute-mer. Voici quelques exemples: une escadre mamlouke après avoir ravagé Chypre en 1425 voulait rentrer à Tripoli, mais arriva à at-Tīna, près de Damiette.

107 Guillaume Adam, «De modo saracenos extirpandi», *RHC, Documents arméniens,* II, p. 523.

108 *Muqaddimah,* trad. Fr. Rosenthal, II, p. 46. Les traductions qu'on a faites de ce passage sont très différentes, v. celles de M. de Slane, *Les Prolegomènes,* Paris 1863–68, II, p. 46; V. Monteil, *Discours sur l'histoire universelle,* Beyrouth 1968, II, p. 525 (l'original dans l'édition de Quatremère, «Notices et Extraits» 17, II, p. 40).

109 *Sulūk,* IV, p. 689.

110 *Diplomatarium Veneto-Levantinum,* II, no 91.

L'historien arabe qui raconte l'épisode explique que le vent avait poussé les bateaux vers l'Egypte[111]. En 1426, quatre bateaux de guerre qui devaient participer à l'attaque finale contre Chypre firent naufrage près de Rosette, sur la côte d'Egypte. Al-Makrīzī relate que le sultan voulait renoncer à l'expédition contre Chypre et qu'il se ressaisit plus tard sous l'influence de l'émir Djerbāsh Ḳāshiḳ[112].

Il va de soi que les Musulmans se rendaient compte de l'état des choses et songeaient à y remédier.

Ils engagèrent ainsi des marins chrétiens. C'est ce qu'on apprend de diverses sources. Selon un document vénitien, en 1357 un navire de Musulmans de Tunis arriva à Tripoli, venant d'Alexandrie; le patron et les marins, tous Génois, emmenèrent comme prisonnier un marchand vénitien[113]. Des marins chrétiens servaient en effet, comme le soutient Guillaume Adam, dans les flottes de guerre des Musulmans. Le chroniqueur vénitien Morosini raconte que la flotte mamlouke allant attaquer Chypre en 1426 comptait 120 bateaux équipés par des Musulmans et des Francs. L'auteur tirait cela d'une lettre de Damas[114]. Toutes les mesures prises par l'Eglise contre les «mauvais Chrétiens» qui vendaient des bateaux aux Musulmans et servaient dans leurs flottes furent vaines. Depuis la fin du XIIe siècle les conciles œcuméniques les condamnaient, les papes s'adressaient aux autorités ecclésiastiques et séculaires, qui devaient punir les transgresseurs, mais l'appât du profit était trop grand[115]. La bulle de Boniface VIII datant d'avril 1299 et répétée dans la même année est particulièrement explicite. Elle condamne les Chrétiens qui «in piraticis Saracenorum navibus curam gubernationis exercerent vel in machinis aut quibuslibet aliis aliquod eis (...) impenderent auxilium vel consilium»[116].

Les souverains musulmans de leur côté, encourageaient les Chrétiens à vendre des navires à leur sujets. Dans de nombreux traités passés entre les souverains de Tunis et les nations marchandes il était stipulé que la vente d'un bateau par un Chrétien à un Musulman était exempte de droits. La vente d'un bateau à un sujet d'un autre Etat chrétien, qui n'avait pas conclu un traité d'amitié avec le souverain musulman, était imposée d'un

111 Ibn Ḥadjar al-Askalānii, *Inbā al-ghumr,* III, p. 345 et s. (al-Maḳrīzī ne mentionne pas cet événement, v. *Sulūk,* IV, p. 695).

112 *Sulūk,* IV, p. 720; *Ibn Iyās,* éd. M. Mostafa, II, Wiesbaden 1972, p. 106; cf. Weil, *Geschichte der Chalifen,* V, p. 173 et s.

113 De Mas Latrie, *Traités,* II, p. 228 et s.

114 Chronique Morosini, c. 437.

115 V. les textes cités dans ma conférence «L'artiglieria veneziana e il commercio di Levante», dans le symposium *Armi e cultura nel Bresciano dal 1420 al 1870,* Brescia 1982, p. 152 et s.; à ajouter Mansi, *Concilia,* 26, col. 336: bulle du pape promulguée à Chypre en 1251 contre ceux qui servent sur les bateaux des Musulmans.

116 *Reg. de Boniface VIII,* Paris 1885-1939, no 3354 cf. 3421.

droit de 10%[117]. On se réservait aussi le droit d'affréter des bateaux chrétiens ancrant dans les ports musulmans. Les accords entre les souverains maghrébins et les Etats chrétiens contiennent presque toujours un paragraphe selon lequel les autorités musulmanes pouvaient faire usage d'un navire chrétien sur trois se trouvant dans un port de leur pays et cela s'il n'était pas encore chargé ou avec le consentement du consul de la nation à laquelle le bateau appartenait[118]. En plus on stipulait que le patron d'un bateau chrétien qui l'avait loué à des Musulmans pouvait effectuer des achats avec le frêt reçu sans payer des droits[119].

Les marchands musulmans ainsi que les autorités des Etats du Maghreb et du Proche-Orient avaient en effet souvent recours aux services des flottes chrétiennes. On n'exagérera pas en soutenant que la plus grande partie du trafic maritime entre le Maghreb et l'Egypte était à cette époque assurée par des bateaux européens. On pourrait évoquer de nombreux documents et textes dans des sources littéraires qui témoignent de cette situation[120]. On comprend que le transport de Musulmans et de leurs marchandises donnait souvent lieu à des conflits et causait de grandes difficultés aux nations marchandes. Quand des patrons trop avides s'emparaient des marchandises de leurs passagers ou que des corsaires attaquaient les bateaux, les Etats musulmans exerçaient des représailles contre la nation des pirates[121]. De tels incidents avaient lieu partout, des côtes du Maghreb au Proche-Orient. Car les Musulmans d'Egypte et de Syrie avaient aussi souvent besoin de bateaux chrétiens. Parfois les nations marchandes interdisaient le transport des passagers musulmans pour éviter des conflits. En 1406 le Sénat vénitien fut saisi d'une proposition de révoquer l'interdiction d'affréter des bateaux aux Musulmans (et à d'autres étrangers) à Alexandrie pour transporter du blé à partir de là et d'autres ports égyptiens vers les échelles du Proche-Orient. Mais la proposition ne fut pas acceptée[122]. D'autre part, les Musulmans ne pouvaient pas se passer des flottes chrétiennes. En 1450 le bateau du Ragusain Mihoč Kisiličić fut mis sous séquestre à Alexandrie par

117 V. la liste des traités où est comprise cette clause chez de Mas Latrie, *Traités,* I, p. 214; v. aussi G. Petti Balbi, «Il trattato del 1343 tra Genova e Tunisi», Civico Istituto Colombiano, Genova, *Saggi e documenti,* I, Gênes 1978, p. 316 et s.

118 De Mas Latrie, *Traités,* II, p. 52, 60 et s., 138 et s., 254, 356.

119 *Op. cit.,* II, p. 197, 200, 213, 218, 234, 246; Petti Balbi, *art. cit.,* p. 319. Dans des traités faits entre le roi de Tunisie et Pise en 1313 et à la fin du XIIIe siècle avec le roi de Catalogne on lit que les patrons sont exempts de la moitié du droit pour des achats faits avec le frêt obtenu de Musulmans, v. *op. cit.,* p. 60 et s., 283, 288; mais depuis 1314 les sujets du roi de Catalogne jouissaient de l'exemption totale, v. p. 319.

120 V. «L'artiglieria veneziana», p. 151 et s. et notes 52, 53; *Le Proche-Orient au bas Moyen Age,* chapitre g; de nombreux autres textes pourraient être cités, v. par exemple *Itinéraire d'Anselme Adorno en Terre Sainte (1470–1471),* éd. J. Heers-G. de Groer, Paris 1978, p. 141; G. P., Sent. 48, f. 112a et ss.

121 De Mas Latrie, *Traités,* II, p. 228 et s.

122 Misti 47, f. 63a et s.

les autorités mamlouks. Le patron fut contraint par le gouverneur de conduire un ambassadeur du sultan à Chypre et d'accepter une certaine somme d'argent pour l'achat de blé à Chypre ou en Asie Mineure. De fâcheux inconvénients s'ensuivirent[123]. Il ne serait pas difficile de citer des relations de conflits plus graves.

Ce qui frappe l'historien qui étudie les rapports entre les civilisations médiévales est le fait incontestable que les Byzantins aussi (et d'autres Grecs) avaient perdu, à la fin du Moyen Age, le goût de la navigation. Il suffit de jeter un coup d'œil sur les documents traitant des rapports entre Venise et l'empereur de Constantinople pour s'en apercevoir. Ce sont les bateaux vénitiens qui approvisionnaient Constantinople en blé acheté en Crimée ou en Bulgarie[124]. Des bateaux vénitiens exportaient aussi du blé de la Turquie pour le compte des Byzantins[125] et l'empereur se trouvant en état de guerre fut contraint de demander aux Vénitiens d'approvisionner Salonique[126]. Et même pour ses déplacements, il eut recours aux services de bateaux vénitiens[127].

Les Turcs certes n'excellaient pas dans la navigation. Il ne faut pas se laisser tromper par les activités des corsaires barbaresques qui sillonnaient au XVIe siècle la Méditerranée. C'étaient des renégats, des Chrétiens européens passés au côté des Musulmans. En 1588, les trente cinq galères d'Algérie étaient commandées par onze Turcs et par vingt quatre renégats, venus de tous les pays chrétiens riverains de la Méditerranée[128].

Armes

La supériorité technologique de l'Occident se manifestait aussi, à la fin du Moyen Age, dans un autre domaine, la production d'armes. Il est vrai que depuis longtemps les épées franques jouissaient d'une grande renommée dans le monde oriental. Mais à l'époque du bas Moyen Age, les manufactures d'armes dans les pays du Proche-Orient, dans le Maghreb et dans des autres régions orientales semblent avoir tellement décliné que l'importation d'armes de l'Europe était devenue nécessaire. De plus, étant donné qu'il s'agissait d'un phénomène lié à la décadence technologique dans la

123 B. Krekić, *Dubrovnik (Raguse) et le Levant au Moyen Age,* Paris 1961, no 1258, cf. no 1192, 1201, 1202.
124 Fr. Thiriet, *Régestes des délibérations du sénat de Venise concernant la Roumanie,* Paris 1958-61, 1, p. 52 (a. 1343), 120 (a. 1368), 136 (a. 1375) et v. aussi 186 (a. 1390); *Diplomatarium Ven.-Lev.,* II, no 49 (a. 1362).
125 Fr. Thiriet, *Régestes,* 1, p. 69 (a. 1350).
126 *Op. cit.* I, p. 68.
127 *Op. cit.* II, p. 39 (a. 1403), 51 (a. 1405), 74 (a. 1407).
128 St. Lane-Poole, *The Barbary corsairs,* Londres 1890, p. 200 et ss.

production industrielle, on avait aussi perdu l'habileté à réparer les armes. On était donc amené à avoir recours aux services des Occidentaux.

Puisque la vente d'armes aux Musulmans était interdite par l'Eglise, et en particulier leur exportation vers les pays du Proche-Orient, on se gardait bien de mentionner ces transactions dans les documents. Mais ça et là on en trouve des mentions. Quand les Génois firent, en 1433, un traité avec le souverain de Tunis, ils s'obligèrent pour racheter des prisonniers chrétiens à lui livrer «gladii parvi»[129]. Et les Génois n'étaient pas les seuls à fournir les Musulmans en armes.

Une série de bulles pontificales attestent qu'on exportait à la fin du XIIIe siècle et au XIVe siècle, à partir de Chypre très souvent, des armes vers l'Egypte et la Syrie. Et c'est en vain que le Saint-Siège s'adressa au roi de Chypre pour lui demander de prendre des mesures efficaces contre cette contrebande et d'accorder son assistance à ceux qui menaient la lutte contre les mauvais Chrétiens[130].

Les textes qui se réfèrent à ce commerce florissant avec l'Orient sont assez nombreux et il semble que les Génois y étaient particulièrement actifs. C'était en effet un commerce très profitable. En 1312 le pape s'adressa au gouvernement de Gênes au sujet du conflit l'opposant aux Hospitaliers qui avaient arraisonné une galère génoise transportant des armes pour les Musulmans[131]. Et les Vénitiens et les Pisans s'adonnaient eux aussi à ces activités de contrebande. Le Maître des Templiers les accusa de ce commerce devant le Pape en 1311, mentionnant les lances et d'autres armes qu'ils avaient fournies aux Musulmans[132]. Benoît XI dut même accompagner l'envoi d'une bulle interdisant ce commerce d'une lettre particulière au gouvernement de Venise[133]. L'importance qu'avait la fourniture d'armes aux yeux des Musulmans est aussi mise en évidence par des auteurs arabes. Un texte dans l'histoire de l'écrivain syrien Abu l-Fidā contenant la constatation que la conquête de Rhodes par les Hospitaliers en 1308 avait rendu difficile aux marchands européens l'accès de la Syrie se rapporte certainement au commerce des armes[134]. Tous ces témoignages datent de l'époque postérieure à la chute de Saint-Jean d'Acre, mais il va de soi que, même plus tard, les Orientaux continuèrent à avoir besoin d'armes occidentales. Au milieu du XVe siècle, Jacques Cœur fût accusé non seulement d'avoir

129 De Mas Latrie, *Traités*, II, p. 141.

130 Baronius-Raynaldi, *Annales ecclesiae*, s. a. 1299 no 38, s. a. 1323 no 12, s. a. 1324 no 43. V. aussi s. a. 1359 no 19.

131 S. Paoli, *Codice diplomatico... Gerosolomitano*, II, Lucques 1737, p. 31 ss.

132 St. Baluze, *Vitae paparum Avinoniensium*, Paris 1693–94, II, col. 180.

133 *Libri commemoriali*, ed. Predelli, I, lib. 1, no 161, 162, 169; cf. C. A. Marin, *Storia civile e politica del commercio de' Veneziani*, V, Venise 1800, p. 322 ss. Des marchands siciliens vendaient eux-aussi, au XIVe siècle, du fer aux Musulmans, v. P. Corrao, in *Medioevo*, (Cagliari), VI, 1981, p. 145.

134 *Abulfeda*, éd. Reiske-Adler, V, Hafniae 1794, p. 211.

fourni au sultan d'Egypte des armes mais de lui avoir aussi envoyé des armuriers pour en enseigner l'emploi[135].

L'infériorité en ce qui concerne le développement des techniques d'armement se manifesta encore plus dans les pays musulmans et grecs quand les Occidentaux réussirent progressivement à perfectionner les armes à feu, employées depuis 1330 environ. On allongea d'abord la canne des «bombardes» (canons primitifs) pour accélérer la vitesse du tir[136]; au XVe siècle on commença à produire des pièces faites de bronze (à 90% de cuivre et 10% d'étain) moins sensibles à la pression de la poudre. A la fin du XVe siècle, on introduisit la «fonte montante», qui améliora considérablement la qualité du canon[137]. On introduisit aussi l'emploi des projectiles de fer (au lieu de pierres) - dont le poids spécifique était plus lourd et donc de plus petite superficie - réduisant d'autant la force de frottement de l'air et permettant un tir plus exact[138]. On réussit enfin au cours de ce siècle à allonger la portée du tir[139].

On se tromperait en croyant que les militaires orientaux, turcs et grecs, ne s'étaient par aperçus du grand progrès réalisé dans la production d'armes à feu en Europe. Bien sûr, les cavaliers turcs dédaignaient l'artillerie à pied et méprisaient les armes mécaniques. Et s'il est vrai que les Mamlouks étaient prêts à les employer, c'était pour en équiper des compagnies composées de renégats européens et de Noirs[140]. Les Grecs se rendaient eux aussi compte de la nécessité d'employer des armes à feu et, en 1452 l'empereur de Byzance fut pourvu par Venise de salpêtre pour en user dans la lutte contre les Ottomans[141]. Venise était en effet un grand centre de la production de poudre à feu, et on savait très bien y raffiner le salpêtre, un de ses composants[142]. De même, leurs ennemis avait recours à des armes fabriquées en Occident. En 1463, lors de la guerre entre les Ottomans et Venise, ce furent les Génois de Caffa qui leur fournirent des armes venant d'Allemagne[143]. Les succès fulgurants des Turcs à l'époque de leur grandeur sont souvent attribués à l'emploi des armes à feu, surtout dans les guerres des Balkans et dans la lutte contre les Mamlouks. Mais leur capacité de les produire, et de les employer, bref leur attitude envers elles n'était pas très différente de celle de leurs adversaires d'Orient. L'histoire du rené-

135 Vallet de Viriville, *Histoire de Charles III,* Paris 1888, II, p. 327.

136 V. Schmidtchen, *Bombarden, Befestigungen, Büchsenmeister,* Düsseldorf 1977, p. 17 et s.

137 *Op. cit.,* p. 29.

138 *Op. cit.,* p. 105.

139 *Op. cit.,* p. 32.

140 V. «L'artiglieria veneziana e il commercio di Levante», p. 142 et note 4 (où sont citées les sources arabes).

141 S. Romanin, *Storia documentata di Venezia,* 3e éd., Venise 1972-75, IV, p. 180.

142 V. mon article «Aspetti della espansione italiana», p. 24 et s.

143 J. Heers, *Gênes au XVe siècle,* Paris, p. 371.

gat hongrois (ou roumain) Orban qui fondit un grand canon pour Mehmed le Conquérant est bien connue[144]. Mais il ne faut pas négliger d'autres témoignages concernant le recours à des Occidentaux pour la fourniture des pièces d'artillerie. Marino Sanuto cite un rapport de Constantinople selon lequel des juifs réfugiés d'Espagne fondirent en 1517 des pièces d'artillerie pour les Ottomans[145]. Ce rapport est confirmé par un témoin qu'on ne peut suspecter (car il n'aimait pas les juifs). Le voyageur français Nicolai de Nicolay raconte que des Juifs, spécialement des Marranes, avaient introduit chez les Turcs plusieurs inventions, artifices et machines de guerre, comme à faire artillerie, arquebuses, poudre à canon, boulets et autres armes[146]. Ces juifs espagnols qui furent, semble-t-il, partout les promoteurs des nouvelles techniques - ou du moins ceux qui les répandirent, - aidaient aussi les Arabes de Tripoli dans leur lutte contre les envahisseurs espagnols.

Evoquons un autre témoignage relevé par Marino Sanuto. Le chroniqueur vénitien cite une lettre de Pelegrin Venier, consul de Venise à Palerme, écrite le 10 novembre 1510 et traitant de la campagne espagnole en Tripolitaine. Parlant des préparatifs du roi musulman de la Tunisie pour reconquérir Tripoli (prise par les Espagnols) il écrit: «E come iera zerti Zudei d'Alemagna renegati quali havea fato de continuo artelarie de diverse qualita»[147]. On se demande qui étaient ces juifs autrefois chrétiens et puis renégats (car c'est le sens du terme) et que faisaient des juifs allemands dans la Tripolitaine? En fait, il n'y a guère de doute que le bon Venier s'est trompé et écrit (ou entend) Alemagna au lieu de Spagna. Et ce devait être, encore une fois, des juifs réfugiés d'Espagne, des Marranes!

Mais les Ottomans, qui employaient des armes à feu et se faisaient construire leurs canons par des étrangers avaient un goût très particulier. Ils aimaient des pièces géantes qui faisaient grande impression, même si elles étaient peu utiles[148]. L'artillerie ottomane était, en effet, peu efficace. Les pièces mises à la disposition des garnisons stationnées en Syrie ne leur permettaient pas de mener à bien la lutte contre les Bédouins. Les commandants se plaignaient à la Sublime Porte que les canons étaient trop courts et que les boulets ne portaient pas assez loin[149].

144 J. v. Hammer, *Geschichte des osmanischen Reiches,* Pesth 1834–36, I, p. 389; N. Jorga, *Geschichte des osmanischen Reiches,* Gotha 1908–13, II, p. 18.

145 Diarii 25, col 147: «schiopeti, archibusi et altre artillerie minute, le qual si fanno in varii lochi de la terra et ne la habitation loro» (sc. de ces juifs).

146 N. de Nicolay. *Les navigations et pérégrinations... faites en Turquie,* Anvers 1586, p. 168.

147 Marino Sanuto, *Diarii,* XI, col 710.

148 C. M. Cipolla, *Guns & sails in the early phase of European expansion, 1400–1700,* Londres 1965, p. 92.

149 U. Heyd, *Ottoman documents on Palestine,* 1552–1615, Oxford 1960, p. 94.

Conclusion

Les témoignages, trouvés dans diverses sources, qu'on a citées ici, ne laissent aucun doute: les civilisations orientales subissaient à la fin du Moyen Age une décadence technologique qui les affaiblissait et leur rendait impossible la résistance à l'expansion de l'Occident. Et combien d'autres relations pourrait-on y ajouter...

Un voyageur flamand raconte que les remparts de Damas, détruits par Tamerlan, avaient été reconstruits par un Florentin qui s'était fait Musulman[150]. Les chroniques arabes relatent la destruction de digues du Nil, et les inondations qui s'ensuivaient, et ajoutent qu'on les laissait en ruines pendant de longues années[151]. Négligence ou incapacité? Les ingénieurs des Mamlouks étaient incapables de réparer un pont et pour restaurer la Grande Mosquée de Damas on dut faire appel à des architectes d'Asie Mineure[152]. Les services du sultan mamlouk émettaient des dinars qui n'avaient pas de poids fixe. C'étaient en effet des pièces d'or de poids irréguliers et estampées par le gouvernement[153]. L'inhabileté technique des Grecs n'était pas moindre à cette époque. Le basileus Comnène de Trebizond s'adressa en 1365 au gouvernement de Venise pour demander deux cloches[154], et un de ses successeurs envoya à Venise une cloche et une horloge pour les réparer[155].

Mais, hélas, si recueillir des témoignages touchant le déclin technologique de civilisations est facile, l'expliquer est plus ardu. Les hypothèses avancées ne sont pas toutes convaincantes. Elles ne peuvent être considérées comme valables que dans certains cas. On ne peut prétendre avoir trouvé des raisons générales.

Le problème est en effet très complexe. Pourquoi des peuples qui ne manquaient pas d'esprits ingénieux ont-ils rejeté des innovations? Pourquoi a-t-on refusé de meilleures méthodes de production, bien qu'on en ait eu les moyens (force hydraulique, par exemple) et qu'on n'ait pas ignoré leurs avantages?

Que la politique fiscale, tout à fait erronée, de certains souverains musulmans ait contribué à la ruine des industries est hors de doute. Il est certain que la monopolisation de plusieurs secteurs industriels et les achats forcés de leurs produits, a enlevé aux manufactures royales la motivation de faire

150 *Itinéraire d'Anselme d'Adorno*, p. 331.

151 Ibn Ḥadjar al-Askalānī, *Inbā* III, p. 422.

152 E. Ashtor, *A social and economic history of the Near East in the Middle Ages*, Londres 1976, p. 309.

153 P. Balog, *The coinage of the Mamlūk sultans of Egypt and Syria*, New York 1964, p. 41 et cf. Ph. Grierson, «La moneta veneziana nell'economia mediterranea del Trecento e Quattrocento», in *La civiltà veneziana del Quattrocento*, Florence 1957, p. 89 et s.

154 Fr. Thiriet, *Régestes*, I, p. 110, 119.

155 *Op. cit.*, II, p. 38.

de coûteuses expériences pour améliorer les méthodes de production. On peut se demander toutefois pourquoi les autorités mamloukes n'avaient pas intérêt à exporter les textiles et le sucre de leurs pays, ce qui leur aurait apporté de gros revenus. En outre, combien de fois des inventions ont été faites par hasard ou par un seul technicien qui travaillait pour son compte! La supposition que la libre concurrence entre des entreprises privées aurait eu pour conséquence l'introduction de meilleures méthodes de production, tandis que les régimes autoritaires amènent le déclin n'est pas satisfaisante non plus. Car on ne comprendrait pas le grand progrès réalisé dans les Etats autoritaires par excellence, comme en Russie à l'époque de Pierre le Grand. L'hypothèse d'un lien entre offre considérable de main-d'œuvre et recul technologique (thèse marxiste), ne tient pas, car Vitruve, le plus grand ingénieur de Rome, ne vécut-il pas quand l'esclavage était à son apogée? On a soutenu aussi que le progrès technologique est un phénomène qui se manifeste en liaison avec une croissance démographique. La pression démographique poussant à développer les techniques, la diminution de la population entraînant dans son sillon le déclin technologique. Mais en acceptant cette façon d'expliquer l'évolution technique on ne comprendrait pas pourquoi l'Inde aujourd'hui n'est pas le pays technologiquement le plus avancé. On a expliqué le progrès technologique opéré en Europe au Moyen Age et plus tard par le caractère du Christianisme occidental, basé sur le libre choix[156]. L'attitude des Chrétiens latins envers les innovations technologiques était-elle vraiment, dès l'abord, différente de celle des Chrétiens grecs-orthodoxes et des Musulmans? Devons-nous donc croire que le recul technologique des vieilles civilisations orientales était la conséquence de leur fatalisme religieux? Mais on a vu que les Musulmans, à certaines époques du moins, avaient acquis des engins occidentaux et qu'ils avaient retenus des techniciens européens pour apprendre et employer leurs méthodes. Toutefois il apparaît que l'opposition aux innovations qui se manifeste dans toutes les civilisations y était particulièrement forte. Le refus d'employer les moulins à vent introduits par les Croisés au Proche-Orient[157] est un exemple caractéristique de cette mentalité. On n'oubliera pas la résistance des populations proche-orientales à accepter le papier-monnaie, émis par le gouvernement tartare en Perse et en Iraq, à la fin du XIIIe siècle. L'introduction de ces billets aurait propagé l'impression chinoise dans le Proche-Orient[158]. Le retour au foulage à pieds observé en Palestine après la ruine du centre industriel établi par les juifs espagnols à

156 Lynn White, «Technology and invention in the Middle Ages», *Speculum,* 15, 1940, p. 156; J. Gimpel, *La révolution industrielle du Moyen Age,* Paris 1975, p. 160.

157 Lynn White, *Medieval technology and social change,* Oxford 1962, p. 88; M. T. Horwitz, «Über das Aufkommen, die erste Entwicklung und die Verbreitung des Windrades», *Technikgeschichte,* 22, 1933, p. 93 et ss.

158 *A social and economic history of the Near East in the Middle Ages,* p. 257.

Safed, démontre lui-aussi que le conservatisme des Orientaux était très prononcé. Suffit-il pourtant, d'expliquer le déclin technologique d'une civilisation par l'ankylose spirituelle? Il est vrai que les républiques marchandes du Moyen Age étaient les foyers du progrès technologique et que leurs gouvernements encourageaient et appuyaient les inventeurs[159]. Mais n'y a-t-il pas eu des Etats dominés par des classes très conservatrices et qui se sont distingués par leur disponibilité à introduire des innovations technologiques (la Prusse au XIXe siècle, par exemple)? La disponibilité des Mamlouks à utiliser des armes à feu, quarante ans seulement après que les Occidentaux eurent commencé à les employer, signifie que leur incapacité à les développer était due à la stagnation technologique régnant dans leurs pays et, d'autre part, à une autre mentalité. L'attitude des Japonais, qui ont adopté les innovations apportées par les Européens, témoigne en revanche d'une réaction tout-à-fait différente de celle manifestée par les peuples du Proche-Orient à la fin du Moyen Age.

159 G. Zanetti, *Dell'origine di alcune arti principali appresso i Viniziani,* Venise 1758, p. 74.

Safed, démontre lui aussi que le conservatisme des Orientaux était très prononcé. Suffit-il pourtant, d'expliquer le déclin technologique d'une civilisation par l'ankylose spirituelle? Il est vrai que les [illegible] du Moyen-Age étaient les [illegible] progrès technologique et que leurs gouvernements encourageaient [illegible] les inventeurs. Mais n'y a-t-il pas eu [illegible] des cas [illegible] très [illegible] et qui se sont distingués par leur disponibilité à introduire des innovations technologiques (la Russie au XIXe siècle, par exemple)? La réticence des Mamlouks à utiliser les armes à feu [illegible] que les [illegible] derniers [illegible] à [illegible] que leur incapacité à les développer était due à la stagnation [illegible] régnant dans leurs pays et, d'autre part, à [illegible] mentalité [illegible] été les innovations apportées [illegible] par ces [illegible] l'Occident [illegible] du Moyen Age?

[illegible]

V

ASPETTI DELLA ESPANSIONE ITALIANA NEL BASSO MEDIOEVO

I

Per spiegare il grande sviluppo del commercio italiano (e anche catalano) nel basso medioevo e l'espansione delle repubbliche marittime nel Levante, gli storici economici hanno addotto parecchie ragioni. La sostituzione di aziende centralizzate e articolate in succursali con compagnie indipendenti, operanti in vari paesi e collegate da un capo comune avrebbe impedito che il fallimento di un ramo del sistema coinvolgesse gli altri. L'uso, diventato quasi generale, di assicurare i trasporti marittimi e l'impiego della lettera di cambio per trasferire considerevoli somme di contanti avrebbe permesso ai grandi mercanti di evitare lunghi e costosi viaggi. Affidando le merci tramite l'accomandita a rappresentanti oltremare, i cosidetti fattori, che facevano affari per molti « maestri », le transazioni sarebbero state più semplici e più facili. Una più dettagliata struttura dei noli marittimi, che distingueva più che prima fra le diverse merci, avrebbe agevolato il trasporto di articoli voluminosi e meno cari. F. Melis non si stancava di ribadire che questa riforma dei noli significava una vera rivoluzione nella storia del commercio internazionale [1]. La notevole efficienza del servizio di informazione assicurata dagli agenti delle grandi ditte negli scali principali del commercio internazionale rendeva possibile previsioni esatte, sicché i rischi del mercante diminuivano. L'uso di fare contratti diretti fra i mercanti, invece di ricorrere a notai che redigevano documenti latini, avrebbe fatto risparmiare molto tempo.

Tutte queste osservazioni sono giuste e potremmo aggiungerne altre. Il servizio veneziano delle galee « a mercato », che funzionava regolarmente, garantiva senza dubbio uno svolgimento molto efficiente delle transazioni. Il fatto che i mercanti di vari paesi sapessero esattamente quando potevano vendere o comprare li induceva a tenere

[1] *Werner Sombart e i problemi della navigazione nel medio evo*, in *L'opera di Werner Sombart nel centenario della sua nascita*, Milano, 1964 p. 132 sgg.; *Mercaderes italianos en España* (siglos XIV-XVI), Sevilla, 1976, pp. 145, 193.

pronti soldi e merci e così risparmiavano tempo e spese. La rigorosa vigilanza delle autorità veneziane sul traffico marittimo impediva che la sfrenata avidità di lucro di mercanti e di padroni di navi sfociasse nella perdita di interi carichi di ricche navi che veleggiavano in acque infestate da pirati.

Bisogna anche soffermarsi sul grande cambiamento che provocò la caduta del gruppo dei Karimiti. Finché questi ricchi, influenti mercanti e banchieri orientali dominavano il commercio internazionale nel Vicino Oriente potevano anche imporre le loro condizioni ai mercanti italiani. Parecchi documenti riferentisi ai passi redatti dai diplomati della Serenissima presso il sultano del Cairo ne fanno testimonianza. Ma quando il sultano mamlucoho Barsbay li rovesciò, i mercanti europei li sostituirono in grande misura e poterono tentare di regolare il commercio fra il Levante e le loro metropoli come meglio desideravano [2].

Tuttavia queste ragioni non sono sufficienti per spiegare l'espansione economica delle «nazioni mercanti» nell'epoca susseguente alle Crociate e anzitutto nel secondo Trecento e nel Quattrocento. Il commercio nel Mediterraneo è allora quasi completamente nelle mani dei mercanti italiani, il traffico marittimo è un affare degli armatori genovesi e veneziani, nessuna nave musulmana approda in un porto cristiano. Le industrie di parecchie regioni in Italia, in Catalogna e nei Paesi Bassi esportano grandi quantità dei loro prodotti nel Levante da cui importano materie grezze. Questo fenomeno sarebbe incomprensibile se non venisse preso in considerazione un grande cambiamento nei paesi del Levante. Era la decadenza delle industrie in alcune regioni di questi paesi che rendeva possibile, in grande misura, l'espansione italiana. La diminuzione della produzione o piuttosto la sua sospensione in vari rami delle industrie orientali lasciò un vuoto che venne riempito da prodotti importati dai mercanti italiani. Se non supponiamo che il tramonto delle industrie orientali sia stato la causa e il sintomo di un vero dumping di prodotti europei, non potremmo spiegare come i mercanti pagassero i cari articoli che acquistavano negli scali levantini.

Questo nesso causale è molto chiaro, benché non fosse stato osservato da molti studiosi europei che consideravano l'espansione italiana soltanto come fenomeno della storia dell'Europa occidentale. Ma è una constatazione che pone altri problemi. Il crollo delle industrie orientali era l'effetto di una sbagliata politica fiscale dei sovrani musulmani, dell'oppressione della concorrenza libera, del predominio dello Stato nella produzione industriale e anzitutto del loro ristagno tecnologico. Ora, la decadenza tecnologica risultava dai fenomeni sovramenzionati, ma non si può sostenere questi ne fossero l'unica ragione. Certo è possibile addurne altre, ma si dovrebbe ricercare

[2] V. il mio articolo *The Venetian supremacy in Levantine trade: monopoly or pre-colonialism*, JEEH III (1974), p. 26 sgg.

una causa che possa essere considerata come principale. Quale era? E poiché la decadenza tecnologica determinava, così pare, la sorte della civiltà orientale, come in generale non è possibile non accorgersi del nesso fra lo slancio tecnologico e la ascesa di civiltà e di potenze politiche e il ristagno tecnologico e la loro discesa, ci troviamo di fronte a un grosso problema a cui i fatti raccolti in questo articolo dovrebbero fornire materiali senza pretendere di trovarne una soluzione [3].

II

Le fonti arabe ci forniscono dati abbastanza esatti circa le fasi successive della decadenza delle più grandi industrie del Levante — le industrie tessili del Basso Egitto. Secondo al-Maḳrīzī Tinnīs, uno dei più importanti centri di queste industrie, fu evacuata e distrutta nel 1277 e non venne ricostruita [4]. Pare che anche altre città del Basso Egitto, ove fiorivano le manifatture del lino e di altri tessili, venissero abbandonate nello stesso tempo, giacché il medesimo scrittore, quando le menziona nella sua Topografia di Egitto, impiega il passato [5]. La cittadina di Dabīḳ, i cui tessili godevano di grande fama all'epoca delle Crociate, a giudicare da molti documenti della gheniza, già era stata abbandonata in una data anteriore, poiché Yāḳūt, che compilò la sua enciclopedia geografica verso l'anno 1220, non conosceva la sua posizione [6]. al-Maḳrīzī afferma che la rovina di Tinnīs era dovuta all'invasione dell'Egitto da parte dei Crociati che minacciarono di conquistare questa regione. È una interpretazione data da un autore medievale che non vedeva lo sfondo economico del declino industriale. Infatti la chiusura delle fabbriche di tessili nel Basso Egitto avvenne dopo la terribile carestia e la peste negli anni 1201-02 che diminuirono la popolazione di Egitto considerevolmente. Ora, la diminuzione della manodopera provocò il rincaro del lavoro, un fatto di cui fanno testimonianza parecchi documenti della gheniza [7]. Certamente la produzione di tessili a Tinnīs e in altre città non rendeva più. Se non fosse il troppo alto costo della produzione almeno una ragione della sua sospensione, le fabbriche sarebbero state riaperte, forse in altre città, dopo la ritirata dei Crociati. Ma si desume dalla relazione di un cronista arabo che nella stessa epoca già cominciò l'importazione massiccia di tessili dall'Europa, un fatto che probabil-

[3] Già ho trattato della decadenza di certe industrie orientali in parecchi articoli (v. infra). Lo scopo di questo articolo non è soltanto di presentare un quadro di insieme, ma anche di fornire molti nuovi dati.

[4] al-Khiṭaṭ I, p. 181^{25}; as-Sulūk I, p. 224.

[5] al-Khiṭaṭ I, p. 182^{2} sg., $185^{25,31}$ sg., 226^{13}, 464 II, p. 104.

[6] Mu'djam al-buldān II, pp. 546, 548.

[7] V. la mia *Histoire des prix et des salaires dans l'Orient médiéval*, Parigi, 1969, p. 224 sg.

mente indica la loro superiore qualità o il più basso prezzo. L'autore arabo Ibn Wāṣil racconta che quando il viziro del sultano Baibars si recò nel 1263 ad Alessandria per preparare la visita del sovrano raccolse ivi 95,000 pezze di panni del Yemen, di Venezia, scarlattini ed altri [8]. Atti notarili, rogati a Lajazzo negli anni 1274 e 1279, si riferiscono a panni di Ypres e della Lombardia ivi importati (e probabilmente riesportati nelle vicine regioni musulmane) [9].

Il fermo governo dei primi sultani mamlucchi determinò tuttavia se non un ricupero almeno un rallentamento del declino industriale. Alessandria, ad esempio, fu nella seconda metà del tredicesimo secolo e fino all'inizio del Quattrocento un importante centro dell'industria tessile. Ma in quest'ultima data un altro cataclisma avvenne. al-Maḳrīzī, testimone oculare, racconta che dopo la crisi economica nel 1403 gli Egiziani cambiarono il loro modo di vestire: tutti abbandonarono gli abiti di lino e cominciarono ad indossare panni di lana importati dall'Europa [10]. D'altra parte, lo stesso autore racconta, in un'altra opera, che il numero dei telai in Alessandria diminuiva da 14,000 nel 1395 a 800 nel 1434 [11]. Benché non possiamo citare testi precisi circa il declino delle industrie tessili nella Siria, vi sono indizi che dimostrano che anche in questo paese si profilava sullo scorcio del Trecento una notevole decadenza. Gli inventari di carichi di navi che veleggiavano dagli scali levantini, nell'ultimo terzo del Trecento, verso i porti dell'Italia, della Provenza e della Catalogna, comprendono sovente preziosi panni di seta. Anche le tariffe di nolo che fissavano le autorità veneziane in quell'epoca testimoniano l'esportazione di tali panni in Italia [12]. Poi, nel Quattrocento, i mercanti europei importano panni di seta nel Levante.

Sarebbe esagerato affermare che le industrie tessili crollassero completamente nel Levante all'inizio del Quattrocento. Molte relazioni dei cronisti arabi dimostrano che la produzione di cotonine fioriva ancora in quell'epoca in Siria, particolarmente nella città di Baalbek. Alessandria aveva ancora un'industria di seta [13]. Ma il volume della produzione di tessili era allora incomparabilmente inferiore a quello di epoche anteriori e neanche la qualità dei prodotti era paragonabile con i fini tessuti dell'epoca delle Crociate.

[8] Quatremère, *Histoire des sultans mamlouks*, I, 1, p. 252.

[9] C. Desimoni, *Actes passés en 1271, 1274 et 1279 à l'Aias (Petite Arménie) et à Beyrouth par devant des notaires génois*, Archives de l'Orient latin I (Paris, 1881), pp. 454, 506.

[10] al-Khiṭaṭ II, p. 98; traduzione francese: R. Dozy, *Dictionnaire détaillé des noms des vêtements chez les Arabes*, Amsterdam, 1845, p. 128.

[11] as-Sulūk, ms. Parigi 1727, f. 416a; bn Taghrībirdī, an-Nudjūm as-zāhira, ed. Popper, VI, p. 714.

[12] ASV (Archivio di Stato, Venezia), Senato, Miste 40, f. 27a 42, f. 111b.

[13] Ibn Taghrībirdī, Ḥawādith, p. 7, 14, 78 sg., 103 sg., 204; Ibn al-Ukhuwwa, Ma'ālim al-qurba, Cambridge, 1938, p. 142; Miste 60, f. 208b; Cronaca Zancaruola, ms. Marciana 1275 (Ital. VII, 9275), f. 584b.

Il crollo delle industrie tessili nel Levante era l'effetto di un nuovo e notevole rincaro del lavoro, conseguenza del progressivo spopolamento dopo la Peste Nera e le epidemie susseguenti. Lo stesso al-Makrīzī ribadisce che era allora molto difficile trovare un operaio [14]. Ma aveva anche altre cause [15]. Anzitutto derivava dal calo del livello della produzione. Due autori arabi, che avevano interesse per i problemi economici, al-Makrīzī e Ibn Khaldūn, raccontano che in quell'epoca, cioè alla fine del quattordicesimo secolo, i ṭirāz, le grandi manifatture reali, non funzionavano più e che la corte era costretta ad acquistare gli abiti di lusso [16]. Ora, i ṭirāz erano grandi fabbriche, sovente appaltate da ricchi imprenditori, e non sbaglieremo dicendo che erano vere imprese capitalistiche. Non bisogna mettere in rilievo che tali fabbriche potevano permettersi innovazioni tecnologiche e i lunghi e costosi sperimenti che ne sono spesso la condizione imprescindibile. Infatti quando la produzione calò sul livello artigianale, tali sperimenti non si poterono fare, superando i mezzi dei produttori.

E in quell'epoca le industrie tessili dell'Occidente già profittavano in ampia misura di tre importanti innovazioni tecnologiche che cambiarono la loro produzione completamente. Queste innovazioni erano l'impiego del filatoio, del telaio messo in funzione da un pedale e della gualcatura per mezzo di mulini ad acqua. Il nuovo filatoio (la ruota) che raddoppiava la produzione si era diffuso nell'Europa occidentale fin dalla seconda metà del tredicesimo secolo, il telaio con pedale fin dall'undicesimo secolo [17]. L'impiego del mulino ad acqua per gualcare i panni dopo la tessitura era senza dubbio l'innovazione più importante. La studiosa inglese E. M. Carus-Wilson non ha avuto torto caratterizzandola come una rivoluzione industriale [18]. Infatti segnava un passo importante nell'impiego della forza idraulica per scopi industriali.

Pare che tutte queste innovazioni non venissero introdotte nell'Oriente musulmano. Finché non siano studiate a fondo le miniature nelle collezioni di manoscritti orientali, una tale supposizione comporta rischi. Ma alcuni testi arabi del Trecento e del Quattrocento dimostrano che mulini ad acqua erano allora nel Levante considerati come una rarità. Quando il generale Djarkas al-Khalīlī costruì, nel 1382, un mulino ad acqua (più esattamente un mulino sul Nilo) per

[14] Traité des famines, trad. Wiet, JESHO V (1962), p. 75. Sul rincaro dei tessuti v. il mio articolo *L'évolution des prix dans le Proche-Orient à la basse-époque*, JESHO IV (1961), p. 39 ed anche Ḥawādith, p. 229 sgg.

[15] V. la mia comunicazione *Les lainages dans l'Orient médiéval*, Atti della IIª settimana di studi, Istituto Datini, Firenze, 1976, p. 682 sgg.

[16] al-Khiṭaṭ II, p. 98 sgg.; Ibn Khaldūn, The Muqaddimah (trad. Rosenthal), II, p. 67.

[17] Lynn White, *Medieval technology and social change*, Oxford, 1962, pp. 117, 119.

[18] *An industrial revolution of the thirteenth century*, « Economic History Review », 11 (1941), p. 29 sgg.

impiegarlo nella molitura, la gente veniva, così racconta al-Maḳrīzī, da lontano per vederlo [19]. Un altro scrittore arabo racconta, nella biografia di un ufficiale ritiratosi nella seconda metà del Quattrocento dalla carriera militare, che quest'ultimo fondò nella provincia di Fayyūm una massaria con un mulino ad acqua che non veniva messo in funzione da animali [20]. Un tale mulino era dunque molto raro.

La rarità di tali mulini certamente non era causata dalla scarsezza di fiumi e dalla ignoranza dei tecnici orientali. Anche nelle regioni attraversate da fiumi il numero dei mulini ad acqua era già molto diminuito quando scrisse il geografo Ibn Ḥauḳal la sua opera, alla fine del decimo secolo [21]. D'altra parte gli Arabi sapevano benissimo trasformare acqua stagnante in acqua corrente, ma lo facevano per altri scopi. In questo si tratta dunque della bene conosciuta opposizione conservatrice contro innovazioni tecnologiche, considerate come un peggioramento della produzione.

Comunque sia, l'effetto della inferiorità tecnologica era l'incapacità di fare concorrenza ai prodotti importati dai paesi europei. L'importazione di questi tessuti diventava sullo scorcio del Trecento un vero dumping. I panni fiorentini, di diversa qualità, tenevano un posto di prim'ordine fra i tessili che venivano importati dall'Occidente. Pare che grazie a perfezionamenti della produzione e per altre ragioni i loro prezzi diminuissero nel corso del Quattrocento [22]. Dalle liste di prezzi che compilavano in Egitto e in Siria gli agenti di Fr. Datini si desume che i mercanti italiani offrivano ivi alla fine del Trecento anche molti panni della Fiandra e del Brabante come panni di Wervicq-sur-Lys e di Malines ecc. Alla stessa epoca i Catalani cominciarono a esportare grandi quantità dei loro panni che costavano molto meno, anzitutto panni di Barcellona e di Perpignan [23]. Sembra che l'esportazione di panni fiamminghi nel Levante musulmano sia considerevolmente diminuita nel Quattrocento, mentre i Veneziani esportavano ivi grandi quantità di panni della Lombardia. La ditta veneziana di Andrea Barbarigo esporta nel 1431 in Acri 2 panni (cioè «pezze» di panni, di circa 30 metri) di Firenze e 20 anni loesti e nel 1433 74 panni loesti, 10 panni scarlattini, 5 panni bastardi, 5 panni di Mantova, 1 gilforte. Nel 1434 esportò nella stessa città 30 pezze di loesti e 4 pezze di mantovano. I panni fiorentini

[19] as-Sulūk III, p. 472.

[20] as-Sakhāwī, aḍ-Ḍau al-lāmi' III, p. 208[11].

[21] Ibn Ḥauḳal, ed. Kramers, p. 219 sg.

[22] V. *Les lainages dans l'Orient médiéval*, p. 679.

[23] V. art. cit., p. 678; il mio articolo *L'exportation de textiles occidentaux dans le Proche Orient musulman au bas Moyen Age*, nella *Miscellanea Fed. Melis*, cap. VII (in stampa). V. anche Miste 38, f. 156a: il senato decide che sia permesso caricare i panni di Fiandra che dovevano arrivare, fino alla partenza delle galee di Beirut, anche immediatamente prima della loro partenza.

e mantovani erano cari, il loro prezzo ammontava a 30-50 ducati la pezza, mentre i panni loesti si vendevano a prezzi bassi. Essi costavano la terza parte del prezzo dei panni suddetti [24]. I loesti (da Lowestoft, una località in Inghilterra, o da lowest), bastardi e gilforte erano probabilmente prodotti italiani, benché originariamente fabbricati in Inghilterra e nella Fiandra [25]. Nella seconda metà del Quattrocento i Veneziani spedivano grandi carichi di panni di Brescia in Siria. Anche questi panni erano di basso prezzo [26]. Ma mercanti veneziani esportavano in Egitto e in Siria anche panni bergamaschi e panni di altre città dell'Italia settentrionale [27]. L'importazione di panni inglesi, via Venezia, Genova e altri porti italiani, o direttamente, aumentava di molto nella stessa epoca [28]. Panni provenienti da tutte le provincie della Francia venivano offerti agli scali del Levante da mercanti francesi e da altri. Mercanti genovesi ivi esportano nell'ultimo terzo del Trecento panni di Beauvais [29], una ditta tedesca vende nel 1470 in Alessandria panni di Linguadoca [30]. L'importazione di panni fiamminghi, benché fosse diminuita, non venne interrotta. I Genoveni li importarono durante tutto il Quattrocento [31]. Ai clienti che appartenevano ai ceti alti della società orientale si offrivano scarlattini che erano molto apprezzati e richiesti, anzitutto dagli ufficiali musulmani [32], panni di seta [33] e broccati, come i famosi «panni di oro» di Cologna [34], velluti [35] e zetanini [36]. D'altra parte i mercanti italiani esportavano nel Levante sargie [37] e altri panni a buon prezzo,

[24] S. Sassi, *Sulle scritture di due aziende mercantili veneziane del Quattrocento*, Napoli, s. d., p. 236 sgg., 242, 248, 250.

[25] V. ASV, Senato, Mar IV, f. 161a; bastardi di Inghilterra: Miste 52, f. 152b.

[26] V. *L'exportation de textiles occidentaux dans l'Orient musulman* ecc., cap. I e v. anche ASV, Giudici di petiziòn (G. P.), Terminazioni V, f. 68b sg., 69b, 208a.

[27] G. P., Terminazioni III, f. 102a sgg. IX, f. 76b sg.

[28] Senato, Mar VI, f. 119b; G. P., Terminazioni III, f. 102a sgg.; ASG (Archivio di Stato, Genova), 2774 C, f. 23b, 33b, 35b. Anche in Sicilia l'importazione massiccia di panni inglesi cominciò nella metà del Quattrocento, v. C. Trasselli, *Fromento e panni inglesi nella Sicilia del XV secolo*, (nella sua raccolta) *Mediterraneo e Sicilia all'inizio dell'epoca moderna*, Cosenza, 1977, p. 321 sgg.

[29] J. Day, *Les douanes de Gênes 1376-1377*, Parigi, 1963, pp. 232, 414.

[30] G. P., Terminazioni VIII, f. 30a sg.

[31] R. Brunschvig, *Deux récits de voyage inédits en Afrique du Nord au XVe siècle*, Parigi, 1936, p. 135.

[32] G. P., Terminazioni III, f. 103a VII, f. 6b; Senato, Mar 11, f. 92a; 12, f. 58a sg. 13, f. 94a sg. 14, f. 4a; Cronaca Zorzi Dolfin, ms. Marciana Ital. VII, 794, f. 394a sg.; Miste 50, f. 83b 55, f. 117b.

[33] Miste 40, f. 72a; 42, f. 111b; 53, f. 89b.

[34] Senato, Mar IX, f. 150b; G. P., Terminazioni V, f. 164a sg.; Miste 50, f. 83b 55, f. 117b.

[35] G. P., Terminazioni X, f. 165a sg.; Miste 53, f. 118b 55, f. 35a, 75a; Senato, Mar II, f. 184a.

[36] Senato, Mar IX, f. 86b; G. P., Terminazioni X, f. 165a sg.

[37] Miste 26, f. 79b, 86a 41, f. 92b 44, f. 120a 45, f. 119b 53, f. 214a sgg 54, f. 72a sgg.

come panni di Polonia[38]. Di più offrivano i fustagni della Lombardia[39] e le tele della Francia e della Germania[40].

Il ricavo dell'esportazione massiccia di tutti questi tessili era senza dubbio considerevole, probabilmente ammontava a centinaia di migliaia di ducati all'anno[41]. Poiché i mercanti italiani non potevano pagare le costose spezierie in contanti, lo svolgimento delle loro attività sarebbe stato impossibile senza l'esportazione dei panni.

III

Il quadro che emerge dello studio dei dati che si trovano nelle fonti arabe sullo sviluppo delle altre industrie orientali è più o meno lo stesso: fin dallo scorcio del Trecento una notevole decadenza si profila in tutti i settori industriali. Le ragioni sembrano essere le stesse — una sbagliata politica fiscale dei governi musulmani, il rincaro del lavoro, l'oppressione della concorrenza e l'eliminazione della industria privata, il ristagno tecnologico. Anche le conseguenze sono uguali: l'importazione di prodotti della industria europea.

L'industria dello zucchero, introdotta nel mondo mediterraneo dagli Arabi, che l'avevano sviluppata notevolmente, inventando metodi di raffinamento e di produzione di cubi di zucchero bianco, fioriva fino all'inizio del Quattrocento. Gli inventari dei carichi delle navi impiegate nel commercio levantino nell'ultimo terzo del Trecento comprendono grandi quantità di zucchero[42]. Ma all'inizio del Quattrocento l'importazione di zucchero levantino diminuisce in Europa, lo zucchero siriano ed egiziano è in grande misura sostituito da zucchero di Cipro e di Sicilia. Le navi degli Italiani (e delle altre nazioni mercanti) esportano ancora zucchero dalla Siria e dall'Egitto, come dimostrano molte tariffe di noli ed ordini dati dal senato veneziano alle navi partenti[43] e talvolta le autorità mamlucche impongono ai mercanti italiani anche in quest'epoca la compra obbligatoria di

[38] Panni grossi teotonici (Miste 57, f. 13b: grossi et teotonici) et de Polana et grisi valoris duc' 5 et ab inde infra singula pecie, pro balla soldi 8 et grossi 9; da una tariffa di noli per le galee di Beirut, a. 1426, v. Miste 56, f. 32a sg. et cf. 57, f. 11b. In quanto al significato di Polana non c'è dubbio, v. re di Polana e di Lituania, Cronaca Morosini, ms. Vienna 6586-87 I, c. 224 cf. 225, 241; v. anche Zancaruola f. 496b.

[39] Miste 35, f. 46a 54, f. 74b; G. P., Terminazioni III, f. 103a.

[40] Miste 26, f. 79b, 86a 34, f. 26b 38, f. 156a.

[41] V. *Les lainages dans l'Orient médiéval*, p. 681.

[42] J. HEERS, *Il commercio nel Mediterraneo alla fine del secolo XIV e nei primi anni del XV*, « Archivio Storico Italiano », 113 (1955), p. 168 sg.; il mio articolo *The volume of Levantine trade in the later Middle Ages*, JEEH IV (1975), pp. 584, 587 sg.

[43] Miste 46; f. 31b, 137b 47, f. 7a sg., 56a, 117b sg. 48, f. 12b sgg., 42a, 82a sgg. 49, f. 32a, 125b 50, f. 4b 52, f. 34b, 101b sgg., 102b sg. 54, f. 116b sgg. 55, f. 31a; v. anche 52, f. 68a 57, f. 11b.

certe quantità di zucchero[44]. I Genovesi esportano ancora nel 1458 zucchero dalla Siria[45]. Ma le quantità di zucchero di cui dispongono i musulmani (gli industriali e le autorità) sono incomparabilmente più ristrette che nella prima metà del Trecento[46] e, d'altra parte, pare che la più grande parte dello zucchero venduto ai mercanti italiani sia polvere[47]. Lo zucchero più fino («di tre cotte») non era mai destinato alla esportazione, ma in quell'epoca i mercanti stranieri non potevano procurarsi neanche lo zucchero di qualità media (chiamato nei documenti italiani babilonio e musciatto). Queste specie di zucchero orientale non sono più registrate nelle liste di prezzi dei grandi mercati europei. Dati in fonti arabe e occidentali dimostrano anche che il prezzo dello zucchero aumentava allora nel Levante considerevolmente[48]. Il suo rincaro era la conseguenza del più alto costo del lavoro e, d'altra parte, della più scarsa offerta.

La diminuzione della produzione dello zucchero nel Levante musulmano, che si intravvede nei documenit riferentisi al commercio levantino degli Italiani, è pienamente confermata dagli scrittori arabi di quell'epoca. Lo storico egiziano Ibn Duḳmāḳ, che scrisse la sua Topografia nei primi anni del Quattrocento, cita un elenco degli zuccherifici nella capitale d'Egitto, compilato negli anni 1320, e aggiunge dati sulle loro vicende. Ibn Duḳmāḳ menziona gli zuccherifici anche in altri capitoli della sua opera, descrivendo i villaggi e le piccole città nelle varie provincie d'Egitto. Questi dati gettano luce sulle strutture di questa importante industria dell'Egitto e sulle ragioni del suo crollo all'epoca dell'autore. Dalle sue relazioni sugli zuccherifici nel Cairo veniamo a sapere che il loro numero era diminuito fin dalla terza decade del Trecento del 42%. Di 66 zuccherifici 40 non funzionavano più[49]. Le indicazioni che ci forniscono Ibn Duḳmāḳ e altri scrittori arabi dimostrano che anche fuori della capitale si profilava un notevole declino di questa industria. Inoltre, si desume dai loro dati che un grande settore era statale o in possesso di feudatari altolocati, come figli di sultani, o ricchissime famiglie di mercanti. I figli del sultano al-Malik an-Nāṣir Ḥasan (1347-1351, 1354-1361) e parecchie famiglie di Karimiti possedevano molti zuccherifici. Anche nella Siria i feudatari erano i padroni della industria dello zucchero[50]. Poiché ottenevano la materia grezza a un prezzo più

[44] Miste 52, f. 119a, 133a.
[45] ASG (Archivio di Stato, Genova), Caratorum veterum 1553, c. 23a, 23b.
[46] V. ad esempio as-Sulūk II, p. 243: 80,000 ḳinṭār (djarwī, di 96,7 chili.) trovati da un viziro caduto in disgrazia.
[47] ASV, Senato, Secreta I, f. 81a sgg.; Cronaca Morosini II, c. 353.
[48] *Histoire des prix et des salaires dans l'Orient médiéval*, p. 316 sgg., 404 sgg. Un ambasciatore veneziano riceve dal sultano zucchero « di tre cotte » in regalo, v. ASV, Libri commemoriali 15, f. 69b.
[49] Ibn Duḳmāḳ, al-Intiṣār IV, p. 41 sgg.
[50] Miste 44, f. 55a.

basso, pagavano meno tasse (o non le pagavano del tutto) e, d'altra parte, potevano imporre agli industriali privati e ai mercanti la compra obbligatoria dei prodotti delle loro fabbriche, erano capaci di opprimere, senza grande difficoltà, la concorrenza. Il tentativo del sultano Barsbay di fare della produzione dello zucchero un monopolio fu un episodio di questa politica della classe dominante [51]. L'amministrazione degli zuccherifici dello Stato era corrotta e poiché sotto il regno dei sultani circassi non vi fu più un settore privato che facesse loro concorrenza, questi non avevano né bisogno né incentivi di migliorare i metodi di produzione e di introdurre innovazioni.

Frattanto una importante innovazione era stata applicata nell'industria dello zucchero in Sicilia. Fin dallo scorcio del Trecento la materia grezza si macinava per mezzo di cilindri messi in funzione da mulini ad acqua e veniva cotta nei cosidetti trappeti e infine raffinata in appositi magazzini [52]. Parecchi documenti notarili dimostrano che questo nuovo metodo di produzione già era stato impiegato molto tempo prima della metà del Quattrocento, data che gli era assegnata [53]. Ecco un altro progresso industriale dovuto all'impiego della forza idraulica che sembra non venisse introdotto nel Levante musulmano [54].

Il declino, quantitativo e qualitativo, della produzione dello zucchero nei paesi levantini aveva come conseguenza che i mercanti europei potevano ivi importare i prodotti dei loro zuccherifici. Ma poiché i paesi orientali già erano molto impoveriti, importarono per lo più la melassa. Molti documenti negli archivi di Venezia e di altre città italiane ne dànno testimonianza [55]. Così i mercanti avevano un altro articolo da barattare con le spezierie...

[51] M. Sobernheim, *Das Zuckermonopol unter Sultan Barsbai*, « Zeitschrift f. Assyriologie », 27, p. 75 sgg.

[52] C. Trasselli, *La canna da zucchero nell'agro palermitano nel secolo XV*, « Annali della Facoltà di economia e commercio », Univ. di Palermo, VII (1953), no. 1, p. 119.

[53] Vedasi un contratto del 1421 citato da C. Trasselli, *Sulla diffusione degli Ebrei e sull'importanza della cultura e della lingua ebraica in Sicilia*, « Bollettino di studi filologici e linguistici siciliani », II (1954), p. 381; AS Palermo, Notai, Aprea, Antonio, 800, sub 18 gennaio 1444; 801, sub 22 marzo 1446; Goffredo, Pietro, 1076, sub 6 febbraio 1446.

[54] Vale la pena di mettere in rilievo, in questo contesto, che il trappeto era nei paesi dell'Etiopia meridionale impiegato anche nei frantoi di olio, v. AS Pal, Notai, Randisi, Giacomo, 1151, sub 6 sett. 1430. Probabilmente il suo impiego era una delle ragioni per cui l'olio di questi paesi era migliore dell'orientale e veniva esportato nel Levante in grandi quantità, v. il mio articolo *Quelques problèmes que soulève l'histoire des prix dans l'Orient médiéval*, negli *Studies in memory of Gaston Wiet*, Gerusalemme, 1977, cap. II.

[55] V. la mia comunicazione *The Levantine sugar industry in the later Middle Ages, a sample of technological decline*, « Israel Oriental Studies » VII (1977), p. 226 sgg.

IV

Quanto all'industria del sapone non possiamo additare le innovazioni che incisero sul suo sviluppo in Italia (e in altri paesi dell'Europa meridionale) nel basso medioevo. Ma in fonti arabe e in documenti conservati negli archivi italiani vi sono molti dati che rendono possibile abbozzare il declino di questa industria nel Vicino Oriente e l'importazione dei prodotti dell'industria saponiera europea come conseguenza.

Nella seconda metà del tredicesimo secolo e anche nella prima metà del Trecento i saponifici fiorivano ancora in Siria. In Aleppo il sapone si produceva in venti fabbriche e poiché il commercio di questo articolo, anche esportato in altri paesi, era molto vivace, si costruirono nuovi «khān» (specie di borsa) per questo [56]. Ma fin dall'inizio del regno dei Mamlucchi circassi il declino di questa industria e i fattori che lo causarono si profilano chiaramente. Uno fu la politica dei sovrani musulmani che aggravava la produzione e la vendita di olio e di sapone. Parecchie iscrizioni che annunziano l'abolizione di tali tasse ne fanno testimonianza [57]. La compra forzosa di olio, imposta agli industriali del sapone, ad un prezzo molto alto, li rovinava [58]. Nello stesso tempo le autorità vendevano ai mercanti italiani, talvolta per forza, grandi quantità di una materia grezza che era necessaria per la specie di sapone che allora si produceva in Siria ed anche in Italia (il cosidetto sapone duro che spumeggia lentamente). Questa materia era la cenere di due piante della famiglia delle Salsole kali L., che veniva portata dai beduini dal deserto siriano. Avidi di barattare la cenere, chiamata dagli Italiani lume o più esattamente lume catina (ma anche allume), con gli scarlattini, importati dai mercanti italiani, i Mamlucchi approvvigionavano in questo modo i saponifici di Venezia, di Napoli, di Gaeta e delle Marche di materia grezza... [59].

Il declino della industria del sapone nel Levante e il suo sviluppo in Italia aveva come conseguenza l'importazione di questo articolo negli scali della Siria e dell'Egitto, come in molte altre regioni del Levante. Certo, questo ramo del commercio levantino non aveva, per il bilancio dei pagamenti del Vicino Oriente, l'importanza che aveva l'importazione dei tessili. Ma non si dimentichi che il ricavo del sapone venduto in Alessandria e al Cairo si addizionava al prezzo di altri prodotti industriali ivi importati.

[56] J. Sauvaget, *Alep*, Parigi, 1941, p. 173.

[57] Kāmil al-Ghazzī, *Nahr adh-dhahab*, Aleppo, 1923-26, III, p. 229; J. Sauvaget, *Décrets mamlouks de Syrie*, BEO III, no. 17 (p. 1 sg.).

[58] Mudjīr ad-dīn al-'Ulaimī, al-Uns al-djalīl, p. 686 sg.

[59] R. Mantran - J. Sauvaget, *Règlements fiscaux ottomans. Les provinces syriennes*, Parigi, 1951, p. 22 sgg.

Il governo veneziano si rendeva conto di questo fatto e non si stancava di prendere misure per aumentare l'esportazione di sapone nel Vicino Oriente. Nel 1391 il senato di Venezia prese la decisione di sussidiare questo commercio di esportazione [60] e mentre molti articoli non potevano essere spediti su tutte le navi, i decreti delle autorità veneziane permettevano la libera esportazione del sapone [61]. Infatti le navi veneziane esportavano considerevoli carichi di sapone in Egitto [62]. Anche i mercanti di Gaeta, di Ancona ed altri esportavano i prodotti dei saponifici delle loro città in Alessandria e a Damasco [63].

Un altro prodotto industriale che i mercanti italiani smerciavano in quell'epoca nel Vicino Oriente, ove la sua produzione era di molto declinata, era la carta. La decadenza di questa industria è forse il fenomeno più caratteristico per dimostrare il ristagno tecnologico dell'Oriente in quell'epoca, poiché furono gli Arabi ad introdurla sotto il regno degli Abbasidi e poi a trapiantarla in Spagna. La produzione della carta fatta con stracci, come lo aveva insegnato un prigioniero cinese venuto nel 751 a Samarcanda [64], si continuò nei paesi del Vicino Oriente per molti secoli fino all'epoca dei Turchi ottomani. Le cartiere di Baghdad e di altre città dell'Irak, della Siria e dell'Egitto producevano vari tipi di carta anche nel basso medioevo [65]. Gli stracci impregnati d'acqua e frantumati venivano pestati con pestoni in mortai, la cartapesta cruda veniva inamidata con cellulosa vegetale e stesa su fusti di canna. Pure la carta prodotta nella Spagna musulmana e poi in Catalogna era dello stesso tipo, cioè grossa e di colore piuttosto scuro.

Ma fin dall'anno 1270 una nuova industria di carta si sviluppava nella città di Fabriano, nelle Marche. Le cartiere di Fabriano erano ricorse alla stessa innovazione che aveva rivoluzionato l'industria tessile e l'industria dello zucchero: l'impiego della forza idraulica. Per mezzo di batterie di martelli messi in moto da mulini ad acqua, la cartapesta veniva triturata molto meglio e invece di cellulosa vegetale, che contiene batteri disfacenti la carta nel corso del tempo, si impiegava cellulosa animale, priva di tali elementi disgregatori. Grazie a queste ed altre innovazioni la carta che si produceva a Fabriano e nelle città ove veniva prodotta con i medesimi procedi-

60 Miste 41, f. 127b.

61 Miste l. c. 42, f. 113b 43, f. 8b, 64b, 130a 44, f. 6a sg., 48 a 45, f. 90a 46, f. 32a 48, f. 13b sg.

62 Vedasi Miste 46, f. 94a; una nave veneziana il cui carico è pressapoco interamente sapone, v. Cronaca Morosini I, c. 320.

63 ASV, Cancelleria inferiore, Notai, Ba 222, Antoniello de Vataciis, sub 18 luglio 1406; il mio articolo *Il commercio levantino di Ancona, nel basso medioevo*, RSI 88 (1976), p. 228.

64 J. Karabacek, *Das arabische Papier*, *Mittheilungen aus der Sammlung des Papyrus Erzherzog Rainer II-III* (1887), p. 108 sgg., 141 sg., 147; Th. Carter, *The invention of printing in China*, 2ª ed., Nuova York, 1955, p. 7 sg.

65 Ṣubḥ al-a'shā II, p. 476.

menti era di qualità molto migliore. Di conseguenza era richiesta nel Vicino Oriente e i mercanti cominciavano ad importarla. Parecchi documenti si riferiscono alla sua importazione in Egitto e in Siria. Secondo questi documenti, confermati da un autore arabo di quell'epoca, mercanti veneziani, anconetani ed altri, offrivano la carta di Fabriano e delle cartiere di altre città italiane in Alessandria e altrove [66].

Lo sviluppo dell'arte del vetro assomiglia molto all'industria della carta. Appresa a Tiro, da vetrai ebrei, i Veneziani perfezionarono quest'arte progressivamente, lavorando migliori materie grezze e impiegando nuovi metodi finché superarono i loro maestri e poterono esportare i loro prodotti nel Levante.

L'epoca in cui iniziò la decadenza dell'arte del vetro nel Vicino Oriente è la stessa in cui crollò l'industria tessile — la fine del Trecento, quando gli Italiani intensificarono i loro scambi col Levante.

Nel tredicesimo secolo e nella prima metà del Trecento l'arte del vetro fioriva ancora in Siria e in Egitto, ove Aleppo e Il Cairo erano i centri principali. I vetrai, influenzati da profughi della città di Raḳḳa e da altre città della Mesopotamia, conquistata dai Tartari, producevano oggetti molto belli di vetro smaltato e dorato con contorni in rosso. Negli oggetti che risalgono al Trecento, d'altra parte, s'intravvede l'influenza cinese, in conformità con i gusti della aristocrazia turco-mongolica allora dominante in questi paesi. Hanno ornamenti naturalistici e calligrafici e quelli che provengono dal Cairo risalenti al Trecento anche iscrizioni intessute con blasoni mamlucchi [67]. I prodotti delle vetrerie aleppine erano molto apprezzati in altri paesi, si esportavano fino in Cina [68]. Anche gli oggetti di vetro fabbricati a Damasco e in alcune cittadine della Palestina, a Hebron anzitutto, venivano smerciati in molti paesi dell'Oriente e dell'Occidente, dalla Cina alla Germania [69].

La sfrenata tassazione della industria e la concorrenza che facevano le vetrerie dello Stato alla industria privata causarono il declino di quest'ultima. Ma anche altri fattori incisero sulla decadenza dell'arte del vetro nel Levante musulmano. L'esilio forzoso di molti artigiani di Damasco, portati via da Timur nel 1401, e l'impoverimento generale della società orientale, che non poteva permettersi di pagare gli oggetti a caro prezzo, come in epoche anteriori, avevano senza

[66] Vedasi Miste 46, f. 94a; 54, f. 74b; MARINO SANUTO, *Diarii*, III, col. 1188, 1199 XI, col. 95; *Il commercio levantino di Ancona* ecc., pp. 228, 236; inoltre il mio articolo negli « Israel Oriental Studies », VII (1977).

[67] C. J. LAMM, *Mittelalterliche Gläser u. Steinschnittarbeiten aus dem Nahen Osten*, Berlin, 1930, p. 247.

[68] Ibn Kathīr, al-Bidāya wa 'n-nihāya 13, p. 120. Sulla produzione di vetro in Aleppo vedasi anche SAUVAGET, *Alep*, p. 121: un suk di vetrai.

[69] LAMM, op. cit., pp. 246, 259, 493; ID., *Oriental glasses of medieval date found in Sweden and the early history of lustrepainting*, Stoccolma, 1941, p. 73; W. PFEIFFER, *Acrische Gläser*, « Journal of Glass Studies », 12 (1970), p. 67 sgg.

dubbio un grande peso. I vetrai del Vicino Oriente avevano anche difficoltà a procurarsi buone materie grezze. Parecchie materie coloranti come il «ferretto», ossido di rame trovato nelle miniere di ferro in Spagna, il verderame e il realgar dovevano essere importate dai paesi dell'Europa meridionale. I mercanti italiani le vendevano in Alessandria e a Damasco a prezzi molto alti [70]. D'altra parte, le autorità mamlucche vendevano agli stessi mercanti italiani, talvolta per forza, per avere eleganti panni, la cenere che era un ingrediente imprescindibile per la fabbricazione del vetro. Molti passi nei ricettari delle vetrerie italiane risalenti al basso medioevo si riferiscono al lume importato dalla Siria [71]. Le sempre più grandi difficoltà contribuirono alla decadenza dell'arte del vetro nel Vicino Oriente. Gli storici dell'arte che hanno studiato le lampade delle moschee cairine di quell'epoca si sono accorti del deterioramento nel gusto delle decorazioni fin dallo scorcio del Trecento [72]. Ma anche viaggiatori occidentali che visitarono le città del Vicino Oriente nella seconda metà del Quattrocento se ne resero conto. Nei loro libri di viaggio non troviamo descrizioni entusiastiche degli oggetti di vetro prodotti nella Siria, come quelle date da viaggiatori in epoche anteriori. Il domenicano bavarese Felix Fabri, che visitò nel 1483 Hebron, racconta che il vetro ivi fabbricato non era trasparente ma piuttosto nero e i colori di qualità mediocre [73].

Nella stessa epoca i vetrai muranesi impararono come aggiungere alle materie grezze il pyrobusito per migliorare la trasparenza e i colori dei loro prodotti. Si chiamava «il sapone del vetraio» [74]. Nella seconda metà del tredicesimo secolo cominciarono anche a produrre vetro smaltato ed a decorare gli oggetti per mezzo della lustratura [75]. Le vetrerie di Murano lavoravano anche materie grezze sempre migliori. Per la fabbricazione del «cristallo», ad esempio, erano ricorsi a materia grezza trovata sul valico del San Bernardo [76]. Per la

[70] *Lettere a Pignol Zucchello*, ed. Morozzo della Rocca, Venezia, 1957, pp. 87, 110; Giovanni da Uzzano, *La pratica della mercatura*, (in) Pagnini, *Della decima*, IV, p. 112.

[71] *Dell'arte del vetro per musaico tre trattatelli*, ed. G. Milanesi, Bologna, 1864, II, 1, 2, 4, 5, 10, 11, 12; III, 65.

[72] Lamm, *Oriental glass*, p. 72.

[73] *Evagatorium in Terram Sanctam, Arabiae et Egypti peregrinationes*, ed. C. D. Hassler, Stoccarda, 1843-49, II, p. 341 (Lamm non conosceva questo passo nel libro latino e cita il suo libro di viaggio nel tedesco il quale è più breve).

[74] R. W. Douglas - S. Frank, *A history of glassmaking*, Hanley-on-Thann, 1972, p. 7.

[75] L. Zecchin, *Un decoratore di vetri a Murano alla fine del Duecento*, «Journal of Glass Studies», 11 (1969), p. 41; Id., *Fornaci muranesi fra il 1279 ed il 1290*, «Journal of Glass Studies», 12 (1970), p. 79 sgg.

[76] W. Ganzmüller, *Hüttengeheimnisse der italienischen Glasmacher des Mittelalters*, (nella sua raccolta) *Beiträge zur Geschichte der Technologie und der Alchemie*, Weinheim, 1956, p. 73.

tintura del vetro impiegavano il cobalto importato dalla Germania[77].

Fin dall'inizio del Quattrocento la superiorità del vetro muranese sul levantino era incontestabile, sicché i mercanti veneziani ed altri cominciarono la sua esportazione nel Vicino Oriente. Un atto notarile, datato in Alessandria 1434, si riferisce alla importazione di tre casse di vetro di Venezia[78]. Secondo un atto giudiziario dell'anno 1444, il mercante veneziano Benedetto Longo esportò nella stessa Alessandria (probabilmente verso il 1440) oggetti di vetro smaltato e dorato, barattati con 12 cantari e 87 ratli di zenzero del valore di 18 ducati (il cantaro), 23 cantari di verzi e 800 mann di noci moscate[79]. Questi oggetti rappresentavano dunque un valore di 1000-1100 ducati[80]. Secondo un altro atto giudiziario i famosi fabbricanti di vetro, Marco e Zuan Barovier, esportavano nel 1459 a Tripoli 97 chili di vetro smaltato[81]. I dibattiti fra gli orientalisti e fra gli storici dell'arte sulla provenienza di lampade di moschee e di altri oggetti che indicano origine veneziana sono perciò vani. Non v'è dubbio che provengono da Murano. Lo stesso sultano del Cairo era un cliente delle vetrerie di Murano. Una deliberazione del senato veneziano del 1466 si riferisce alla richiesta del sultano di aver vetro per finestre[82].

V

Il quadro è dunque completo. In seguito alla politica economica sbagliata dei sovrani musulmani, al rincaro del lavoro risultante dalla mancanza di manodopera, alla grande difficoltà di procurarsi migliori materie grezze e anche ad altri fattori, le industrie orientali declinarono e sullo scorcio del Trecento pressapoco tramontarono. Un vuoto si era creato che necessariamente, come tutti i vuoti, veniva riempito. I Veneziani, Genovesi, Fiorentini, Anconetani ed altri importavano nei paesi levantini prodotti industriali, con il ricavo dei quali era loro possibile pagare il prezzo del pepe, dello zenzero, del cotone, della seta e di molte altre merci orientali. Se non avessero smerciato loro prodotti sui mercati levantini, non avrebbero potuto pagare queste merci. Tutti i dati che troviamo nei documenti e in fonti letterarie dimostrano che pagavano soltanto una parte del prezzo delle spezierie in contanti.

[77] GANZMÜLLER, *Über die Verwendung von Kobalt bei den Glasmachern des Mittelalters*, (nella stessa raccolta) p. 171.

[78] ASV, Cancelleria inferiore, Notai, Ba 211, Niccolò Turiano V, f. 8a sg.

[79] ASV, Giudici di petiziòn, Sentenze a giustizia 96, f. 151a.

[80] Vedasi la mia *Histoire des prix et des salaires dans l'Orient médiéval*, pp. 336, 342.

[81] G. P., Sentenze 130, f. 45b sgg. Cf. sulla esportazione di vetro in Siria L. ZECCHIN, *L'arte vetraria muranese all'inizio del 1469*, « Rivista della stazione sperimentale del vetro », VI (1976), p. 256.

[82] Senato, Mar VIII, f. 97b, cf. f. 103b. V. anche Cronaca Zancaruola f. 584a: un ambasciatore veneziano presenta al sultano cristalli.

I fatti sembrano essere indiscutibili, la loro spiegazione solleva molte questioni.

Le relazioni di cronisti arabi sulla incapacità degli ingegneri di scavare canali di irrigazione [83] e di Ibn Khaldūn sul declino dei cantieri navali [84] sono una testimonianza chiarissima. Il declino tecnologico dei paesi orientali si profila infatti in molti settori e in tutte le regioni. Alcuni protocolli delle deilberazioni del senato veneziano si riferiscono ad una domanda dell'imperatore di Trebisonda di restaurare una campana e un orologio che aveva spediti a questo scopo alla Serenissima [85].

D'altra parte le spiegazioni che possiamo dare di questo fenomeno di declino ci lasciano in qualche misura insoddisfatti. Benché l'eliminazione della concorrenza da parte delle industrie private avesse reso più facile alle manifatture statali e alle fabbriche dei feudatari lo smerciare dei loro prodotti, ci domandiamo perché non avessero introdotto nuovi metodi per migliorare la produzione e vendere le loro merci ai mercanti occidentali, come in epoche anteriori. I mercanti italiani erano anche nel Quattrocento avidi di aver lo zucchero « di tre cotte » e avrebbero comprato volentieri buoni tessuti di seta. Invece di comprare la carta importata dall'Italia potevano inamidare la cartapesta con cellulosa animale come facevano a Fabriano. Certo non avrebbero avuto grande difficoltà a ottenere i segreti industriali per mezzo di rinnegati e di altri. Neanche l'abolizione delle manifatture statali potrebbe spiegare in modo davvero convincente la mancata introduzione di innovazioni tecnologiche. È vero che semplici artigiani non potevano fare lunghi esperimenti, ma quante grandi invenzioni sono state fatte da singoli e senza l'aiuto delle autorità o di ricche ditte? I sostenitori del materialismo storico sono inclini a interpretare il declino tecnologico come un effetto di sovrabbondanza di manodopera a buon prezzo, ad esempio di schiavi. Ma Vitruvio visse in un'epoca in cui la schiavitù era al suo apogeo e nell'epoca in cui le industrie del Vicino Oriente tramontarono la manodopera era scarsa.

Si tratta della ben conosciuta opposizione alle inonvazioni provocata da un atteggiamento conservatore da parte di gente che considerava le innovazioni come la causa di un peggioramento della qualità dei prodotti? È indubbio che una tale opposizione esisteva. Quando Gaikhatu, il sovrano tartaro della Persia e dell'Irak, emise, nel 1294, banconote stampate da tipografi cinesi in parecchie città del suo regno, la popolazione si rivoltò e lo costrinse a rinunciare

[83] Vedasi la mia *Social and economic history of the Near East in the Middle Ages*, London 1976, p. 144 sg.
[84] The Muqaddimah (trad. Rosenthal), II, p. 46.
[85] Miste 45, f. 6b (molto breve e incompleto da Fr. Thiriet, *Régestes des délibérations du Sénat de Venise concernant la Romanie*, II, p. 11).

al suo tentativo [86]. L'insuccesso del sovrano tartaro significava la soppressione della tipografia (cinese) che fu introdotta nel Vicino Oriente, duecento anni prima di Gutenberg! Se avesse avuto successo, le conseguenze per lo sviluppo della civiltà levantina sarebbero state incalcolabili.

Ma anche gli industriali che introducevano in Francia, in Germania ed in Inghilterra i mulini ad acqua per la gualcatura urtarono contro coloro che consideravano tale gualcatura causa di deterioramento della qualità dei tessuti. Tuttavia gli industriali occidentali riuscirono a superare l'opposizione.

Forse l'ipotesi di un rapporto fra sviluppo demografico da una parte e ascesa e discesa tecnologica dall'altra può spiegare il fenomeno del ristagno tecnologico del Vicino Oriente nel basso medioevo. Supponendo, come alcuni studiosi, che le innovazioni tecnologiche siano in relazione con l'incremento della popolazione e il ristagno tecnologico con lo spopolamento, si capirebbe la decadenza delle industrie orientali alla fine del medioevo. La diminuzione della popolazione fu infatti un fenomeno fondamentale della storia sociale ed economica di questi paesi in quell'epoca [87].

Pure anche questa supposizione non è più di una ipotesi. Per forza dobbiamo concludere con un grande punto interrogativo.

VI

Il notevole sviluppo delle armi da fuoco in Italia, fin dalla metà del Trecento, e la superiorità militare sugli Stati musulmani che ne derivava era un altro aspetto della relazione fra ascesa tecnologica da una parte e decadenza dall'altra.

Diversi tipi di cannoni, allora chiamati bombarde, sono in uso in Italia, come in altri paesi dell'Occidente, fin dalla prima metà del Trecento. Si producevano bombarde il cui calibro era piccolo ed anche bombarde a più canne che potevano gettare proiettili molto pesanti, fino a 100-150 chili di pietre [88]. Molte, piccole e grosse, avevano l'anima lunga e tiravano orizzontalmente, altre ad anima corta tiravano in parabole di grande elevazione e spesso anche pietre molto grosse [89]. Fra i primi a ricorrere alle armi da fuoco furono, in tutti i paesi dell'Occidente, i comuni e anzitutto quelli che erano centri mercantili ed industriali: nella Fiandra e nel Brabante Bruges, Ma-

[86] K. Jahn, *Das iranische Papiergeld*, « Archiv Orientální », X (1938), p. 308 sgg.

[87] Vedasi *Social and economic history of the Near East in the Middle Ages*, p. 302 sgg.

[88] A. Angelucci, *Documenti inediti per la storia delle armi da fuoco italiane*, Torino, 1869, pp. 69, 82 e v. Miste 57, f. 156a.

[89] Angelucci, op. cit., p. 78 sgg.

lines, Bruxelles, Tournai e infine Mons nel Hainaut[90]. Lo stesso fenomeno si profila in Italia. Non di rado i principi si rivolgono alle città per chiedere di dare loro in prestito le bombarde[91].

Fra le stesse città italiane che si provvedono di armi da fuoco e spendono molti soldi a questo scopo, Venezia e le altre città mercantili hanno un posto di primo rango.

Alla metà del Trecento le guarnigioni delle provincie di Venezia, come Capodistria ed altre, sono munite di bombarde. Nel 1349, ad esempio, il podestà di Capodistria riceve ordini di inviare a Venezia due spingarde (bombarde minute ad anima lunga) per ripararle[92]. L'esercito veneziano impiega bombarde anche nel campo, come si desume da ordini dati nel 1376 alle truppe nel Friuli[93]. Durante la guerra fra Venezia e Genova che culminò nella battaglia di Chioggia ambedue le parti facevano molto uso delle nuove armi da fuoco. Nel gennaio 1379 Vettor Pisani bombarda Zara dalle sue galee con bombarde[94]. Quando i Padovani avanzano verso Mestre, nel luglio 1378, impiegano molte e grosse bombarde per l'attacco ed anche i difensori tirano con bombarde e uccidono molti uomini[95]. Poi, quando i Genovesi occuparono Chioggia, grazie all'impiego delle loro bombarde, tiravano sul Lido avendo istallato bombarde sulle galee ed i Veneziani si difendevano con la stessa arma[96]. Mentre Antonio Morosini e Zorzi Dolfin scrivevano le loro cronache alla metà del Quattrocento, cioè 60 anni dopo la guerra di Chioggia, Daniele di Chinazzo era un testimone oculare. La sua relazione sulla sconfitta dei Genovesi e l'impiego delle armi da fuoco nella battaglia decisiva ha perciò grande valore. Secondo lui i Veneziani, tirando con una grande bombarda, rovesciarono nel gennaio 1380 il campanile di Brondolo, a sud di Chioggia, causando la morte del comandante genovese. Poi il muro del monastero di Brondolo colpito dalle bombarde crollò ed uccise molti Genovesi[97].

Pare che i Veneziani raddoppiassero, dopo il successo della loro artiglieria nella guerra di Chioggia, i loro sforzi per munirsi di bom-

[90] Cl. Gaier, *L'industrie et le commerce des armes dans les anciennes principautés belges du XIIIe à la fin du XVe siècle* (Bibl. de la faculté de phil. et lettres de l'Univ. de Liège 102), Parigi, 1973, pp. 117, 129, 131 sgg., 136, 143 sgg. e v. anzitutto p. 92 sg.

[91] Angelucci, op. cit., p. 74.

[92] Miste 25, f. 38b. Questo riferimento come parecchi altri e anche indicazioni bibliografiche mi sono stati forniti dal dott. Franco Morin, eccellente storico delle armi da fuoco, e vorrei ringraziarlo anche in questo modo.

[93] ASV, Senato, Alfabetico, Reg. L sub 3 ottobre 1376.

[94] Daniele de Chinazzo, *Cronica della guerra da Veniciani a Zenovesi*, a cura di Vitt. Lazzarini (Monumenti storici pubbl. dalla Deputazione di storia patria, N. S. 11), Venezia, 1958, p. 38. Infatti l'autore non dice che venivano usate bombarde ma racconta che la città fu « bombardata ».

[95] Op. cit., p. 33.

[96] *Cronaca Dolfin*, f. 236b sg., 237a, 238a, 238b, 240b, 244b, 245a, 246a; *Cronaca Morosini*, I, c. 105, 106.

[97] Daniele de Chinazzo, p. 103 sg. e cf. *Cron. Morosini*, I, c. 112.

barde. Durante la guerra contro i Carrara e i loro alleati spesero grandi somme per ingrandire il numero delle bombarde di cui disponeva l'esercito [98]. Anche i loro avversari erano ricorsi alle armi da fuoco. Avendo conquistato nel 1405 la fortezza di Castrocaro i Veneziani vi trovarono 20 grosse bombarde, tra cui 3-4 molto grosse, atte a gettare pietre di 400-500 libbre [99]. Per conquistare Monselice dovettero superare il fuoco delle bombarde impiegate dai difensori [100]. Poi, nel 1412, nella guerra contro gli Ungheresi nel Friuli erano ricorsi alle bombarde nel campo e per la difesa delle fortezze [101]. Le città che la Serenissima possedeva nella Grecia venivano alla fine del Trecento munite sistematicamente di questa nuova arma [102].

Nella stessa epoca i Veneziani cominciarono ad impiegare le bombarde nella guerra navale e a munirne le navi mercantili e le navi di scorta. Usando una forcella di ferro, messa sul parapetto della nave, la bombarda aveva un campo abbastanza largo di tiro. Già nel 1374 una flottiglia di cocche partenti per Alessandria era munita di « sclopi », cioè piccoli pezzi di artiglieria. Ogni nave aveva 10 sclopi, 10.000 verrettoni e 500 pallottole di ferro [103]. Nel 1382 il governo di Venezia manda a Tenedo una galea grossa e una cocca munite di bombarde [104]. Quando il senato decise, nel 1398, di mandare due cocche a Beirut per caricare una grande quantità di spezierie, ognuna dovette essere munita di tre bombarde [105]. Le decisioni riferentisi alle cocche che partivano nella prima metà del Quattrocento due volte all'anno per la Siria per caricare il cotone comprendono non di rado l'ordine di munire ognuna di quattro bombarde [106]. Anche le cocche inviate a combattere contro i pirati avevano quattro bombarde ognuna [107]. Pure le galee che assicuravano il traffico regolare col Levante avevano talvolta bombarde [108].

Le altre grandi citta mercantili d'Italia munivano, nello stesso modo, i loro eserciti di bombarde e anche le loro navi di trasporto

[98] ASV, Senato, Alfabetico, Reg. R, f. 15b (a. 1388).
[99] *Cron. Morosini*, I, c. 171.
[100] Op. cit., c. 183 sg.
[101] Op. cit., c. 257, 260.
[102] ASV, Collegio Notatorio, Reg. III, f. 10b; Thiriet, Régestes II, p. 43. Nel corso del tempo le guarnigioni veneziane venivano munite di pezzi di artiglieria più numerosi e variati. Nel 1430 il governo di Venezia manda a Negroponte una grossa bombarda e 25 bombardelle, v. Miste 57, f. 239a (incompleto da Thiriet, *Régestes*, II, p. 277).
[103] Miste 34, f. 47a.
[104] *Cron. Dolfin*, f. 275b.
[105] Miste 44, f. 27b sg.
[106] Miste 47, f. 7a sg. (cf. *Cron. Morosini*, I, c. 173), 25b 55, f. 181a sg. 58, f. 60b.
[107] Miste 49, f. 75a sg. 52, f. 15a 53, f. 86a, 198b e cf. Collegio Notatorio V, f. 68b (ove è detto che debbano averne due soltanto); *Cronaca Morosini*, II, c. 575.
[108] AS Messina, Notai, Mallono, Franc., f. 96a (a. 1431).

e da guerra. I Genovesi ne avevano molte [109] ed anche le navi anconetane erano munite della nuova arma. Una descrizione, allegata ad un atto notarile del 1479, della caravella di Rainaldo e Pellegrino, figli di Dragutto di Sebenico, comprende una bombarda [110]. Secondo un atto del 1486, Bartolino Quiriaci de Nassinis, abitante di Ancona, ricevette da Giovanni de Turiglionibus, anconetano anche lui, in prestito 4 bombarde di ferro, con forcelle di ferro ed affusti e anche 14 bombardelle a retrocarico (cauda) [111].

I governi europei si adoperavano in vari modi per provvedersi di bombarde e agevolare la loro fabbricazione. La Serenissima prendeva molte misure per approvvigionare la città di sufficienti quantità di ferro, acquistava da vari paesi rame per fabbricare bombarde [112] e ordinava la fabbricazione di pezzi anche in altre città, come a Brescia, uno dei centri dell'industria di armi [113]. I quaderni degli atti rogati dai notai di quest'epoca comprendono contratti di governi con artigiani specializzati nella fabbricazione di bombarde. Un tale contratto redatto nel 1430 fra il governo reale di Sicilia e Mgr. Johan Pazes de Fetreres lo obbliga a lavorare un anno per le autorità incaricate dell'armamento [114].

Anche l'approvvigionamento di sufficienti riserve di munizioni diventa in quell'epoca una preoccupazione permanente dei governi. Parecchie decisioni del senato veneziano testimoniano dei provvedimenti presi per gli artigiani che fabbricavano verrettoni e polvere da sparo [115]. Altrettanto, dovendo approvvigionare i loro arsenali di polvere da sparo, si dànno premura per procurarsene gli ingredienti. Fin dalla seconda metà del Trecento il salnitro (la materia grezza trovata in giacimenti) era un articolo di cui si faceva un vivace commercio. Atti di notai siciliani si riferiscono a transazioni di Ebrei che, in quest'isola, erano specializzati nel raffinamento di tale materia. La Sicilia era in quell'epoca un centro di produzione di salnitro raffinato e pare che gli Ebrei avessero un posto di primo rango in quest'arte. Artigiani ebrei forniscono il salnitro anche al governo [116]. Pure Venezia era un centro del commercio di salnitro, la cui materia grezza proveniva anzitutto dalla Puglia [117]. Secondo gli atti della can-

[109] V. *Cronaca Morosini*, II, c. 593.
[110] AS Ancona, Notai, Alberici, Giacomo, I, f. 30a.
[111] Stesso notaio III, f. 55a.
[112] Ph. Braunstein, *Le commerce de fer à Venise au XVe siècle*, « Studi Veneziani », VIII (1967), p. 289 sgg.; Miste 60, f. 57b; Senato, Secreta 19, f. 82b.
[113] Braunstein, art. cit., p. 278.
[114] AS Palermo, Notai, Randisi, Giacomo, 1151, sub 6 sett. 1430.
[115] Miste 49, f. 107b 60, f. 248a.
[116] AS Siracusa, Notai, Pidono, Antonino, 10245, f. 272a sg.; AS Palermo, Notai, Di Marco, Giacomo, 762, sub 16 gennaio 1416; C. Trasselli, *Gli Ebrei in Sicilia*, « Nuovi Quaderni del Meridione », VII (1969), p. 49.
[117] Anche salnitro raffinato viene esportato dalla Puglia, vedasi Miste 53, f. 132a.

celleria reale di Napoli, la Serenissima chiese nel 1492 al re il permesso di esportare dal suo regno 200 milliaria di salnitro [118]. Il salnitro raffinato a Venezia veniva esportato in parecchi paesi dell'Europa centrale, come la Germania, via Nürnberg, e i Paesi Bassi [119]. All'inizio del Quattrocento il governo veneziano preoccupato di non aver sufficienti riserve richiedeva un permesso speciale per l'esportazione di salnitro. Di conseguenza la materia grezza non veniva importata, mentre i mercanti l'esportavano dalla Puglia in Sicilia dove non vigeva tale divieto. D'altra parte il salnitro raffinato veniva esportato da Venezia segretamente, sicché nel 1409 il senato dovette prendere misure in merito [120]. Poi nel 1412 il senato permise che due terzi del salnitro importato potessero essere riesportati. Per il terzo rimanente era necessario un permesso, condizionato dalla dichiarazione dell'Arsenale che non v'era deficienza di questa materia [121]. Ma anche questa liberalizzazione non era sufficiente per indurre i mercanti ad aumentare l'importazione e nel 1420 si permise che fosse esportata liberamente [122]. Nel 1421 il dazio di 5 ducati per l'esportazione di un milliario, fissato nel 1408, fu ridotto a 30 grossi [123].

Tutti questi decreti sono una eloquente testimonianza del fatto che fin dallo scorcio del Trecento Venezia già aveva un posto di avanguardia nella produzione di armi da fuoco, di proiettili e di salnitro. Principi ed altri si rivolgono alla Serenissima domandando in prestito alcuni pezzi di artiglieria per loro guerre. Lo fa la « Maona » di Chio nel 1409 [124] e il Conte di Segna nel 1424 [125]. Il Conte di Segna, che apparteneva alla famiglia dei Frangipan, già aveva chiesto nel 1387 che il governo di Venezia gli permettesse la compra di 2000 libbre di salnitro, 2000 libbre di zolfo e 1500 libbre di verrettoni [126]. Nel 1400 il duca Federico di Asburgo chiedette dalla Serenissima il permesso di comprare a Venezia 100 centenari di salnitro e zolfo e 25 milliaia di verrettoni. Gli fu accordato soltanto l'acquisto dello zolfo [127]. Il Conte di Segna domandò anche nel 1424 l'autorizzazione di comprare a Venezia il salnitro [128].

118 Fr. Trinchera, Codice Aragonese II, parte 1 (Napoli 1868-1870), no. 40 (p. 42).
119 V. Miste 46, f. 57a (esportazione di salnitro falsificato in Germania nel 1402); B. Rathgen, *Das Geschütz im Mittelalter*, Berlin, 1928, p. 96; Cl. Gaier, *L'industrie et le commerce des armes* ecc., p. 182.
120 Miste 48, f. 91b.
121 Miste 49, f. 59b.
122 Miste 53, f. 43a.
123 Miste 153, f. 132a.
124 Senato, Secreta IV, f. 12b.
125 Miste 54, f. 170b.
126 Miste 40, f. 86a.
127 Senato, Secreta III, f. 120a. È Federico IV, chiamato « delle tasche vuote », duca del Tirolo e dell'Austria « anteriore ».
128 V. supra.

Mentre gli Stati occidentali e anzitutto le repubbliche marittime svolgevano febbrili attività per munire i loro eserciti delle nuove armi da fuoco e per riempire i loro arsenali di riserve di munizioni, la classe dominante nel Levante musulmano, composta da cavalieri turchi e circassi, fautori del guerreggiare tradizionale, disprezzava le armi da fuoco. Infatti l'impiego della artiglieria cominciò in Egitto nella settima decade del Trecento, ma si usava soltanto nell'assedio (e nella difesa) di fortezze [129]. Le brigate che impiegavano l'archibugio alla fine del Quattrocento e all'inizio del Cinquecento erano truppe di secondo rango, composte da negri, ad esempio [130].

L'artiglieria mamlucca era nettamente inferiore alle forze armate delle varie potenze dell'Europa meridionale. Ogni scontro portava per forza ad una sconfitta dei Mamlucchi. L'assedio di Rodi, nel 1444, lo dimostra. Ambedue le parti belligeranti impiegarono bombarde, ma secondo un cronista contemporaneo i Mamlucchi persero 16 navi per i tiri delle bombarde dei cavalieri [131]. Da altre fonti occidentali veniamo a sapere che le bombarde impiegate nella difesa di Rodi provenivano in parte dai Paesi Bassi ed erano state trasportate nell'isola appositamente da Anversa [132]. Il fatto essenziale che emerge chiaramente dalle fonti è l'inferiorità tecnologica dei Mamlucchi che non sapevano maneggiare le nuove armi. Il parallelo è ovvio con il ristagno delle industrie di tessili, dello zucchero, della carta e del vetro.

VII

La decadenza delle industrie orientali, l'importanza che aveva per l'economia del Levante l'esportazione di materie grezze destinate alle industrie europee (il cotone, il lume) e l'inferiorità della artiglieria dei Mamlucchi ebbero come conseguenza un rapporto nuovo fra le potenze occidentali ed il Vicino Oriente. Questo nuovo rapporto presenta parecchi tratti che furono caratteristici, nell'epoca moderna, delle relazioni fra l'Europa occidentale e i paesi coloniali. Tuttavia è soltanto una somiglianza. Perciò guardiamoci dall'esagerare e dal sostituire la supposizione che vi fosse dipendenza coloniale dei Mamlucchi dall'Orda d'Oro (il Kiptčak), fatta dall'orientalista A. N. Poliak [133], con la supposizione che tale rapporto sussistesse con i

[129] D. Ayalon, *Gunpowder and firearms in the Mamlūk kingdom* (Londra, 1956), pp. 46, 96.

[130] Op. cit., pp. 63, 65.

[131] *Cronaca Dolfin*, f. 401 sg.; *Cronaca Zancaruola*, f. 593b.

[132] Gaier, op. cit., p. 146 sg.

[133] *Le caractère colonial de l'Etat mamelouk dans ses rapports avec la Horde d'Or*, « Revue des études islamiques », IX (1935). p. 230 sgg. e vedasi la sua conclusione p. 244: il regno dei Mamlucchi era un impero coloniale di feudatari e di mercanti dei paesi a nord del Mar Nero, nel senso in cui i principati dei

Veneziani, affermando che il colonialismo è iniziato in Oriente un lungo tempo prima delle capitulazioni. Ma se di colonialismo non si può parlare, pure di esso c'erano le prime manifestazioni. Siamo agli albori dell'imperialismo moderno.

Benché fin dall'ultimo terzo del Trecento il rapporto fra il Levante musulmano e le repubbliche marittime d'Italia somigliasse alla relazione fra paesi coloniali e potenze occidentali nell'epoca moderna, i dirigenti delle nazioni mercantili già avevano come mira l'occupazione di certi scali levantini che dovevano servire come basi sicure per le loro attività commerciali. Nel 1383 i Genovesi assalirono Beirut e secondo la relazione dello storico libanese Ṣaliḥ b. Yaḥyā, il cui padre partecipò alla battaglia, tentarono di piantare la loro bandiera su di una torre della città [134]. Benché non sia sicuro che questo attacco fosse stato sferrato per gli ordini del governo genovese, è certo che si trattò di un tentativo di conquistare questo importante porto e farne una colonia. È vero che i Genovesi erano più propensi ad agire *manu forte* contro i musulmani. Ma anche i Veneziani avevano tali mire. Nel 1401 il senato di Venezia deliberò la proposta di chiedere al sultano del Cairo che vendesse loro l'isola di Tortosa, presso la costa di Siria, affinché servisse come emporio sicuro alla Serenissima [135]. Forse non a caso si tratta di un antico possesso dei cavalieri dell'Ospedale. La proposta fu respinta. Tuttavia in occasione di un'altra crisi negli scambi commerciali col Levante una tale proposta fu di nuovo fatta al senato. Nel 1505, secondo un cronista contemporaneo, « molti volevano che si domandasse al sultano un porto sicuro » (nell'Egitto) [136]. Gli atti del senato che contengono le istruzioni date allora ad un ambasciatore veneziano per le trattative col sultano e le discussioni relative comprendono infatti la proposta che egli si rivolga al sovrano musulmano in questo modo: per tanto ... farai intender ala Excellentia sua che i marcadanti nostri non havendo porto libero ti existimi non sera più alcuno se metti tanto pericolo... [137].

D'altra parte, la politica veneziana era molto cauta e la lezione avuta dall'assalto di Alessandria nel 1365 non era stata dimenticata. La potenza militare dei Mamlucchi era ancora notevole e la Serenissima non aveva il desiderio di aver masse di musulmani sotto la sua dominazione. Pure il sultano del Cairo doveva prendere in considerazione la potenza militare delle repubbliche marittime e dei Catalani. Egli non poteva dimenticare la lezione di Rodi. Senza

Crociati erano un impero di feudatari e di mercanti dell'Europa occidentale, ambedue senza una dipendenza amministrativa.

134 E. Ashtor - B. Z. Kedar, *Una guerra fra Genova e i Mamlucchi negli anni 1380*, « Archivio Storico Italiano », 1975, p. 21 sg. e v. p. 33 sgg. su altri tentativi genovesi di creare colonie nel Levante.

135 Jorga, *Notes et extraits pour servir à l'histoire des Croisades au XV siècle*, ROL IV (1896), p. 243.

136 Priuli, *Diarii*, II, p. 384.

137 Senato, Secreta 40, f. 114a.

dubbio i dirigenti del Cairo erano consapevoli della debolezza della loro artiglieria che li metteva in uno stato di inferiorità di fronte alle potenze occidentali. Ogni tanto accadevano altri scontri che rammentavano la loro propria inferiorità. Quando nel 1505 le galee veneziane partirono da Alessandria senza aver avuto il permesso e vennero bombardate dai Mamlucchi, i tiri quasi non fecero danno alle navi [138]. Perciò il maltrattamento che subivano i mercanti italiani, non di rado battuti e talvolta imprigionati, non dovrebbe stupirci. Le atrocità dei Mamlucchi non rispecchiavano fedelmente la realtà storica.

La conquista del Vicino Oriente da parte dei Turchi ottomani e la fondazione del loro impero poté ritardare di 150 anni il principio dell'autentico imperialismo in questa parte del mondo. Ma il sultanato ottomano dimostrava fin dall'inizio gli stessi tratti dei Mamlucchi, suoi predecessori — anzitutto l'inferiorità tecnologica e la lentezza di introdurre le innovazioni fatte nell'Occidente, come le nuove armi da fuoco. Anche la sua artiglieria era inferiore alla artiglieria delle potenze cristiane. Come i Mamlucchi impiegavano i cannoni anzitutto per bombardare fortezze mentre nel campo la loro artiglieria era meno efficiente di quella delle potenze cristiane. I loro cannoni erano troppo grossi e perciò meno mobili [139].

Il vero rapporto fra i Mamlucchi e Venezia era così ovvio che anche i dirigenti di altri paesi se ne rendevano conto. Nella prima metà del Quattrocento quando l'imperatore Sigismundo tentò di accerchiare la Serenissima mediante alleanze tra i nemici di questa, il regno dei Mamlucchi già era considerato come strettamente alleato a Venezia [140]. Poi, all'inizio del Cinquecento, quando si temeva a Venezia che le spedizioni portoghesi nell'India portassero alla rovina il suo commercio levantino e il sultano del Cairo preparava la guerra navale contro gli invasori nei mari del sud, l'intervento veneziano a favore del sultano si profilò chiaramente. Le relazioni che si trovano nelle fonti veneziane sono piuttosto laconiche ma non possono ingannare lo storico. Si intravvede che il sultano richiese dalla Serenissima di provvederlo di esperti artiglieri. Marino Sanuto racconta che prima della partenza dell'ambasciatore Domenico Trevisan al Cairo il Consiglio dei Dieci e la commissione che era incaricata delle questioni del commercio levantino gli dettero istruzioni segrete in merito della

[138] Priuli, *Diarii*, II, p. 272. Parecchie notizie su navi musulmane prese per corseggio dai Veneziani e da altri Europei fin dagli ultimi anni del Trecento testimoniano la stessa superiorità delle loro armi, v. Miste 43, f. 53b 44, f. 38b, 39b.

[139] Carlo M. Cipolla, *Guns and sails in the early phase of European expansion, 1400-1700*, London, 1965, pp. 92, 98.

[140] W. v. Stromer, *Die Schwarzmeer- und Levante-Politik Sigismunds von Luxemburg*, *Miscellanea Charles Verlinden*, Bruxelles, 1974, p. 609 sg.; v. anche il suo articolo *Diplomatische Kontakte des Herrschers vom Weissen Hammel, Uthman genannt Qara Yuluq, mit dem deutschen König Sigismund*, (in) « Südost-Forschungen », 20 (1961), p. 267 sgg.

« richiesta de armada et artilleria per le cose de Colocut »[141]. Secondo un altro cronista contemporaneo l'ambasciatore dovette promettere quello che il sultano aveva richiesto per quanto fosse stato possibile « et sopra tuto secretamente cum magior silentio se poteva et mancho etiam strepito »[142]. Ma questa relazione è falsa e rispecchia quello che si diceva allora a Venezia. Infatti le autorità avevano deciso di rifiutare al sovrano musulmano l'aiuto se avesse richiesto un ufficiale per addestrare le sue unità d'artiglieria o avesse fatto altre simili domande[143]. Una proposta di suggerire al sultano che mandasse emissari a Candia per prendere in servizio tali esperti o di offrire che la stessa Serenissima li mettesse alla sua disposizione venne respinta[144].

Questi testi sono eloquenti. Era l'ora della verità.

[141] *Diarii*, 13, col. 362.

[142] Priuli apud R. FULIN, *Girolamo Priuli e i suoi diarii*, « Archivio Veneto », 22 (1881), p. 246.

[143] R. FULIN, *Il canale di Suez e la repubblica di Venezia*, « Archivio Veneto », II (1871), p. 189 sg.

[144] Art. cit., p. 191.

VI

L'APOGÉE DU COMMERCE VÉNITIEN AU LEVANT. UN NOUVEL ESSAI D'EXPLICATION

Le rôle des Vénitiens dans le commerce international au bas Moyen Age et au début de l'époque moderne a suscité l'intérêt de beaucoup de savants qui en ont donné d'explications variées. Mais si nombreux que ces aperçus et hypothèses soient, il y reste toujours un point d'interrogation. Sur les pages suivantes un essai sera fait d'expliquer l'essor du commerce de Venise au Levant par la supposition qu'il était, dans une grande mesure, la conséquence de changements dans les structures économiques et sociales des pays musulmans du Proche-Orient. Presque tous les savants qui ont traité de l'histoire de Venise n'ont pas pris en considération que l'expansion vénitienne était étroitement liée à l'évolution de la société proche-orientale. En effet elle était un phénomène de l'histoire du Proche-Orient de même qu'elle faisait part de l'histoire de l'Europe méridionale.

La supposition que les Vénitiens réussissaient à monopoliser le grand commerce avec le Levant est partagée par de si nombreux auteurs qu'on puisse parler d'un véritable axiome. Mais des sources récemment publiées et des recherches qu'on a faites depuis la deuxième guerre mondiale touchant le commerce levantin des Vénitiens et des autres nations marchandes de l'Europe méridionale nous imposent, semble-t-il, une nouvelle évaluation. Peut-on en effet parler d'un monopole vénitien dans le commerce du Levant à la fin du Moyen Age? C'est la deuxième question dont nous voudrions traiter dans cette communication.

En essayant de répondre à ces questions on doit, cela se comprend, encore une fois définir ce qu'on peut considérer comme monopole vénitien dans le commerce du Levant et surtout en déterminer la chronologie.

Les chroniques et d'autres sources arabes et, d'autre part, les cahiers des notaires vénitiens qui étaient souvent aux échelles d'Orient les seuls répresentants de leur métier, nous fournissent bon nombre de données dont on se peut servir pour un essai d'éclaircir ces problèmes.

I.

A la fin du XIVe siècle et au début du XVe siècle les Vénitiens n'étaient pas encore la puissance dirigeante dans le commerce européen avec le Levant. De nombreuses données dans des sources différentes démontrent que les relations commerciales avec l'Egypte et la Syrie étaient alors un champs libre pour les activitées de plusieurs nations de l'Europe méridionale. La concurrence entre les nations marchandes était très forte, aucune n'avait une espèce d'hégémonie.

F. Melis a recueilli, dans les archives de Fr. Datini, des notices relatives aux navires européens qui fréquentaient le port de Beyrouth à cette époque. Il y a constaté que dans les années 1399-1408 le nombre des bateaux vénitiens mouillant à Beyrouth se montait à 278, tandis que Gênes était représentée par 264 et la Catalogne par 224.[1] Selon les actes d'un notaire vénitien à Alexandrie une seule coque vénitienne jetait l'ancre dans ce port dans la deuxième moitié de l'an 1404, tandis qu'il y avait trois génoises. Dans les actes du même notaire datant de l'an 1405 mention est faite de 7 coques catalanes, de 6 génoises, de 4 siciliennes et – d'une vénitienne.[2] Des documents génois témoignent de l'existence d'un service de galées qui faisaient le voyage de Chypre et d'Alexandrie.[3]

---

[1] *Note sur le mouvement du port de Beyrouth d'après la documentation florentine aux environs de 1400*, dans *Sociétés et compagnies de commerce en Orient et dans l'océan indien, Actes du huitième colloque international d'histoire maritime*, Paris 1970, pp. 371-73.

[2] ASV (Archivio di Stato, Venise), *Cancellaria Inferiore, Notai*, Busta 222: Antoniello de Vataciis (les feuillets ne sont pas numérotés, mais arrangés, plus ou moins, selon l'ordre chronologique).

[3] ASG (Archivio di Stato, Gênes), *Antico Comune* 26, pp. 36, 40, 44, 48 etc. Ces textes contredisent la supposition de J. Heers qui niait l'existence de convois de galées génoises allant en Egypte, v. *Types de navires et spécialisation du trafic en Méditerranée à la fin du Moyen Age*, dans

Quant à l'intensité des relations commerciales qui liaient à cette époque la Catalogne avec le Proche-Orient musulman, on peut citer les résultats de Cl. Carrère qui a fouillé les archives de Barcelone. On en apprend que 3-5 galées catalanes visitaient, à la fin du XIVe siècle, les ports de Syrie et d'Egypte. Au début du XVe siècle, le nombre des coques et des galées catalanes mouillant chaque année dans ces ports se serait monté à 7 en moyenne.[4]

Le nombre des fondachi où séjournaient les marchands européens porte lui-aussi témoignage du volume des échanges commerciaux entre diverses nations de l'Europe méridionale et les pays dominés par les Mamlouks. Il semble que les Génois aient eu à cette époque deux fondachi à Alexandrie.[5] Les marchands français en avaient encore plus. Car il y avait un fondaco des marchands « d'Avignon et de France »,[6] un fondaco de Marseille et enfin un fondaco de Narbonne.[7] Ces trois groupes de marchands français avaient à leur tête des consuls à eux.

Pour démontrer l'équilibre entre les nations marchandes on peut aussi citer la lettre d'un fattore, écrite à Alexandrie en 1424. Il rapporte à sa firme à Venise que les marchands vénitiens ont à leur disposition, au mois de mars, 5000 dinars en espèces et 40.000 en marchandises, les Génois en tout 30.000 et les Florentins – 14.000.[8]

Pourtant les conditions dans le commerce avec le Levant changeaient beaucoup après le tournant du siècle. L'époque caractérisée par la concurrence de diverses nations marchandes, suite de leur participation au commerce levantin à l'époque des Croisades et s'appuyant sur des privilèges alors obtenus, touchait à sa fin. Plusieurs facteurrs amenaient le ralentisse-

Le navire et l'économie maritime du Moyen Age au XVIIIe siècle, principalement en Méditerranée (*2e colloque international d'histoire maritime*, 1957), Paris 1958, p. 114. Toutefois il n'y a pas de doute que ce service n'était pas si régulier comme le vénitien et fut plus tard aboli.

[4] *Barcelone centre économique 1380-1462,* Paris 1967, pp. 644, 851.

[5] Heyd, *Histoire du commerce du Levant*, II, pp. 432.

[6] Ant. de Vataciis, 6 juillet 1404, 4 octobre 1404, 6 octobre 1404, 30 octobre 1404.

[7] *Ibid.* 8 nov. 1404, 29 juillet 1404.

[8] F. Melis, *Documenti per la storia economica dei secoli XIII-XVI*, Florence 1972, p. 190.

ment des activités commerciales de certaines nations au Proche-Orient. Pour la plupart de ces nations c'était un déclin lent mais progressif.

La regréssion du commerce génois en Syrie et en Egypte ressort avec netteté des documents datant du XVe siècle. En effet les Génois avaient moins d'intérêt à l'achat des épices que n'en avaient les Vénitiens. Les connaissements des bateaux génois qui rentraient du Proche-Orient à la fin du XIVe siècle comprenaient de quantités d'épices beaucoup plus petites que celles qu'apportaient les galées vénitiennes.[9] En effet les marchés où les Génois pouvaient écouler les épices étaient beaucoup plus limités que ceux auxquels elles étaient exportées par les Vénitiens. Les Génois n'étaient pas réussis à remplacer les marchands de la Provence et du Languedoc dans la France septentrionale et en faire un grand marché pour les épices qu'ils importaient du Levant. Quant au coton, les Génois en acquéraient de grandes quantités en Turquie, ainsi que la Syrie ne fût pour eux qu'une source d'approvisionnement secondaire.[10] D'après les régistres des douanes de Gênes, il y arrivèrent en 1445 4 bateaux qui avaient visité les ports d'Egypte et de Syrie. Mais ces bateaux avaient continué leus voyages à Chios, Rhodes et Tunis et y chargé d'autres marchandises. En 1458 et en 1507 un seul bateau vint de Beyrouth à Gênes.[11] Les autorités de Gênes ne pouvaient pas ne s'apercevoir du déclin du commerce avec le Levant musulman. En 1496 on conférait aux officiales Alexandriae le droit de nommer le consul d'Alexandrie « propter que negociatio loci illius et totius Egypti ac Syrie solitam frequentationem et

---

[9] V. mon livre *Les métaux précieux et la balance des payements du Proche-Orient à la basse-époque*, Paris 1971, pp. 75 et s.

[10] Par conséquent de grandes quantités de coton furent chargées sur des navires génois à Chios, v. ASG, *Carat. vet.* 1552, f. 125a, 126b, 127a, 143a, 148a; G. Musso, *Nuovi documenti dell'archivio di Stato di Genova sui Genovesi e il Levante nel secondo Quattrocento*, dans « Rassegna degli archivi di Stato », 27 (1967), pp. 484, 488; M.-L. Heers, *Le commerce de l'alun à la fin du moyen-âge*, dans « Rev. d'hist. écon. et soc. », 32 (1954), p. 36.

[11] ASG, *Carat. vet.* 1552, f. 45a, 124a, 127a, 131a, 134a et cf. J. Heers, *Gênes au XVe siècle*, Paris 1961, pp. 374, 376 à être corrigé; ASG, *San Giorgio, Sala 38/54*, f. 4b, 17b; *Carat. vet.* 1556, f. 36a et ss.

cursum habere possit que a longo tempore nec dum plurimum diminuta sed in toto extincta videtur ».[12] On ne doit oublier non plus que Gênes ne pouvait pas offrir aux Egyptiens et aux Syriens de grandes quantités d'argent et de cuivre dont ils avaient grand besoin. Les Vénitiens les obtenaient en Bosnie, en Serbie et en Allemagne.

On fera des constatations semblables en étudiant l'évolution du commerce levantin de Marseille et d'autres villes marchandes de l'Europe méridionale.

E. Baratier a démontré que les activités commerciales des Marseillais dans le Proche-Orient musulman furent interrompues depuis un essor en 1380-85. Elles furent reprises au début du XVe siècle, mais pour peu de temps.[13] On trouve cependant de textes se référant à leur commerce en Egypte et en Syrie à des époques postérieures du Moyen Age et le consulat de Marseille existait à Alexandrie jusqu'à la fin du XVe siècle.[14] Pourtant les marchands provençaux et français qui sont mentionnés dans les actes dressés par des notaires vénitiens à Damas et à Alexandrie dans la deuxième et la troisième décennie du XVe siècle sont peu nombreux. Le commerce des Marseillais et des autres Français en Orient revêtait à cette époque toujours un caractère sporadique. L'entreprise de Jacques Coeur qui essayait au milieu du XVe siècle d'établir des échanges plus réguliers et intenses échouèrent. Bien que les voyages des galées françaises aient été renouvelés en 1456, le volume du commerce français en Egypte et en Syrie resta assez modeste.

Florence avait des colonies marchandes à Alexandrie et à Damas depuis le début du XVe siècle et même à une époque antérieure. Ayant obtenu en 1422 un privilège de la part du Sultan Barsbay elle avait un consulat à Alexandrie.[15] Au

[12] ASG, *San Giorgio, Primi cancellieri,* Ba 88, p. 322.

[13] *Histoire du commerce de Marseille,* II, Paris 1951, pp. 229 et ss., 240 et s.

[14] ASV, *Cancellaria Inferiore,* Notai, Ba 230, Nicolo Venier, fasc. B, 2, f. 45a et s.; ASG, *Arch. Segr.* 2774 C, cf. mon article *Salaires dans l'Orient médiéval, à la basse époque,* dans « Rev. des étud. isl. », 39 (1971), pp. 106 et ss.

[15] ASV, *Cancellaria Inferiore,* Notai, Ba 83, Cristofore del Fiore I, f. 13a et ss.; ASV, *Giudici di petizion,* Sentenze 54, f. 36a et ss. 107, f. 133b et ss.

milieu du XVe siècle la Signoria établit un service de galées qui devait visiter régulièrement les ports de Syrie et d'Egypte. En 1460 le tarif de cargaisons fixé en 1444 fut réduit,[16] sans doute pour encourager les marchands à intensifier leurs activités en Orient. Pourtant les efforts faits par le gouvernement de Florence étaient en vain. Il ne réussit pas à maintenir un service régulier de galées liant Porto Pisano avec les échelles d'Orient.[17] Mais ce n'était pas cet echec qui explique le petit volume du commerce florentin en Orient. Comme les Génois, les marchands de Florence n'avaient pas de grands marchés où ils pouvaient vendre les épices. D'autre part ils ne pouvaient offrir aux Orientaux que les produits de leur industrie textile, tandis que les Vénitiens payaient une grande partie des marchandises orientales en métaux bruts, obtenus dans des pays voisins à leur métropole.

II.

Alors que le commerce levantin des autres nations marchandes déclinait depuis le début du XVe siècle ou avait un caractère sporadique, tel qu'avaient les activités commerciales de Raguse et de plusieurs autres villes de l'Europe méridionale, les Vénitiens poursuivaient une politique tenace visant à se saisir du commerce des épices et à ériger une suprématie commerciale dans le basin oriental de la Méditerranée.

Ils s'appliquaient, en première ligne, à maintenir un service régulier de galées liant leur métropole avec Alexandrie et Beyrouth La ligne Venise-Alexandrie fonctionnait régulièrement depuis 1345, la ligne Venise-Beyrouth depuis 1374. Rarement le service fut interrompu, pour des raisons politiques ou pour d'autres, pour une année ou plus. En étudiant les données qu'on trouve dans les régistres du « Senato Mar » et des « Incanti » on s'aperçoit que jusqu'à la huitième décennie du XVe siècle le nombre des galèes allant à Beyrouth était plus grand, puis les galées d'Alexandrie l'emportaient. Ce changement dé-

---

[16] G. Müller, *Documenti sulle relazioni delle città toscane coll'Oriente cristiano e coi Turchi*, Florence 1879, pp. 351 et s., 358 et s.

[17] M. E. Mallet, *The Florentine galleys in the fifteenth century*, Oxford 1967, pp. 63 et ss., 153 et ss.

montre que le commerce du poivre, l'article principal parmi les épices exportées d'Egypte, augmentait toujours. Ce qui plus est, le sénat de Venise destinait toujours pour le convoi d'Alexandrie de « galées grosses », tandis que les galées de Beyrouth avaient un tonnage plus petit. Une deuxième observation qui s'impose à quiconque étudie ces textes se réfère au total des galées. Il s'élevait, à la fin du XIVe siècle et au début du XVe siècle, jusqu'à 38-40 par lustre. Quoiqu'il y ait eu d'oscillations, dues aux vicissitudes politiques et commerciales, les Vénitiens réussirent à maintenir le volume de la navigation des galées. A la fin du XVe siècle, en 1471-75, 1481-85 et 1491-95, le total des galées allant à Alexandrie et à Beyrouth était à peu près le même.[18]

Pourtant on se tromperait en concluant de ces données que le volume des épices transportées par les galées de Venise ne changeait pas au cours de cette époque. Car les galées envoyées dans la deuxième moitié du XVe siècle en Egypte et en Syrie étaient beaucoup plus grandes que celles qu'on avait employées au siècle précédant. Les grandes galées avaient un tonnage de 1000-1500 boutes (600-900 tonnes), tandis que les galées allant en Orient au XIVe siècle n'en avaient que 600-700.[19]

De nombreux renseignements dans des sources diverses justifient la conclusion que la quantité d'épices que les Vénitiens exportaient de l'Egypte et de la Syrie augmentait considérablement depuis la fin du XIVe siècle.

Les archives de la firme Francesco Datini nous fournissent des indications pour le volume du commerce des épices à la fin du XIVe siècle et au début du XVe siècle. Plusieurs rapports trouvés dans ces archives indiquent les quantités des

---

[18] V. F. C. LANE, *The Merchant Marine of the Venetian Republic*, dans le recueil de ses articles *Venice and history*, Baltimore 1966, p. 148; F. THIRIET, *Quelques observations sur le trafic des galères vénitiennes d'après les chiffres de incanti* (*XIVe-XVe siècle*), dans *Studi in onore di Amintore Fanfani*, Milano 1962, III, pp. 511, 516; R. ROMANO-A. TENENTI-U. TUCCI, *Venise et la route du cap 1499-1517*, dans *Mediterraneo e Oceano Indiano*, *Atti del Sesto Colloquio Internazionale di Storia Marittima* (*1962*), Florence 1970, p. 111; A. TENENTI-C. VIVANTI, *Le film d'un grand système de navigation: les galères vénitiennes XIVe-XVIe siècles*, dans « Annales E. S. C. », 16 (1961), pp. 83-86.

[19] THIRIET, *art. cit.*, p. 513.

épices exportées d'Alexandrie et de Beyrouth par les galées vénitiennes, d'autres documents dans les même archives contiennent des renseignements sur leurs prix.[20] Bien que ces rapports ne soient pas complets ils nous rendent possible d'avancer quelques hypothèses quant au total du commerce vénitien. Voici des résumés touchant le commerce des deux épices les plus importantes:

date		quantité			valeur		total
1394	poivre	Alexandrie	2190	pondi	65,700	dinars	
		Beyrouth	1586	»	44,408	»	
	gingembre	Alexandrie	138	»	12,420	»	
		Beyrouth	246	»	44,280		
							166,808
1395	poivre	Alexandrie	2100	»	63,000		
		Beyrouth	1000	ḳinṭār	60,000	»	
	gingembre	Alexandrie	190	pondi	19,000	»	
		Beyrouth	323	ḳinṭār	64,800	»	
							206,800
1396	poivre	Alexandrie	1573	pondi	47,728	»	
	gingembre	»	221	»	19,890	»	
							67,618
1399	poivre	Alexandrie	2100	»	52,920	»	
		Beyrouth	220	»	6,600	»	
	gingembre	Alexandrie	130	»	6,890	»	
		Beyrouth	2420	colli	65,340	»	
							131,750
1404	poivre	Beyrouth	1724	pondi	77,580	ducats	
	gingembre	»	920	»	46,000	»	
							123,580
1405	poivre	Beyrouth	820	»	36,900	»	
	gingembre	»	828	»	41,150	»	
							78,050

[20] Les renseignements dans les documents Datini ont été publiés par J. Heers, *Il commercio nel Mediterraneo alla fine del secolo XIV e nei primi anni del XV*, dans « ASI », 113 (1955), pp. 205 et ss. Quant aux prix des épices selon lesquels les calculs suivants ont été faits v. nos ouvrages *Les métaux précieux*, p. 73; *Histoire des prix et des salaires dans l'Orient médiéval*, pp. 414 et s. (avec quelqes corrections). Les pondo ou colli dans lesquels les documents Datini indiquent les exportations de Beyrouth et d'Alexandrie ont été considérés comme le même poids et equivalant à 50 raṭls damascènes ou 90 kg.

Toutes ces données démontrent apparemment que les galées vénitiennes exportaient, à la fin du XIVe siècle et au début du XVe siècle, d'Alexandrie et de Beyrouth du poivre et du gingembre valant, en moyenne, de 140.000 à 150.000 dinars (équivalant à 180.000 ducats).

Le volume des exportations d'épices à la fin du XVe siècle était beaucoup plus grand. Evaluant les quantités indiquées dans les chroniques vénitiennes de la fin du Moyen Age[21] on trouve les totaux suivants:

date		quantité			valeur		total
1496	poivre	Alexandrie	950	colli	101,240	ducats	
		Beyrouth	2600	»	71,500	»	
	gingembre	Alexandrie	600	»	60,000	»	
		Beyrouth	550	»	15,125	»	
							247,865
1497	poivre	Alexandrie	1250	»	150,000	»	
		Beyrouth	993	»	39,610	»	
	gingembre	Alexandrie	776	»	93,315	»	
		Beyrouth	709	»	28,360	»	
							311,285

En comparant ces données on constate que la valeur des cargaisons de poivre et de gingembre que les Vénitiens achetaient en Syrie et en Egypte avait augmenté au cours du XVe siècle de 50% à peu près!

Une autre branche, dont l'importance pour les activités commerciales des Vénitiens était de premier ordre était l'exportations de coton de Syrie et d'Egypte. Surtout en Syrie la production de coton était considérable et les marchands vénitiens en acquéraient de grandes quantités. Dans cette branche aussi leur suprématie était nette. La Sérénissime envoyait chaque année deux convois de coques en Orient, l'un en mars allant en Egypte et en Syrie pour la foire (mudda) de coton,

---

[21] Priuli, *Diarii*, I, pp. 59, 73. Selon Lane dans « AHR », 38, p. 228 le collo égyptien était, à cette époque, égal à 1120 libbre sottili de Venise. Pourtant d'après ASV, *Senato Mar*, 12, f. 136b (de l'an 1488) un pondo (ou collo) était considéré comme quatre fois autant le collo de Beyrouth. De nombreux renseignements dans les Terminazioni des Giudici di petiziòn confirment cette équation, savoir: 1 pondo = 1200 libbre sottili de Venise.

l'autre en septembre.[22] Le convoi de coques visitant les ports de Syrie au printemps comptait la plupart du temps 6-7 bateaux. Bien que les navires ronds aient transporté aussi des quantités considérables d'un autre produit syrien, la potasse si nécessaire pour la fabrication du savon, le coton était toujours l'article le plus important de leurs cargaisons.

Des comptes et d'autres documents provenant des archives de marchands vénitiens démontrent que beaucoup de firmes achetaient chaque année en Syrie (ou en Palestine) du coton valant 600-800 ducats. Mais il y avait de grands marchands qui en acquéraient chaque année de quantités valant 2000 ducats et plus.[23] Un rapport compris dans la grande chronique de Girolamo Priuli nous fournit une précieuse indication quant au volume total du coton exporté par les Vénitiens de Syrie. On y lit qu'en 1495 deux bateaux vénitiens venant de Syrie coulèrent dans l'Adriatique, leur cargaisons comprenant 1000 sacs de coton, en dehors d'autres articles.[24] Supposant que le convoi consistait de 5 bateaux seulement on conclurait qu'ils transportaient du coton valant 50.000 ducats. Car un sac contenait la plupart du temps 80-90 raṭls tripolitains et, d'autre part, un ḳinṭār valait de 22 à 25 ducats.[25]

Pour démontrer que le commerce levantin de Venise augmentait toujours, jusqu'à la fin du XVe siècle, qu'il nous soit permis d'évoquer d'autres faits qui portent témoignage de la grande expansion ou même d'une suprématie vénitienne. Les données statistique qu'on vient de citer indiquent l'augmentation des exportations, des autres rapports témoignent de la consolidation des colonies vénitiennes aux échelles d'Orient.

De nombreux textes se référant aux activités commerciales que les Vénitiens poursuivaient au XVe siècle en quelques

---

[22] Ce que dit Heyd, II, pp. 460 et s. sur une mudda en juin doit être corrigé. Mais parfois des coques vénitiennes allaient en été (juillet) en Syrie pour charger du coton, v. *Giud. di pet.*, Sentenze 34, f. 4a et ss.

[23] V. *Giud. di pet.*, Sent. 29, f. 34a 34, f. 4a et ss. 73, f. 114b, 125a et ss. 104, f. 84b et ss. 107, f. 169a et ss.; S. Sassi, *Sulle scritture di due aziende mercantili veneziane del Quattrocento*, Naples 1950, pp. 76, 107, 109, 111 et ss.

[24] *Diarii*, I, p. 42.

[25] *Giud. di pet.*, Sent. 50, f. 23a et ss. 52, f. 135b et s. 97, f. 116b et s. 100, f. 127a et ss. 106, f. 66b et ss. 107, f. 154b et ss., 185a et ss. 123, f. 53b et ss. 127, f. 27b et ss.

villes de la Palestine, jadis sans aucune importance pour le commerce international. Parmi ces villes Acre tenait sans doute la première place et en effet la sénat vénitien décida que deux d'un convoide neuf coques allant en Syrie jétassent l'ancre dans son port.[26] La petite ville de Ramla avait aussi à cette époque une colonie vénitienne. On y achetait du coton et des épices.[27] Hamath avait, au début du XVe siècle, un vice-consul vénitien, mais puis, au milieu du siècle, un consul y résidait.[28] Tripoli hébergeait certainement la plus grande colonie vénitienne dans la Syrie septentrionale et les activités commerciales des Vénitiens y étaient intenses. Cette ville était le siège de fattori qui procuraient à leurs firmes des grandes quantités de coton et les expédiaient à la métropole. En 1442, le sénat créa un consulat à Tripoli. On lit dans un texte se rapportant à cette décision que cela était un fait tout à fait nouveau (« nova et inusitata »).[29]

Il semble qu'en Egypte aussi les colonies vénitiennes croissaient. Car on trouve à la tête de la colonie vénitienne à Damiette en 1420 un vice-consul et en 1440 un consul.[30]

Ces changements dans l'administration coloniale indiquent apparemment que dans le deuxième quart du XVe siècle Venise était réussie à ériger sa suprématie dans le commerce du Levant.

III.

Il n'y a pas de doute que la régularité du service des galées et l'emprise des Vénitiens sur les débouchés des régions productrices de grandes quantités d'argent et de cuivre facili-

---

[26] ASV, *Senato Mar*, III, f. 23b et s., 30b et ss.; *Miste*, 60, f. 158b (a. 1439, 1447).

[27] *Libri Commemoriali*, ed. PREDELLI, IV, p. 40 où la citation du texte n'est pas correcte); *Giud. di pet.*, Sent. 19, f. 2a et s., 28b et s. 21, f. 37a et s. 28, f. 92a et s.

[28] Plusieurs lettres à Donà Soranzo, vice-consul à Hamath, dans ASV, *Miscellanea di carte non appartenenti a nessun archivio*, Ba 8; *Senato Mar*, III, f. 31b (a. 1447) V, f. 113a (a. 1455).

[29] N. JORGA, *Notes et extraits pour servir à l'histoire des Croisades au XVe siècle*, dans « Rev. de l'Or. Latin », VII, p. 77.

[30] NICOLO VENIER A, f. 8b; *Giud. di pet.*, Sent. 119, f. 64a et ss. et cf. HEYD, II, p. 427 et s.

taient leurs activités commerciales dans le Proche-Orient musulman. Pourtant leur succès dans le commerce du Levant était aussi la conséquence de certains changements dans les structures économiques et sociales des pays proche-orientaux eux-mêmes. C'est ce que la plupart des historiens de Venise s'ont laissé échapper.

Deux grands changements ont été survenus dans le monde proche-oriental depuis la fin des Croisades: la plupart des vieilles industries étaient tombées en decadence et la classe des grands marchands, qui avait été engagé dans le commerce international, fut supprimé par les sultans mamlouks. Sans prendre en considération les suites de ces deux phénomènes on ne pourrait comprendre le grand essor du commerce vénitien en Orient.

La décadence des industries textiles avait la plus grande portée pour le développement économique du Proche-Orient au bas Moyen Age. Car ces industries jadis rénommées pour la qualité de leurs produits en avaient exporté de grandes quantités en d'autres pays.

Il va sans dire que l'invasion de l'Irak par les Tatares, au milieu du XIIIe siècle, avait eu de conséquences néfastes pour ses manufactures. Les industries de Syrie avaient perdu bon nombre de leurs ouvriers par leur déportation en Asie Centrale, sur l'ordre de Tamerlan. Mais on se tromperait en expliquant la ruine des industries textiles dans le Proche-Orient médiéval comme suite des invasions par des armées ennemies. C'est l'explication donnée par les anciens chroniqueurs et répétée par quelques orientalistes. On nous apprend que l'industrie textile de la Basse-Egypte disparut quand les Croisés invahirent le Délta au début du XIIIe siècle. Pourtant on se demande: Si ces manufactures étaient profitables, pourquoi on ne les a pas rouvertes après la retraite de l'ennemi?

Le déclin industriel était en effet la suite de la stagnation technologique. La plupart des industries proche-orientales n'étaient plus capables de faire la concurrence aux produits des manufactures occidentales, importés par des marchands italiens et d'autres. Or le grand essor des industries dans l'Europe occidentale avait été rendu possible par des innovations technologiques. C'étaient elles qui avaient pour conséquence que les produits des manufactures fussent de meilleure qualité et aussi meilleur marché.

Dans l'industrie textile, la plus importante innovation était sans doute le moulin à fouler, opéré par d'eau. Inventé en Toscane ou dans la Lombardie, dans la deuxième moitié du Xe siècle ou dans la première moitié de l'XIe siècle, le moulin à fouler s'était répandu dans tous les pays de l'Europe occidentale. Le changement produit par cette innovation, surtout en Angleterre au XIIIe siècle, était si grand qu'on a pu parler d'une véritable « révolution industrielle ».[31] Le moulin à eau n'était pas inconnu en Orient où il était souvent appelé « moulin persan », mais il semble qu'on ne l'employait pas dans l'industrie. On foulait les draps avec les pieds comme autrefois. Apparemment deux autres innovations dans l'industrie textile de l'Europe occidentale ne furent pas introduites en Orient non plus: le rouet à filer et le métier mis en mouvement par un pédale.

L'importation de draps occidentaux revêtait à la fin du XIVe siècle et au début du XVe siècle le caractère d'un véritable dumping. Les marchands européens écoulaient de grandes quantités de draps en tous les pays d'Orient. Les Italiens vendaient les produits de l'industrie de Florence et de Flandres, les Catalans les draps grossiers de Barcelone et d'autres villes de cette région. Les auteurs arabes ne pouvaient pas ne s'apercevoir de ce phénomène. al-Maḳrīzī se lamente du changement survenu dans l'habillement des Egyptiens au début du XVe siècle: au lieu de bons vêtements égyptiens on portait des habits de drap grossier d'Europe.[32] Ibn Taghrībirdī nous fournit des éléments statistiques quant au déclin de l'industrie textile à Alexandrie: le nombre des métiers y avait diminué de 14.000 dans la dernière décennie du XIVe siècle à 800 en 1434.[33]

---

[31] LYNN WHITE Jr., *Medieval technology and social change*, Oxford 1965, p. 83; C. M. CIPOLLA, *Storia economica dell'Europa pre-industriale*, Bologna 1974, p. 223; A.-M. BAUTIER, *Les plus anciennes mentions de moulins hydrauliques industriels et de moulins à vent*, dans « Bulletin philologique et historique du comité des travaux historiques et scientifiques », II (1960), pp. 581 et ss.; E. M. CARUS-WILSON, *An industrial revolution of the thirteenth century*, dans ses *Essays on Economic History*, I, London 1954, pp. 41 et ss.

[32] V. R. DOZY, *Dictionnaire détaillé des noms des vêtements chez les Arabes*, Amsterdam 1845, pp. 127 et ss.

[33] IBN TAGHRĪBIRDĪ, *an-Nudjūm az-zāhira*, éd. POPPER, VI, p. 714; trad. POPPER, IV, p. 112.

Le développement d'autres industries du Proche-Orient s'inscrivait sur la même ligne. Car la stagnation technologique était sans doute la conséquence de l'établissement de monopoles par les régimes féodaux ou de la préponderance des manufactures qui étaient en possession de grands aristocrats et s'étaient érigés en de véritables trusts. Les régimes des califes orthodoxes et fatimidex se caractérisaient par la liberté d'entreprise et, par conséquent, par la concurrence des manufactures royales et privées. Quand la concurrence avait été plus ou moins supprimée, les manufactures royales n'avaient le besoin d'introduire des innovations pour lesquelles on devait faire de nombreux et coûteux expériments.

Jusqu'à la fin du XIVe siècle la Syrie et l'Egypte pouvaient exporter, en des pays d'Orient et d'Occident, des grandes quantités de sucre.[34] Mais puis, au XVe siècle, la production de sucre diminuait considérablement dans les pays du Proche-Orient et, d'autre part, on y importait de la mélasse et aussi du bon sucre de Chypre, de la Sicile et d'autres pays.[35] Sans doute le déclin de l'industrie du sucre en Egypte et en Syrie était la suite d'une stagnation technologique. Les produits des sucreries européennes étaient devenus meilleur marché quand on y avait fait des innovations technologiques, telle que l'introduction du trappetto en Sicile.[36]

On fera des observations semblables en étudiant l'évolution de l'industrie du papier. Les papeteries d'Orient avaient fournit leurs produits et aussi des ouvriers experts aux pays de l'Europe méridionale depuis de longs siècles. Mais quand les papetiers de Fabriano, une petite ville dans les Marches, avaient introduit dans leurs manufactures les moulins à eau et avaient appris à écraser la pâte par des batteries de marteaux, leurs produits étaient de meilleure qualité et meilleur marché. Ils faisaient aussi une autre innovation: en lieu de l'amidon végétale ils se servaient de matières animales.[37] Un grand essor

---

[34] V. Heers, *Il commercio mediterraneo* etc., pp. 172, 174, 175, 185.

[35] *Giud. di pet.*, Sent. 48, f. 5a et s. 54, f. 31b et ss. 34a et s., 36a et ss. 96, f. 66a et ss. 98, f. 117b et ss.; Marino Sanuto, *Diarii*, X, col. 95.

[36] Sur ce sujet v. ma conférence au Colloque international d'histoire économique du Proche-Orient, en juin 1974 à Princeton, à être publié dans les *Proceedings* de ce colloque.

[37] *Zonghi's watermarks*, Hilversum 1953 (*Monumenta chartae papyraceae historiam illustrantia*, III), pp. 70 et ss.

de l'industrie du papier s'ensuivit et on en exportait les produits aussi en Orient. De nombreux documents vénitiens en portent témoignage.[38]

Bref, la décadence des industries orientales avaient pour conséquence l'augmentation des importations de produits européens. Les marchands européens pouvaient échanger une grande partie des épices et des autres articles orientaux contre les produits industriels. Parmi les marchands européens qui tiraient parti de ce changement les Vénitiens tenaient la première place.

Un autre changement qui rendait possibile le grand succès des Vénitiens était la chute des Kārimites.

Depuis l'époque des Croisades un groupe de riches marchands, appelés « marchands de Kārim » (tudjdjār al-kārim) prédominait dans le grand commerce d'épices du Proche-Orient. Mais ils ne s'occupaient pas seulement de l'importation des articles indiens en Egypte et en Syrie, mais aussi étaient très actifs dans d'autres branches du commerce international, telle que la traite. Les sources arabes nous ne fournissent pas des indications sur les structures de leur commerce, c'est-à-dire les modalités de leurs transactions et de l'organisation de leur groupe. Pourtant on apprend des rapports des auteurs arabes que les Kārimites étaient un groupe de grands capitalistes qui souvent donnaient des prêts aux souverains proche-orientaux. C'est pourquoi le sultan du Caire les protégeait. Or l'époque des sultans mamlouks de la dynastie baḥrite (1250-1381) était l'apogée des Kārimites· Zaki 'd-dīn Abū Bakr b. ʻAlī Ibn al-Kharrūbī (m. 1385) est appelé « le dernier des Kārimites ». D'après d'autres sources arabes Burhān ad-dīn Ibrāhīm Ibn al-Maḥallī (m. 1403) était le dernier grand Kārimite.[39] Sultan al-Malik al-Mu'ayyad Shaikh (1412-19) avait encore un Kārimite parmi ses courtisans.[40] Pourtant après la mort de ce sultan le déclin des Kārimites s'ensuivit. Bien que des marchands appelés Kārimites soient mentionnées dans les

---

[38] *Giud. di pet.*, Sent. 45, f. 33a et ss. (a. 1419) 70, f. 11' et s. (a. 1412) 96, f. 81a et ss. (a. 1441) etc.; MARINO SANUTO, *Diarii*, X, col. 95.

[39] W. J. FISCHEL, *Über die Gruppe der Kārimī-Kaufleute*, dans *Studia Arabica* (« Analecta Orientalia », 14, Rome 1937), p. 71.

[40] E. ASHTOR, *The Kārimī merchants*, dans « JRAS », 1956, pp. 46 et s.

chroniques arabes du milieu et de la deuxième moitié du XVe siècle, ils disparurent comme un groupe. Leur chute était sans doute la conséquence de la politique économique de Barsbay (1422-38), visant à un monopole sultanien dans le commerce des épices. Il est vrai que sa politique n'était pas couronnée de succès, mais il abolit les privilèges des Kārimites et les remplaça par ses agents commerciaux.[41] Quelques Kārimites entraient dans le service du sultan, d'autres émigraiente aux Indes ou ailleurs.[42]

Les documents vénitiens jettent de la lumière sur ce grand changement dans le commerce international du Proche-Orient.

Dans des textes se référant aux activités commerciales des Vénitiens aux échelles d'Orient, au début du XVe siècle, mention est faite de marchands musulmans qui leur vendaient de grandes quantités d'articles indiens. Un marchand appelé Shaikh 'Alī vendit, au Caire en 1412, au Vénitien Clario Arcangeli d'épices valant 56.000 dinars.[43] Mais dans documents datant du milieu du XVe siècle il est toujours parlé du « marchand du sultan ». Trait caractéristique, plusieurs de ces agents du sultan étaient des étrangers, tel que Khawādjā Ghālib Rufā'īl de Valence, mentionné dans un acte notarié à Alexandrie en 1456.[44]

D'autres textes démontrent que des grands marchands privés étaient contraints à entrer au service du sultan.

Des actes d'un notaire vénitiens à Damas et des autres documents datant de l'an 1413 se rapportent aux activités d'un grand marchand musulman, Aḥmad Ibn al-Muzalliḳ. Il avait beaucoup d'affaires avec les marchands italiens, par exemple l'échange de textiles européens contre clou de girofle.[45] Puis en 1421 le sénat de Venise décida d'envoyer au sultan du Caire des ambassadeurs qui devaient, en dehors d'autres sujets, traiter avec

---

[41] I. M. Lapidus, *Muslim cities in the later Middle Ages*, Harvard Press 1967, pp. 126 et ss.

[42] S. Y. Labib, *Handelsgeschichte Ägyptens im Spätmittelalter*, Wiesbaden 1965, pp. 402 et s.; A. Darrag, *L'Egypte sous le règne de Barsbay*, Damas 1961, pp. 233, 235 et s.

[43] *Giud. di pet.*, Sent. 35, f. 56a et ss.

[44] Cristofore del Fiore, V, f. 17b et s.

[45] ASV, *Notarile 14832*, Giacomo della Torre, n. 16, 17; *Giud. di pet.*, Sent. 46, f. 63a et ss.

lui de l'ingérence de «Ben-Emuslach» (Ibn al-Muzalliḳ) dans le commerce des Vénitiens à Damas. Les ambassadeurs devaient expliquer au sultan qu'un marchand privé, tel qu'Ibn al-Muzalliḳ, ne pouvait donner des ordres aux Damascènes quant aux échanges commerciaux avec les Vénitiens.[46] Or, au début de la troisième décennie du XVe siècle, Ibn al-Muzalliḳ était un marchand privé. Dans les sources arabes on trouve des renseignements additionels sur ce marchand. Il était le fils d'un riche marchand, Shams ad-dīn Muḥammad b. 'Alī Ibn al-Muzalliḳ (m. 1444), qui est appelé dans un recueil de biographies du XVe siècle, « le plus grand marchand de Damas ». Aḥmad lui-même mourut, d'après la même source arabe, en 1468. Il avait deux frères, Sirādj ad-dīn 'Umar et Badr ad-dīn Ḥasan.[47] Quand Barsbay fit volte face et amena par sa politique monopoliste la chute des Kārimites, les Ibn al-Muzalliḳ devenaient des agents du sultan. Parmi les actes du tribunal vénitien des Giudici di petiziòn il y a quelques uns qui se réfèrent à des transactions en 1436 et en 1440 à Damas et où il est parlé du marchand du sultan, appelé Ibn al-Muzalliḳ. Une lettre du sénat vénitien au consul à Damas, écrite en 1443, comprend des instructions touchant les menaces d'« Ebenemusalach », qui veut arrêter les marchands vénitiens et confisquer leur biens. Puisque le prénom n'est pas indiqué dans ces documents, on ne peut savoir s'il s'agit d'Aḥmad, de son père ou d'un de ses frères. Peu l'importe. Quiconque ce soit, ces textes démontrent que les Ibn al-Muzalliḳ n'étaient plus de marchands privés. Quant à Muḥammad Ibn al-Muzalliḳ, le premier de cette famille, on peut évoquer un texte arabe qui démontre que lui restait jusqu'à la fin de sa vie un marchand privé. Le grand recueil de documents arabes, Ṣubḥ al-a'shā fī ṣinā'at al-inshā, contient un ordre sultanien touchant l'exemption d'impôts qu'on accorde à Muḥammad Ibn al-Muzalliḳ, en raison de ses activités au service du sultan. Puisque l'auteur de ce recueil, Shihāb ad-dīn al-Ḳalḳashandī, mourut en 1418, ce document date de l'époque antérieure au règne du sultan Barsbay.[48]

---

[46] JORGA, *Notes et extraits*, dans « ROL », V, p. 115.

[47] AS-SAKHĀWĪ, *aḍ-Ḍau al-lāmi'*, II, p. 147; III, p. 126; VI, p. 120; VIII, pp. 173 et s.

[48] *Giud. di pet.*, Sent. 76, f. 51b et ss. 90, f. 133a; JORGA, *Notes et*

Pour comprendre la portée de la chute des Kārimites pour le commerce des Vénitiens en Orient, on doit prendre en considération que les grands marchands d'épices s'occupaient aussi d'autres transactions. Selon les actes d'un notaire vénitien Aḥmad Ibn al-Muzalliḳ importait à Damas du corail.[49] D'un acte d'un notaire génois se référant à des transactions dans la cinquième décénnie du XVe siècle on apprend qu'il vendait des diamants.[50]

Après la chute des Kārimites les Vénitiens pouvaient élargir leurs activités commerciales aux échelles d'Orient. Déjà au début du XVe siècle ils avaient acquis du coton directement des paysans dans la province d'Alep.[51] Sans doute ils pouvaient agrandir ces transactions depuis la disparution des Kārimites. Les Vénitiens s'occupaient aussi du commerce d'esclaves, en important des nègres en Syrie et e Egypte. Nicolo Contarini importa à Tripoli, en 1434, d'esclaves noirs.[52] Un autre marchand vénitien vint à Alexandrie, en 1480 (environ), avec 188 nègres et quelques esclaves noires.[53]

Le synchronisme de la chute des Kārimites et de l'apogée du commerce vénitien au Levant est un fait éclatant. Il ne laisse aucun doute quant à la causalité.

IV.

Depuis la quatrième décennie du XVe siècle la suprématie des Vénitiens dans le commerce du Levant était un fait incontestable. Des phénomènes divers, qui en étaient les conséquences, portent témoignage de leur hégémonie.

Tout d'abord on doit mettre en relief le succès des Vénitiens en contrecarrant les projets de plusieurs sultans du Caire qui visaient à la suppression de la prédominance des marchands

---

extraits, dans « ROL », VII, p. 73; Ṣubḥ al-a'shā 13, p. 40. La supposition que le document cité par al-Kalḳashandī se rapporte au début du XVe siècle est plus probable que l'hypothèse d'une interpolation.

[49] Nicolo Venier B, 2, f. 6a et s.

[50] ASG, *Notai*, Branco Bagnara 10, n. 20.

[51] *Giud. di pet.*, Sent. 15, f. 48a et ss.

[52] Même série 70, f. 132a et ss.

[53] Même série 80, f. 103b et s.

européens, Venitiens et d'autres, dans le commerce du Levant. Ni sultan Barsbay, ni son successeur Djaḳmaḳ réussissaient à ériger un monopole de poivre et devaient se contenter d'imposer aux nations marchandes l'achat annuel d'une certaine quantité à l'agence sultanienne. D'autres tentatives de limiter la liberté de commerce ou la durée du séjour des marchands dans les pays du sultan s'heurtaient à l'opposition résolue de la Sérénissime et échouaient. Les répresentants de Venise protestaient aussi auprès du sultan contre des activités arbitraires de fonctionnaires et obtenaient leur relèvement.[54]

Le rôle que jouait le ducat vénitien dans la vie monétaire du Proche-Orient au bas Moyen Age démontre lui aussi la suprématie des Vénitiens dans le commerce du Levant. Le ducat était en effet la monnaie d'or partout accepté et en circulation dans tous les pays du Proche-Orient, les musulmans et les chrétiens. Il était devenu aux marchés d'Egypte et de Syrie plus en vogue que les dinars musulmans et c'est pourquoi sultan Barsbay prit la décision, en 1425, de remplacer ces derniers, bien que considérés par les musulmans comme monnaie de poids et d'aloi canonique, par une nouvelle monnaie d'or équivalante au séquin. Certes, ce n'était pas la seule raison et peut-être non pas la plus importante. Mais on ne peut douter que le gouvernement du sultan ne pouvait tolérer la circulation de grandes quantités de monnaies d'or portant des emblèmes chrétiens, mais préferées au dinar en raison de leur poids exact et aloi excellent. La monnaie d'or frappée par sultan Barsbay en 1425 était du même poids et avait la même valeur que le ducat. Il est vrai que les monnaies d'or italiennes étaient, pour la plupart, appelées par les Arabes « ifrantī », c'est-à-dire florin. Mais cela ne démontre que le florin avait pénétré en Orient avant le ducat.[55]

En effet on peut dire que la suprematie vénitienne dans le commerce du Levant ne date pas du deuxième quart du XVe siècle. C'était à cette époque qu'elle fût consolidée, tandis que les activités commerciales des autres nations marchandes

---

[54] JORGA, *Notes et extraits*, dans « ROL », IV, pp. 552 et ss.

[55] A. RAUGÉ VAN GENNEP, *Le ducat vénitien en Egypte*, dans « Revue Numismatique » IVe série, I (1897), pp. 373 et ss., 494 et ss.; W. POPPER, *Egypt and Syria under the Circassian sultans 1382-1468 A. D.*, II (Univ. of California Press 1957), pp. 48 et ss.

en Syrie et en Egypte diminuaient considérablement. Venise avait déjà obtenu de la part du sultan ayyoubide al-Malik al-ʿĀdil II, en 1238, le privilège que son consul à Alexandrie fût le juge dans des litigations entre ses sujets et d'autres marchands européens.[56] Les Vénitiens jouissaient aussi d'un status privilégié en ce qui concerne les impôts. Ils payaient moins que ne devaient payer d'autres marchands européens.[57]

On comprend donc des autres nations marchandes entamant des négotiations avec le sultan du Caire pour conclure un traité de commerce s'efforçaient d'obtenir des copies authentiques de ses traités avec Venise. Car elles voulaient demander des privilèges semblables à leurs. On a démontré que le traité conclu en 1487 entre Florence et le sultan mamlouk indique l'emploi d'un modèle vénitien. C'était le traité entre Venise et le sultan datant de l'an 1442. Les traités successifs, datant de 1489 et de 1497, se réfèrent expressément aux privilèges des Vénitiens.[58]

D'autre part Venise n'érigeait jamais un monopole dans le commerce du Levant. Les autres nations marchandes, telles que les Génois, Florentins, Français, Ragusains, continuaient leurs activités en Orient, bien qu'elles aient diminué ou aient été irrégulières. Les Génois acquéraient jusqu'à la fin du règne des Mamlouks des épices en Egypte et du coton en Syrie et exportaient en ces pays des produits de l'industrie textile de l'Occident, du corail et d'autres articles.[59]. Les Florentins exportaient de la Syrie du poivre, du gingembre, du coton et de la soie.[60] Des bateaux français apportaient aus échelles d'Orient des lourdes cargaisons de textiles et d'autres produits de l'Occident.[61]

Bref, il y eut une suprématie vénitienne dans le commerce du Levant, non pas un monopole.

---

[56] Tafel-Thomas, *Urkunden*, II, p. 338.

[57] Heyd, *Histoire du commerce du Levant*, II, p. 450.

[58] J. Wansbrough, *Venice and Florence in the Mamluk commercial privileges*, dans « BSOAS », 28 (1965), pp. 483 et ss.

[59] ASG, *Carat. vet.* 1553, f. 23b, 24a, 28a; G. Musso, *Nuovi documenti* etc., pp. 461, 490 et ss.; Marino Sanuto, *Diarii*, X, col. 95; F. Lucchetta, *L'« affare Zen » in Levante nel primo Cinquecento*, dans « Studi Veneziani », X (1968), p. 189.

[60] Mallet, *op. cit.*, p. 118.

[61] Musso, *art. cit.*, p. 492.

VII

Levantine Alkali Ashes and European Industries

This paper will describe the European imports of a Levantine product that provided an indispensable raw material for soap and glass making from time immemorial. While it is true that these industries did not have an economic importance comparable to that of the textile industries, for example, they were still important, and the story of this import trade constitutes a very long chapter in European economic history, covering 1200 years in so far as the documents and other known data allow us to trace it. The paper will also refer to these industrial activities in various countries of Southern and Western Europe. The documentation on which it is based is rich, especially that in the archives of Venice which was a major centre of these industries and also of world trade.[1]

---

* Sections II-III, V-VIII were written by E. Ashtor, sections I, IV by G. Cevidalli, Professor of Applied Chemistry at the Hebrew University of Jerusalem. The authors of the paper express their thanks to Mr. Nissim Crispin and to Mr. David Heller who supplied the plants from the sea coast and the herbarium of the Hebrew University. They also express their sincere thanks to Professor J. Lorch of the Department of Botany at the Hebrew University.

1 Series of documents which are quoted throughout are the following: ASV (Archivio di Stato, Venice)

Maggior Consiglio. - M. C.

Salsola soda L.

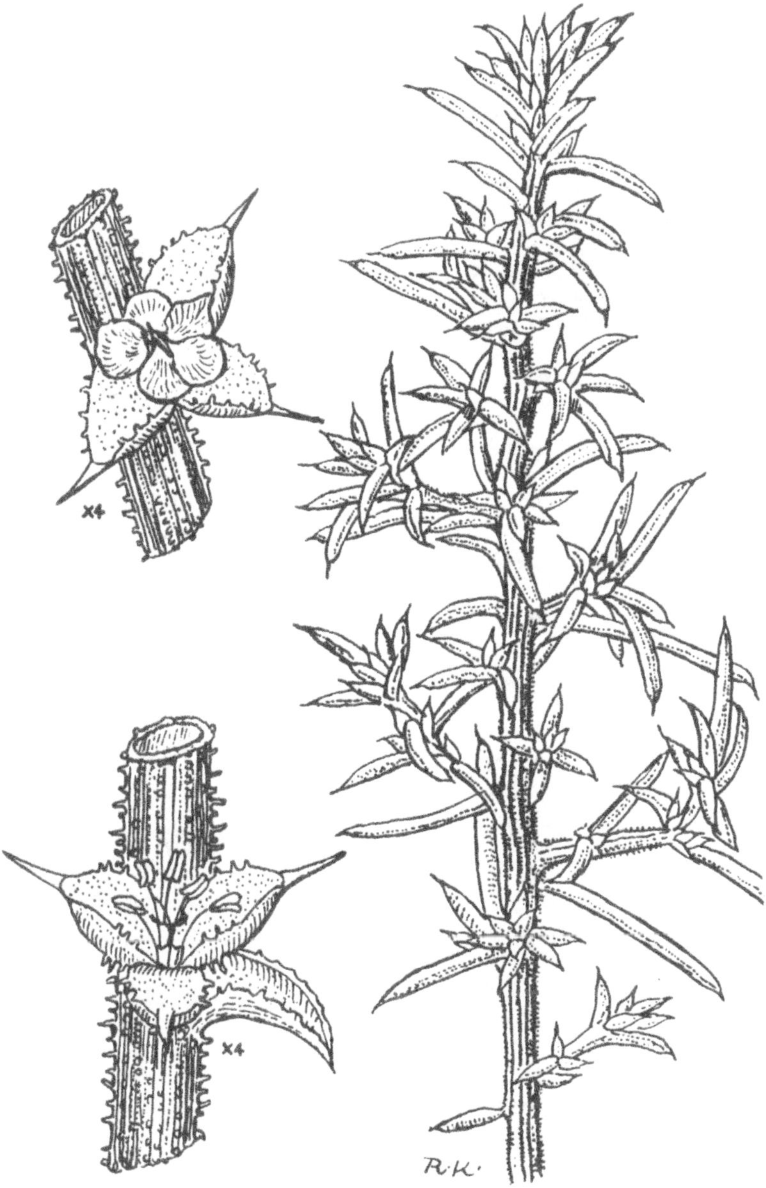

Salsola kali L.

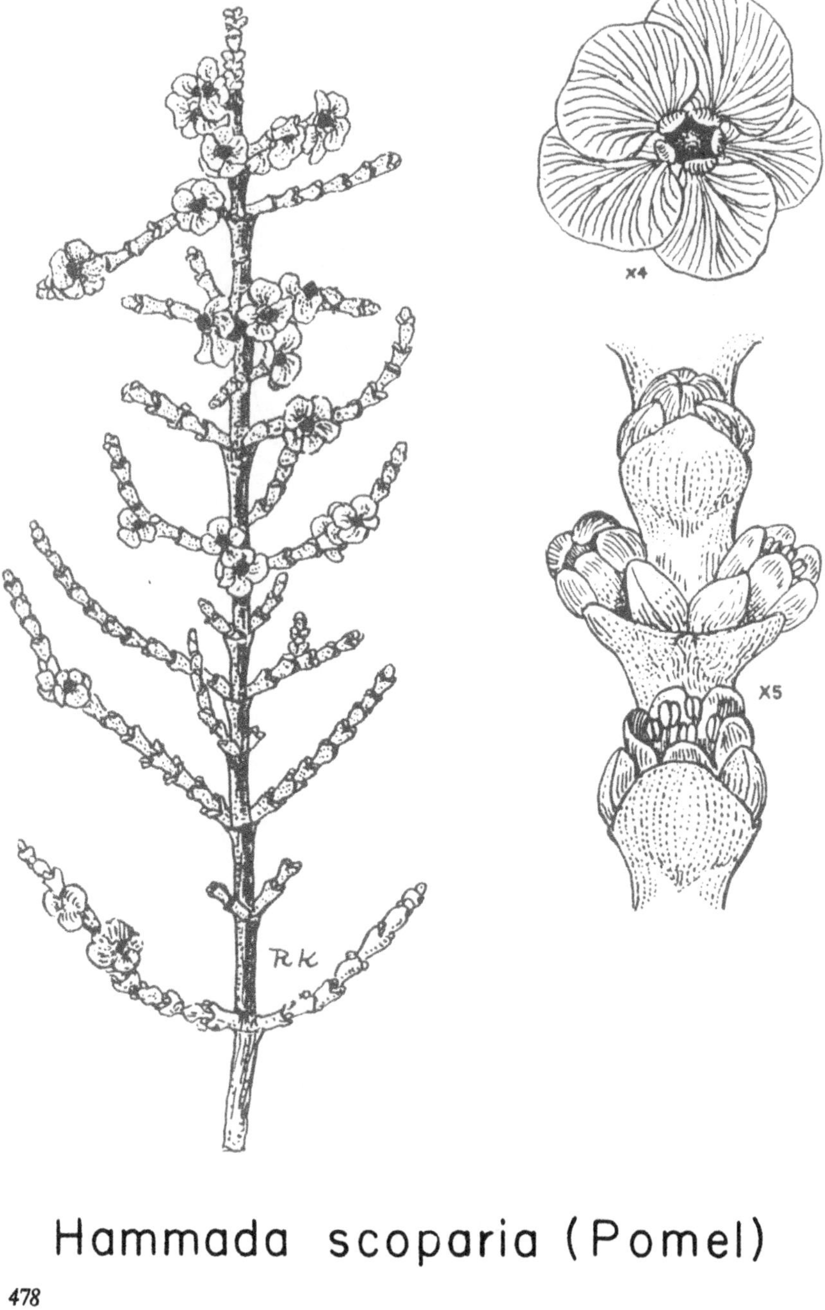

Hammada scoparia (Pomel)

I. The Raw Materials for Soap and Glass Making

Soap and glass are among the most ancient " industrial products " used by mankind. The latter is of entirely inorganic composition, that is to say the raw materials used today are apparently much the same as those employed in Egypt 14,000 years ago [2], are of mineral nature. These are primarily silica (from sand or sand stones), limestone and alkali carbonates, largely sodium carbonate (plus other constituents). The latter component is found in natural deposits only in arid regions, remote from populated areas.[3] " Natron " residue was left from the Nile floodings and contains Na_2CO_3, $CaCO_3$, NaCl and traces of copper oxide, responsible for the beautiful blue colour of ancient Egyptian glass.[4] It seems that at the beginning of the first century A.D. natron was also shipped to Palestinian ports from Alexandria for glass manufacture in Galilee.[5] But in the Middle Ages and later, the alkali carbonates were obtained by burning wood or plants.

Soap preparation required one component that is the same as that used for the manufacture of glass, namely, alkali carbonates, while the other components, the fatty acids, are contained in triglycerides which are found as fats in all animals and as oils

---

Senato, Misti. - Misti.
Senato, Terra. - S. Terra.
Senato, Mar. - S. Mar.
Giudici di petiziòn, Sentenze a giustizia. - G.P., Sent.
Giudici di petiziòn, Terminazioni. - G.P., Ter.
Cinque savi alla mercanzia, N.S. 145. - Savi, N.S. 145.
ASG (Archivio di Stato, Genoa)
Caratorum veterum. - Car. Vet.
ASPr (Archivio di Stato, Prato)
Fondo Datini. - Dat.
Le deliberazioni del Consiglio dei Rogati (Senato), serie Mixtorum, ed. R. Cessi-P. Sambin I-II (Venice 1960-61). - Misti ed. Cessi.

[2] W.M. Petries, in *Trans. Newcomen Society V* (1924), p. 72.

[3] Kirk Othmer, *Encycl. of Chem. Techn. I* (1947), p. 385.

[4] *Op. cit.*, 3rd ed. 11 (1980), p. 807.

[5] It was probably even shipped to European countries, see below.

in a great variety of plants. A third component used for soap-making in the preindustrial era was lime, which was obtained from limestone, in a process that we call today the "caustification" of alkali carbonates, because only caustic alkali may be used for the saponification of oils or fats, namely sodium hydroxide ($NaOH$) or potassium hydroxide (KOH), and not the carbonates (Na_2CO_3 or K_2CO_3).

To summarise, in the preindustrial era the following were the main raw materials used for glass and soap:

plant ashes and limestone, for both;
for glass: silica;
for soap: fats and oils.

Some preliminary technical facts about the manufacture of soap should be recalled. As we have already said, alkali hydroxides ($NaOH$ or KOH) must be used for the decomposition (saponification) of fats or oils. Today these products are obtained by the direct electrolysis of salt ($NaCl$) or potassium chloride (KCl), respectively. But in the last century they were still obtained (especially $NaOH$) by caustification of the alkali ashes (or carbonates) with lime, in the same way that they were obtained from plant ashes in the most ancient times. A clear reference to caustification for soap making is made by Galenus.[6] Both the sodium and potassium salts of fatty acid provide effective soaps (as opposed to calcium and magnesium salts). The difference between them consists in the fact that sodium soaps are of solid consistency and may be formed into suitable shapes, whereas potassium soaps are liquid or gelatinous.[7]

The nature of the fatty acids obtained from fats or oils also has an influence on the consistency of the soap. Long-chain saturated acids, like stearic acid obtained from animal fat, produce harder soaps. Oleic acid, for instance from olive oil, gives a clean,

---

[6] GALEN, *Opera omnia*, ed. Kühn, X (Lipsia 1825), p. 569.

[7] KIRK OTHMER, 2nd ed., 18 (1969), p. 415.

white, odourless soap that is easily scented and also tends to give softer, more liquid soaps, unless a high proportion of NaOH versus KOH is used. The existence of solid and liquid soaps was known to Plinius who wrote in his *Naturalis historia*: " Sapo... fit ex sebo et cinere, optimus fagino et caprino, duobus modis, spissus et liquidus, uterque apud Germanos majore in usu viris quam feminis... ".[8] The Italian chemist Ballarati mentioned the possibility that the forest ashes used by the Germans were rich in potash and gave a gelatinous soap, whereas the Gauls used ashes of marine plants and obtained solid soaps.[9] It is clear, therefore, that the composition of the plant ashes used, the amount of Na_2CO_3 and K_2CO_3 they contained, and, most important, their ratio, have a great influence upon the nature of the soap obtained.

Peculiarly enough, the ratio of K_2CO_3 to Na_2CO_3 is also very important for the glass industry. The main component of ancient and modern glass is silica (SiO_2), which constitutes between 65 to 75% of glass. The second major component is the alkali oxides, and the third, calcium oxides; but many other minor products, colorants, oxidizers, etc., were and are used. Minor amounts of extraneous matter (iron, copper, titanium, oxides, etc.) may impair the transparency and colour of glass. These impurities may be contained in the ashes, but much more frequently they are found in the sand used.[10] The effect of potash in glass-making, besides influencing the final physical properties, is to increase the viscosity if melted at a given temperature, making the complex manufacture of glass more difficult.[11]

Of course, in the gradual development of glass manufacture, changes in components and their ratios did not result in abrupt

---

[8] PLINIUS, *Naturalis historia* XXVIII, 191 (ed. Harvard Univ. Press VIII, 1963, p. 128 f.).

[9] M. BALLARATI, *Grassi e saponi* (Pavia 1908), p. 69.

[10] KIRK OTHMER, 3rd ed., 11 (1980) p. 846.

[11] KIRK OTHMER 1. c.; G.W. MOREY, *The Properties of Glass* (New York 1954), p. 77; S.R. SHOLES, *Modern Glass Practice* (Chicago 1952), p. 32.

changes of properties, because unlike soap, glass is not a chemical compound, but a solid solution of its components.[12]

II. The Period of the Crusades

The ashes of certain plants which grow in the Levant on saline soils, such as the fringes of the desert or the sea coast, were used for industrial purposes in that region and exported to Europe in the period of Roman rule and later at the dawn of the Middle Ages, and a high percentage of sodium carbonate was recognized to be of great value in the production of high-quality soap and glass. The Arabic geographer al-Muḳaddasī, who wrote his work in (about) 985, mentions *ushnān* as an export of the province of Aleppo.[13] This was *Haloxylon articulatum*, today called Hammada scoparia, and Anabasis, plants that are still widely used in Near Eastern countries. Very probably the term included salsola and other plants belonging to the large family of the *Chenopodiaceae*, which is also to be found in various regions (mainly coastal) in Europe.[14] *Ushnān* is the name in literary Arabic, but in the vernacular it is still called *Kali* in the Near East to this day. In the Middle Ages, it was used for the fulling of textiles,[15] and more extensively for the production of soap and glass, and the advanced level of the ancient glass industry was certainly due to a great extent to the quality of this raw material.

Even in Roman times these ashes were apparently exported

---

[12] W.A. Weil - E.C. Marbol, *The Constitution of Glasses I* (New York 1962), p. 249.

[13] Aḥsan at-takāsīm, ed. de Goeje (Leiden 1906), p. 181. The name, which means both the plant and its ashes, is also spelled *ishnān*, see E.W. Lane, *Arabic-English Lexicon I*, p. 62 and cf. on its meaning R. Dozy, *Supplément aux dictionnaires arabes I*, p. 25 f.

[14] On its identification see M. Zohary, *The Plants of the Bible* (Cambridge University Press 1982), p. 151 and on its use today Cl. Bailey - A. Danin, " Bedouin Plant utilization in Sinai and the Negev ", (in) *Economic Botany* 35 (1981), pp. 149, 161; cf. G.E. Post - J. Dinsmore, *Flora of Syria, Palestine and Sinai* (Beirut 1932-1933) II, pp. 445, 452.

[15] Cf. Ushnān al-kaṣṣārīn Edrisi, *Description de l'Afrique et de l'Espagne*, ed. transl. R. Dozy-M.J. de Goeje (Leiden 1866), p. 37, note 1.

to certain European countries where centres of the glass industry had developed. When the economic unity of the Mediterranean broke up after the Arab conquests, the imports were discontinued and the European glassmakers had to use ashes from their own forest and meadow plants which rendered less valuable fluxants. In the Rhineland, in the Merovingian period, Syrian ashes were still used for the production of glass. But the analysis of glass manufactured in that region in the VIIIth-IXth centuries shows that producers had to make do with the ashes of local forest plants.[16] The same observation has been made by archaeologists studying old English glass. Whereas Anglo-Saxon glass was produced by the fusion of silica and the ashes of sea plants, they maintain that the glass that can be dated to the ninth and tenth centuries has a high potassium content and was more susceptible to decay: obviously they must have been using ashes from bracken and woodland.[17] The archaeologists speak vaguely about ashes of plants from the sea coast and of those of the forests. The former must have been Levantine ashes, for those of the plants of the European coasts obviously could still be obtained. Ashes from beech wood (fagus), containing a high level of potash, were used and in the German-speaking countries, the glass produced from it was called *Waldglas* [18] and in the French-speaking countries, where ashes of fern (filix) were used, *verre de fougère*.[19] At the end of the tenth century and in the first half of the eleventh century, local ash was used everywhere, as is clearly borne out by the description of glassmaking provided by the Byzantine monk Theophilus, who after long travels settled in Cologne in

---

[16] D.B. Harden, (in) Singer-Holmyard-Williams, *A History of Technology* II (Oxford 1956), p. 325.

[17] J.R. Hunter, "The Medieval Glass Industry", (in) *Medieval Industry*, ed. D.W. Crossley (Council for British Archaeology, Research Report no. 40) (London 1981), p. 145.

[18] W.B. Honey, *Glass* (London 1966), p. 2.

[19] J. Barrelet, *La Verrerie en France de l'epoque gallo-romaine à nos jours* (Paris 1953) p. 32.

the first half of the eleventh century and here wrote his work.[20] The German glassmakers and soap manufacturers used ashes of plants from Eastern Europe and tallow. This is also documented in various commercial treaties between German traders and certain Russian princes like those of Polozk, Witebsk, Smolensk and Novgorod, in the thirteenth century.[21] It goes without saying that the use of these raw materials resulted in the decay of the glass industries in Northern and Central Europe.

Meanwhile new centres of the glass industry developed in Italy and followed another trend. Remnants of glass found in Torcello can be dated to the seventh or eighth century.[22] In the tenth and eleventh centuries there were glass factories in Venice, as is illustrated by the references to glassmakers in documents of the years 982, 1083, 1090 and 1092.[23] At the same time, another centre of the glass industry had come into being in the Ligurian town of Altare.[24] But what raw materials were used there? The Venetian scholar B. Cecchetti concluded from a document of 1072 that Egyptian ash was used in Venice, but the document (which he had in mind although he does not refer to it) undoubtedly refers to alum.[25] However, since trade with

---

20 *On diverse arts, the Treatise of Theophilus*, transl. by J.G. Hawthorne and C. St. Smith (Univ. of Chicago Press 1963), p. 49 cf. p. XVI.

21 W. Rennkamp, *Studien zum deutsch-russischen Handel bis zum Ende des 13.* Jahrhunderts, Nowgorod und Dünagebiet (Bochum 1977), p. 171, 347 f.

22 L. Leciejewicz - E. Tabaczyńska - S. Tabaczyński, *Torcello*, scavi 1961-1962 (Rome 1977), p. 63 ff., 72 f.

23 A. Gasparetto, *Il vetro di Murano dalle origini ad oggi* (Venice 1958), p. 43; A. Santi, *Origine dell'arte vetraria in Venezia e Murano, cenni storici* (Venice 1886), p. 16.

24 L. Zecchin, " Sull'origine dell'arte vetraria in Altare ", *Vetro e Silicati* IX (1965), p. 19 ff.

25 B. Cecchetti, " Sulle origini e sullo svolgimento della vetreria veneziana e muranese ", (in) B. Cecchetti - V. Zanetti - E. Sanfermo, *Monografia della vetreria veneziana e muranese* (Venice 1874), p. 7. The document is that published by R. Morozzo della Rocca - A. Lombardo, *Documenti del commercio veneziano nei secoli XI-XIII* (Rome 1940), no. 11 (I, p. 10 f.) (nove sporte di allume da Alessandria). In that period, alum was an important export from Egypt, see Ibn Mammātī, Kawānīn ad-dawāwīn (Cairo 1943), p. 328 f. - Were the ashes of plants growing in the " Levante " of Spain perhaps used in Italy? D. Goitein lists " potash alum " as a commodity exported in that period

the Moslem Levant was expanded in the second half of the tenth century, it may be that some shipments of Levantine ashes containing high levels of sodium carbonate arrived in Venice and other towns of Italy. However even the products of the Italian glass factories of the Crusader period were rather crude vessels.[26]

One cannot of course estimate the volume of the activities of these producers to determine whether they constituted real industries. But the soap factories probably did. In England, Bristol was a great centre of soap making in the second half of the twelfth century, so that a Latin author of that period could write: Apud Bristollum nemo est qui non sit vel fuerit saponarius.[27] In the thirteenth century, the soap industry also flourished in London and Coventry.[28] In Italy, Savona had an excellent soap industry,[29] as did Venice and its province. This is clearly shown by the frequency of the family name Saponarius or Savonario in documents of the period of the Crusades and of the first years of the Trecento.[30] Another testimony to the existence

---

from Spain, see *Letters of Medieval Jewish Traders* (Princeton University Press 1973), p. 25, but since this article does not appear in the documents which he translates one cannot know what he had in mind.

26 G. LUZZATTO, *Storia economica di Venezia dall'XI al XVI secolo* (Venice 1961), p. 68; L. ZECCHIN, "Prodotti vetrari nei documenti veneziani (1268-1331)", *Rivista della Stazione Sperimentale del Vetro* (Murano) VIII (1978), p. 160.

27 Chronicle of RICHARD of DEVIZES, *De rebus gestis Ricardi primi* (*Rerum Britannicarum medii aevi scriptores* 82, part III) (London 1886), p. 438 and cf. on the author p. LXXII.

28 F.W. GIBBS, "The History of the Manufacture of Soap", *Annals of Science* IV (1939/1940), p. 171.

29 I SCOVAZZI - F. NOBERASCO, *Storia di Savona* (Savona 1926-1928) I, p. 259.

30 In the second half of the eleventh century Johannes Saponarius was patriarch of Grado, see JACOPO FILIASI, *Memorie storiche de' Veneti, primi e secondi*, 2nd ed., VI (Padua 1812), p. 386; the name Pancracius Saponarius is to be found in documents of 1157, 1167, and 1179, see MOROZZO DELLA ROCCA-LOMBARDO, *op. cit.*, no. 127, 185, 186, 304. That of Johannes Savonarius in a document of the Rialto of 1243, see *op. cit.*, no. 762, and Jacobus Saponario, a Venetian too, is to be found in a document of 1180, see *op. cit.*, no. 372. A Joh. Savonarius appears in documents of the years 1305 and 1306, see *I capitolari delle arti veneziane*, ed. G. Monticoli - G. Besta I (Rome 1896), p. LXXII, f.; M.C., Magnus et Capricornus, f. 5a. Petrus Savonarius is known from documents of 1294, 1305, 1307 and 1317, see *Deliberazioni del Maggior Consiglio di Ve-*

of the soap industry in Venice is the name given to a canal in the first half of the thirteenth century — the Rio Saponario in S. Cassiano.[31] In that district of Venice, there were apparently several soap factories located over a very long period. The data that have come down to us, however, leave little doubt that in this period the European soap industries used the ashes of plants that grew in their countries almost exclusively. The use was so intensive that there was large-scale destruction of woodland in some regions of France for instance. In England by the end of the thirteenth century, Russian ash was being used.[32]

Despite the lack of high-grade raw materials both the soap and glass industries developed at a reasonable pace. In the middle of the thirteenth century, the glassmakers' guild in Venice was a sizeable one[33] and they also began to export glass and glass vessels.[34] Another sign of the high reputation that this Venetian industry already had in those days is the fact that Venetian glass-makers were in demand elsewhere and emigrated to many other

---

nezia, ed. R. Cessi, III (Bologna 1934), p. 366; M.C. Magnus et Capricornus 1. c.; Misti, ed. Cessi-Sambin I, p. 120, 181. Nicolo Savonario appears in documents of 1312 and 1317, see *Museo Correr*, MS. Cicogna 3248 (= 2986), no. VII, a writ of the Doge Marino Zorzi, cf. Catalogue MSS. Cicogna V, f. 118b; Misti, ed. Cessi-Sambin, I, p. 181. Dominicus a Sapone is to be found in a notarial act of the year 1314, see *Domenico prete di S. Maurizio, notaio in Venezia*, ed. M. Fr. Tiepolo (Venice 1970), no. 407. Angelo Savonario, at the beginning of the fourteenth century had much property in Venice, including houses in the parishes of S. Geremia, S. Giovanni Crisostomo, S. Ermagora (this latter today called S. Marcuola) (at the corner of the Canal Grande and the Canal of Canareggio, cf. G. Tassini, *Curiosità veneziane*, 6th ed., Venice 1933, p. 413), see ASV, Proc. di S. Marco, Misti, b. 134. Franciscus Savonarius is mentioned in a deed of 1319, see Misti, ed. Cessi-Sambin I, p. 214 and finally Marcus Saponario lives in 1330, see op. cit., p. 424.

[31] G. Galliccioli, *Delle memorie venete antiche, profane ed ecclesiastiche* (Venice 1795) I, p. 196; Morozzo della Rocca-Lombardo, *op. cit.*, no. 651 (of a 1231).

[32] Gibbs, *art. cit.*, p. 172., W. Stieda, *Revaler Zollbücher und Quittungen* (Halle a. S. 1887), p. XCIX note 6.

[33] See B. Cecchetti, *Sulle origini e sullo svolgimento della vetraria veneziana e muranese*, p. 7; idem, "Le industrie in Venezia", *Archivio Veneto* IV (1872), p. 625.

[34] L. Zecchin, "Vetrerie muranesi dal 1276 al 1200", *Riv. Staz. Sper.* I (1971), no. 4, p. 18; idem, "Fornaci muranesi fra il 1279 ed il 1290," *Journal of Glass Studies XII* (1970), p. 81.

Italian towns despite the prohibitions promulgated by the government.[35] However there was no major expansion before the end of the thirteenth century.

III. The Imports of Levantine Ash

Certain Venetian documents which refer to the import of " allumen " and date from 1233 and 1255, are rather puzzling.[36] It may really have been alum, but in documents of the last quarter of the thirteenth century there are references that establish beyond doubt the importation of Levantine ash into Venice.[37] This raw material was imported from both Syria and Egypt in the last years of the thirteenth century,[38] but the greater part came from Syria.

It seems that from ancient times the Bedouin collected these plants in the Syrian desert and brought them to the towns to sell them. Most of these were probably the ushnān that grows on the fringes of the desert and is on sale in all Levantine markets to this day. But undoubtedly the Bedouins collected more than one herb, and the trade was conducted over many centuries. The Bedouin of Northern Syria sold the ashes of plants which they had burnt in the form of solid lumps (in Arabic vernacular *hağer*, i.e. stone) or pebble (*zerab*). The residue, which was rich in inorganic components (obtained by drying the plants without burning them) (*zahra*), was also sold and used for soap making.[39] In more modern times the Bedouin came to Aleppo ten times

---

35 *I capitolari*, ed. Monticolo-Besta, II, part a (Rome 1905), p. 88 f.

36 R. Predelli - A. Sacerdote, *Gli statuti marittimi veneziani fino al 1255* (Venice 1903), p. 73, 160.

37 L. Zecchin, *Vetrerie muranesi dal 1276 al 1300*, p. 19; idem, " Cronologia vetraria veneziana e muranese dal 1286 al 1301 ", *Riv. Staz. Sper.* III (1973), p. 64.

38 Deliberazioni del Maggior Consiglio, ed. Cessi, III, p. 298. The medieval documents referring to imports from Egypt leave us in doubt, however, whether ashes containing alkali carbonates were really meant or perhaps natron.

39 See Albert de Boucheman, " Une petite cité caravanière: Suḫné " (*Documents d'etudes orientales de l'Institut francais de Damas* VI) (Damascus s.d.), p. 77 f.

a year in great caravans to sell these ashes.[40] The caravans were called " caravans of the *keli* " (North Syrian form of kali).[41] The Bavarian physician and botanist Leonhart Rauwolff, who stayed in Tripoli in 1573, has left us a very interesting account of this trade in his day. He describes how the Bedouin obtained two kinds of *shinan*, (i.e. *ushnān*) by burning plants on a mountain near the town. They sold the products to the Venetians who eagerly acquired entire ship loads.[42] There were also " *ushnān* mills " in Damascus where the ashes were prepared, as can be learned from the description of the town by Ṣalāḥ-ad-dīn al-Kutubī, an author of the fourteenth century.[43] The well-known French traveller, Volney, who visited Southern Palestine at the end of the eighteenth century, also recounts how the Bedouin used to supply the soap factories of Ghaza with " kali ".[44]

According to Turkish documents dating from the sixteenth century, the sale of these ashes was a monopoly in Syria. A great part of it was destined for sale to European merchants,[45] but there can be no doubt that the monopoly had been established a long time before the conquest of Syria by the Ottomans. Many Venetian documents show that the predecessors of the Ottomans, the Mamluks, also sold this product to the European merchants. The fact the Venetians often bought the ashes from the Mamluk authorities, such as the governor of Tripoli or of some other Syrian town, or were even compelled by them to buy them,

[40] *Op. cit.*, p. 89.

[41] *Op. cit.*, p. 88. The literary form is *kily*.

[42] Aigentlich beschreibung der Reiss (Lavingen 1583), p. 37. On the two kinds of *ushnān*, see below.

[43] MS. Istanbul, Topkapu Saray, R. 2027 (8966), f. 55a f. (We have quoted a copy made by Dr. Y. Sadan of Tel Aviv University, who, believes that this treatise was meanwhile published from another MS. by Ṣalāḥ ad-dīn al-Munadjdjid).

[44] C. - F. Volney, *Voyage en Egypte et en Syrie*, publ. par J. Gaulmier (Paris 1959), p. 347 f.

[45] J. v. Hammer, *Staatsverfassung und Staatsverwaltung des osmanischen Reichs* (Vienna 1815) I, p. 228; R. Mantran - J. Sauvaget, *Règlements fiscaux ottomans, Les provinces syriennes* (Paris 1951), p. 22 ff., 69.

or also heeded their permission to export them, leaves no doubt of this.[46] The documents referring to a Venetian embassy to the sultan of Cairo in the year 1449 are explicit: in the negotiations in Cairo the sultan insisted that the Venetians must buy ashes from his stocks, until a compromise was reached, whereby the Venetians undertook to buy a certain quantity from the governor of Tripoli every year.[47] But even in later years the Venetians were still compelled to buy ashes from the Mamluk authorities.[48] The Mamluks of course ruined the local industries in this way by depriving glass and soap makers of the raw materials. They also harmed the industry in other ways, for example by the imposition of taxes on the sale of the raw materials as well as compulsory purchases.[49]

The European merchants were eager to purchase the Levantine ashes, however. Venetian documents refer to shipping ashes from Syria and Egypt to Crete in 1296 [50] and in 1300,[51] or directly to Venice from Egypt.[52] At the end of the thirteenth century and the beginning of the fourteenth century Alexandria was a major market for these ashes.[53] When the papal embargo on trade with the Moslem Levant was strictly enforced in the first half of the fourteenth century, some shipments could certainly still be obtained via Cyprus, Crete, or Little Armenia.[54]

---

[46] See G.P., Sent. 54, f. 40a 71, f. 55a ff. 124, f. 63b ff.; G.P., Cap. publ. VII, f. 2a.

[47] See the sources quoted in E. Ashtor, *Levant Trade in the Later Middle Ages* (Princeton University Press 1983), p. 307.

[48] See *op. cit.*, chapter VII and the sources quoted in note 112.

[49] Corpus Inscr. Arab. II, part 1, Syrie du Nord par M. Sobernheim (Cairo 1909), p. 59 f. (where the material is called b'l's). Cf. E. Ashtor, " Le Proche-Orient au bas moyen âge — une région sous-développée ", *Istituto Franc. Datini (Prato), Settimane di studio 1978* (Florence 1983), p. 404 f., 419.

[50] Misti, ed. Cessi-Sambin, I, p. 4.

[51] *Pietro Pizolo, notaio in Candia*, ed. S. Carbone, I (Venice 1978), no. 321; Deliberazioni del Maggior Consiglio, ed. Cessi, III, p. 398.

[52] Misti, ed. Cessi-Sambin, I, p. 104.

[53] *Zibaldone da Canal*, ed. A. Stussi (Venice 1976), p. 66.

[54] A Stussi, *Testi veneziani del Duecento e dei primi del Trecento* (Pisa 1965), p. 103; *Lettere di mercanti a Pignol Zucchello*, ed. Morozzo della Rocca (Venice 1957), p. 32,

The importance that the government of Venice attached to the purchase of the Levantine ashes may be inferred from a decree enacted in 1308, when it was stipulated that cogs departing from Alexandria, Damietta or Tinnis for Venice should load only this commodity.[55] This decree shows clearly that the supply of sufficient quantities of the Levantine ashes was considered to be a vital matter for the Venetian economy. On the other hand, it was also forbidden to export this raw material from Venice. The prohibition was made first in 1275 [56] and again in 1282,[57] but it was revoked in the year 1283 [58] and then re-enacted in 1315.[59] More convincing evidence of the importance of Levantine ashes for the economy of Venice is a law promulgated in the same period to forbid the use of fern ashes for glass-making — only Levantine ashes were permitted and the authorities rarely made an exception.[60]

The ashes of the Levantine plants from which the alkali car-

---

56 f.; L. Zecchin, " Cronologia vetraria veneziana e muranese dal 1302 al 1314, " *Riv. Staz. Sper.* III (1973), p. 122.

55 *Misti,* ed. Cessi-Sambin, I, p. 129.

56 M.C., Fractus, f. 52; quoted by B. Cecchetti, " Delle origini e dello svolgimento dell'arte vetraria muranese, nuove ricerche ", *Atti del R. Istituto Ven. di scienze, lettere ed arti, ser.* IV, vol. I, p. 21.

57 M.C., Avogaria di comun, Bifrons, f. 12a; cf. Cecchetti, *ibidem.*

58 M.C., Luna (copy), f. 79a f.

59 L. Zecchin, " Materie prime e mezzi d'opera dei vetrai nei documenti veneziani dal 1348 al 1438 ", *Riv. Staz. Sper.* XI (1981) p. 77. What Zecchin says, in " Materie prime e mezzi d'opera dei vetrai nei documenti veneziani dal 1233 al 1347 ", *Riv. Staz. Sper.* X (1980), p. 173 about a renewal of the decree in 1285 is mistaken — this reenactment dates from 1282. The same error is made by Cecchetti, *Sulla storia dell'arte vetraria muranese* (Venice 1865), p. 10.

60 M.C., Magnus et Capricornus, f. 11b (a. 1306), printed by Cecchetti, *op. cit.*, p. 32 and quoted by L. Zecchin, " Cronologia vetraria veneziana e muranese dal 1302 al 1314 ", *Riv. Staz. Sper.* III (1973), p. 120. A glassmaker who obtained sodium carbonate from a mixture of Levantine ashes and that of fern was granted exceptional permission to use it in 1318, see M.C., Clericus Civicus, f. 136a and L. Zecchin, " Materie prime e mezzi d'opera dei vetrai nei documenti veneziani dal 1233 al 1347 ", *Riv. Staz. Sper.* III, p. 174; idem, " Cronologia vetraria veneziana e muranese dal 1315 al 1331 ", *Riv. Staz. Sper.* III, p. 166 f.

bonates for the production of soap and glass were obtained had a variety of Venetians names: *cenere*, *botassa*, *allumen* and most commonly *lume* (from allumen) or *lume catina* (or *catino*) or *lume de savon*.[61] In Tuscany they were called *cenere grevellera*[62] or *soda da bicchieri*.[63]

But of far greater importance for our subject is that in the first half of the fifteenth century a method of purifying the ashes to obtain a high-grade alkali carbonate was known in Italy.[64] The greatest progress was probably made in Venice, but elsewhere the use of Syro-Egyptian ashes for the production of soap and glass was widely used as well.[65]

IV. Chemical Aspects

One must not be misled by the use of the term " soda " and " potash " in the sources of the later Middle Ages and the Early Modern period. Both words were very often used without any clear distinction or even a basic knowledge of their chemical meaning. The terms " potassium carbonate " and " sodium carbonate " were used in a confused way, as thorough research

---

61 See the texts quoted in notes 175-180 of E. ASHTOR, " Le Proche-Orient au bas moyen âge — une région sous-développée ". The word *lume* (which is Venetian vernacular) is used by the Syro-Palestinian Arabs down to the present. *Catina* was sometimes pronounced catína and others cátina. For *lume catina* see also *Misti* 34, f. 110a. In fact, the term *lume* was also used for other products, such as burnt tartar called *lume di feccia*, sodium chloride was called *lume di gemma*; *lume scaiola* means the cristalline form of calcium sulphate.

62 Fr. B. PEGOLOTTI, *La pratica della mercatura*, ed. Evans (Cambridge Mass. 1936), p. 380. The Florentine author also lists among the Oriental commodities *sale arcali* (i.e. *kali*), see p. 296 and cf. Evans p. 428 f.

63 GIOVANNI DA UZZANO, " La pratica della mercatura ", (in) Pagnini, *Della decima* IV (Lisbon-Lucca 1746), p. 25; *El libro di mercatantie*, ed. Borlandi (Turin 1936), p. 22.

64 L. ZECCHIN, " Ricette vetrarie d'ispirazione muranese nel Quattrocento, " *Riv. Staz. Sper.* XI, p. 265.

65 See the text quoted in note 63 from Giov. da Uzzano referring to the customs to be paid on import into Florence. Cf. L. ZECCHIN, " Ricette vetrarie toscane nel Quattrocento ", *Riv. Staz. Sper.* XI (1981), p. 214.

in this field was not to be made before the beginning of the nineteenth century. It seems that the first observations on the difference between the crystals obtained from soda and potash were made by G.E. Stahl in 1702.[66] Later, in the middle of the eighteenth century, Henri Duhamel carried out studies on salsola kali (" common saltwort "),[67] but it was not before 1807 that a chemist established the exact distinction between the two elements; potassium and sodium. Humphry Davy separated a " new element by electrolysis of caustic potash and gave it the name "potassium " and the chemical symbol K (Latin *Kalium*), from the Arabic *kali* or *keli* — that is the ash of the plant from which the alkali metal compounds were obtained. In the same way, he discovered the sister alkali which he named sodium, whose symbol is Na (*Natrium*, from natron).

Although the technicians of the Middle ages had no knowledge of the chemical composition of the ashes they used for the production of soap and glass, they were well aware of the differences in behaviour due to their composition. They used to purify the ashes by a process of solution, filtration, concentration and crystallisation, obtaining a mixture of white salts, mainly Na_2CO_3 and K_2CO_3 which they called " the salt ", and they could compare the total amount of alkali carbonate contained in the various ashes.[68] They had no way of measuring the ratio of Na_2O/K_2O, but they knew very well the technical effect of this ratio. The same is true for the soap and glass producers of the sixteenth and seventeenth centuries. At the end of the seventeenth century Haudicquer de Blancourt, in his work on the glass industry, emphasizes that the difference between various ashes was due to

[66] M.E. Weeks - H.M. Leicester, *The Discovery of the Elements* (San Francisco 1967), p. 438.

[67] G. Troost, " Description of the American Petalite from Lake Ontario ", *Acad. Nat. Sc.* (Philadelphia) III (1824), p. 234 ff.

[68] G. Rossetti, *Notandissimi secreti de l'arte profumatoria*, ed. Fr. Brunello - Fr. Facchetti (Vicenza 1973), p. 47, 164.

the diversity of the plants and of the regions in which they grow, " and even to the mixture of heterogeneous salts ".[69]

Modern chemists who have undertaken research on soap-making have made various observations on the Levantine ashes in their historical introductions. E. Marazza claims that the salsola soda ash contains 41 % of Na_2CO_3 and those of salsola kali 44 %, and he also states that the ashes of saline plants which grow in Spain and were used for soap-making (and glass), such as those coming from the region of Alicante, Cartagena, and Malaga, contain 25-30 % Na_2CO_3 or even much less, such as 6-10 %. He also mentions other ashes known from ancient times as " soda of Vareque " and collected on the Mediterranean coast of France, which are supposed to be those of algae (*Fucus serraltus*, *Fucus vesciculosus*, etc.).[70] V. Scansetti claims that the Spanish plants contain only 20-25 % sodium carbonate and those growing on the coast of Southern France 10-15 %.[71]

We therefore thought it would be useful to analyse the ashes obtained by burning some plants of the Chenopodiaceae family, which grow spontaneously in arid or semiarid zones in areas now within the borders of Israel. Before doing that we took branches of beech wood (Fagus Silvatica) from the forest of the plateau of Cansiglio (in the province of Treviso in Italy). This is now a mixed forest of beechs and firs, whereas in the past it was a pure beech forest, covering about 15-20,000 ha, situated about 60 km north of Venice. In the past it was maintained with lavish care by the government of the Republic of Venice and called " la foresta da reme del Cansiglio ", because its timber was used for the construction and outfitting of ships. It could also have provided a very abundant and easily accessible sources of ash. The analysis gave the results reported in Table I.

As can be seen, the total amount of alkali is negligible, and the

---

69 HAUDICQUER DE BLANCOURT, *De l'art de la verrerie* (Paris 1697), p. 51.
70 E. MARAZZA, *L'industria saponiera* (Milan 1907), p. 7 ff.
71 V. SCANSETTI, *L'industria dei saponi*, 5th ed. (Milan 1933), p. 5.

TABLE I

BEECH OF THE CANSIGLIO FOREST*

Ashes, % of wood			2.7%
Ashes, composition, % of weight			
	Na_2O	0.11	
	K_2O	1.1	
	CaO	34	
	MgO	6.5	

* This Table contains the analysis of plant ashes collected by G. Cevidalli.

Experimental detail: plants dried at 40° for two days, ashes obtained by burning at 500°-550° for six hours.

Caution: ashes dissolved in dilute HCl, then analysed by atomic absorption spectrophotometry, Perkin Elmer 405.

Cl^- – Vohlard method.
SO_4^{--} – $BaSO_4$ gravimetric
SiO_2 – Feigl and Krumholz method.

ratio of Na_2O/K_2O is 0.1. Although such a small sample from a vast forest is certainly not representative we can conclude that these ashes would be a most unsuitable raw material for making either glass or soap, which may well be the reason that Venice did not use them for its industries.

In order to establish the quality of Levantine ash, we decided after consultation with botanist colleagues to analyse two small bushes both belonging to the Chenopodiaceae family: *salsola kali* L. and *salsola soda* L. We believe that these were indeed the two plants described in the second half of the sixteenth century by the German botanist (and physician) L. Rauwolff in the chapter of his travelogue dealing with his visit to Tripoli, Syria.[72] The chapter contains a long passage on the Levantine ashes which were used in Europe as raw materials for soap and glass-making. Although he called them by the Arabic name *shinan* (that is *ushnān*), the fact that he records that they were burnt into ashes near Tripoli suggests that they grew in that region, on the sea coast, and not on the fringes of the desert. Two further facts were decisive for our choice. On one hand, the Arabic name of at least one of

[72] *Aigentlich beschreibung der Reiss,* l.c.

the plants used was (and is) " *kali* " and, on the other Haudicquer de Blancourt stated [73] that this plant was the same as the one called by other names by various authors: " alkali, soda, salicornia, anthilloides, kelp, antillis ". And Karl Linnaeus in his fundamental work ' *Critica Botanica* ' adopted some " barbarous names ", that is names used outside of Europe, and among them *kali*, now known as *salsola kali L.*

Salsola kali and salsola soda are small annual bushes (20-60 cm), belonging to the Chenopodiaceae family, and are not very different, at least for a non-specialist, from one another. Both grow on the sandy sea shores of the Acre and Sharon plains; salsola kali also grows in the western Negev and in the vicinity of the Dead Sea.

A salsola kali specimen was collected from the northern coastal plain of Israel, near the town of Acre. The salsola soda was taken from the *herbarium* of the botanical department of our university. It had been collected in the same location mentioned above.

The results of analysis are shown in Tables II and III. On the basis of this analysis, Professor Michael Zohary expressed verbal doubts that salsola soda could have been used in the Middle Ages and at the beginning of the modern period for ash production, as it is today a rather rare plant. Since in the Near East even in our day ashes are still used for soap-making, he believes that these are ashes of the *Hammada scoparia* (formely known as *Haloxylon articulatum*). This plant also belongs to the Chenopodiceae family and grows in deserts, in the lower Jordan Valley, the Negev, etc., and also on alluvial soils[74] (see fig. 3). So we also took a sample of this plant from the university *herbarium*. It had been collected in the Negev, in the Wadi 'Aslūdj.

Analysis follows in Table IV.

---

[73] Haudicquer de Blancourt, *op. cit.*, p. 53.

[74] M. Zohary, *Flora Palaestina* (Jerusalem 1966) I, p. 164, 170.

TABLE II

SALSOLA KALI

Ashes: 26%	
Ashes analysis	% Weight
Na_2O	14.3
K_2O	15.5
CaO	14.4
MgO	9
Cl^-	1.4
So_4^{--}	5.5
SiO_2 (qualitative)	< 1

TABLE III

SALSOLA SODA

Sample 1 — Ashes 23%		Sample 2 — Ashes 20%
Ashes analysis	% Weight	% Weight
Na_2O	44	42
K_2O	6	7.5
CaO	3.3	3.8
MgO	1.6	2
Cl^-	3.2	2.8
SO_4^{--}	0.8	1
Si_2O (qualitative)	< 1	< 1

TABLE IV

HAMMADA SCOPARIA

Ashes 11%.	
Ash analysis	Weight %
Na_2O	9.8
K_2O	7.8
CaO	22.6
MgO	12.6
Cl^-	0.8
SO_4^{--}	4
SiO_2 (qualitative)	< 1

Before commenting on these results, we shall first consider the analysis of other ashes that have been examined in the *Stazione Sperimentale del Vetro* (Experimental Glass Laboratory) in Murano, with its very kind permission. These include a) ashes obtained from ferns (whose specific species we do not know) growing on the Lido of Venice; b) " Soda di Catania ", obtained from plants growing in that area of Sicily; c) " ashes of Vareque ". from the Mediterranean coast of France and believed to be produced by marine algae. The results of the analysis are given in Tables V-VII.

In the following comments we shall attempt to sacrifice scientific precision to clarity; we will calculate the ash composition by attributing all the Cl^- to Na_2O (when enough is present) the remaining Na_2O being considered as belonging to Na_2CO_3 and all K_2O as K_2CO_3, except for the Vareque ashes (see below). Obviously plant composition may change, according to place of origin, climate and microclimate, age, etc., and therefore large numbers of samples really need to be collected and analysed. As this is beyond the scope of the present research, the following comments should be taken with some reserve.

The six group of ashes examined can be schematically divided into three main groups:

I) The ashes of fern: these are relatively rich in alkali carbonates (about 30%), but practically all is due to potash, and none to soda, making them unsuitable for either glass or (solid) soap. This was obviously the reason for the repeated prohibitions of their use by the Venetian government (see above and below).

II) The ashes of salsola soda contain almost 80% of alkali carbonates, predominantly sodium carbonate. The weight ratio of Na_2O/K_2O (subtracting NaCl) is — in these two samples — respectively 6.85 and 5.2. This is an excellent raw material both for glass and soap, and much more suitable than the following group.

TABLE V

FERN ASH

	Weight %
Na_2O	0.41
K_2O	25.5
CaO	17.9
MgO	8.1
Cl^-	3.37
SiO_2	8
Al_2O_3	1.4
Fe_2O_3	0.75
MnO	0.5
P_2O_5	4

TABLE VI

SODA DI CATANIA

	Weight %
Na_2O	23
K_2O	9.6
CaO	9.3
MgO	2
Cl^-	8.23
SO_3	1.1
S^{--}	0.04
SiO_2	1.35
Al_2O_3	1.35
Fe_2O_3	1.32
P_2O_5	0.58

TABLE VII

"VAREQUE" ASHES

	Weight %
Na_2O	19.8
K_2O	17.5
CaO	9.17
MgO	6.75
Cl^-	15.5
SO_3	20.82
SiO_2	3.50
CO_2	5

III) We include in this group the ashes of salsola kali, of Hammada scoparia, the soda of Catania and Vareque ashes. These last are very rich in sodium chloride. It is difficult to comment on their composition, because the amount of CO_2 (the only case where this direct analysis is made) is highly insufficient to balance the $K_2O + Na_2O$ (after subtracting NaCl), if they were present as carbonates. Tentatively one may calculate the amount of their carbonates as between 15 to 25 %, largely potash, the ratio Na_2O/K_2O (with the caution due to above considerations) being about 0.3. Very probably ashes of this composition were not suitable for producing a good quality glass, although they could perhaps have been used for manufacturing inferior quality semi-solid soaps made from animal fats, but certainly not for those made from olive oil.

There is some resemblance between the ash of salsola kali and di Catania. The Catania soda is much richer in table salt and the total amount of alkali carbonate (about 41 %) is slightly lower than in the salsola kali (45 %). On the other hand, the ratio of available Na_2O to K_2O is much higher in Catania ashes (1.6) than in salsola kali (0.84). Both these ashes are undoubtedly greatly inferior to the outstanding salsola soda, but perhaps by adopting different techniques they could have been used for various kinds of glass and soap.

The ashes of Hammada scoparia have a ratio of Na_2O to K_2O of 1.16, intermediate between the two discussed above. The total amount of alkali carbonates is rather low (27 %), slightly more than half of that of salsola kali. This means that almost double the amount of ashes would have to be used to obtain the same amount of soap. In today's terms, we could say that transport costs would have discriminated heavily against this raw material.

After analysing the composition of all these plants, one asks oneself which was used in Syria in the Middle Ages and in the early Modern period for producing the ashes to be exported as raw material for the European soap and glass industries. Again we should turn first to the statements of same authors of those times.

Giovanventura Rossetti says that the ashes used for making soap from oil were a mixture of one part Levantine ash and one part ashes of local plants. But when calf or pig fat was used, he says, two parts of ashes of " cervo " (*quercus cerri* L.) and half a part of Levantine ashes were used.[75] This statement suggests that in the middle of the sixteenth century Levantine ashes were so rich in Na_2CO_3 that it was possible to mix or " dilute " them with European ashes, containing a negligible amount of this alkali.

Haudicquer de Blancourt [76] in 1697 described a very ingenious and sophisticated technique used by the Orientals. They dissolved the ashes in water and sprinkled the solution on the burning bushes, obtaining by this partial recycling an enrichment of the more soluble alkali carbonates in the ashes eventually produced. But it is worth noting that the very precise Rauwolff did not allude to this method of improving the quality of the ashes.[77]

Since Professor Zohary has pointed out that the salsola soda is now a rare plant and it is the Hammada scoparia that is mainly used by Levantine populations for domestic use, the following conjectures may be made, with no claim that they have been proved by the facts known so far.

The plants used since ancient times in Syria were a mixture of several Chenopodianceae, among which the salsola soda was probably predominant. The continuous destruction of this plant in the delicate desert ecosystem, made it more and more difficult to find the plant. The sophisticated technique used by the Bedouin

---

75 Rossetti, *op. cit.*, p. 47, 65.

76 Haudicquer de Blancourt, *op. cit.*, p. 51.

77 Rauwolff, *op. cit.*, 1.c.

at the end of the seventeenth century (and never referred to before that time, as far as we know) was dictated by the necessity of overcoming the decreasing quality of the ashes, due to the declining proportion of salsola soda in the mixture of the plants used. The quality of ashes shipped to Venice and other European ports was not constant over the centuries, but tended to decline. This may have been one reason for the declining competitiveness of Levantine ashes.

Much further research would be necessary to validate this hypothesis, but the scarcity of reliable chemical and botanical information before the beginning of the last century (when the synthesis of Na_2CO_3 by the Leblanc process caused a rapid decline in the commercial importance of plant ashes) will make this a very difficult task.

V. The Expansion of the Soap and Glass Industries

Southern European imports of large quantities of Levantine ash which began at the end of the thirteenth century ushered in the expansion of the soap and glass industries. One need only glance at the Merchant Guides compiled in Italy in the first half of the fourteenth century to be aware of the volume of the soap exports from Italy and other countries as well. By the beginning of the fourteenth century soap was exported from Italy to Syria which had had a well developed soap industry from ancient times.[78] From the work of Pegolotti we learn that large shipments of soap were sent to Cyprus, Rhodes and Constantinople[79] and to the provinces of Asia Minor under Turkish rule.[80] The Genoese exported great quantities of soap

[78] Marucelliana Library (Florence), C 226, Anonymous Merchant Guide, apud R. - H. Bautier, "Les relations économiques des occidentaux avec les pays d'Orient, au moyen âge, points de vue et documents," (in) *Sociétés et compagnies de commerce en Orient et dans l'Océan Indien*, Actes du VIII colloque int. d'histoire maritime, Beyrouth 1966 (Paris 1970), pp. 318, 319.

[79] p. 33, 158, 318 f.

[80] p. 56.

from Naples and Gaeta to Egypt in the second half of the fourteenth century.[81] Savona too had a flourishing soap industry in the fifteenth century and exported its products.[82] The Venetians greatly increased their exports of soap to the Moslem Levant in the fifteenth century.[83]

TABLE VIII

SOAP EXPORTS ON VENETIAN ALEXANDRIA GALLEYS ABOUT 1500

Year	Quantity	Source
1498	573 sacks	Malipiero, p. 646 *
1500	62 sacks	Marino Sanuto, Diarii III, col. 1188; Priuli II, p. 74 **
1503	378 boxes	Priuli II, p. 255
1511	502 boxes	Marino Sanuto, Diarii XII, col. 78

* *Annali Veneti*, ASI VII, part 1 (1843) .
** GIROLAMO PRIULI, *Diarii* (Bologna 1912-1936).

Part of these shipments was soap manufactured in Gaeta, another great centre of this industry.[84] Ragusa, the growing commercial town on the Eastern coast of the Adriatic also exported soap to Egypt.[85] The March of Ancona was a major centre for the soap industry, which used Apulian and local olive oils with Levantine ashes. The Anconitans exported great quantities of soap to the Greek and Moslem Levant in the fourteenth and fifteenth centuries.[86] As the export of soap became an important sector of the industrial production and foreign trade of the South European countries, measures were taken to foster it.

[81] J. DAY, *Les douanes de Gênes 1376-1377* (Paris 1963), pp. 268, 351, 527.

[82] F. NOBERASCO, "I commerci savonesi del sec. XV", *Atti della Società Savonese di Storia Patria VII* (1924), p. 76.

[83] See E. ASHTOR, "Observations on Venetian Trade in the Levant in the XIVth century", *JEEH V* (1976), p. 579.

[84] See the documents quoted in E. ASHTOR, "The Proche-Orient au bas moyen âge — une région sous-développée", note 21.

[85] Dat 1171, price list of February 26, 1396.

[86] E. ASHTOR, "Il commercio levantino di Ancona", *RSI* 88 (1976), p. 227 ff., 235 ff.; see also about the customs tariff C. CIAVARINI, *Statuti anconitani del mare, del terzenale e della dogana* (Ancona 1896), p. 144 f. and cf. p. 35.

Venice granted subsidies to the exporters in 1374 and 1391,[87] and even the Provencals exported soap to the Near East.[88]

The new expansion of the glass industry was no less spectacular, and Venice especially, where Levantine ashes were used exclusively, became a renowned centre of glassmaking. The use of fern was strictly forbidden.[89] Whereas in the period of the Crusades only crude vessels had been produced and an effort was made to imitate Orient glass work, in the fourteenth century the manufacture of new types of transparent, coloured and enamelled glass began in Murano. In addition, the production of mirrors was begun,[90] and spectacles were also produced from the end of the thirteenth century.[91] In the fifteenth century, the Levantine glass industry decayed while that of Murano reached its apogee. In the middle of the century, Angelo Barovier invented the " cristallo " and perhaps also chalcedony, which resembled agate.[92] It seems that he also invented the *lattimo*.[93] All these achievements were due to the use of the high-grade alkali ash, rich in sodium, obtained from the Levant, and to the progress made in its purification.[94] These are facts borne out by decrees of the Venetian authorities, and also by other documents. Documents from the first half of the

---

87 Misti 41, f. 127b and see *Capitolari dei Visdomini del fontego dei Tedeschi a Venezia*, ed. G.M. Thomas (Berlin 1874), p. 95 ff. i Savi N.S. 145, Commercio.

88 *ASV*, Cancellaria Inferiore, Notai, Ba 229, Leonardo de Valle, sub 7 Febr. 1403.

89 M.C., Spiritus, f. 48b.

90 M.C., Clericus et Civicus, f. 136a; cf. B. Cecchetti, *Sulle origini e sullo svolgimento della vetraria veneziana e muranese*, p. 10.

91 L. Zecchin, " Prodotti vetrari nei documenti veneziani (1333-1400) ", *Riv. Staz. Sper.* IX (1979), p. 22.

92 L. Zecchin, " Angelo Barovier, vetraio del rinascimento ", *Vetro e Silicati* X (1966), no. 58, p. 26; idem, " Il vetro " cristallino " nella carte del Quattrocento ", *Vetro e Silicati* VII (1963), no. 38, p. 21 ff.

93 L. Zecchin, " I " segreti " dei vetrai muranesi del Quattrocento ", *Riv. Staz. Sper. XI* (1981), p. 169.

94 L. Zecchin, " Prodotti vetrari nei documenti veneziani (1457-1468) ", *Riv. Staz. Sper.* X (1980), p. 17; idem, " Nascita del cristallo veneziano ", *Vetro e Silicati XI* (1967), no. 66, p. 21.

fourteenth century prove that in Murano Levantine sodium carbonate was used exclusively.[95] It was also used for the production of artificial jewels.[96] But it was not only in Murano that there was a great upswing in the glass industry. Tuscan craftsmen came to Murano, and after working there for some time then introduced Muranese methods of production into their own country.[97] In Tuscany, too, producers began to use Syrian ashes for the manufacture of glass.[98] Muranese glassmakers were also invited to work in other towns, or, more exactly, were enticed to emigrate from Venice against strict prohibition by the *Serenissma.* This was an old phenomenon, for the emigration of Muranese glassmakers had begun at the end of the thirteenth century when new glass factories were founded in Treviso, Vicenza, Mantua, Ferrara, and Bologna.[99] In the fourteenth and fifteenth centuries, when the reputation of the Muranese became very great, they were everywhere well thought of and well paid, and other rulers tried to bring them to their dominions.[100] Others left Murano on their own to try their luck elsewhere, and in 1392 some Muranese glassmakers or their apprentices introduced the glass industry into Ancona.[101] The

---

95 L. Zecchin, "Cronologia vetraria veneziana e muranese dal 1332 al 1345", *Riv. Staz. Sper.* III (1973), p. 215; idem, "Materie prime e mezzi d'opera dei vetrai nei documenti veneziani dal 1348 al 1438", *Riv. Staz. Sper. XI* (1981), p. 76; *Dell'arte del vetro per musaico tre trattatelli dei secoli XIV e XV*, ed. G. Milanesi (Bologna 1864), p. 69, 72, 79, 81, 83 f., 86 f. (the second and third treatise published by Milanesi are of Muranese origin, see L. Zecchin, "Ricette vetrarie d'ispirazione muranese nel Quattrocento", *Riv. Staz. Sper.* XI, p. 265 ff.); cf. L. Zecchin, "Ricette vetrarie del '400 (reprint from Giornale Economico, Venice 1954) (Venice 1955), p. 29 f.

96 *Dell'arte del vetro per musaico*, pp. 90, 128.

97 L. Zecchin, "Forestieri nell'arte vetraria muranese (1276-138)", *Riv. Staz. Sper.* VII (1977), p. 275 ff.

98 *Dell'arte del vetro*, pp. 39, 60 (the first of these treatises is of Tuscan origin, see L. Zecchin, "Ricette vetrarie toscane del Quattrocento", *Riv. Staz. Sper.* XI, p. 213).

99 A. Gasparetto, *Il vetro di Murano dalle origini ad oggi*, p. 53.

100 L. Zecchin, "Vetrerie muranesi fra il 1446 ed il 1447", *Riv. Staz. Sper. IX* (1979), p. 152 f.

101 C. Albertini, *Storia d'Ancona*, MS. of the Bibl. Comunale of Ancona, IX, part 2, f. 155a.

Muranese founded glass factories in that period even in Germany.[102] The same is true for the glassmakers of Altare, who were also well received in other countries and in the course of the fifteenth century founded factories in France and Belgium.[103]

In that period, the flourishing glass industries of several regions of Southern Europe began to export their products to other countries. This began as early as the first half of the fourteenth century. In the second decade of the fourteenth century, Murano glass was to be found in Egypt;[104] in the 1340's, if not earlier, Italian glass was marketed in Greece, Rhodes and other regions that had once belonged to the Byzantine empire;[105] glass vessels were also exported to Constantinople and to the commercial towns on the coasts of the Black Sea and the Sea of Azov.[106] In the fifteenth century, the Venetians sold the products of their glass industry in Egypt and Syria, where they had originally learnt the craft of glassmaking.[107] The export of Murano glass and glass vessels to Constantinople went on after the town became the capital of the Ottoman Empire.[108]

VI. Import of Levantine Ash in the XIVth-XVth Centuries

As the soap and glass industries of several European countries developed rapidly and production increased, ever greater quantities of Near Eastern ash were needed and its import be-

---

102 L. Zecchin, "Cronologia vetraria veneziana e muranese dal 1444 al 1454", *Rev. Staz. Sper.* VI (1976), p. 63.

103 J. Barrelet, *La verrerie en France de l'époque gallo-romaine à nos jours*, pp. 65, 171 f., 178 ff.

104 See E. Ashtor, *Levant Trade in the later Middle Ages*, p. 25, note 122.

105 *Lettere a Pignol Zucchello*, p. 38.

106 L. Zecchin, "Prodotti vetrari nei documenti veneziani (1333-1400)", *Riv. Staz. Sper.* IX, p. 22.

107 E. Ashtor, "Aspetti della espansione italiana nel basso medioevo", *RSI* 90 (1978), p. 19.

108 L. Zecchin, "Prodotti vetrari nei documenti veneziani (1469-1482)", *Riv. Staz. Sper.* X (1980), p. 61.

came a not insignificant branch of trade with the Levant. But even in this period when large volumes of this material were imported, the ashes of local plants were also used almost everywhere in Europe to prepare soda ash for the soap and glass industries, since the ashes of European plants were of course more easily available and cheaper. Competition between Levantine and European ashes therefore also characterised soap and glass production at the end of the Middle Ages.

In the fifteenth century it was mainly fern ash from the local forests and meadows, that was used in Tuscany,[109] in Sicily, the ashes of plants of the local Chenopodiaceae were used,[110] since they grew everywhere in the province of Catania,[111] and were called *shebba*.[112] Some Italian manufacturers and merchants also tried to introduce Spanish ashes; letters written by a Florentine firm in Ancona in 1406 to the Datini company in Majorca and Barcelona contain a request for a supply of Spanish ashes.[113] In Germany, in the fifteenth century, large quantities of plant ashes from the forests of Eastern Europe were imported via Reval, Riga and Danzig. From the Hanse towns Russian ashes were reexported to the Low Countries.[114] Levantine ashes were supplied by the merchants of the South European "trading nations" who engaged in all branches of the trade with the Levant.

---

[109] See L. ZECCHIN, "Ricette vetrarie del '400", p. 9.

[110] Fr. D'ANGELO, "Produzione e consume del vetro in Sicilia", *Archaeologia Medievale* III (1976), p. 388.

[111] See M. BONNANO - Fr. D'ANGELO, "La vetreria di Cefalà Diana ed il problema del vetro siciliano nel medioevo", *Archivio Storico Siciliano*, series III, 21/22 (1972), p. 346.

[112] Ibidem. *Shabb* means alum in Arabic. So, as a result, in Sicily, as in Venice, sodium carbonate was called by a name derived from alum (*lume*).

[113] Dat 844, letter of Gianni di Freduccio e Giovanni di Pietri of 10 April 1406; Dat 1044, letter of the same of 4 June, 1406.

[114] Fr. SIEWERT, *Geschichte und Urkunden der Rigafahrer in Lübeck im 16. und 17. Jahrhundert* (Berlin 1897), p. 147 f.; A. ATTMAN, *The Russian and Polish Markets in International Trade, 1500-1650* (Göteborg 1973), pp. 35, 43, 57, 58 and cf. p. 18. The ashes were often called potash because they were packed in boxes called pot. See Gasparetto, *Il vetro di Murano*, p. 24.

Immediately upon the renewal of direct trade with the Mamluk dominions in the middle of the fourteenth century, the Venetians began to ship great quantities of Levantine ashes to their metropolis.[115] In that period, the preferred places for these purchases were the Syrian towns of Aleppo,[116] Sarmin,[117] Latakia,[118] Tripoli,[119] Beirut,[120] and Ramla.[121] Sometimes they were also bought in Egypt,[122] but Egyptian ashes were considered to be inferior. Pegolotti says that they were black and were transported to Europe as large blocks without being put in sacks. According to him, they were a third of the value of those of Syria. At the beginning of the sixteenth century, a Venetian merchant maintained that they could be used only for the production of soap, but not of glass.[123] The Venetians had no monopoly in this trade, and all the European Levantine traders had an interest in the purchase of the ashes of the *ushnān* and *salsola* growing in the Levant and eagerly acquired them. The Genoese exported them from Egypt and Syria, often shipping them directly to Flanders and England.[124] Certain clauses in

---

115 See *Misti* 23, f. 23b (a. 1345), 58a (a. 1346) 24, f. 20b (a. 1347) 26, f. 89a (a. 1352).

116 G.P. Ter. IX, f. 13a.

117 *Misti* 40, f. 117b.

118 *Cronaca Dolfin*, MS. Marciana Library of Venice, Ital. VII DCCXCIV, f. 378a, 400a.

119 G.P. Sent. 18, f. 85b ff. 54, f. 40a 71, f. 55a ff. 79, f. 118b ff. 84, f. 136b ff. 95, f. 75b f. 97, f. 116b ff. 99, f. 26a ff. 123, f. 53b ff. 140, f. 58b 165, f. 183b 187, f. 101a ff.; G.P., Ter VII, f. 2a f.

120 *Misti* 52, f. 34a f.; G.P. Sent. 20, f. 122a 30, f. 74b 53, f. 23a 124, f. 63b ff. 153, f. 28b ff.; G.P., Ter. III, f. 82a; ASV, Cancelleria Inferiore, Notai, Ba 83, Cristoforo del Fiore VI, f. 5b; Marino Sanuto, *Diarii* I, col. 604.

121 G.P., Sent. 23, f. 75b. Ashes bought in Ramla were shipped from Jaffa, see *Misti* 47, f. 7a f.

122 *Misti* 23, f. 23b, 58a 24, f. 20b f. 26, f. 89a.

123 Pegolotti, p. 180; see further the merchant letters quoted by G. della Santa (according to note 157) p. 1550.

124 See the freight inventories in E. Ashtor, "Il volume del commercio levantino di Genova nel secondo Trecento", (in) *Saggi e documenti I* (Studi e testi, serie storica 2) Civico Istituto Colombiano (Genova 1978), p. 432; Car. Vet. 1552, f. 125a, 127a 1553, f. 23b. *ASG*, notary Battista Airolo, 13, sub 3 July 1483. Cf. E. Ashtor, "Le

the commercial treaties between Florence and the Mamluk sultan refer to the purchase of these ashes in Syria.[125] The Anconitans, too, carried heavy shipments of Syrian ashes to their town,[126] while the Provencals did not lag behind them, buying the ashes of the ushnan and salsola in the Near Eastern markets.[127]

The price of the ashes on the Levant was low; in the fifteenth century, in Syria, the price of a kinṭār of 180 kg. was 2 ducats or even less [128] (Table IX), but the freight of this cheap commodity

TABLE IX

PRICES OF SYRIAN ASH IN THE MIDDLE OF THE FIFTEENTH CENTURY

Date	Place	Price of a Kinṭār	Source
1426	Tripoli	2 ducats	G.P., Sent. 65, f. 129a f.
1440	»	2 ducats	same series 88, f. 30b ff.
1441	»	1.7-1.87 ducats	same series 97, f. 116b ff.
1468	»	1.2 duc. (60 dirh.)	same series 165, f. 183a
before 1473	»	0.63-0.725 ducats	same series 158, f. 43a, f.
1473	Damascus	1.4 duc. (70 dirh.)	same series 169, f. 172b ff.
1476 (or 1477)	Aleppo	2.5 ashrafīs *	G.P., Ter. IX, f. 13a

* The *ashrafī* generally had the same value as the ducat, see E. ASHTOR, 'Etudes sur le système monétaire des Mamlouks circassiens,' *Israel Oriental Studies VI* (1976), p. 272.

Proche-Orient au bas moyen âge - une région sous-développée", p. 407 and notes 182-184.

[125] J. WANSBROUGH, "A Mamluk Commercial Treaty Concluded with the Republic of Florence 894/1489", (in) *Documents from Islamic Chanceries*, ed. S.M. Stern (Oxford 1965), p. 65; idem, "Venice and Florence in the Mamluk Commercial Privileges", *BSOAS* 28 (1965), p. 505. In the treaty quoted in the first place, the ashes are called kily (*kali*), but in the second one there appears the name buls (here vocalised, and cf. above note 49). This latter word seems to have been the official name of the commodity. It does not appear in the Arabic dictionaries.

[126] F. MELIS, *Documenti per la storia economica dei secoli XIII-XVI* (Florence 1972), p. 144; *ASV*, Cancelleria inferiore, notai, Ba 229, Leonardo de Valle sub 19 Aug. 1402.

[127] Dat 1171, freight inventory of the ship of M ... Luziano which arrived on 28 April, 1397, in Marseilles.

[128] See E. ASHTOR, "Le Proche-Orient au bas moyen âge — une région sous-développée", p. 409 The data in the following table should be added.

was relatively costly, although the ashes were used as ballast; in the course of time it decreased. As can be seen in table X, the freight of a Syrian kinṭār of ashes decreased from three ducats at the beginning of the fifteenth century to 1.5 in the second half. The decrease in the freight charges for the Levantine ash was considerable and was the consequences of a well planned policy by the Venetian government, as is evident from comparison with the prices paid for the transport of cotton. Whereas the freight cost of ashes decreased by 50%, that of cotton went down by only 20% (see Table XI). This is a clear proof that the Senate

TABLE X

FREIGHT COSTS OF LEVANTINE ASH ON VENETIAN COGS
(for a migliaio of 477 kg.)

	Year	Syrian cogs	Alexandrian cogs	Source
	1371		4 ducats	Misti 33, f. 110b
	1373		3 "	" 34, f. 48a
	1374	3 ducats		" 34, f. 76b f.
	1378	6 "		" 36, f. 59b
	1384		4 "	" 38, f. 127b
	1385		3 "	" 39, f. 92a
	1395		3 "	" 43, f. 65a f.
	1396		3 "	" 43, f. 130b f.
	1400		3 "	" 45,f. 144b f.
	1404		3 "	" 46, f. 144b f.
fall	1405	3 "		" 47, f. 7a f.
spring	1406	2.5 "		" 47, f. 25b
fall	1417	2.5 "		" 52, f. 24a f.
spring	1426	2.5 "		" 55, f. 182a
fall	1426	2 "		" 56, f. 16b f.
fall	1427	2 "		" 56, f. 105a
spring	1428	2 "		" 56, f. 142b
fall	1430		2 "	" 57, f. 233a cf. 232a
fall	1431	3 "		" 58, f. 60a ff.*
fall	1456	2 "		S. Mar V, f. 154b f.
	1468	1.5 "		G.P., Sent. 165, f. 183b
fall	1473	1.5 "		S. Mar IX, f. 174a f.**

* Because of great insecurity on the sea, special measures were taken, and freight charges increased.
** In fact this is only a proposal; the decision is missing.

TABLE XI

FREIGHT COSTS OF COTTON ON VENETIAN COGS
(for a migliaio of 301 kg.)

	Year	Syrian cogs	Alexandrian cogs	Source
	1368		2 ducats	Misti 32, f. 131a
	1371		8 "	" 33, f. 110b
	1373		6 "	" 34, f. 48a
	1374		6 "	" 34, f. 76b f.
	1384		6 "	" 38, f. 127b
	1385		6 "	" 39, f. 92a
	1395		6 "	" 43, f. 65a f.
fall	1405	12 ducats		" 47, f. 7a f.
spring	1406	7 "		" 47, f. 25b f.
fall	1417	6 "		" 52,f. 24a f.
spring	1426	7 "		" 55, f. 182a
fall	1426	6 "		" 56, f. 16b
fall	1427	5 "		" 56, f. 105a
spring	1428	6 "		" 56, f. 142b
fall	1439	6 "		" 60, f. 119a
fall	1456	6 "		S. Mar V, f. 165a
fall	1473	5.5 "		S. Mar IX, f. 164a f.

TABLE XII

PRICES OF LEVANTINE ASH IN ITALY

Year	Town	Price of a migliaio	Source
1428	Venice	10.5 ducats	G.P., Sent. 73, f. (between 86 and 87) *
1444	Ancona	25 "	Same series 104, f. 63a **
1449	Venice	18 "	Accounts Fr. Contarini, f. 45a ***
1452	Venice	16 "	G.P., Sent. 129, f. 84b ff.

* This is a barter price.
** The migliaio of Ancona was of 346 kg.
*** Venice, Museo Correr, PD C 912/I.

of Venice considered the import of large quantities of Levantine ash to be vital for her economy. But although the price of the article in the Near East was low and freight charges went down, its price in Southern Europe remained high.

The data we have cited seem to point to at least a 200% gross profit. However, the merchants had relatively high expenses,[129] as is clearly shown by the accounts that have come down to us of certain Venetian firms (see Table XIII). The profits in any case were considerable, and as the demand for the article was brisk the Levant traders eagerly engaged in this sector of trade.

Venetian merchants bought 400-500 kinṭārs or more in a single year.[130] The total amount of the shipments the Venetian cog convoys carried from Syria in certain years can be found in some sources. The greatest part of the Levantine ashes was shipped to Venice by the cotton cogs, whereas the galleys loaded them only when they had empty space. Of course, sometimes other ships brought the "*lume*" to Venice,[131] but the bulk of the Levantine salsola ashes arrived on the cog convoys, and Venice held the lion's share of this import trade. Data on the shipments of ashes by these convoys are therefore of great value (see Table XIV).

The data available are not sufficient to draw firm conclusions, but they give the impression that at the end of the fourteenth century and the beginning of the fifteenth century the spring convoys of the Venetian cotton cogs carried no more than 400-800 sacks to the metropolis. The quantity carried to Venice by the autumn convoy of 1396 may perhaps have been more characteristic of the volume of the Venetian shipments of this commodity. Yet there is a great discrepancy between the evidence on the purchases of Levantine ashes made by single Venetian merchants in the fifteenth century and these shipments. On the other hand, certain data of the late fifteenth century point to 1000-1200 sacks being loaded on one Venetian cog.[132] One could therefore con-

---

129 See S. Mar I, f. 125b about the consular dues.

130 See E. Ashtor, "The Venetian Supremacy in Levantine Trade", *JEEH* III (1974), p. 45; to be added G.P., Sent. 54, f. 40a f. 153, f. 28b ff.; G.P., Ter. IX, f. 13a.

131 See G.P., Sent. 146, f. 47b ff. On the transport of the ashes on the cogs, see (besides the texts quoted in note 115) *Misti* 32, f. 131a.

132 See Girolamo Priuli, *Diarii I*, p. 42; Domenico Malipiero, *Annali Veneti*, p. 629.

TABLE XIII

ACCOUNTS OF VENETIAN TRADERS

a) Luca & Andrea Vendramin	a. 1441 purchase of 2184 ḳinṭār ashes in Tripoli net price 4905 duc.
G.P., Sent. 97, f. 116b ff.	expenses in Syria 1389 duc. expenses 34.7%
b) Domenico Erizo	a. 1468 purchase of 282.4 ḳinṭār in Tripoli price (with expenses in Syria) 542.5 duc. freight 175 " expenses in Venice 20.5 "
G.P., Sent. 165, f. 183b	(expenses 36%)

TABLE XIV

VOLUME OF IMPORTS TO VENICE

Year		Quantity	Source
1386	spring fair	160 migliaia	Dat 548, letter of Zanobi di Taddeo Gaddi of 15 May 1386
1394	spring fair	790 sacks	Dat 797, letter of the same of 30 April 1394
1395	spring fair	1200 migliaia	Dat 926, letter of the same of 26 May 1395
1396	fall fair	2000 sacks	Dat 550, letter of the same of 26 Oct. 1396
1406	spring fair	500 sacks	Dat 929; letters of the successors ("commessaria") of Zanobi and of Ant. di Ser Bartolomeo of 14 and 21 Aug. 1406; Ibid., letter of Giannozzo Ant. degli Alberti of 7 Aug. 1406 *

* The last letter states that the cogs carried 563 sacks of ashes to Venice.

clude that in the course of the fifteenth century the volume of the Venetian ash trade increased very greatly as the data for the end of the fifteenth century point to the import of 10,000 sacks a year.[133]

It is certainly true that Venetian merchants supplied Constantinople, and especially Gaeta,[134] with the Levantine ashes, just as did the Genoese,[135] and that sometimes the stocks in Venice were so great that there were requests to export it [136] but this was in fact conceded only as an exception,[137] because the policy of the Venetian government was to forbid the supply of this excellent raw material to the industries of other countries. Time and again the *Maggior Consiglio* or the Senate decreed that the export of " *lume* " was forbidden (e.g., in 1332,[138] 1384, [139] and 1468.[140] The attitude of the Venetian government was very rigid because some merchants carried Levantine ash to Gaeta and Gallipoli (in Apulia), which were centres of the soap industry, as an investment in order to market the soap produced with it in the Near East. This was strictly forbidden in 1489.[141] Proposals to allow the export of the ashes were seldom carried in the Senate,[142] and the *Serenissima* took no notice when the prohibition aroused the anger of princes. In the year 1394, Gian Galeazzo Visconti, prince of Milan, sent an ambassador to Venice to request the re-

133 *G.P.*, Sent. 78, f. 57b ff. 165, f. 93b f.

134 *G.P.*, Sent. 20, f. 122a 71, f. 55a ff.

135 *Car. Vet.* 1552, f. 125a.

136 *Misti* 39, f. 58b.

137 *Misti* 47, f. 161a; L. Zecchin, " Materie prime e mezzi d'opera dei vetrai nei documenti veneziani dal 1439 al 1452 ", *Riv. Staz. Sper.* XII (1982), p. 65.

138 M.C., Spiritus, f. 48b; published by B. Cecchetti, Sulla storia, p. 32; cf. L. Zecchin, " Materie prime e mezzi d'opera nei documenti veneziani dal 1233 al 1347 ", *Riv. Staz. Sper. X* (1980), p. 174.

139 *Misti* 38, f. 117a.

140 *S. Terra* VI, f. 20b.

141 Malipiero, *Annali Veneti*, p. 685; S. Terra X, f. 170a f. The decree was repeated in 1492, see S. Mar. 13, f. 92b.

142 See L. Zecchin, " Materie prime e mezzi d'opera dei vetrai nei documenti veneziani dal 1348 al 1438 ", *Riv. Staz. Sper.* XI (1981), p. 77.

vocation of this prohibition, because Levantine ashes were a raw material necessary for the production of majolica. As a reprisal he threatened that he would forbid the export of the pebbles of the river Ticino to Venice. Since these pebbles were the most important component of glass the Venetians were very keen indeed to obtain this particularly excellent kind.[143] The German merchants who traded in Venice also tried to purchase the precious Levantine ashes, but this was forbidden in 1469.[144]

VII Levantine and European Ashes, 1500-1650

The competition between the Levantine ashes and the ashes of local European plants continued in the sixteenth and seventeenth centuries. In some countries of Western and Central Europe, the ashes of local plants or those from other parts of Europe were largely, if not exclusively, used for the production of soap and glass. In other centres of these industries the Levantine ushnān and salsola ashes were still used.

In sixteenth century England, there were various kinds of soap: coarse soap, made from train oil (obtained from the blubber of whales); sweet soap made from olive oil; and speckled soap made from tallow. The ashes used for the production of these soaps were imported from Denmark. Perfumed soap from Bologna and Naples was imported, as well as soap from Spain, in the production of which the ashes of the local plants were certainly used.[145] Ashes of plants growing in Russia and the neigh-

---

[143] *Libri Commemorali* VIII, no. 415 (ed. Predelli III, p. 225 f.)

[144] L. ZECCHIN, *Nuovi appunti di storia vetraria muranese* (Venezia 1958), p. ff.; idem, "L'arte vetraria muranese all'inizio del 1469", *Riv. Staz. Sper.* VI (1976), p. 253 f.

[145] GIBBS, "The History of the Manufacture of Soap," *Annals of Science* IV, p. 173 f. Concerning the salsoleae plants in Spain, see M. WILKOMM - J. LANGE, *Prodromus florae Hispanicae* (Stuttgart 1861-1880) I, p. 257 ff. On the imports of Spanish soap into England in earlier periods see R. DOEHAERD - Ch. KERREMANS, *Les relations commerciales entre Gênes, la Belgique et l'Outremont* (Brussels-Rome 1952), no. 643.

bouring regions of Eastern Europe were also widely used in the soap industries of Central and Western Europe in the sixteenth century. They were imported via Riga, Königsberg, and Danzig through the sixteenth and seventeenth centuries to Lubeck and farther to the Netherlands and to England.[146] However, certain quantities of Levantine ashes were imported into Germany from Venice.[147]

As in earlier ages, much high-quality soap was manufactured in Italy, using various raw materials. Genoa and Venice were the main centres of the industry. The renown of Venetian hard soap was very great everywhere and accordingly people in other countries tried to imitate its production. In the year 1622, a patent was granted in England to two manufacturers, Jones and Palmer, for the production of this article, called Venetian or Castille soap.[148] In Venice, use was made of olive oil and also the fat of oxen and cattle, together with ashes of the bitter oak [quercus cerris] and the Levantine *ushnān*, as can be learned from treatises on the subject written in the sixteenth century.[149] A well-informed author in the middle of the sixteenth century says that for soap-making ashes from Beirut were the best, and those of Tripoli which were second only to them: the third place in terms of quality was held by that of the West, the ashes of Alicante. The lowest quality were the ashes coming from Egypt.[150] There can be no doubt that in sixteenth-century Venice considerable

---

[146] Fr. Siewert, *Geschichte und Urkunden der Rigafahrer*, p. 199, 237, 286, 309; H. Rachel, *Die Handels-, Zoll- und Akzisenpolitik Brandenburg-Preussens bis 1713* (Berlin 1911), p. 368; A. Attman, *The Russian and Polish Markets in International Trade, 1500-1650*, pp. 43, 46, 47, 49, 51 ff., 54, 55, 56 ff., 58, 60.

[147] H Simonsfeld, *Der Fondaco dei Tedeschi in Venedig* (Aachen 1968) II, p. 196.

[148] Gibbs, "The History of the Manufacture of Soap", p. 175.

[149] Giovanventura Rossetti, *Notandissimi secreti de l'arte profumatoria*, p. 47 f., 64 ff., 102, 104 f., 111 f. The oak tree is called cerro in Italian, that is, quercus cerris, cf. P. Zangheri, *Flora Italica I* (Padua 1976), p. 82; A. Fiori, *Nuova flora analitica d'Italia* (Florence 1923-1929) I, p. 364.

[150] Tomaso Garzoni, *La piazza di tutte le professioni nel mondo* (Venice 1665), p. 605 (The first edition of the book is of Venice 1587).

quantities of Levantine ash were needed as the soap industry was flourishing and its export reached a sizeable volume. There were many soap factories in Venice, on both sides of the Grand Canal, in the parish of S. Giobbe (where the name Ponte della Saponella remains to this day), in that of S. Pantaleone (where there is a Calle della Saoneria), in S. Polo (Calle seconda dei Saoneri) and in S. Barnaba (Calle dei Saoneri).[151] The Venetian soap for which Levantine ash was used was a high-quality product, and when, in 1566, Teodoro Spinola proposed introducing into Venice the manufacture of soap such as that produced in Lombardy, Genoa, Rome, Naples, Sicily, Provence, France and Savoy, the "*Provveditori di comun*" refused to grant him a licence, mantaining that the production of such soap, (for which the ashes of Provençal and Spanish plants would be used) would be prejudicial to the reputation of the Venetian industry.[152] As in earlier ages, the Senate of Venice maintained a strict prohibition of the export of these Levantine ashes.[153] The volume of production at the end of the sixteenth century was about 13 million pounds a year.[154] The olive oils of Apulia and the ashes of Syrian and Egyptian herbs were still preferred. The production of 18,000 lb. of soap required 3000 lb. of Syrian ashes plus 1500 of Egyptian.[155] The prosperity of the Venetian soap industry continued in the first half of the seventeenth century and in the 1620's 6 million pounds a year were exported.[156]

That considerable quantities of Levantine ashes were imported to Venice and other industrial and commercial centres in the sixteenth century is borne out by documents referring to this trade.

---

[151] G. Tassini, *Curiosità veneziane*, p. 624 f.

[152] G. Mandich, "Privilegi per novità industriali a Venezia nei secoli XV e XVI", *Deputazione di Storia Patria per le Venezie, Assemblee*, 8 Sept. 1963, p. 31.

[153] *Savi* N.S. 145, Commercio, part 2, decision of the Senate of 8 Nov., 1553.

[154] D. Sella, *Commerci e industrie a Venezia del secolo XVII, notizie sull'industria del sapone* (Venice 1961), p. 132 ff.

[155] Ibidem.

[156] Ibidem.

Letters of Venetian merchants at the beginning of the sixteenth century deal with the import of various kinds of Levantine ashes into the metropolis which were purchased in Tripoli and Beirut.[157]

However, high-grade soaps were also produced from other raw materials in that period in Italy. A sixteenth-century author reports that a lye prepared from the ashes of poplar and quicklime was used,[158] and in place of Levantine ashes a good deal of oak ash was used for the production of certain kinds of soap. In the first half of the seventeenth century, new soap industries were founded in various provinces of Italy — in Ferrara, Mantua, and Liguria — all of them using the ashes of local plants.[160] The soap industry of Venice began to decay when owing to the decline of Venetian trade and of her fleet, the supplies of Levantine ashes were no longer sufficient. Perhaps the qualitative decline of the Levantine ashes also played a part in this. Competition from the new soap industries of other towns was another reason. The soap-makers of Venice began to emigrate although government tried in vain to induce them to return.[161] On the other hand, soap produced outside the Venetian territory began to be imported. In the middle of the sixteenth century, the Senate began to take measures against these infringements of the law.[162] Most of the soap produced by the new industries was of inferior quality, but nevertheless it was imported into the Venetian dominions despite the prohibition by the government.[163]

---

157 D. DALLA SANTA, " Commerci, vita privata e notizie politiche dei giorni della Lega di Cambrai, da lettere del mercante veneziano Martino Merlini ", (in) *Atti del R. Istituto Ven. di scienze, lettere ed arti* 76 (1916/7), p. 1549 f.

158 *The Secrets of Alexis of Piedmont* (London 1615), f. 50a.

159 See above *MS.* TIMOTEO ROSELLI, *De' secreti universali* (Venice 1644), f. 86b, 89b.

160 Sella, *Commerci e industrie*, p. 133 f.

161 See the decree: Parte presa nell'eccellentissimo Senato 1613 a 19 genaro in materia di savoni, stampata per Ant. Pinelli, stampator ducal.

162 H. KALLFELZ, Die venezianische Seifenindustrie im 17. und 18. Jahrhundert, *Zeitschrift f. Bayerische Landesgeschichte* 29 (1966), p. 440.

163 Ibidem.

As far as the glass industry is concerned, Venice reached the apogee of a long development in the sixteenth century and the production of her workshops was renoved and imitated all the world over. This was undoubtedly to a great extent the consequence of the use of high-grade raw materials, among them the ashes of the Levantine *ushnān* and *salsola*. This fact is clearly shown by treatises written in the sixteenth century by specialists. These authors explain that ashes of Spanish plants produce a bluish glass.[164] Glass made from ashes of fern, they say, is yellow and fragile.[165] Even the methods of production used in Murano were considered exemplary.[166] In the glass exhibition in the Correr Museum (Venice) in October, 1982, an unpublished manuscript of about 1700 was exhibited which reads: « Da molti paesi vengono ceneri che si adoprano in Murano. Da Spagna, e questi sono buonissime da vetro come ancora quelle che vengono da Tripoli di Soria, ma quelle che vengono d'Aleppo, da Acris, da Cartagine sono inferiori, e s'addimandano magre... stentano a far vetro, ma vengono anco d'Alessandria, ma queste non sono buone a far altro che negro ». The author of the compendium (of the kind of those " Ricettari " so popular in those days [167]) considered the ashes brought from Tripoli in Syria and those coming from Spain as the best. But he held not all Syrian ashes in esteem. Haudicquer de Blancourt who published a comprehensive and scientific work at the end of the seventeenth century had another opinion. He emphasizes that crystal is always made from Syrian ash because the sodium carbonate obtained from it is white and blue tinge and ren-

---

[164] ANTONIO NERI, *L'arte vetraria* (Florence 1612, reprint Milan 1980), cap. I.

[165] LEONARDO FIORAVANTE, *Specchio di scientia universale* (Venice 1564), f. 68a.

[166] *Op. cit.*, f. 67b. See further on the use of Levantine ashes the " Ricettario di Montpellier " dating to 1536 and of Muranese inspiration, published by L. ZECCHIN, *Bollettino della Staz. Sper. del Vetro* VII, no. 5 (1963), p. 8, 12 and cf. " Le ricette vetrarie di Montpellier ", *Journal of Glass Studies* VI (1964), p. 75 ff.

[167] The MS is property of Dr. Mario Barbini of Florence. Cartagine is of course Cartagena in Spain.

ders the glass as beautiful as it is. The author also says that in his day Levantine ash was still used in Murano.[168]

So through the sixteenth and seventeenth centuries the ashes of the Levantine *ushnān* and *salsola* held a preeminent place among the raw materials used in Southern Europe for the production of high-quality merchandise. Even in that period they were used not only for the production of soap and glass, but also of artificial jewels such as beads of different colours.[169] The soda obtained from the Levantine ashes was also used for cleaning teeth and hands.[170] However the use of Levantine ash was very limited or even rare in the glass factories that had sprung up in the sixteenth and seventeenth centuries in Western and Central Europe. In England in the sixteenth century fern ash was used and although Levantine ashes were imported from Venice later, attempts were made to use potash (instead of the ashes of plants growing on sea coasts). In France the ashes of local plants were used; in the sixteenth century it was those of ferns growing on the banks of the Rhone. Haudicquer de Blancourt says that at the end of the seventeenth century Levantine ash was not used any more in France: the Royal glass manufacturers in Saint-Gobain normally used Spanish ashes.[171] Even the new glass factories in some towns of Italy used either ashes of Spanish plants [172] or those of plants growing on the coasts of the Adriatic or in the marshes of Tuscany.[173]

---

168 De l'art de la verrerie, p. 49 ff.

169 Neri, *L'arte vetraria*, cap. 102.

170 Rosetti, *De' secreti universali*, f. 96a; *Ricettario galante del principio del secolo XVI*, ed. O. Guerrini (Bologna 1883), p. 66, 72.

171 Vannuncio Biringucci, *Pirotechnia* (Venice 1559), f. 98b; Haudicquer de Blancourt, p. 52. The *vareque* was used a great deal, see P. Fournier, *Les quatre flores de la France* (Paris 1961), p. 135; Cl. Pris, *La manufacture royale de glace de Saint-Gobain, 1665-1830* (Université de Lille 1975) I, p. 197.

172 G. Taddei, *L'arte del vetro in Firenze* (Florence 1954), p. 29.

173 De' discorsi di M. Pietro Andrea Matthioli Senese, part II (Venice 1604), p. 1430 (first edition 1554) (Matthioli lived 1500-1577).

VIII. The Decline of the Levantine Ash Trade

In the seventeenth century both the soap and the glass industries of Italy (mainly those of Murano) which produced high-quality articles began to decline. This decline resulted in a further decrease in the import of Levantine ash and later it was no longer necessary because new inventions made its use superfluous and anachronistic.

In the year 1714, of the 30 soap factories with 90 boiling-vats that had existed in Venice, only 7 plants with 21 boiling-vats remained. The decay of the once famous soap industry of Venice was the sequel of the upswing of the soap factories of Naples, Apulia, Milan, Mantua and Genoa.[174] But it was also the consequence of the imposition of a tax on olive oil first introduced in 1625, abolished in 1635, 1649 and 1715, but each time reestablished.[175] At the end of the seventeenth century and at the beginning of the eighteenth century the decline was rapid; whereas in March-July 1641, 499,000 lb. had been exported to Germany (via the *fondaco*), between 1713-1715 only 36,000 lb. on average were exported.[176] When the decline became obvious, there were attempts to replace Levantine by local ash, but these attempts did not prove successful.[177] Ashes imported from the Levant were still used for producing high-grade soaps, and export accounts in the years 1697-1706 show that the quantity of the inferior " black soap " exported from Venice was less than half of that of the " white soap ".[178] At the same time, a flourishing soap industry developed in Crete and its products were exported to Turkey, Syria, Egypt, and also to Italy. This industry, whose

---

174 KALLFELZ, Die venezianische Seifenindustrie im 17. und 18 Jahrhundert, p. 438. But in another document referring to the olive oil used by the soap factories in 1715-1717, eight are listed, see *Savi* N.S. 145, Commercio, part 2.

175 Art. cit., p. 435. The (printed) decrees of the abolitions in 1634 and 1715 are to be found in *Savi*, N.S. 145.

176 Art. cit., p. 450.

177 Art. cit., p. 436.

178 *Savi* N.S. 145, Commercio, part 2.

success was a severe blow to that of Venice, used Sicilian ash,[179] but in order to improve its quality (it was very poor in alkalis) it was shipped to Tripoli where Syrian ash (as much as a fourth of the weight) was added to it. This was reported by the Swiss traveller, J.L. Burckhardt, who had embraced Islam and visited Syria in 1811.[180]

The reason for the decay of the famous Venetian glass industry was the development of new industries in several countries of Western and Central Europe, most of them founded by glassmakers who had emigrated from Murano or Altera. They had founded glass factories in France in the fifteenth century, and in the sixteenth and seventeenth centuries they worked in England and elsewhere.[181] No Levantine ash was used by these factories. Then, around 1680 in Bohemia, a new method of using potash (instead of soda) together with a great quantity of chalk was invented: the glass produced by this method was colourless and strong , and it began to be exported to Venice.[182]

In Venice attempts at recovery were made by introducing other raw materials. In the year 1739, the brothers Mazzola proposed to use in Murano certain Silesian materials which were also used in England, and made the glass white and transparent. The Venetian government hesitated and finally allowed its use in one furnace producing *lattimo*.[183] The enterprising glassmaker Giuseppe Briatta suceeded in bringing the decline of the famous industry of Murano to a halt through the use of this material on a large scale.[184] Then in 1776, Giorgio Barbaria, back from long travels in Western Europe, proposed the use of Spanish plant ash.[185]

---

179 Y. Triantafyllides, " L'industrie du savon en Crète au XVIIIe siècle, aspects économiques et sociaux ", (in) *Etudes Balkaniques* XI (1975), p. 78.

180 J.L. Burckhardt, *Travels in Syria and the Holy Land* (London 1882), p. 168.

181 G. Mariacher, *L'arte del vetro* (Milan 1954), p. 116 ff.

182 A. Gasparetto, *Il vetro di Murano dalle origini ad oggi*, p. 115.

183 B. Cecchetti, *Sulla storia dell'arte vetraria muranese*, p. 231.

184 *Op. cit.*, p. 24.

185 Gasparetto, *op. cit.*, p. 191.

Three years later, in 1779, Pietro Arduino, a botanist and professor of agriculture in Padua (1728-1805) suggested cultivating the local plant called *roscano* systematically and published instructions on how to obtain soda for glassmaking from its ashes.[186] Another Venetian, the engineer Lorgna, suggested using fern ashes.[187] None of these proposals, however, had any success. The times when the Venetian cogs had carried thousands of sacks of Levantine ashes to Venice and Murano glass had enjoyed an unchallenged reputation were over. But ashes imported from other regions were still used in Venice. A French traveller who visited Venice in 1785 recounts that ashes from Spain were used in Murano for producing the glass.[188] At the beginning of the nineteenth century there was a shift to the use of Sicilian ashes coming from Catania.[189]

Meanwhile new methods of producing the alkali carbonates for manufacturing soap and glass had been discevered and imports of ashes of *ushnān* from the Levant or ashes from other regions were no longer necessary.

---

[186] The Senate decreed its publication in 1780, see S. Terra 398, f. 150. It was published with the title: *Istruzione dei modi da praticarsi per coltivare il kali maggiore o sia salsola* soda erba communale nota col nome toscano e di formare la soda, cenere che impiegasi nella composizione di vetri, e di sapone ... stanpata ... aprile 1700, Figliuoli di Ant. Pinelli.

[187] B. Cecchetti, " Sull'origine e sullo svolgimento della vetraria veneziana e muranese ", p. 32.

[188] Joseph-Jerôme Le Français de Lalande (ou de la Lande), *Voyage en Italie*, 2nd ed., (Geneva 1790) VII, p. 83. Lalande (1732-1807) was an astronomer.

[189] V. Zanetti, *Guida di Murano e delle celebri sue fornaci vetrarie* (Venice 1866), p. 24.

VIII

The Factors of Technological and Industrial Progress in the Later Middle Ages

The great progress made by technology and industrial production in the Middle Ages has attracted the attention of many distinguished historians. It may now be timely to elaborate the factors which made this progress possible. But because social conditions in that era were very different from those of today, one cannot apply the theories developed by modern economists and other interpretations must be sought.

Modern economists have distinguished between invention and innovation, the former referring to novelties in technology and the latter to new elements in economic organisation.[1] The economic historian who deals with technological progress in the Middle Ages soon becomes aware of the fact that the distinction between the role of the inventor and the entrepreneur is often blurred. Even when considering the range of the inventions, he cannot be as exact as the historian of a modern economy. In order to draw a clear picture of industrial progress, he cannot isolate it from the general advance of technology. The same is true for chronological and geographical delimitation. The great progress made in industrial production in the later Middle Ages

[1] See V. RUTTAN, *Usher and Schumpeter on invention, innovation and technological change*, in *The economics of technological change*, ed. N. Rosenberg (Middlesex, 1971), p. 74, 79.

lends itself more to historical and sociological interpretation because of the relative wealth of sources. However one cannot ignore developments in earlier periods, as the picture would be inaccurate. In order to put into perspective the great progress made by European industries at the end of the Middle Ages, it should be compared with the stagnation and industrial decline in the neighbouring Near Eastern countries.

I

One of the factors which was considered to have promoted technological progress in the Middle Ages is Western Christianity. This argument was put forward by Lynn White who claimed that there is no evidence to support the view that social conditions (such as the scarcity of labour) were important for technological advance in the later Middle Ages.[2] To understand the factors which promoted technological progress in medieval Europe, one should consider the different ideas about labour amongst Western (Latin) Christians, Greek-Orthodox Christians and Moslems. From the beginning Christianity showed a different attitude from the Greeks and Romans towards labour, and placed much greater value on it. But Western Christianity was distinguished in particular by its voluntarist tradition. Physical work acquired a spiritual value, akin to worship. Mastering nature was close to collaboration with the Creator. Thus even the most degraded labour became dignified. Lynn White, argued that this was a distinctive feature of the religious approach and the piety of Western Christianity, which emphasizes good work, in contrast to the contemplativeness of Eastern Christianity and explained the favourable attitude towards technological progress in Western Europe in the Middle Ages.[3]

[2] LYNN WHITE JR., *Technology and innovation in the Middle Ages,* (in his volume) *Medieval Religion and Technology* (Univ. of California Press 1978), p. 22; idem, *Cultural elements and technological advance in the Middle Ages,* (in the same volume), p. 227.

[3] *Technology and innovation,* l.c.; *Cultural elements and technological advance in*

The connection between intellectual attitudes and technological development may be valid for the later Middle Ages, but fails to take account of the great advance of Byzantine and Islamic technology in the early Middle Ages. When the Byzantines constructed their superb domes and the Moslems invented the refining of sugar and introduced Chinese paper production into the Levant, their style of piety was already very different from that of Western Christianity.

Many historians have argued that the influence of foreign civilisations was an important factor in the development of technology in medieval Europe. Many innovations may have followed the transmission of inventions from the Near or even the Far East. However, most of these arguments lack archival evidence or are simply erroneous. One prominent orientalist has claimed, for instance, that the lateen sail and the compass, two important innovations of medieval shipping, were taken over by the Europeans from the Moslem world.[4] In fact the lateen sail was used in the Mediterranean in Roman times and came into use again in the Byzantine navy between the sixth and the ninth centuries.[5] The mariner's compass was originally a Chinese invention. However the Chinese used a floating compass, whereas in southern Europe the magnetic needle was amalgamated with the windrose that is attached to a compass card, so that it moved together with it and turned when the ship changed direction.[6]

the Middle Ages, p. 246 ff.; idem, *The iconography of Temperantia and the virtuousness of technology*, (in the same volume) p. 204; idem, *The expansion of technology, 500-1500*, (in) *The Fontana Economic History of Europe, The Middle Ages* (London 1972), p. 170 f.

[4] W. Montgomery Watt, *The influence of Islam on Medieval Europe* (Edinburgh 1972), p. 20, 21.

[5] Lynn White, *The diffusion of the lateen sail*, (in his volume quoted above), p. 212 ff.; Paul Adam, *A propos des origines de la voile latine*, (in) *Mediterraneo e oceano indiano, Atti del Sesto Colloquio Int. di Storia Marittima*, Venezia 1962 (Florence 1970), p. 212.

[6] K. Kretschmer, *Die italienischen Portolane des Mittelalters* (Berlin 1909), p. 70, 74, 80 f.; Bachisio R. Motzo (ed.), *Il compasso da navigare* (Cagliari 1947) (Annali della Facoltà di lettere e filosofia della Università di Cagliari VIII), p. LXXXIV.

The phenomenon of "parallel" invention, that is, inventions made independently of each other but stemming from the same needs, played a great role in the development of technology in the past when communication was much slower than today. Lynn White, who is a great authority in this field, is also aware of this fact.[7] Nevertheless he is inclined to assume the Central Asian origin of the new horse collar, used in Europe from the early Middle Ages.[8] Nor does he admit that printing by means of moveable cast types which was developed in the mid-XVth century in the Rhineland, was a Korean invention transmitted to the Europeans or that firearms had a Chinese origin.[9] Neither does he believe that the mechanical crank was taken over from the Far East.[10] However, Lynn White does believe firmly in a more or less steady flow of technological inventions from India and China to Western Europe. King Alfred the Great, for example, sent a mission to India [11] and in the later Middle Ages Tatar slaves would have been the vehicle of transmission of technology.[12]

One cannot deny that technological innovations were transmitted from one geographical region to another. Despite chronic warfare the countries of the Christian Occident,Byzantium, the Caliphate and their successor states formed a region. Cotton planting and the growing of sugar cane were certainly introduced in Sicily by the Moslems and it is well known that the

[7] See his paper *Medieval borrowings from Further Asia,* (in) *Medieval and Renaissance Studies,* ed. O.B. Hardison Jr. (Chapel Hill, Univ. of North Carolina Press 1971), p. 5.

[8] *Art. cit.,* p. 10 f.

[9] *Technology and innovation in the Middle Ages,* p. 8 ff.

[10] *Medieval borrowings from Further Asia,* p. 11.

[11] *Art. cit.,* p. 6; in fact this assumption is due to the error of a medieval copyist who wrote *India* instead of *Judaea* (which the emissaries visited), see *The Anglo Saxon Chronicle,* ed. B. Thorpe (London 1861) I, p. 152 II, p. 66; Willelmi Malmesburensis monachi, *De gestibus regum Anglorum,* ed. W. Stubbs (London 1887) I, p. 130; M. Kratochwill, *Eine Reise von Sendboten K*önig Alfreds des Grossen nach Indien, "Mitt. der Geogr. Gesellschaft zu Wien" 81 (1938), p. 227 ff.

[12] *Medieval borrowings from Further Asia,* p. 20 f.

Swabian Emperor, Frederick II, invited Syrian technicians to improve the sugar production in Sicily.[13] But it is questionable whether the methods of production were transferred from Arabic cotton weavers in Sicily to those on the Italian mainland. M.F. Mazzaoui, in her excellent book, surmises that slaves or Jews fulfilled this role. She also believes that the bow used for beating cotton travelled from Sicily to the Italian mainland.[14] These suppositions, however, are not substantiated by documented facts.[15] Mazzaoui also assumes that the treadle-loom was of Oriental origin, while she sees the use of Oriental names for cotton fabrics as evidence of the transmission of methods of production. She also argues that Italian cotton weavers took over only some of the methods of the Orientals, since famous fabrics like the mulham cloth were not produced in Italian workshops.[16] But the texts used by Professor Mazzaoui to prove the Sicilian origin of the Italian cotton industry do not refer to cotton weaving but to cotton planting and linen production.[17] The assumption that the treadle-loom was transmitted from the Near East via Sicily to Italy is a mere hypothesis,[18] while the use of Oriental names for certain textiles does not prove that production methods were copied. Finally, the fact that mulham cloth (a textile whose warp was of silk and the woof of cotton) was not produced in Italy, does not point to a "funnel effect" (transmission of a part of the production

[13] W. Heyd, *Histoire du Commerce du Levant au Moyen-Âge* (Leipzig 1885-86) II, p. 686.

[14] *The Italian Cotton Industry in the Later Middle Ages* (Cambridge Univ. Press 1981), p. 66, 76.

[15] As to the use of the bow, the author can produce only one document dating from 1110 and Apulia.

[16] *Op. cit.*, p. 82 f., 89 f.

[17] al-Mukaddasi, *Ahsan at-takasim*, p. 145; M. Amari, *Storia* [2] (Catania 1933-37), III, p. 826; D. Abulafia, *The Two Italies* (Cambridge Univ. Press 1977), p. 38, 47, 48, 218, 221, 255, 283; R.B. Serjeant, *Material for a history of Islamic textiles up to the Mongol conquest,* "Ars Islamica" 15/16 (1951), p. 55 f.

[18] A. Geijer, *Technical Viewpoints on Technical Designs* (in) *Artigianato e tecnica nella società dell'alto medioevo occidentale, 18ª Settimana di studio, Centro italiano di studi sull'alto medioevo* (Spoleto 1971), p. 694.

methods only) as Professor Mazzaoui supposes, since the mulham cloth was a typical product of Eastern Persia only.[19]

Marxist historians generally believe that slavery (and forced labour) impeded technological progress. But it is essential to set this problem in its context, because both in Near Eastern Moslem civilisation and in medieval Western Europe slavery and forced labour (in various forms) played a great role.[20] If the Marxist thesis is correct, the replacement of slavery and serfdom by free labour would have generated technological progress.

Marx and Engels outlined their views on technological progress and decline when dealing with the civilisation of the Ancients. They argued that Greco-Roman civilisation was essentially a slave-holder society, and the employment of great numbers of slaves for manual work resulted in the debasement and general disdain of physical labour causing technological stagnation. These arguments are maintained by Marxists to this day.[21] Although Marxist economic historians are not consistent about the character of Roman society and the impact of slave labour upon the development of technology, some Marxist scholars have admitted that free labour represented a major sector of production in the Roman Empire, although even these historians emphasised the negative influence of slavery upon technological advance.[22] Another team of Marxist archaeologists concluded from a detail study of Roman ceramics and other sec-

[19] See ATH-THA'ALIBI, *Laṭa'if al-ma'arif*, transl. C.E. Bosworth (Edinburgh 1968), p. 28, 145; AL-MUKADDASI, p. 323, 325; R. DOZY, *Dictionnaire détaillé des noms des vêtements chez les Arabes* (Amsterdam 1845), p. 113; idem, *Supplément aux dictionnaires arabes*, II, p. 522. (But of course *mulham* appears sometimes in documents of the Near East, see E. ASHTOR, *Histoire des prix et des salaires dans l'Orient médiéval*, [Paris 1969], p. 152).

[20] E. ASHTOR, *A Social and Economic History of the Near East in the Middle Ages* (London 1976), p. 201 (for forced labour employed in State industries).

[21] See F. VITTINGHOFF, *Die Theorie des historischen Materialismus über den antiken "Sklavenhalterstaat"*, "Saeculum" 11 (1960), p. 89 ff., 127 f.

[22] E. CICOTTI, *Le declin de l'esclavage antique* (Paris 1910), p. 284 f., 287 ff., 295, 413 ff., 419; see further K. KAUTSKY, *Sklaverei und Kapitalismus*, (in) "Die Neue Zeit" 29, part 1 (1911), p. 720, 722, 723.

tors of industrial production that at the heyday of Roman power, slavery reached its apogee and that the employment of slaves in great enterprises impeded technological advance.[23]

But non-Marxist historians have time and again emphasized that slavery was never the predominant system of production in either sector.[24] A more persuasive argument which disproves the Marxist analysis is that Roman technology made the greatest progress especially in methods of agricultural work during the first century B.C.,[25] while the finest Roman pottery, produced in the same period in Arezzo, was manufactured by slaves. Even Soviet historians admit to this fact.[26] One must also ask why Roman technology made insignificant progress in the early republican period when there was relatively little slavery, while it is obvious that the decline of slavery in the later empire did not result in technological advance.[27]

A Dutch historian has maintained that technology did not advance in the Roman Empire because the availability of labour made labour-saving devices almost unnecessary.[28] This thesis has great importance for the interpretation of technological progress (and stagnation) in the medieval period. But if it were correct, one would have difficulty in explaining the considerable advance of technology in the Caliphate. In fact when the Barme-

[23] A. Carandini, *Sviluppo e crisi delle manufatture rurali e urbane*, (in) *Società romana e produzione schiavistica* III, ed. A. Carandini e A. Schiavone (Bari 1981), p. 250, 258.

[24] M.L. Finley, *Ancient Slavery and Modern Ideology* (London 1980), p. 79, 81, 85; A.H.M. Jones, *The Later Roman Empire* (Oxford 1964) II, p. 851, 860, 862.

[25] B. Gille, *Lents progrès de la technique*, "Revue de synthèse", n.s. 32 (1953), p. 76 f.; M.L. Finley, *Technical innovation and economic progress in the ancient world*, "Economic History Review" 2nd series, 18 (1965), p. 35, 43; Fr. Kiechle, *Sklavenarbeit und technischer Fortschritt im* römischen Reich (Wiesbaden 1969), p. 170 f.

[26] E.M. Štaerman, *Die Blütezeit der Sklavenwirtschaft in der römischen Republik* (Wiesbaden 1969), p. 110.

[27] Fr. Kiechle, *Sklavenarbeit und technischer Fortschritt*, p. 173; Finley, *Ancient Slavery and Modern Ideology*, p. 138.

[28] H.W. Pleket, *Technology and society in the Graeco-Roman world*, "Acta Historica Nerrlandica" II (1967), p. 13.

kids introduced Chinese paper production in the Abbasid Caliphate and later when the Egyptians learned to refine sugar, the availability of labour was so great that the price of labour went down steadily and continuously.[29] The same Dutch historian provided another explanation for technological stagnation in the ancient world when he claimed that the emphasis of Greek and Roman education on rhetoric and literature was an obstacle to technological progress. This is an interpretation that is widely shared among classical scholars. But others have argued that the Ancients were interested in technological progress in order to increase luxury.[30] This interpretation is again pertinent for the analysis of medieval economies, since in Moslem countries new techniques were invented mainly for the sake of luxury and pleasure.[31]

Another interpretation of technological development has stressed the decisive impact of demographic change. Population growth encouraged the advance of technology, while depopulation had the reverse effect. Considerable technological progress was made in Athens — particularly in mining and shipbuilding — in the sixth and fifth centuries B.C., while the technological advance of the Roman Empire in the first century B.C. and the first century A.D. was also concomitant with population growth. In the Middle Ages technologies were greatly improved in the XIth-XIIIth centuries when population increased everywhere, while these developments ended towards the end of the XIIIth century when population declined.[32] In short, the need to feed greater numbers of people encouraged the introduction

[29] E. Ashtor, *I salari del medio oriente durante l'epoca medievale*, RSI 78 (1966), p. 329.

[30] Fr. Kiechle, *Das Problem der Stagnation des technischen Fortschritts in der römischen Kaiserzeit*, (in) "Geschichte in Wissenschaft und Unterricht" 16 (1965), p. 97.

[31] E. Wiedemann, *Aufsätze zur arabischen Wissenschaftsgeschichte* (Hildesheim 1970) I, p. 75 note a, 100 ff. II, p. 48 ff., 471 ff., cf. 478; Carra de Vaux, *Les mécaniques ou l'élevateur de Héron d'Alexandrie*, "Journal Asiatique" 1893, I, p. 419, II, p. 499, 505, 507.

[32] B. Gille, *Lents progrès de la technique*, p. 74, 76, 79, 81.

of labour-saving machines and innovations which increased the supply of commodities.[33] The data concerning the development of technology in the Caliphate could certainly be an additional argument for this hypothesis. Even there, methods of industrial production were considerably improved and new industries were founded when population increased.

However, important innovations were made in late medieval Europe when the curve of demographic development was at an ebb. From the end of the XIIIth century the use of the spinning wheel spread in Western Europe; in about 1330 the mechanical clock was invented; from the middle of the XIVth century the use of water-power in various sectors of industrial production became general and in the XVth century there was a great upswing in mining and mechanics due to the invention of the bit and brace and the reverberatory furnace (*seigern*).[34] Historians who claim that demographic development was the decisive factor in technological changes are surely aware of the critical importance of capital supply. Why is it that present-day India, which enjoys a true demographic boom, is not one of the most technologically advanced countries? There are indeed different responses to population growth, which may result either in an outburst of innovations or in the fall of per capita income.[35]

The spectacular upswing of technology which took place in Western and Central Europe in the period after the Black Death may be explained by the fact that many people enjoyed great well-being so that high quality commodities were in demand. This could explain the improvement of the production of woollens with the introduction of carding.[36] However, this inter-

[33] F.M. Feldhaus, *Die Technik der Antike und des Mittelalters* (Potsdam 1931), p. 425.

[34] Lynn White, *The expansion of technology, 500-1500*, p. 160.

[35] J.A. Schumpeter, *The creative response in economic history*, "Journal of Economic History", VII (1947), p. 149 f. (But it also happens that population growth brings about both phenomena, e.g., in the Caliphate...).

[36] G. Gille, (in) M. Daumas, *A history of Technology & Invention* II (New York 1969), p. 92.

pretation is not tenable for the development of other industries in late medieval Europe. W. von Stromer's work on the birth of the South German fustian industry at the end of the XIVth century, rightly raised the question of how the founders of this new industry overcame the opposition of the linen weavers, who were very much attached to their craft. The answer, according to W. von Stromer, was that the Black Death and subsequent epidemics had decimated the linen weavers, leaving a vacuum which made it possible to found a new industry.[37] This hypothesis is contrary to the supposed correlation between demographic growth and technological advance. But the decline of Near Eastern industries in the later Middle Ages, when the region suffered from a great shortage of labour, would also disprove this hypothesis and points to the impact of government policies on industrial development, since in the period immediately subsequent to the Black Death the Near Eastern countries still had a strong class of capitalists who were certainly interested in improving production methods and increasing their profits.

II

Against the all-embracing theories which single out one factor as decisive for the development of technology in the preindustrial period, one should emphasize the importance of other phenomena such as the migration of workers and the introduction of new raw materials, two occurrences which were often correlated. In the Middle Ages foreign workers introduced new techniques everywhere, while the use of new raw materials was often conditioned by the employment of foreign workers. They brought with them new methods adapted to the use of certain raw materials.[38] Even in the Moslem countries in the days of the

[37] W. von Stromer, *Die Gründung der Baumwollindustrie in Mitteleuropa* (Stuttgart 1978), p. 138 f.

[38] Mazzaoui, *The Italian Cotton Industry*, p. 67, 70; G. Mandich, *Privilegi per*

Caliphate and in the XIVth century, techniques were transmitted by workers who emigrated.[39]

Much data can be provided to show the great importance of worker migrations for the development of textile industries in medieval Europe. Flemish weavers developed the woollen industry in England in the 1330's [40] and worked in Vienna at the beginning of the XIIIth century.[41] Later, in the XVth century Flemish weavers were engaged in Saxony in order to raise the level of the wool production.[42] French clothmakers were employed in the wool industry of Genoa in the XIIIth century.[43] There was frequent migration of workers from one industrial centre to another in the same country. For various reasons weavers and other textile workers left their homes and went to another town where they introduced the production methods with which they were familiar. This happened very often in Italy in the later Middle Ages. The Florentine woollen workshops employed weavers, dyers and finishers from Lombardy and also from Germany.[44] When the Florentine industrialists decided to introduce the production of Perpignan cloth, foreign workers

novità industriali a Venezia nei secoli XV e XVI, (in) Deputazione di storia patria per le Venezie, Atti Asemblee 8. sett. 1963, p. 31.

[39] Serjeant, *Material for a history of Islamic textiles,* "Ars Islamica" X (1943), p. 74 (about *dabiki* produced in Fars); C.J. Lamm, *Mittelalterliche Gläser und Steinschnittarbeiten aus dem Nahen Osten* (Berlin 1930), p. 247; E. Ashtor in *Xe Settimana di Studio, Istituto Fr. Datini* (Florence 1983), p. 417 f.

[40] H.-E de Sagher, *L'immigration des tisserands flamands et brabançons en Angleterre sous Edouard III,* (in) "Mélanges d'histoire offerts a H. Pirenne" (Bruxelles 1926), p. 109 ff.

[41] H. Ammann, *Deutschland und die Tuchindustrie Nordwesteuropas* (in) "Hansische Geschichtsblätter" 72 (1954), p. 61.

[42] R. Sprandel, *Zur Geschichte der Wollproduktion in Nordwestdeutschland,* I^a^ Settimana di studio, Istituto Fr. Datini (Florence 1974), p. 101.

[43] R. Doehaerd, *Les relations commerciales entre Gênes, la Belgique et l'Outremont d'après les archives notariales génoises aux XIIIe et XIVe siècles* (Bruxelles-Rome 1941), I, p. 175, 197.

[44] G.A. Brucker, *Florentine Politics and Society, 1343-1378* (Princeton University Press 1962), p. 150; about the role of the Umiliati in Florence see A. Doren, *Die Florentiner Wollentuchindustrie vom vierzehnten bis zum sechzehnten Jahrhundert* (Stuttgart 1901-08), II, p. 28 ff.

were once more brought to the town.[45] In fact most medieval textile centres not only produced a characteristic type of cloth, but also imitated the products of other towns. For this purpose they had, at least in the beginning, recourse to the skill of foreign workers. When the Venetians embarked on the imitation of Florentine *garbo* cloth, they engaged Florentine textile workers.[46] Silk weavers of Lucca introduced their own local methods to Venice in the beginning of the XIVth century.[47] On the other hand, Venetian weavers worked in Padua [48] and Venetian dyers were employed in the Swabian linen industry. They taught the Germans to use dyes according to the Venetian fashion.[49]

Sometimes workers who later introduced production methods of their town to another industrial centre and spread what was considered a professional secret, had left home for political reasons, for example when a certain political party was defeated and its members persecuted or exiled. This happened often in medieval Italy. But various townships and princes who ruled industrial towns made efforts to induce foreign workers to settle on their territory and to develop industries and promised them privileges such as tax exemption, if they wished to accept their invitation.[50] The township of Bologna in the XIIIth century granted several privileges, including financial assistance, to foreign textile workers from Verona and other towns.[51]

45 Doren, *op. cit.*, p. 96.

46 H. Hoshino, *L'Arte della Lana in Firenze nel Basso Medioevo* (Florence 1980), p. 247.

47 T. Bini, *Su i Lucchesi a Venezia. Memorie dei secoli XIII e XIV*, "Atti della R. Accademia Lucchese" 16 (1857), pp. 174, 185, 238, 244 f.

48 R. Cessi, *Le corporazioni dei mercanti di panni e della lana in Padova fino a tutto il secolo XV*, (in) "Memorie del R. Istituto Veneto di scienze, lettere ed arti" 28, no. 2 (1980), p. 48.

49 W. von Stromer, *Die Gründung der Baumwollindustrie in Mitteleuropa*, p. 92.

50 See Cessi, *art. cit.*, p. 48 f. about a decree of Francesco da Carrara, ruler of Padua, in 1365; Mazzaoui, *op. cit.*, p. 71.

51 M.F. Mazzaoui, *The emigration of Veronese textile artisans to Bologna in the*

Thus great and even minor centres of the textile industry employed a considerable number of foreign workers, who contributed by introducing the manufacturing methods of their home towns to the development of the cloth industries. In Vicenza there were workers from Bergamo, Como, Crema, Verona and even from Germany and Flanders. In the middle of the XVth century the influx of German clothmakers to Vicenza was particularly strong.[52]

The intense migratory movement of textile workers resulted in the same raw materials and manufacturing methods being used in various towns. In cloth manufacturing in Venice the same types of wool as those of Verona and Bologna were used.[53] On the transmission of manufacturing methods one might also mention the role of the textile workers of Verona who emigrated in 1230/1 to Bologna, where they introduced the measurements of Veronese cloth.[54] The introduction of new methods of cloth-making was certainly most important for the medieval textile centres. The dyeing of textiles learned from foreign craftsmen had enormous importance in the Middle Ages. The numerous shades of different colours were very much sought after and the employment of foreign dyers had a great impact on the textile manufacturers in all countries.

There is a great deal of information on the activities of textile workers who emigrated to other countries, and the influence of migrant skilled workers in other branches of medieval industry can also be traced.

The Germans played a major role in the development of mining in numerous European countries, and were also consi-

thirteenth century, "Atti e Memorie della Accademia di Agricoltura, Scienze e Lettere di Verona", ser. VI, vol. 19 (1967-68), p. 275 ff. 279.

52 G.B. Zanasso, *L'arte della lana in Vicenza (secoli XIII-XIV)*, (in) "Miscellanea di storia veneta", ser. III, t. VI (Venice 1914), p. 70, 97, 314 ff., 353 ff., 369 ff.

53 E. Rossini-M.F. Mazzaoui, *Società e tecnica nel medioevo. La produzione di panni di lana a Verona nei secoli XIII-XIV-XV*, (in) "Atti e Memorie della Accad. di agricoltura, scienze e lettere di Verona", ser. VI, vol. 21 (1971), p. 592 f.

54 Mazzaoui, *The Italian cotton industry*, p. 84.

dered great experts in many branches of metallurgy and were readily engaged everywhere.[55] The production of mirrors was introduced into Venice by German and French craftsmen,[56] while the skill of German cannonmakers ("bombardieri") was highly appreciated in Italy in the XVth century. Many townships employed them.[57] German gunmakers were also employed in France.[58] In Italy, after 1461,[59] French and German printers spread the new art of using moveable types, while Italian papermakers introduced the art of producing rag paper for Nuremberg.[60]

The importance of the migration of skilled workers for the spread of technological innovations (which were often considered as professional secrets) was brought home with a vengeance by the measures taken against it by various governments. The great number of decrees enacted to this effect bears testimony to the apprehension of the industrial centres. The Senate of Venice even forbade the teaching of glassmaking to foreigners,[61] and ship-patrons were warned not to accept as passengers skilled artisans who wanted to emigrate from Venice.[62] Craftsmen who emigrated were threatened by many governments with heavy punishment,[63] and sometimes they were even threatened with the death penalty and those who would kill

[55] *Itinerario di Marino Sanuto per la terraferma veneziana nell'anno MCCCCXXXIII* (Padua 1847), p. 123.

[56] A. Casparetto, *Il vetro di Murano dalle origini ad oggi* (Venice 1958), p. 161 ff.

[57] B. Rathgen, *Das Geschütz im Mittelalter* (Berlin 1928), p. 29.

[58] R. Gandilhon, *Politique économique de Louis XI* (Paris 1941), p. 205.

[59] H.F. Brown, *The Venetian Printing Press, 1469-1800* (London 1891), chapter I.

[60] E. Marabini, *Die Papiermühlen im Gebiet der weiland freien Reichsstadt Nürnberg* (Nürnberg 1894), p. 17 ff.

[61] ASV (Archivio di Stato, Venezia), Senato Terra X, f. 177a f.

[62] Senato Terra 1. c.

[63] Florence: Doren, *Die Florentiner Wollentuchindustrie* II, p. 76, 570 f.; Venice: G. Monticolo, *I capitolari delle arti veneziane*, vol. II, part. 1, (Rome 1905), p. 88 f.; B. Cecchetti, *Sulla storia dell'arte vetraria muranese* (Venice 1865), p. 31, 32; L. Zecchin, *Nuovi appunti di storia vetraria muranese* (Venice 1958), p. 5 ff.

them were promised a reward.[64] However, there were also numerous decisions to grant the emigrated workers facilities in order to induce them to return.[65]

While the emigration of workers was an event which affected the population of both the town (or country) they left and the town where they settled, there is much less data about the introduction of new raw materials in a particular industrial centre, although this often had a major impact on industrial production and often made it necessary to adopt new methods of production.

The importance of English wool in the cloth industry of Florence is well known. In other Italian textile centres in the later Middle Ages, the kind of wool used for the manufacturing of various cloth also changed from time to time.[66] A great variety of dyes were also employed in the European textile industry,[67] and the import of Oriental dyes was accompanied by the transmission of methods of dying. The Orientals were great experts in the use of mineral mordants. At first they used old olive oil mixed with a soda solution, so that a precipitate of sodium oleate (especially of cotton) remained on the fibres. This sediment reacted during the following treatment by salts, calcic or tin salts. When madder was then added, the red colour was particularly durable.[68] The introduction of alum, of which great quantities had been imported into Southern Europe from the Levant since the Crusades, brought great improvements to the manufacture of textiles. There is much evidence that the Europeans esteemed the Oriental dyers as great experts [69] and in both the

[64] A. Schwarz, *Der Haspel*, "Ciba-Rundschau", Heft 64 (1945), p. 2357.

[65] L. Zecchin, *Cronologia vetraria veneziana e muranese*, "Rivista della Stazione sperimentale del vetro (Murano)" III (1973), p. 165, 213, 216, 257.

[66] N. Fano, *Ricerche sull'arte della lana a Venezia*, "Archivio Veneto", ser. V, vol. 18 (1936), p. 153 f.

[67] See E. Ashtor, *L'ascendant technologique de l'Occident medieval*, "Revue suisse d'histoire" (1983), p. 392.

[68] E.E. Ploss, *Ein Buch von alten Farben* (Heidelberg 1962), p. 39 ff.

[69] See A. Lombardo, *Un testamento e altri documenti in volgare siciliano del*

textile and glass-making industries the European dyers did their best to imitate them. Successful dyeing was of major importance even for this flourishing medieval industry,[70] and Venice, the leading commercial town in the Levant trade, played a major role in the transmission of Oriental dyeing methods to the West.

The variety of raw materials used in the famous glass industry of Murano was particularly great and induced the glaziers to develop new methods. The glassmakers of Murano used pebbles from the river Ticino, which contained high quantities of silicate, for producing fine crystal glass.[71] To make the glass clear, manganese from Piedmont was also used.[72] For the dyeing of glass, the Muranese used cobalt from Germany,[73] and Italian glassmakers in the later Middle Ages also commonly used *ferretto* (oxide of copper) to produce green enamelled glass.[74]

The great advantages that came from using new raw materials is clearly seen in the outstanding work of the Muranese glassmakers in the XVth and XVIth centuries. The great progress that resulted from the use of high quality raw materials also made other achievements possible, such as the invention of spectacles, an instrument of major importance for the intellectual development of mankind, which followed the production of clear glass in about the year 1280 in Italy.[75] The date of the in-

secolo XIV a Venezia, "Bollettino del Centro di studi filologici e linguistici siciliani" 10 (1969), p. 59.

[70] L. ZECCHIN, *I "segreti" dei vetrai muranesi del Quattrocento*, "Riv. Staz. sper. del vetro" 11 (1981), p. 167 f.

[71] ANT. NERI, *L'arte vetraria, 1612*, ed. R. Barovier Mentasti (Milan 1980), p. 4; *Dell'arte del vetro per musaico tre trattatelli*, ed. G. Milanesi (Bologna 1864) I, chap. 6 (the first and the second treatise are of Muranese inspiration).

[72] L. ZECCHIN, *Materie prime e mezzi d'opera dei vetrai nei documenti veneziani dal 1439 al 1452*, "Riv. Staz. sper. del vetro" 12 (1982), p. 65.

[73] W. GANZMÜLLER, *Uber die Verwendung von Kobalt bei den Glasmachern des Mittelalters*, (in his volume) *Beiträge zur Geschichte der Technologie und der Alchemie* (Weinheim 1956), p. 171.

[74] *Dell'arte del vetro*, chapter 88 (this is a Florentine treatise).

[75] L. ZECCHIN, *I "roidi da ogli"*, "Giornale economico" (of the Camera di commercio, industria e agricoltura di Venezia) 1962, p. 438 ff.; idem, *I "rodoli di vero"*, ibidem,p. 688 ff.; idem, *Cronologia vetraria veneziana e muranese dal 1286 al 1301*,

vention coincides with the first references to the import of the excellent Syrian alkali ashes which formed the basic raw material of the Murano glass industry.[76]

In discussing the impact of the introduction of new raw materials on the progress of technology in medieval Europe, it is important to emphasize once more the great difference between conditions of industrial production in Western Europe and in the Near East in this period. Although the Near Easterners imported high quality raw material from far-away regions, such as saffron from Southern Europe, which was used for dyeing, oxide of copper and others, these were small shipments of very expensive articles. The importing of large quantities of other basic raw materials was unthinkable under the economic and social conditions of the late medieval Levant.

III

As well as the migration of skilled craftsmen and the use of new raw materials, the economic policy of the State in the later Middle Ages was another decisive factor in technological and industrial progress. Whereas in the modern period entrepreneurship probably played the greatest role in modernising industry, it was princes and governments of comunes who in the Middle Ages held the key to industrial development. This has already been argued by other historians, but requires fuller documentation.

There were numerous good reasons for princes and city governments to foster technological and industrial progress. Princes wanted to immortalize their names by erecting famous buildings, which gave a strong impetus to technology. Architects had

"Riv. Staz. sper. del vetro" III (1973), p. 66, 120. But according to F.M. Feldhaus this invention was made in Germany, see his *Die Technik der Antike und des Mittelalters*, p. 305.

[76] E. Ashtor-G. Cevidalli, *Levantine alkali ashes and European industries*, JEEH 12 (1983), pp. 487-90.

to improve methods and engineers invented new instruments while it was also necessary to ensure sufficient supply of the commodities needed by the subjects and to supply work. Full employment of the population was at the top of the agenda of medieval rulers just as it is today. But although other political reasons, such as conflicts with other countries, also induced princes to foster industrial enterprises, the strongest incentive came from the desire to increase stocks of money by increasing exports and to reducing imports. This was probably the major consideration for the rulers.

Sometimes different objectives were combined, such as improving economic conditions and achieving fame. This was surely true of Francesco Sforza, the ruler of Milan (1450-66), who embarked on great hydraulic projects to control the level of the river Po and open navigable waterways for his capital. In the years 1457-60 the Martesana canal, connecting Milan with Lake Como, was constructed and then another canal, leading from Milan to Pavia. Important innovations accompanied the construction of these canals, such as locks with moveable gates.[77] But the Montefeltro rulers of Urbino had different motives. They were primarily interested in military engineering and their team of splendid technicians and architects scored great achievements in the building of fortifications and palaces, which also led to important inventions in hydraulics and mechanics.[78]

The patronage of engineers and architects was typical of the Renaissance princes who were imbued with the ideas of humanism, while the measures taken by other princes and communal governments show the growing influence of mercantilist ideas. Princes and townships sought to protect local products from foreign competition either by imposing or increasing import duties or by forbidding the imports altogether. They also attempted to increase the supply of raw materials and to im-

[77] B. Gille, (in) M. Daumas, *A history of technology & invention* II, p. 27.
[78] *Op. cit.*, p. 27 f.

prove their quality, while measures were taken to encourage import of capital and to inhibit export, and new industries were fostered by inviting foreign skilled workers and entrepreneurs. The strict supervision of industrial production was another aspect of this new departure.

There is ample evidence of the ways in which princes and cities in the late Middle Ages attempted to foster technological progress. As textile manufacturing was the most important sector of medieval industry, the measures taken by different governments were aimed principally at its promotion.

The German kings of the Luxemburg dynasty took a number of steps to strengthen the trade and industry of their countries. Sigismund, King of Germany and Hungary (and later Emperor) founded a privileged cotton industry in Košice [Eastern Slovakia] in 1411.[79] Louis XI of France, who systematically pursued a mercantilist policy, introduced the silk industry in his country by employing Italian specialists.[80] The Angevins of Naples made efforts to develop a woollen industry which could compete with those of other countries. Charles I of Naples gave orders to import sheep from North Africa in order to provide the workshops with better wool.[81] His son and successor Charles II made agreements with the Umiliati and Florentine industrialists to establish workshops in Naples.[82] Then King Robert brought Florentine industrialists to Naples to establish the manufacture of woollens.[83] In 1327 the town council of Na-

[79] W. von Stromer, *Die Gründung der Baumwollindustrie in Mitteleuropa*, p. 92.

[80] Gandilhon, *Politique économique de Louis XI*, p. 176 ff.

[81] C. Minieri Riccio, *Nuovi studi riguardanti la dominazione angioina nel regno di Sicilia* (Naples 1876), p. 14.

[82] G. de Blasiis, *La dimora di Giovanni Boccaccio a Napoli*, "Arch. Stor. per le prov. nap." 17 (1892), p. 97; see also Cerone, "Arch. Stor. Nap." 27, p. 492 f.; G. Yver, *Le commerce et les marchands dan l'Italie méridionale au XIIIe & au XIVe siècle* (Paris 1903), p. 86 f.; G. Coniglio, *L'arte della lana a Napoli*, "Samnium" 21 (1948), p. 62.

[83] M. Camera, *Annali delle due Sicilie*, II (Naples 1860), p. 215; N.F. Faraglia, *Storia dei prezzi in Napoli dal 1131 al 1860* (Naples 1878), p. 95; Yver, *op. cit.*, p. 88

ples granted facilities to a Florentine for industrial activities.[84] In the second half of the XVth century King Ferrante of Naples made further efforts to foster the textile industry of his country. In 1465 he forbade the import of foreign cloth and in 1480 he granted privileges for establishing workshops in Naples to Spanish, Florentine, Bolognese and Milanese industrialists.[85] Like his father before him, he also invited silk production experts to Naples.[86] Even the Aragonese kings of Sicily tried to develop the production of high quality cloth in their country. In 1309 a contract was made with the Umiliati to establish a workshop in Palermo[87] and in 1322 another attempt was made, this time by the town council of Palermo.[88] The governments of the Renaissance period not only invited foreign industrialists to settle in their territories, but also took measures to raise the technological level of production. For instance fulling the cloth by the feet was forbidden.[89]

So far we have quoted measures taken by powerful kings to foster industrial progress, but princes of lower rank and small communes did the same. The measures taken by these rulers and lawgivers referred expressly to technological innovations.

The statutes of the silk guild of Florence contained the stipulation that foreign inventors be encouraged to settle in the

f.; R. CAGGESE, *Roberto d'Angiò e i suoi tempi* (Florence 1922), I, p. 531; CONIGLIO, *art. cit.*, p. 62 f.

84 CAMERA, *op. cit.*, p. 332.

85 FARAGLIA, *op. cit.*, p. 99; CONIGLIO, *art. cit.*, p. 64 f.

86 G. TESCIONE, *L'arte della seta a Napoli e la colonia di S. Leucio* (Naples 1932), p. 16 ff.; about an agreement of the duke of Salerno with Sienese clothmakers to establish a woollen industry in Amalfi see M. AYMARD, *Commerce et consommation des draps en Sicile et en Italie méridionale*, IIª Settimana di studio, Istituto Fr. Datini (Florence 1976), p. 137 f.

87 G. GIULINI, *Memorie spettanti alla storia, al governo ed alla descrizione della città e della campagna di Milano ne' secoli bassi* (Milan 1760), VIII, p. 585; cf. Sac. I. CARINI, *Le pergamene cremonesi nel Grande Archivio di Palermo*, "Archivio Storico Siciliano", n.s. II (1877), p. 227 f.; C. TRASSELLI, *Tessuti di lana siciliani a Palermo nel XIV secolo*, "Economia e Storia", III (1956), p. 304 f.

88 G. PIPITONE-FEDERICO, *Di un lanificio palermitano della prima metà del secolo XIV*, "Arch. Stor. Sic.", n.s. 37 (1913), p. 303 ff.

89 FANO, *Ricerche*, p. 196.

town.[90] Specialists of other crafts were also invited to come to Florence.[91] Venice granted facilities such as housing and workshops to those who came to found workshops in its territory.[92] Foreign shipbuilders who claimed to have invented new schemes were encouraged to settle in Venice.[93] The rulers of Verona, the Scaligeri family, made great efforts to encourage foreign textile workers to settle on their territory.[94] Even small towns such as Udine tried to develop a cloth industry in the XIVth century by encouraging foreign workers to settle amidst their subjects.[95] In Germany too some city councils attempted to establish textile industries by engaging foreign weavers. The councils of Munich, Speyer and Dinkelsbühl made agreements to this effect at the beginning of the XVth century.[96]

The granting of privileges to entrepreneurs was only one of the measures taken by different governments to foster industrial progress. Some governments placed machinery at the disposal of industrialists which guaranteed the high quality of products. In the year 1332, for example, it was decided in Venice to grant a plot of land and a loan for the construction of a windmill to Bartolomeo Verdi.[97] In 1375 the senate of Venice allowed 1000 ducats for the construction of a fulling mill in order to promote the woollen industry.[98] The Carrara rulers of Padua, too, constructed fulling mills for the town's cloth industry.[99] In Germany some townships took similar measures, and the town

[90] Doren, *op. cit.* II, p. 542 f.

[91] G. Gaye, *Carteggio inedito d'artisti dei secoli XIV, XV, XVI* (Florence 1839-49) I, p. 547.

[92] *Le deliberazioni del Maggior Consiglio di Venezia* (Bologna 1931-50), II, p. 62.

[93] ASV, Senato Misti 60, f. 17.

[94] Rossini-Mazzaoui, *Societa e tecnica nel medioevo*, p. 606 f.

[95] A. di Prampero, *Il dazio dei panni e l'arte della lana in Udine dal 1324 al 1368* (Udine 1881), p. 25 f., 27 ff.

[96] W. von Stromer, *Die Gründung der Baumwollindustrie in Mitteleuropa*, p. 95, 96, 98 f.

[97] G. Zanetti, *Dell'origine di alcune arti principali appresso i Veneziani* (Venice 1758), p. 74.

[98] ASV Senato Misti 34, f. 140b.

[99] R. Cessi, *Le corporazioni dei mercanti di panni e della lana in Padova*, p. 46.

council of Breslau, for instance, built a bleachery for the linen industry in 1359.[100]

The policy of promoting technological and industrial progress was by no means restricted to the textile industry. With the development of the new rag paper industry and later the art of printing in several advanced countries, further government measures were taken to promote these initiatives. Venice, for instance, forbade the export of rags in 1373, so that the papermakers would not suffer a shortage of raw material.[101] The importance of the new art of printing also quickly aroused the interest of farsighted governments, and Charles VII of France sent a gifted technician, Nicolaus Jenson of Sommevoire (near Troyes), to Mainz in 1458 to learn the secrets of printing so that he could later open a printing press in his own country.[102]

IV

In the XVth century the promotion of technological and industrial progress had become an integral part of the economic policy of the more advanced countries of Western and Southern Europe. It even had a distinctive term: *pro introducenda arte*. In the course of time the tendency of innovative governments to draw foreign technicians and industrialists to their countries, resulted in the granting of monopolies and patents. This was however a gradual development. Before the great step of fostering technological innovation was taken, the perception that inventors and innovators ought to enjoy certain privileges evolved slowly.

When the Venetian authorities granted permission to an entrepreneur in 1281 to build a windmill, he received no special

[100] H. Aubin, *Die Anfänge der grossen schlesischen Leinenweberei u.-handlung*, "VSWG" 35 (1942), p. 120.

[101] H.F. Brown, *The Venetian printing press, 1469-1800*, p. 24.

[102] *Op. cit.*, p. 11.

rights.[103] But in 1323 a German engineer proposed to the Venetian government the construction of mills which would be sufficient for all the needs of the town and the Great Council agreed to pay the expenses.[104] In the year 1378 Giacomo da Albertin and Giuliano Sacchetto who proposed the building of windmills, were granted loans and the property of the plot of land where they were located.[105] Several licences for the use of dredging engines, so important for the town of the lagoons, were conceded by the Venetian authorities in the XIVth century and at the beginning of the XVth century with no special rights. Working tools were given to some of the technicians or housing facilities and tax exemption were granted to them.[106] The privileges granted in Bologna in 1341 to the son of Borghegnano for the use of a twisting mill for silk cannot be considered as a patent.[107] These technicians did not claim inventors' rights or monopolies. However, in the year 1416 an engineer from Rhodes obtained a monopoly for a new kind of fulling mill in Venice, which is probably the first case of a patent granted to an inventor.[108] Five years later Filippo Brunelleschi, the architect who built the dome of Florence, received a monopoly for three years of transportation on the river Arno by a vehicle invented by him.[109] However, in the first half of the XVth century the granting of patents and monopolies was still the exception rather than the rule. But the governments of some Italian towns readily granted privileges to foreign technicians and industrialists *pro*

[103] *Deliberazioni del Magg. Consiglio*, II, p. 170.

[104] H. Simonsfeld, *Der Fondaco dei Tedeschi in Venedig und die deutsch-venezianischen Handelsbeziehungen* (Stuttgart 1887), II, p. 292.

[105] B. Cecchetti, *La vita de' Veneziani nel 1300* (Venice 1885), II, p. 58 f.

[106] *Op. cit.* I, p. 58, 61 f.

[107] W. Endrei-W. von Stromer, *Textiltechnische und hydraulische Erfindungen und ihre Innovatoren in Mitteleuropa im 14./15. Jahrhundert*, "Technikgeschichte" 41 (1974), p. 45. Already in 1236 Bonafusio de S.ta Columbia had obtained a licence for the production of new kinds of cloth in Bordeaux, see Mandich, *Privilegi*, p. 29.

[108] G. Mandich, *Primi riconoscimenti veneziani di un diritto di privativa agli inventori*, "Riv. di diritto industriale" VII (1958), p. 114.

[109] G. Gaye, *Carteggio*, p. 547 ff.

arte introducenda, for instance that of Milan in 1442 to a Florentine for the establishment of a silk industry [110] and that of Ferrara in 1446 to a Venetian for running a workshop of gold leaf. In the year 1462 a monopoly for silk production was granted in Ferrara for five years.[111]

In the middle of the XVth century a change in the character of these concessions occurred. In the year 1442 a Frenchman, Antoine Marin, proposed the construction of 24 mills which were not operated by waterpower to the government of Venice. He asked for a patent for 20 years and exemption from taxes. His offer was accepted.[112] Then in 1446 he obtained a privilege for his dredging machines in Venice.[113] Later in 1456 the same Frenchman, together with a fellow-countryman and a Venetian, obtained from Frederick III, archduke of Styria, a monopoly for the production of bricks of lime and the construction of mills and water canals. The concession was valid for 25 years and was to be passed on to their heirs and partners.[114]

The Venetian authorities granted several privileges in that period: in 1450 a privilege for building mills that was valid for 60 years, in 1460 a patent for dyeing engines and another for a machine which would raise water to be used by mills, and in 1469 a patent was granted to the German printer Johann of Speyer. In the year 1471 a gunmaker obtained a patent for 15 years and in 1472 once more a patent for building mills was issued.[115] The time was ripe for a formal law of patents. In 1474 Venice promulgated such a law, a hundred and fifty years before the English Statute of Monopolies. The Venetian Senate had in

110 G. Mandich, *Privilegi per novità industriali a Venezia*, p. 29.

111 L.N. Cittadella, *Notizie relative a Ferrara* (Ferrara 1864), p. 479 ff., 502.

112 Mandich, *Primi riconoscimenti*, p. 117.

113 G. Casoni, in *Venezia e le sue lagune*, ed. G. Correr, I, part 2 (Venice 1847), p. 218.

114 E. Birk, *Urkunden-Auszüge zur Geschichte Kaiser Friedrich des Dritten in den Jahren 1452-1467*, "Archiv f. Kunde Österr. Geschichts-Quellen" X (Vienna 1853), p. 196.

115 Mandich, *Primi riconoscimenti*, p. 121 f., 128 f., 130, 132.

fact previously, in 1453, passed a resolution to promote invention, but this was decision in principle.[116] The law of 1474 was the first patent law, and a major step in the encouragement of technological innovation.

The Senate of Venice decided that inventors should be granted exclusive rights for their innovations for ten years, and they threatened those who imitated them with a heavy fine and the destruction of the equipment. The inventors were also entitled to cede their rights to whomever they wished, but the Venetian government retained the right to use the invention.[117] A historian of jurisprudence who made a thorough study of the development of the patent law, concluded that the Venetian law of 1474 aimed only at the protection of the inventor's right and did not seek to create any monopoly,[118] but G. Mandich maintained that the law had both purposes [119] and he was right. A study of the patents quoted in the registers of the Venetian Senate (*Senato Terra*) shows clearly that such distinctions were not made. It has also been claimed that the law was passed on the occasion of the decision to build a big new dockyard [120] and that its main purpose was to foster the invention of new hydraulic and mechanic engines necessary in the complicated conditions of the lagoon.[121] This is questionable and the Venetian Senate did not have to reckon with any strong opposition from the craft guilds. Indeed, their relative weakness made the passing of the law possible.[122]

The patent law of Venice proved to be a complete success.

[116] MANDICH, *Privilegi per novità industriali*, p. 17.

[117] The text is printed in G. MANDICH, *Le privative industriali veneziane (1450-1550)*, "Rivista di diritto commerciale" 34 (1936), p. 518.

[118] M. SILBERSTEIN, *Erfindungsschutz und merkantilistische Gewerbeprivilegien* (Winterthur 1961), p. 18.

[119] MANDICH, *Le privative*, p. 519.

[120] SILBERSTEIN, *op. cit.*, p. 22 and see p. 32 for another hypothesis for the reason of passing the law.

[121] SILBERSTEIN, *op. cit.*, p. 27 and see also p. 29.

[122] Cf. *op. cit.*, p. 28.

The registers of the Venetian Senate contain a great number of patents granted at the end of the XVth century and in the first half of the XVIth century. Most of the patents were for the construction of water-mills and windmills or for water-pumps and dredging engines.[123] The great majority of the inventors or those who proposed the introduction into Venice of inventions made elsewhere were not Venetians. Some came from other provinces of Italy and others were German, Flemish or French.[124] The conditions stipulated by the Venetian authorities which granted the patents differed-especially with regard to their duration. But the incentive was the protection of the inventor's rights, and this was considerable. Capable technicians from many countries flocked to Venice, hoping to reap the benefits of their genius, so that Venice became a major centre of technological progress thanks to the wisdom of her law-givers.

In the last quarter of the XVth century technicians from many countries lived and worked in Venice and on its territory. The gunmakers in particular are often mentioned in the registers of the Senate because of the contracts signed with them. There were people from France,[125] Brabant,[126] Germany [127] and water engineers from France [128] and Germany.[129] When negotiating a contract of employment with a highly skilled technician the government stipulated that they would teach others.[130] The Venetian authorities also promoted experiments [131] and, as in

[123] See the statistics *op. cit.*, p. 27 and see also MANDICH, *Privilegi per novità industriali*, p. 34; R. BERVEGLIERI-C. PONI, *Three centuries of Venetian patents, 1474-1796*, paper presented at the symposium "Sources for the history of technology: national comparisons" (of the Int. Cooperation in history of technology committee) (Smolenice 1982). An appendix to Mandich, *Le privative*, comprises a synopsis of the patents granted from 1475 to 1549.

[124] MANDICH, *Privilegi per novità industriali*, l. c.

[125] Senato Terra XI, f. 131a; XIII, f. 60b.

[126] Ibid. VII, f. 186a.

[127] Ibid. IX, f. 59a.

[128] Ibid. XI, f. 86a.

[129] Ibid. XI, f. 110a; XII, f. 63a.

[130] Ibid. IV, f. 145b (this contract dates from the period preceding the patent law).

[131] Ibid. IV, f. 119b. (as 130).

earlier periods, took various measures to ensure that the high quality of industrial production, particularly of woollens, would not be impaired.[132]

The impact of the systematic encouragement of technological innovation by the Venetian government can be demonstrated by the role Venice played in the last quarter of the XVth century in the development of printing. From 1469 onwards a relatively large number of German printers came to Venice where they obtained patents for their art.[133] But Greek typographers also came to Venice and worked there.[134] The Venetian government granted all these printers monopolies for printing and selling certain books or for technical improvements and later also copyrights.[135]

V

Although very important for technological and industrial advance, economic policy was only one of the factors promoting it. In certain major commercial towns the great capitalists and entrepreneurs also played a decisive role in promoting technology. The enterprising merchants of Nuremberg developed the linen industry in Silesia, through the putting-out system. They drew up collective contracts with the guilds of different towns and granted the workers social security and advance payments.[136] The invention of the water driven wire-drawing bench was another case of technological advance obtained by the efforts of entrepreneurs. From 1390 mechanics of Nuremberg who produced metal wire engaged in experiments aimed at the invention of automatic machines. After 1401 they enjoyed the help of the town council and later of entrepreneurs. Sometime around the year 1410 the wire-drawing bench operated by water power was invented and thereafter metal wire became one of the famous ex-

[132] Ibid. X, f. 14a ff.; XI, f. 50a; see further XI, f. 30a ff.; cf. supra n. 89.

[133] H.F. Brown, *The Venetian Printing Press, 1469-1800*, p. 29 ff. 50 ff.; see also R. Fulin, *Documenti per servire alla storia della tipografia veneziana* (Venice 1882), (reprint from "Archivio Veneto" 23, 1882, p. 84 ff.), p. 19; C. Castellani, *La stampa in Venezia* (Venice, 1889), p. XXXIII ff. (list of printers in Venice).

[134] Brown, *op. cit.*, p. 44.

[136] H. Aubin, *Die Anfänge der grossen schlesischen Leinenweberei*, p. 144 ff.

ports of Nuremberg.[137] The foundation of the South German cotton industry was certainly connected with the economic war that raged between the markets of Upper Germany on the one side, and Milan and Venice, on the other. But those who founded the new factories were private entrepreneurs, again great merchants who used the putting-out system.[138] The birth of the new industry was to a great extent the outcome of capital accumulation in Upper Germany.[139]

Beside the entrepreneurship of capitalists, the craftsmen's and workers' guilds often played an important role in the foundation of new industries. In some minor centres of the new South German cotton industry, local weavers guilds had taken the initiative and production was organised according along existing patterns.[140]

That war and military needs create novelties is a truism. Herodotus begins his work with a statement to this effect. Technological innovations were not the least amongst them.

In the XVth century, the art of warfare was a major concern of engineers,[141] and in the treatises written by the engineers of that period technology and military art occupied a prominent place. It was certainly not by chance that the first modern treatise about technology to be printed was that of Roberto Valturio concerning military art.[142] The most important progress in military techniques in this period was the invention of moveable firearms. In the well known book by Kyeser (which dates from the last decade of the XIVth century) there is a depiction of a

[137] W. von Stromer, *Innovation u. Wachstum im Spätmittelalter: die Erfindung der Drahtmühle als Stimulator*, "Technikgeschichte" 44 (1977), p. 92 ff.; cf. O.H. Döhner, *Geschichte der Eisendrahtindustrie* (Berlin 1925), p. 26, 34, 40.

[138] W. von Stromer, *Die Gründung der Baumwollindustrie in Mitteleuropa*, p. 128 ff., 138 f.

[139] *Op. cit.*, p. 144.

[140] J. Kallbrunner, *Zur Geschichte der Barchentweberei in Österreich im 15. und 16. Jahrhundert*, "VSWG" 23 (1930), p. 76 ff., 80.

[141] B. Gille, (in) M. Daumas, *A History of Technology & Innovation*, II, p. 21, 16 ff.

[142] It was printed in 1472.

gun of this kind, but moveable firearms were mentioned earlier, although it was only in the XVth century that they came into general use.[143] But the first moveable firearms, the so-called arquebuses, were so heavy that they were not very practicable. During the Hussite wars much lighter muskets were invented and thereafter became the principal firearms.[144] In the same period military experts were very much preoccupied to improve the efficiency of bullets. New hollow bullets that were filled with powder which scattered the pieces on the bursting of the ball were devised and the bomb had come into being.[145] In the first half of the XVth century Jacopo Mariano of Siena invented the modern mine for the purpose of destroying fortresses.[146] A remarkable advance of military technology which involved major progress in metallurgy came with the increased use of cast iron. From the middle of the XIVth century, pieces of artillery and bullets made of cast iron were used everywhere in France and Germany.[147] At the beginning, cast iron was produced mainly for artillery. The techniques of the bronze founders were used first in an attempt to increase the liquidity of the metal by adding tin and antimony to it. Later the pig-iron of blast-furnaces was used which could be liquified more easily, and this also facilitated the development of iron bullets.[148] The techniques for casting iron, which were probably developed in the first half of the XIVth century in the Rhineland, marked a major step forward in the technological progress of the later Middle Ages.[149] For our purposes it is important to stress that at the be-

[143] B. Gille, *op. cit.*, p. 109.

[144] B. Rathgen, *Das Geschütz im Mittelalter*, p. 62 ff.

[145] B. Gille, *op. cit.*, p. 107.

[146] *Op. cit.*, p. 25.

[147] O. Johannsen, *Die Quellen zur Geschichte des Eisengusses im Mittelalter und in der neueren Zeit bis zum Jahre 1530*, (in) "Archiv f. die Geschichte der Naturwissenschaften u. der Technik" III (1911/12), p. 367.

[148] O. Johannsen, *Geschichte des Eisens*, 3rd ed. (Düsseldorf 1953), p. 203 f.

[149] Fr. Klemm, *A History of Western Technology* (Cambridge, Mass. 1964), p. 102.

ginning iron founderies were mainly engaged in the production of artillery pieces and it was only later, in the second half of the XVth century, that they acquired other and more peaceful purposes.[150] Military needs gave other technological innovations greater momentum. The crank-and-connecting-rod system was a major innovation of the later Middle Ages, for example, which appeared in the manuscript of Kyeser's treatise. Later a flywheel was used in order to overcome the difficulties posed by the fact that the device had two dead ends.[151]

* * *

The data we have drawn on relates mainly to two countries, Germany and Italy, but the often contradictory opinions which we have quoted show convincingly that it is impossible to explain technological and industrial progress in the pre-industrial period as the result of any single or principal factor. The impact of economic policy upon technological advance was very great, and the formidable effects of the *ṭarḥ* system (compulsory purchase of the products of State factories or its goods by the subjects) which was in vogue in the Moslem countries, is clear proof of this. But there were other factors which also played a great role. How many inventions were made by single persons who, seized by inspiration, conceived a new idea and how many innovations were made by chance! Man's mind cannot be given orders.

[150] Rathgen, *op. cit.*, p. 27 ff.; Johannsen, *Geschichte des Eisens*, p. 207.
[151] Gille, *op. cit.*, p. 42 ff.

IX

The Jews in the Mediterranean Trade in the Later Middle Ages

The paper should show that in the later Middle Ages the Jews of the Mediterranean countries did not live from money lending, as in Western and Central Europe, but engaged in maritime trade, as well as in crafts and other branches of trade.

Many documents in the archives of Catalonia disclose that the Jews of this country were, until the end of the fourteenth century, very active in the trade with the Maghreb, Sicily and the Levant. In that period the Jews of Marseilles too carried on seaborne trade, exporting wine, cloth and coral, mainly to the Maghreb. But they also invested in the Levant trade. From documents which have become known recently it appears that in the fifteenth century there were in Genoa Jews who took part in the maritime trade and that Jews travelled on Genoese ships. However, in the later Middle Ages the Sicilian Jews were apparently the most active in the sea trade. They traded with all Mediterranean countries. The Jews of Apulia and the Marches had close commercial connections with other regions of the Adriatic. It does seem that altogether the Jewish sea trade in the Western and central Mediterranean declined at the end of the Middle Ages. On the other hand, the Jews who lived in the Genoese and Venetian dominions in the eastern Mediterranean took a lively part in the sea trade. Jews living in Syria and in Egypt had transactions with the Italian merchants.

In the last centuries of the Middle Ages the Jewish communities in a number of western and central European countries lived almost exclusively from money lending. This phenomenon was the outcome of the pressure brought by the craft and merchant guilds, which used religious discrimination as a means to hit competitors. Even more, it was the result of the Church's prohibition of lending money at interest, an interdiction in opposition to the needs of broad strata of the Christian population. These are well-known facts, stated by most historians, but nevertheless the role of the Jews in the economic life had a tremendous impact upon the consciousness of Christian peoples. To this day, the Jew is often identified with the usurer. A certain school of historical analysis has even constructed a theory of Jewish history, maintaining that from the dawn of history the Jews had an inborn inclination to financial transactions

(*) We note with sadness that Professor Ashtor died on November 2, 1984. He had asked his colleague at the Hebrew University, Professor Benjamin Z. Kedar, to serve as his literary executor. We are grateful to Professor Kedar for reading proofs on this article. — ED.

and that later they therefore fulfilled the function of bankers in the preindustrial age and made an important contribution to the development of modern capitalism. According to this theory, when the capitalist order is replaced by a classless society, the Jewish people will no longer have a function and will vanish.[1] Fifty years ago, I contested these ideas in a booklet published in German[2] and I now come back to the subject, sincerely believing that the thesis of these authors is a gross falsification of Jewish history.

In fact, even in the later Middle Ages when the attitude of the Christian peoples towards the Jews was characterized by strong religious hostility and their position in the framework of the feudal-bourgeois society was weak, in a number of countries there were large Jewish communities that made their living mainly from crafts and trade. In the towns where the power of the craft guilds was not dominant, a broad stratum of the Jews were artisans, and in towns where international trade was not in the hands of a ruling oligarchy of merchants, the Jews also participated. In two papers published some years ago, I collected data that show clearly that in the later Middle Ages the Jews had a share in the sea-borne trade of the eastern Mediterranean[3] and in its central basin.[4] The present paper contains additional data, in large part referring to the Jewish trade in the western and central Mediterranean. They have been culled from various sources, mostly from the collections of notarial acts to be found in the archives of Spain and Italy. Presenting the data to the reader interested in the economic history of the Jews, one must of course emphasize that conclusions drawn from them as to the role of the Jewish merchants in the Mediterranean economies of that period will be to some degree conjectural. One would like to know, if the share of the Jews in the maritime trade increased or diminished during this period, in which region they were more active, and in which less active, and if they engaged in all branches of the international trade or if they carried on a peculiar "Jewish" trade. But the historian depends very much on his sources and, alas, so many archives of commercial towns have been destroyed in wars and otherwise, sometimes even purposely, as is the case of the rich archives of Naples burnt by the Germans in the second

(1) This is the thesis of O. Heller, *Der Untergang des Judentums* (Vienna 1931), the first systematic analysis of Jewish history from the viewpoint of historical materialism.

(2) E. Strauss (my former name), *Geht das Judentum unter?* (Vienna 1933).

(3) E. Ashtor, "New Data for the History of Levantine Jewries in the Fifteenth Century," *Bulletin of the Institute of Jewish Studies* (London) III (1975), pp. 67 ff.

(4) E. Ashtor, "The Jews in the Mediterranean Trade in the Fifteenth Century," (in) *Wirtschaftskräfte und Wirtschaftswege, Festschrift für H. Kellenbenz* (Nürnberg 1978) I, p. 441 ff. Both papers were republished (with some corrections) in my volume, *The Jews and the Mediterranean Economy, 10th–15th Centuries* (London 1983).

world war. So our picture may be blurred, because we must rely on the available data.

I

Until the end of the fourteenth century, the Catalan Jews were very active in the sea-borne trade. There can be no doubt that they held first place among Mediterranean Jews in the maritime trade, both as far as the number of merchants engaged in it is concerned and as to the capital invested. These facts are borne out by various sources.

The Jews of Barcelona carried on trade with other seaports of the Iberian peninsula. Notarial acts refer to commendas given to Jews of Barcelona by coreligionists for travels to Sevilla[5] and to investments made by Jews in the trade with Valencia, by commendas given to ship patrons.[6] But the enterprising Jewish merchants of Catalonia also engaged in trade with Sardinia and Sicily. Sardinia had been an Aragonese-Catalan dominion since 1324 and a branch of the Aragonese dynasty reigned in Sicily. A royal order of 1285 refers to a commercial journey of Abraham Mosse and Abraham Sachar to Sicily.[7] The commercial activities of the Catalan Jews in the exchanges with Sicily and Sardinia must have been intense. Some effaced and incomplete notarial deeds (obviously drafts) of the year 1385 bear evidence of commendas for a trip to Sardinia which Juceff, a Jew of Barcelona, received from coreligionists, Bonjuha Duran, Maimono and Beniuha Moses Dellel, the latter a silk trader.[8] The commendas were, at least partly, invested in saffron and woollen cloth, two typical Catalan export goods. Of course these Jews took a lively part in the close relations between Catalonia and the Maghrebin countries. From a deed drawn up in the year 1300 in Candia, one learns, for instance, that two Jews of Barcelona, Iosep Gavio and Isaac Ligon, received from Abraham Bono and Aymbrano Shulel, Jews of Majorca, a commenda for a trip to Cagliari and Tunis.[9] The acts of the Barcelonan notary Pere Marti, who had many Jewish clients, also contain a commenda contract, drawn up in 1381 between Isaac Catan and Beniuha Moses Dellel, the silk trader mentioned above, concerning

(5) AHPB (Archivo Histórico de Protocolos, Barcelona), Pere Marti, V, manual 1371–72, sub 17 Febr. 1372.

(6) Pere Marti, V, manual 20 June–17 Aug. 1373, sub 4 Aug. 1373.

(7) J. Régné, *History of the Jews in Aragon, Regesta and Documents*, ed. Y.T. Assis-A. Gruzman (Jerusalem 1987), no. 1382.

(8) Pere Marti, VIII, manual 15 Apr.–13 Aug. 1385, f. 124a, 134a, 134b f. The name of Dellel (obliterated in the MS) is completed according to another deed of the same notary (see below).

(9) *Pietro Pizolo, notario in Candia*, I, ed. S. Carbone (Venice 1978), no. 60.

a trip to Majorca and Tunis.[10] It is likely that the Catalan Jews also had close contacts with Jewish merchants of the Maghrebin commercial towns, for they too were much engaged in the exchanges between the countries of North Africa and the Iberian peninsula. Some orders of the king of Aragon and Catalonia that date from 1319, 1324, and 1325 testify to the commercial activities of Jews of Ceuta and Cherchel in his dominions.[11]

The Jewish traders of Catalonia also carried on a very lively trade in the eastern basin of the Mediterranean in that period, frequently traveling to all the countries on the coast. In 1316 Bonjuha Bonavia and Isaac Bonavia, both Jewish merchants of Barcelona, received commendas for journeys to "Romania", the name by which the occidential Christians called the territories formerly or still belonging to the Byzantine empire.[12] Some of them used the commercial towns of Crete as points of support, as indicated in several documents. In 1300, Salomon Serot, a Jew of Barcelona, received a certain quantity of wool in Candia, undertaking to carry it on a Genoese ship, from the port of Standea to Alexandria.[13] In the same year Isaac Gracian, another Jewish trader of Barcelona, received a loan in Candia and obliged himself to repay it within four months, or if a ship would arrive from Alexandria before this date to make the payment within the fifteen days after its arrival.[14] This undertaking obviously shows that he carried on trade with Egypt.

There is a great deal of information concerning the activities of the Jewish merchants of Catalonia in Egypt around 1300 and in the first quarter of the fourteenth century. An order of King Jaime II of 1302 refers to the Jews Bonsenyor, son of the late Astrug, Santo Desforn, and Mosse Thoros Gracian, all of Barcelona, who were accused of having behaved in a church in Alexandria in such a manner as to profane it.[15] This order bears evidence of the Jews having been in Egypt around the years 1300 certainly for business purposes. In 1302, the king who had made peace with the Holy See bowed to the papal prohibition of trade with the Mamluk dominions and promulgated a decree to this effect: nobody was to travel or send merchandise there.[16] This decree,

(10) Pere Marti, VIII, manual 21 June–3 Oct. 1381, f. 98a.

(11) Régné, no. 3110, 3284, 3330.

(12) AHPB, Pere de Torre, V, 2, f. 102a, 106a, 108b, 109b f., 110b.

(13) *Pizolo* I, no. 73. Standea, now called Dia, is an island opposite Candia (now called Heraklion).

(14) *Ibid.*, no. 101.

(15) Régné, no. 2781.

(16) M. Fernández de Navarrete, "Disertación histórica sobre la parte que tuvieron los españoles en las guerras de ultramar," *Memorias de la R. Academia de la historia* V (1817), p. 180 ff.

however, did not bring the commercial relations between Catalonia and Egypt to a standstill. Many Catalan merchants, among them Jews, continued their activities in Egypt, and they were fined by the king for whom these payments became a source of revenue. But his attitude towards trade with the Mamluk dominions was two-faced, for he engaged in it himself and sold permits for doing so to private merchants. Several embassies, which he sent to Egypt to make various claims concerning the interests of Christianity, were also commercial expeditions. When he sent Eymeric Dusay as ambassador to the sultan of Cairo in 1305, he allowed him to carry merchandise on the ship. In addition, nineteen merchants received permission to trade, of course for sizeable fees; and among them there were four Jews: Bernardo Sala, Astrugo Abamari, Gaujo, and the latter's son-in-law.[17]

The proceedings against the merchants who went on trading with Egypt despite the royal decree shed bright light on the intensity and the volume of the Jewish trade with the Moslem Levant. The proceedings are well documented. The correspondence of the king with the judicial authorities and his decisions contain many data concerning the travels of Jewish merchants and the fines they had to pay.

In the year 1305, a pardon was granted to the Jewish traders Juceff Besers of Villafranca and Astrug Biona of Barcelona, who had travelled several times to Alexandria, via Cagliari and other routes.[18] Isaac Vives of Barcelona must have been a very rich and enterprising merchant. The copious correspondence between the judicial authorities and the royal chancery in the year 1307, after the merchant's death, bears testimony to the importance attached to squeezing a sizeable sum from his heirs.[19] In 1313, the king granted pardon for transgression against his prohibition to the crew of the cog Santa Eulalia and to the Jewish merchants who had shipped merchandise on it to Egypt. They were Abraham Bisbe, Salomon Faquin, Maymon Abraham, and Benvenist Salomon, all of Barcelona. The fine was 18,500 shillings.[20] As the fines were usually levied according to the tariff of two shillings for merchandise of the value of one Barcelona pound, the commodities shipped on the Santa Eulalia were worth 9,250 pounds, according to the estimate of the royal authorities. So the four merchants engaged in rather large

(17) *Op. cit.*, p. 182. About the king's participation in this trade, see A. Masía de Ros, *La corona de Aragón y los estados del Norte de Africa* (Barcelona 1951), doc. no. 109.

(18) Régné, no. 2840.

(19) Masía de Ros, *op. cit.*, doc. no. 18, 22; Régné, no. 2878.

(20) Régné, no. 2983.

transactions.[21] The value of the commodities imported by the Jewish merchants, Salomon Bisbe and Salomon Jaffie, who in 1312 travelled on another ship to Alexandria, was estimated at 327 l and 10 sh.[22] A royal order of 1319, concerning the pardon granted to the heirs of the Jew Juceff Ferrer for his crimes is interesting for another reason: the king forgives, for a great sum, the crimes of the dead man, but with the exception of journeys he may have made to Egypt.[23] That means that in the first quarter of the fourteenth century Jewish merchants of Catalonia were a priori suspect of carrying on trade with Egypt. In fact, several names of other Jewish traders appear in the documents referring to the fines collected in that period from Catalan merchants who continued commercial exchanges with the dominions of the sultan of Cairo.[24]

The numerous documents testifying to the intense activities of the Catalan Jews in the maritime trade, and especially with the Levant, in the first quarter of the fourteenth century should not mislead us, however. Actually, the Jews had only a small part of the trade between Catalonia and the Levant. The royal orders referring to the fines collected in 1305–1325 contain no less than 163 names of merchants who went on trading with the dominions of the Mamluks despite the royal prohibition.[25] So the Jewish merchants were a small minority among them.

In the middle of the fourteenth century and then in the 1360's, Catalonia's Levant trade underwent a crisis owing to the strict embargo laid upon it by the Church and later by the effects of the attack on Alexandria in 1365 by King Peter I of Cyprus. But some documents show that when trade was taken up again, the Jewish merchants of Catalonia took part in it. In 1365, for instance, Samuel Calidis (or de Calides) and Ferrario Avengana, Jewish merchants of Barcelona, obtained a royal license to go to Alexandria, Damietta, and Beirut, but of course not permitting trade in the "forbidden articles" (iron, timber and pitch, considered as war materials).[26] The said Samuel Calidis was certainly a rich merchant, for one learns from a notarial act drawn up in

(21) On the value of the pound of Barcelona in that period, see Ch. E. Dufourcq, *L'Espagne catalane et le Maghreb aux XIIIe et XIVe siècles* (Paris, 1966), p. 529.

(22) Régné, no. 2975.

(23) Régné, no. 3104.

(24) See Fr. Giunta, *Aragonesi e Catalani nel Mediterraneo* (Palermo 1972–73) II, p. 126: J. David, T. and B. Juceff.

(25) Giunta l. c.

(26) M. Sáez Pomés, "Los aragoneses en la conquista saqueo de Alejandría por Pedro I de Chipre," (in) *Estudios de Edad Media de la Corona de Aragón* V (1952), p. 367.

Barcelona in 1381 that he sold to a merchant of Sant Feliu de Guixols 2 quintals and 6 pounds of coral of Alghero, which is a very considerable quantity.[27]

The general persecution of Spanish Jews in 1391 and especially the slaughter of the Jewry of Barcelona rang the death knell of their flourishing international trade. However, even in the fifteenth century they were not wholly excluded from the seaborne trade. Jews came by sea from Portugal to Catalonia and carried on trade, probably contacting the local Jewries.[28] Jewish merchants of Catalonia, such as Simon Vazquez of Barcelona, still travelled to Egypt in 1414.[29]

II

The attitude adopted by the two great commercial centers on the northern coast of the Tyrrhenian sea, Marseilles and Genoa, towards Jewish seaborne trade was not favorable. As in other great commercial towns of southern Europe the Christian merchants who ruled over these emporia were interested in eliminating the Jewish competition. However, there were different degrees of this policy. Some commercial centers did not allow the Jews to live in their territory at all, others restricted their activities more or less.

The policy of Marseilles towards the Jews was characteristic of this latter attitude. The Jews enjoyed the right of citizenship in Marseilles and had autonomy. When Charles I of Anjou became count of Provence in 1246, he adopted a very friendly attitude towards them, protecting them from vexations. The same is true for his successors of the Anjou dynasty.[30] Most Jews of Marseilles were craftsmen or petty merchants; those who engaged in seaborne trade encountered some difficulties. According to the statutes of the town, only four Jews could embark on a given ship and they could not travel to Alexandria at all on ships of Marseilles.[31] However, when the statutes were revised in 1253 (probably) the latter restriction was practically abolished.[32] Among the Jews of Marseilles there were indeed merchants who carried on maritime trade, mainly with other countries of the western Mediterranean.

(27) Pere Marti, VIII, manual 21 June–30 Oct. 1381, f. 84b.

(28) Cl. Carrère, *Barcelone, centre économique à l'époque des difficultés 1380–1462* (Paris 1967), p. 256.

(29) A. Boscolo, "La politica italiana di Fernando d'Aragona," (in) *Studi Sardi* 12–13 (1952–54), p. 93.

(30) G. Lesage, *Marseille angevine* (Paris 1950), p. 92 f.

(31) A. Crémieux, "Les juifs de Marseille au moyen âge," *REJ* 46 (1903), p. 28.

(32) *Histoire du commerce de Marseille I, moyen âge*, par R. Pernoud (Paris 1949), p. 166.

Several documents of the fourteenth century indicate that Jews exported coral to Barcelona.[33] They also exported wine to Catalonia.[34] The coral, which was worked in Marseilles to a great extent by Jewish craftsmen, came from Sardinia and consequently the Jews frequently travelled to the big island, so near Marseilles, to acquire the raw material. A part was paid in cash, but the Jews also marketed various kinds of cloth in Sardinia and could buy coral with its price.[35] In the middle of the thirteenth century, the Jews of Marseilles still engaged in a lively trade with the Maghrebin countries, especially with the great emporium that Bougie had become in that period.[36] Later their share in this sector of the Mediterranean trade decreased, and from the beginning of the fifteenth century they were virtually excluded from it.[37]

The share of the Jews of Marseilles in the trade with the Levant was insignificant. In the rich archives of Marseilles there are few references to a Jewish merchant travelling to a Levantine port. But probably such journeys were not yet exceptional in the second half of the thirteenth century. In 1278, Sauve, son of Davin, a Jew of Marseilles, travelled to Alexandria.[38] Later, at the end of the fourteenth century and at the beginning of the fifteenth century, the Jews of Marseilles participated in the Levant trade only by giving commendas. In the year 1385, for instance, Leon Passapayre gave a commenda to Philippe de Prads of Avignon who departed for Rhodes and Alexandria. The investment consisted of cloth of Perpignan, burel "of Albay", and linen of Constance — typical export goods of the Provençal Levant traders.[39] Leon Passapayre belonged to a group of rich Jewish merchants, rather distinct from the bulk of the Jewish commercial class of Marseilles. Studying the documents where the investments of the Jewish merchants of Marseilles in the sea trade are indicated, one becomes aware that these investments ranged mostly between 100 and 500 fl.; that is, rather modest outlays.[40] But Leon Passapayre, in 1383, could afford to give coral worth 880 fl. to two Christians departing for Alexandria.[41] Documents of the first years

(33) *Histoire du commerce de Marseille II*, par E. Baratier et F. Reynaud (Paris 1951), p. 92, 93.

(34) Baratier, *op. cit.*, p. 92, note 3.

(35) *Op. cit.*, p. 96.

(36) I. Loeb, "Les négociants juifs de Marseille au milieu du XIIIe siècle," *REJ* 16 (1888), p. 74 ff.

(37) Baratier, *op. cit.*, p. 93.

(38) L. Blancard, *Documents inédits sur le commerce de Marseille au moyen âge* (Marseilles 1884–85) II, no. 14.

(39) Baratier, *op. cit.*, p. 245, note 5.

(40) *Op. cit.*, p. 96.

(41) *Op. cit.*, p. 96, note 2.

of the fifteenth century show that he continued investing in the Levant trade. Other rich Jews of Marseilles who made investments in the Levant trade in the first decenny of the fifteenth century were Cregut Profach and Abramet de Bedarrides.[42] These rich Jewish traders also invested in the corsair activities, just as their Christian fellow citizens did, as indicated by a document of the year 1391.[43]

It seems that for a long period Genoa, the leading commercial town of the Tyrrhenian, did not allow Jews to live within its boundaries. But many documents leave no doubt that in the later Middle Ages the attitude of the Genoese toward the Jews became more flexible. One may assume that the prohibition against Jews living in Genoa was not abolished, but it is sure that Jews visited the town for commercial and perhaps other purposes and that some lived there permanently. Probably they were admitted de facto, not de jure. It was apparently a kind of infiltration, just as happened in Venice,[44] and not a few of these Jews engaged in the maritime trade.

The custom registers of Genoa of 1376–1377 contain a note to the effect that Joseph Judeus imported two pondi (a standard parcel) of pepper on the ship of Antonio Vignolo coming from Alexandria.[45] This is an isolated fact; but judging from the mention of Jews in the acts of the Genoese notaries of the fifteenth century, their presence in the town cannot have been a rare phenomenon. Through the fifteenth century Jews appear in notarial deeds as engaged in various commercial activities, in the trade of cloth and in pepper.[46] In a document of the year 1463 there appears Rabi Josef "collector drictorum et comerchi."[47] The fact that a Jew held this position would point to the Genoese Jews engaging in the Levant trade. In other deeds referring to the commercial activities of the Jews, their debts are indicated in Egyptian gold dinars.[48] A decree of 1492 is explicit as far as the engagement of Jews in the maritime trade is concerned: they are allowed to carry on trade of cloth, on condition that they pay all the custom dues.[49]

That Genoa was a port where Jews not infrequently carried on trade in the later Middle Ages is also borne out by documents referring to the

(42) *Op. cit.*, p. 96, note 3, 239.

(43) *Op. cit.*, p. 95, note 1.

(44) See my paper "Gli inizi della comunità ebraica a Venezia," *Rassegna Mensile di Israel* 44 (1978), p. 694 ff.

(45) J. Day, *Les douanes de Gênes 1376–1377* (Paris 1963), p. 357.

(46) G.G. Musso, "Documenti su Genova e gli ebrei tra il Quattro e il Cinquecento", *Rassegna Mensile di Israel* 36 (1970), p. 428.

(47) *Art. cit.*, *l. c.*

(48) *Art. cit.*, *l. c.*

(49) *Art. cit.*, p. 431.

commercial activities of Jews of other countries. For not only did the Jews of Genoa use its port facilities, but those of other towns of the western and central Mediterranean did so likewise.

In 1287, Samneto, a Jewish money changer of Messina, made a loan to Marchisio Spatario, a fellow-citizen, who obliged himself to repay it in Genoa where he was about to go.[50] Obviously the Jew of Messina had business connections with Genoa. The Jewish merchants of Marseilles, too, had such connections with Genoa. They exported coral to Genoa and gave commendas to travellers departing for the latter town. This is shown by several documents of the fourteenth century.[51] The Jews of Sicily also carried on trade in Genoa. Bracone (i.e. Barhūn), a Jew of Mazzara who engaged in trade in Genoa, appears in a notarial act drawn up in Trapani in 1416.[52]

From the fact that Jews were transported in Genoese ships, one may also conclude that the attitude of the Genoese toward the Jews in the later Middle Ages was more flexible (without being friendly, at least as far as the metropolis itself was concerned). The fact that Genoese ship patrons accepted Jews as passengers of course was of great importance for their commercial activities. Not a few carried merchandise with them. A deed drawn up by a Venetian notary in Candia in 1300 indicates that merchandise was transported by a Jewish trader from Candia to Alexandria on a Genoese ship.[53] In 1481 Meshullām di Volterra went from Italy to Egypt on a Genoese ship. A Flemish traveller (himself of Genoese origin) who embarked in Tunis in 1470 on a Genoese ship sailing to Alexandria recounts that it carried Jewish passengers.[54] Certainly they were Jewish merchants of the Maghreb who were travelling to Egypt on business.

Dealing with the seaborne trade of the Jews in the Tyrrhenian one should not overlook the Jews of Sardinia and Naples. In the middle of the fifteenth century, some Jews of Cagliari and Alghero carried on trade with Barcelona. For in the registers of the insurance contracts to be found in the archives of Barcelona, their names appear as those who had insured their shipments of cloth.[55] It is impossible to estimate the

(50) R. Zeno, *Documenti per la storia del diritto marittimo nei secoli XIII e XIV* (Turin 1936), no. 1.

(51) Baratier, *op. cit.*, p. 94, note 2, 95.

(52) C. Trasselli, "Frumento e panni inglesi nella Sicilia del XV secolo," (in his volume) *Mediterraneo e Sicilia all'inizio dell'epoca moderna* (Cosenza 1977),p. 318.

(53) See above, note 13.

(54) *Massa' Meshullam Mivolterra*, ed. A. Yaari (Jerusalem 1949), p. 3. *Itinéraire d'Anselme d'Adorno en Terre Sainte (1470–1471)*, ed. J. Heers-G. de Groer (Paris 1978), p. 140.

(55) Carrère, *op. cit.*, p. 615.

share of the Jews of Naples in maritime trade. The almost total destruction of the archives of Naples is an irreparable loss. But documents found in the archives of other commercial towns referring to the maritime trade of the Jews show at least that Jews often came to Naples with their merchandise. From a deed in the Bouches-du-Rhône archives, one learns that in 1391 four Jewish merchants, Astrug of Aix, Calb of Arles, Jacques de Grasse and Salomon de Digne, chartered a ship of Marseilles to carry their merchandise to Naples. They themselves sailed on the ship.[56] A document of the year 1477 refers to the import of coral to Naples by a Jewish merchant. The merchant, called Isaac, obtained exemption from the custom dues for the coral, which was imported from Trapani and was destined for the fair of Lanciano (in the Abruzzi).[57]

III

In the later Middle Ages among the Jews of the western and central Mediterranean, those of Sicily were probably the most active in the maritime trade. Their number was relatively large, perhaps 30–35,000, and the royal authorities did not put obstacles in the way of their commercial activities. On the other hand, the island was a crossroads for the Mediterranean trade, connecting the network of commercial relations in the western basin with that of the eastern, and the commercial towns of the North African coast with the emporia of Southern Europe. Certainly, the bulk of Sicily's international trade was in the hands of the Catalans, but Sicilian merchants, and among them many Jews, were also involved.

The Jews of the commercial towns of eastern Sicily carried on a lively trade with all the countries of the eastern Mediterranean as well as with the Adriatic coasts. Two documents of the year 1308 refer to the bequest of Juda Leonus Turtovidi, a Jew of Syracuse who died in Zara. Upon the request of his heirs the king of Sicily intervened with the government of Venice (then ruling over Zara) and the latter gave orders to the local authorities. From these orders we learn that the merchandise the Jewish merchant had left in Zara consisted of such spices as pepper, which suggests that he imported Levantine commodities in Dalmatia.[58] Around

(56) Baratier, *op. cit.*, p. 94, note 2.

(57) G. Tescione, *Italiani alla pesca del corallo ed egemonie marittime nel Mediterraneo*, 2nd ed. (Naples 1968), p. 172. About the fair of Lanciano see A. Grohmann, *Le fiere del regno di Napoli in età aragonese* (Naples 1969), pp. 88 ff.

(58) M. Lattes, "Di un mercantante ebreo siracusano," *Archivio Veneto* VI (1873), pp. 322 ff.; one of the documents had been printed before by S. Ljubić, *Monumenta spectantia historiam Slavorum meridionalium* I, p. 235.

1300, Jewish traders of Sicily engaged in commercial activities in Cyprus. Some deeds of a Genoese notary, who exercised his profession in Famagusta at the turn of the century, refer to them. In September, 1300, Raffaele "of Palermo", a Jewish merchant, appointed his son Macalufo (i.e. Makhlūf) his plenipotentiary to collect from five Jews of Crete the sum he had spent for their ransom. The said Cretan Jews undertook to make the payment in Candia.[59] Then on September 11, 1301, Musa de Guao of Messina appointed Giacomo, son of Bonavita of Messina, his attorney to collect his share from the 700 "white besants", the price of some Jewish slaves (probably captives), sold to the same Raffaele of Palermo by three Genoese.[60] The role of Raffaele of Palermo is not clear. He may have engaged in the ransoming of Jewish captives, but Musa de Guao was certainly a slave dealer. Another Jewish merchant of Messina who carried on trade in Acre in the last quarter of the thirteenth century was Menaḥem al-Masînî. A Judaeo-Arabic letter written in 1276 mentions a payment he had made to an Egyptian Jew, Abu 'l-ᶜAlā Ibn Hilāl al Bannā.[61] To what extent the Jews of Sicily engaged in the Levant trade in that period can be understood from a rather singular decree of King Pedro of Aragon, issued soon after he occupied Sicily. On March 1, 1283, the king ordered the authorities of the port of Syracuse to allow a Genoese to export cheese, wool, honey and other commodities to Alexandria on his ship. But neither Sicilians, except Jews, nor Catalans or Aragonese were to embark on the vessel.[62] The reason for the decree may have been that the king wanted to impede contacts between Sicilians and Catalans with his enemy Charles I of Anjou, whereas he could not make impossible such relations between the Genoese and the French king. But it is more probable that his intention was to avoid the capture of his Sicilian or Catalan subjects by the Provençals. If the interpretation of the king's decree given in the second place is correct, one might assume that the king believed that Jews would not be considered by the corsairs of Charles I of Anjou as his enemies. Whatever the case may have been, the clause concerning the Jews is evidence of their engagement in the maritime trade, or very possibly, the trade with the Levant.

The collections of acts of the Sicilian notaries that have come down to us from the thirteenth and the fourteenth centuries are very few,

(59) *Atti rogati a Cipro da Lamberto di Sambuceto*, ed. V. Polonio (Genoa 1982), no 13, 14.

(60) *Op. cit.*, no. 94.

(61) E. Ashtor-Strauss. *History of the Jews in Egypt and in Syria Under the Mamluks* (in Hebrew) (Jerusalem 1944–1970) III, no. 27.

(62) *De rebus regni Siciliae*, no. 591.

whereas those of the fifteenth century are numerous and contain plenty of data concerning the activities of the Jews in maritime trade. These data are complemented by those found in other sources. Those quoted here are only examples.

Of course the Jewish merchants living in various towns and townlets of Sicily carried on trade among the numerous ports of the island. In the year 1444, for instance, Juda de Vita (i.e. Y'huda b. Ḥayyim) chartered a small ship (of Marsala) for the transport of wheat from Mazzara to Palermo.[63] The Jews also engaged in the export of wheat and other agricultural products of Sicily. The registers of the maestro portulano, who collected fees for permits to export the agricultural products, contain data referring to the activities of the Jews in this sector of maritime trade. In the registers of the year 1408, one finds the names of two Jews of Trapani, Saya Iuda and Sabbei Chujnu, and that of Josip Cuscara of Marsala, all of whom exported wheat.[64]

The Sicilian Jews also had a share in the intense commercial exchanges between the island and the Italian mainland. A deed of the late fourteenth century refers to nine quintals of Sicilian wool, part of a commenda, carried by a Jew to Pisa in 1392, on a ship of Trapani.[65] In the year 1439, Jacob, "de Acri", a Jew of Agrigento, had leased a ship in order to transport cheese to Gaeta. When the ship patron did not depart from Trapani, Jacob "de Acri" lodged a protest against him.[66] A third deed referring to the Jews' trade with the Italian mainland dates from the year 1443. It deals with a commenda that Nissim Lupresti (Cohen) had received from three merchants, one Christian and two Jews, Musa Isaac and Brachone Lupresti, for a journey to Naples.[67] A deed of 1452 refers to the charter of a ship by two merchants of Palermo, Josip de Manichio and Musa of Syracuse (that is a Jew of Syracuse but living in Palermo), for the transport of a great quantity of merchandise to Talamone or Porto Pisano.[68] In the fifteenth century, the Jewish merchants of Sicily also engaged in the trade with the Levant. In 1453, Benedictus (Mevōrakh) Ajeni of Palermo acknowledged the receipt of a certain sum due to him from a merchant of Alexandria. He had received it from the latter's attorney.[69] As Alexandrian merchants, even Italian and

(63) ASTrap (*Archivio di Stato, Trapani*), Francesco Milo 8626, f. 82a.

(64) ASPal (*Archivio di Stato, Palermo*), Maestro Portulano 95, c. 141, 152, 154.

(65) C. Trasselli, "Tessuti di lana siciliani a Palermo nel XIV secolo," *Economia e Storia 3* (1956), p. 305.

(66) ASTrap, Giacomo Miciletto 8588, f. 102a.

(67) Franc. Milo 8625, f. 47a f.

(68) ASPal, Giacomo Comito 848, sub 11 Aug. 1452.

(69) ASPal, Antonino Aprea 811, f. 174b.

Catalan, residing in Alexandria, rarely visited Palermo, one may consider this document as an indication that the Palermitan Jew himself carried on trade in Egypt.

All these data show that the Jewish merchants of Sicily were very active in the sea-borne trade at the end of the Middle Ages. They also strongly emphasize the fact that almost all of these sea traders were not very rich. They belonged to the middle class of the commercial hierarchy.

The Jews of Sicily had close contacts with the Jewry of Malta, and Jewish merchants of Syracuse especially carried on trade with the small island. Jewish merchants of Malta came to the Sicilian ports. But the Jews of Malta also engaged in trade with the North African coast. A deed drawn up in Ragusa (Dubrovnik in Dalmatia) in the year 1382 refers to a quantity of cotton handed over by a Jew of Malta to Milos Gugnević for the latter to transport to Tripoli (in Lybia). There he gave the merchandise to a Jew for whom it was intended, but he could not bring to the Maltese Jew the merchandise, olive oil and sturgeon, due him as the price of the cotton.[70]

IV

In the later Middle Ages there were still many merchants, some of them engaged in maritime trade, in the Jewish communities of Apulia. The royal authorities, both those of the Angevin kings of Naples and their Aragonese successors, did not hinder them, while the Venetians, who were in control of the international trade of the region, often had recourse to their services as agents.

The commercial relations of the towns of the Adriatic coast of Italy with those of Dalmatia, and especially Ragusa, were intense, and the Jewish merchants took part in these exchanges. They travelled to Ragusa and engaged in commercial activities there. In 1431, for instance, Bonaventura Leonis (Meshullam b. Yehuda), a Jew of Trani sojourning in Ragusa, stood surety for the Catalan Johan Ferrer, living in the same town, who received a commenda of coral for a trip to Syria and Egypt.[71] The Jewish merchants of Apulia also carried on trade with Venice. They imported into Venice saltpeter, a raw material for the production of gunpowder badly needed by the Venetians; and therefore a special status was granted them by the Serenissima, otherwise rather antagonistic to Jewish merchants coming to the metropolis. When the

(70) B. Krekić, *Dubrovnik (Raguse) et le Levant au moyen âge* (Paris 1961) no. 361.
(71) Krekić, *op. cit.*, no. 790.

Jews were expelled from Venice and it was then decided (in 1402) that they could come to the town only after having been absent four months, the senate decreed in 1408 that this decision should not be applied to the Jews of Romagna, the Marches, the Abruzzi and Apulia.[72] The visits of Apulian Jewish merchants to Venice must have been not infrequent. In the year 1436, for instance, David son of the late Elijah, a Jew from Otranto and living in Conversano (south of Bari) obligated himself to pay a debt to Andrea Mocenigo in Venice as soon as the ship of Ieronimo Lio arrived in Brindisi or S. Cataldo. He gave, among others, cloth of Mantua as guarantee.[73]

The Jewish merchants of the Marches, which in that period had a considerable number of thriving communities, took part in the seaborne trade. However, one should distinguish between those of Ancona, the capital of the Marches, and those of the other towns. Like Genoa and Venice, Ancona apparently excluded the Jews from the maritime trade. This attitude toward the Jewish merchants seems to have been shared by the leading commercial towns that were independent republics. Or, in other words, there the urban bourgeoisie could implement their wishes to eliminate the Jewish competition. If that had not been the case, the relatively rich documentation of the Jewish presence in fifteenth century Ancona would contain deeds bearing evidence of the Jews' engagement in the sea trade. In fact, one rarely finds hints of it. However, the exclusion of the Jews from the international trade must not have been total. A deed of the year 1451 refers to a sea loan given by Sulam Signoretti, a Jew of Ancona, to Jacobus Pasquale, who travelled to Alexandria on the ship of the Genoese Leonardo Doria. Sulam Signoretti was a rich Jew, whose activities as a banker are known from many documents, but the sum he invested in the expedition to Egypt was rather small — 12 ducats.[74] Another notarial act, which has the date 1462, contains the charter of two ships of Jacobus Petrucci by Salomone Ventura, a Jewish merchant of Chieti (a town south of Pescara) for the transport of wheat and olive oil from Ancona to some other ports of the Adriatic.[75]

(72) E. Ashtor, *Gli inizi della comunità ebraica e Venezia*, pp. 692 f.

(73) ASV (Archivio di Stato, Venezia), Cancelleria inferiore, notai, Ba 213, Odorico Tabarino, f. 7b. S. Cataldo-Porto Adriano is south of Brindisi.

(74) ASAn (Archivio di Stato, Ancona), notary Tommaso Marchetti VIII, f. 194a. f.; about Sulam Signoretti see E. Ashtor, "Gli ebrei di Ancona nel periodo della repubblica," (in) *Atti e Memorie della Deputazione di storia patria per le Marche*, n. s. 82 (Ancona 1978), p. 349 f. It is however true that also many other Anconitans invested such small sums in the maritime trade, see E. Ashtor, "Il commercio levantino di Ancona nel basso medioevo," *Riv. Storica Italiana* 88 (1976), p. 248.

(75) ASAn, notary Antonio Giovanni di Giacomo 11 (75), f. 477b ff.

The attitude of the other towns of the Marches, all of them very small ones, toward Jewish sea-borne trade was more lenient. These towns made great efforts to compete with Ancona or more exactly to keep their modest share in the maritime trade of the Adriatic against the encroachments of the Anconitans. They could not afford to exclude enterprising Jewish merchants. This was particularly true for Recanati which always saw itself threatened by Ancona. The customs registers, which have come down to us from the last years of the fourteenth century, testify to the fact that the Jews used the port of the town for exporting and importing various commodities. In 1396, a certain Vitalis Iudeus exported colored pottery.[76] In the "registro delle bollette del 1396/97", one finds a Jew Musceto who shipped woollen cloth of Verona, a sack of flax, and a barrel of fish. According to the same register the Jew Aleuccio d'Aleuccio imported a barrel of powdered sugar, and Sabbatucio, a Jew of the little town of Osimo (in the Marches) exported a sack of flax and "a box" (sic!).[77]

V

Although the data referring to Jewish merchants who lived in the countries of the western and central basin of the Mediterranean and engaged in the maritime trade in the later Middle Ages are rather numerous, there can be no doubt that as a whole their activities then decreased. This was mainly the effect of the decline of the Catalan Jewries after the tragic events of the year 1391. In that period, only Jewish merchants of Sicily and Maghrebin communities still carried on maritime trade in the western Mediterranean. The activities of the Jews in the international trade in the eastern basin of the Mediterranean in that period must have been more voluminous. The two leading commercial powers in the eastern Mediterranean, the Genoese and the Venetians, pursued toward their Levantine Jewish subjects an essentially friendly policy as distinct from their attitude to the Jews in the metropolis; at least, they protected the interests of their Jewish subjects in the Levant when the latter engaged in sea-borne trade. Meanwhile, the rising star of the Ottoman power changed conditions radically. It opened new horizons for Jewish maritime trade.

Chios and Crete were the two turn-tables where the Jewish merchants

(76) L. Zdekauer, "La dogana del porto di Recanati nel 1396," (in) *Le Marche* IV (1904), p. 68.

(77) L. Zdekauer, *La Dogana del porto di Recanati nei secolo XIII e XIV* (Fano 1904), pp. 8, 18.

carried on international trade under the benevolent suzerainty of the Genoese and the Venetians, respectively. The share the Jews of other emporia had in the maritime trade seems to have been secondary, but not insignificant.

The position of the Jews in Chios, which was ruled by the Genoese Mahona company, was rather favorable. They were not obliged to bear distinctive signs or to live in a closed quarter.[78] They held positions in the government body responsible for the wheat supply of the island, the officium provisionis. So they had the possibility of fostering Jewish maritime trade by placing orders with Jewish merchants. There were indeed some enterprising merchants among the Jews of Chios who undertook to import great quantities of wheat from other countries.[79] Other Jewish merchants of Chios engaged in trade with Rhodes, Cyprus, Ephesus, Damascus, and Alexandria at the end of the fourteenth century.[80] It is true, however, that, mostly, the Jews carried on trade with the neighboring coastal towns of Asia Minor and the other islands of the Archipelago. Anyhow, some Jews of Chios were rich and could invest considerable sums in maritime trade, as did a certain R. Elias; others took part in the business of insurance for shipping.[81]

In the other Genoese colonies and especially in the great emporium of Pera, the role of the Jews in international trade was apparently very modest.[82] But in Constantinople, in the first half of the fifteenth century almost the last remnant of the Byzantine empire but still a flourishing commercial town, the Jews were in various ways connected with the great international trade. They were agents of foreign firms or marketed the commodities imported from western Europe in the Balkans and elsewhere. A Jew whose name was Joel, was the agent of a great Damascene firm, Ibn al-Muzalliḳ. He sold spices to the Venetian merchants in Constantinople and bartered or bought cloth from them.[83] The name of Jacob, the Jew of Sofia, figures in the accounts of a Vene-

(78) M. Balard, *La Romanie génoise (XIIe-début XVe siècle)* (Genoa 1978) I, p. 281 f.

(79) Balard, *op. cit.* I, p. 336, 389; Ph. P. Argenti, *The Occupation of Chios by the Genoese and Their Administration of the Island* (Cambridge 1958) III, p. 629 (a Jew "of Nicosia" is spoken of, but probably he lived in Chios).

(80) Ph. P. Argenti, *The Religious Minorities of Chios* (Cambridge 1970), p. 127.

(81) Balard, *op. cit.* I, p. 336.

(82) *Op. cit.* I, p. 337.

(83) *Il libro di conti di Giacomo Badoer* (Costantinopoli 1436–1440), ed. U. Dorini-T. Bertelè (Rome 1956), p. 25, 27, 56, 64. About Ibn al-Muzalliḳ see E. Ashtor, "L'apogée du commerce venitien au Levant," (in) *Venezia centro di mediazione tra Oriente e Occidente (secoli XV-XVI), Atti del II Convegno int. di storia della civiltà veneziana* (Florence 1977), I, p. 322 ff.

tian merchant in Constantinople of the 1430's as a customer of cloth, bartered for wax.[84]

The base of Venetian trade in the eastern Mediterranean was Crete and even there the Jews took part in the international exchanges through this period. In the acts of a Venetian notary, who exercised his profession in 1300 in Candia, one finds the name of a Cretan Jew, Sambateus (i.e. Shabbetai), son of David, who made investments in the trade with Egypt.[85] A decree of the Venetian governor in the year 1324 sheds light on the role of the Jews of Crete in the maritime trade. After the Serenissima in January, 1323, had issued an absolute prohibition agaagainst travel to Egypt and Syria and against trade with these countries, a similar decree was promulgated by the "Duke" of Crete in the same year. Later, in 1324, another decree forbade Jews, sc. of the island, to trade with the dominions of the sultan or to go there.[86] The Jews of other Venetian colonies in the eastern Mediterranean engaged in sea-borne trade too, for instance those of Negropont (Euboea). In 1452, they complained that because of the activities of pirates their income had diminished so much that they could not afford to pay the taxes.[87]

The professional structure of the Jews of Syria and Egypt changed greatly in the course of the later Middle Ages. At the beginning of Mamluk rule, there were still merchants belonging to the middle class who engaged in sea-borne trade among the Jewish communities of these countries. Later they were ousted from the trade by the powerful Kārimīs who almost monopolized the international exchanges of the Near East. But in the fifteenth century a new class of Jewish merchants who carried on maritime trade emerged. They were Jews hailing from the countries of southern Europe.

According to a Judaeo-Arabic letter written in 1284, Mūsā ar-Raḳīḳ came to Alexandria on a ship from Marseilles, and it states that "the other companions, a big group, is coming".[88] Those companions of Mūsā ar-Raḳīḳ could of course have been "ᶜolim" on their way to the Holy Land, but it is more likely that they were merchants. Also some

(84) *Badoer*, p. 743.

(85) *Pizolo* I, no. 73.

(86) *Duca di Candia, Bandi (1313–1329)*, ed. P. Ratti-Vidulich (Venice 1965), no. 371.

(87) See. D. Jacoby, "On the Status of Jews in the Venetian Colonies in the Middle Ages," *Zion* 28 (1963), p. 59.

(88) E. Ashtor-Strauss, *The Jews in Egypt and Syria Under the Mamluks* III, no. A 30. S.D. Goitein, *A Mediterranean Society* I, p. 67 reads the date 1235 C.E. and see my remarks l. c. If the date Goitein fixes were right this Moses could be Moses of Alexandria who was in Marseilles in 1248; see Blancard II, no 657 and cf. Loeb, *Les négociants juifs*, p. 74.

Catalan documents apparently refer to the activities of Egyptian Jews in the maritime trade in the late thirteenth century. In the year 1270, King Jaime I granted a safe-conduct to two Jews, brothers, from Alexandria, Barchet (Brākhōt) and Mancer (Manṣūr) Avenmenage (Abu Munadjdja); the safe-conduct applied to their families and goods as well.[89] This document may be interpreted in different ways, as intended for merchants or for immigrants.[90] But a deed of 1289 is clearer: King Alfonso III decides in a litigation between Thebat, a Jew of Alexandria (i.e. Thābit) and Bernardo Marchet, son of R. Marchet, concerning a debt of the latter. Although those who are travelling are not liable to answer to claims, the king says, he makes a decision in the case because of the intervention of the sultan (on behalf of his subject).[91] Apparently both of the litigants were Jewish merchants sojourning in Sicily or elsewhere outside Egypt and Catalonia.

Many of the Jewish merchants whose names are mentioned in the sources of the fifteenth century were customers of the Italian fattori or brokers. Some of them may have been indigenous Jews, others of European origin. Such a Jewish merchant in Beirut was Abraham Cohen who in 1485 had dealings with the Venetian Jacopo Dolfin.[92] Others used their connections with the Italian merchants to engage in international trade. In the 1470's, a Jew whose name was Moses served the Genoese colony in Alexandria as interpreter. He also imported European commodities, as is borne out by the payment of 28 ducats he made to the Genoese consulate as import dues.[93] The amount of the consular dues, namely 1800 ducats, points to the great value of the merchandise he had imported.

Summing up the data collected, one may suggest some conclusions. The numerous documents testifying to the activities of Jews of various Mediterranean countries in the maritime trade disprove convincingly the thesis of a strong inclination of the medieval Jew to money lending. These data show that the Jews of the Mediterranean countries engaged in sea-borne trade everywhere they could.

They took part in almost all the branches of maritime trade. Jewish

(89) Régné, no. 443.

(90) In my book, *The Jews in Egypt and Syria Under the Mamluks* I, p. 199 I have followed the opinion of Baron, *A Social and Religious History of the Jews*, 2nd ed. 12 (New York 1967), p. 291, believing that these Jews were merchants. In the paper, "New Data for the History of Levantine Jewries in the Fifteenth Century," p. 69, note 5, I expressed another view.

(91) Régné, no. 2003.

(92) ASV, Senato Mar XII, f. 28a ff.

(93) ASG (Archivio di Stato, Genova), 2774 C., f. 36b.

merchants of the later Middle Ages also engaged in the wheat trade, in contradistinction to the Jewish traders in the Moslem countries in the period of the Crusades, when they had no share in it. It seems that there were very few sectors in which the Jews did not participate. Such a sector was apparently the trade of alum and soda ash, two commodities that frequently served as ballast. Thus only rich merchants who chartered whole ships or large parts of ships could transport these articles. Besides, alum and soda ash, which were raw materials for some European industries, were mostly either bought from the authorities of the Levantine States or produced by European entrepreneurs who had obtained concessions from these states.

One also becomes aware of the fact that only very few of these Jewish merchants were really rich. In fact, it was only some Jewish merchants of Catalonia who engaged in the trade with the Levant around the year 1300 who might be so designated.

Lastly, it emerges clearly from our data that the Jews' international trade, or more correctly the share of the Jews in it, depended upon the general political constellation. Owing to the deterioration of their status in the Iberian peninsula, the role of the Spanish Jews in the great Mediterranean trade diminished considerably. On the other hand, the Jews kept their place in the trade in the eastern basin of the Mediterranean until the rise of the Ottomans granted them new chances.

INDEX

For Product Safety Concerns and Information please contact our EU representative GPSR@taylorandfrancis.com Taylor & Francis Verlag GmbH, Kaufingerstraße 24, 80331 München, Germany

Printed and bound by CPI Group (UK) Ltd, Croydon, CR0 4YY
01/05/2025
01858437-0002